ST/HR/1/Rev.4 (Vol. I/Part 2)

Centre for Human Rights
Geneva

Human Rights

A Compilation of International Instruments

Volume I (Second Part)
Universal Instruments

United Nations
New York, 1993

NOTE

Symbols of United Nations documents are composed of capital letters combined with figures. Mention of such a symbol indicates a reference to a United Nations document.

ST/HR/1/Rev.4
(Vol. I, Part 2)

UNITED NATIONS PUBLICATION

Sales No. E.93.XIV.1 (Vol. I, Part 2)

ISBN 92-1-154091-7
ISSN 0251-7035

Complete set of two volumes: ISBN 92-1-154092-5
First and Second Parts of Volume I not to be sold separately

SUMMARY CONTENTS

VOLUME I: Universal instruments

First Part

Second Part

VOLUME II: Regional instruments

INTRODUCTION

A. ORGANIZATION OF AMERICAN STATES

B. COUNCIL OF EUROPE

C. ORGANIZATION OF AFRICAN UNITY

D. CONFERENCE ON SECURITY AND CO-OPERATION IN EUROPE

CONTENTS

Volume I (First Part)

Volume I (Second Part)

Introduction

This compilation is published by the Centre for Human Rights in connection with the convening of the 1993 World Conference on Human Rights, in Vienna. The first compilation of international instruments in the field of human rights was issued in 1968. Subsequent editions were issued in 1973,[1] 1978,[2] 1983[3] and 1988,[4] the latter marking the fortieth anniversary of the Universal Declaration of Human Rights.

At its first session in September 1991, the Preparatory Committee of the World Conference adopted decision PC/5 entitled "Studies and documentation for the World Conference", recommending the General Assembly to request the Secretary-General to prepare, *inter alia*, "an update of *A Compilation of International Instruments* and *Status of International Instruments* including also texts of regional instruments on human rights". The Preparatory Committee's decision was endorsed by the General Assembly in its resolution 46/116 of 17 December 1991. In accordance with this request, the present edition, consisting of two volumes, the first devoted to instruments of universal character and the second to regional instruments, was produced.

The first volume, which is published in two parts, contains documents adopted up to 31 March 1993. The list of international instruments has been broadened to include additional United Nations documents and instruments adopted by the International Labour Organisation, the United Nations Educational, Scientific and Cultural Organization and the Office of the United Nations High Commissioner for Refugees. Furthermore, a chapter concerning Humanitarian Law and including the four Geneva Conventions and the Protocols thereto has been added. All the instruments, grouped by subject

---

[1] *Human Rights: A Compilation of International Instruments of the United Nations* (United Nations publication, Sales No. E.73.XIV.2).

[2] *Human Rights: A Compilation of International Instruments* (United Nations publication, Sales No. E.78.XIV.2).

[3] *Human Rights: A Compilation of International Instruments* (United Nations publication, Sales No. E.83.XIV.1).

[4] *Human Rights: A Compilation of International Instruments* (United Nations publication, Sales No. E.88.XIV.1).

and organized in chronological order of adoption, appear in a list at the end of each part.

The second volume contains a selection of instruments which have been adopted within the framework of regional intergovernmental organizations up to 31 March 1993. This collection of regional instruments is being issued for the first time. The order of listing of the organizations is that of the date of their establishment, and that of the instruments is the chronological order of their adoption.

The legal status of the instruments contained in the compilation varies. Those referred to as *declarations, principles, guidelines, standard rules* and *recommendations* have no binding legal effect.

Nevertheless, these instruments have an undeniable moral force, and provide practical guidance to States in their conduct. The value of such instruments rests on their recognition and acceptance by a large number of States, and, even without binding legal effect, they may be seen as declaratory of broadly accepted principles within the international community.

International treaties, which are referred to variously as *covenants, protocols* or *conventions*, are legally binding for those States that ratify or accede to them. Treaties adopted within the United Nations are open for signature and ratification by all States, while those adopted within the framework of regional organizations depend for acceptance on membership of the organization concerned.

A *Chart of Ratifications*, containing the status of all treaties appearing in the first part of the Compilation, is issued by the Centre for Human Rights every six months. Information on reservations, declarations, observations and notifications relating to the same treaties is contained in the publication *Human Rights: Status of International Instruments*, which is issued—together with the Compilation—every five years.

The two volumes together constitute a comprehensive catalogue of the existing human rights instruments adopted at both universal and regional level. It is hoped that the compilation will contribute to a wider knowledge and increased awareness of international human rights standards and will be a valuable resource for all those engaged in the promotion and protection of human rights and fundamental freedoms.

I. FREEDOM OF INFORMATION

54. Convention on the International Right of Correction

Opened for signature by General Assembly resolution 630 (VII)
of 16 December 1952

Entry into force: 24 August 1962, in accordance with article VIII

Preamble

The Contracting States,

Desiring to implement the right of their peoples to be fully and reliably informed,

Desiring to improve understanding between their peoples through the free flow of information and opinion,

Desiring thereby to protect mankind from the scourge of war, to prevent the recurrence of aggression from any source, and to combat all propaganda which is either designed or likely to provoke or encourage any threat to peace, breach of the peace, or act of aggression,

Considering the danger to the maintenance of friendly relations between peoples and to the preservation of peace, arising from the publication of inaccurate reports,

Considering that at its second regular session the General Assembly of the United Nations recommended the adoption of measures designed to combat the dissemination of false or distorted reports likely to injure friendly relations between States,

Considering, however, that it is not at present practicable to institute, on the international level, a procedure for verifying the accuracy of a report which might lead to the imposition of penalties for the publication of false or distorted reports,

Considering, moreover, that to prevent the publication of reports of this nature or to reduce their pernicious effects, it is above all necessary to promote a wide circulation of news and to heighten the sense of responsibility of those regularly engaged in the dissemination of news,

Considering that an effective means to these ends is to give States directly affected by a report, which they consider false or distorted and which is disseminated by an information agency, the possibility of securing commensurate publicity for their corrections,

Considering that the legislation of certain States does not provide for a right of correction of which foreign governments may avail themselves, and that it is therefore desirable to institute such a right on the international level, and

Having resolved to conclude a Convention for these purposes,

Have agreed as follows:

Article I

For the purposes of the present Convention:

1. "News dispatch" means news material transmitted in writing or by means of telecommunications, in the form customarily employed by information agencies in transmitting such news material, before publication, to newspapers, news periodicals and broadcasting organizations.

2. "Information agency" means a press, broadcasting, film, television or facsimile organization, public or private, regularly engaged in the collection and dissemination of news material, created and organized under the laws and regulations of the Contracting State in which the central organization is domiciled and which, in each Contracting State where it operates, functions under the laws and regulations of that State.

3. "Correspondent" means a national of a Contracting State or an individual employed by an information agency of a Contracting State, who in either case is regularly engaged in the collection and the reporting of news material, and who when outside his State is identified as a correspondent by a valid passport or by a similar document internationally acceptable.

Article II

1. Recognizing that the professional responsibility of correspondents and information agencies requires them to report facts without discrimination and in their proper context and thereby to promote respect for human rights and fundamental freedoms, to further international understanding and co-operation and to contribute to the maintenance of international peace and security,

Considering also that, as a matter of professional ethics, all correspondents and information agencies should, in the case of news dispatches transmitted or published by them and which have been demonstrated to be false or distorted, follow the customary practice of transmitting through the same channels, or of publishing corrections of such dispatches,

The Contracting States agree that in cases where a Contracting State contends that a news dispatch capable of injuring its relations with other States or its national prestige or dignity transmitted from one country to another by correspondents or information agencies of a Contracting or non-Contracting State and published or disseminated abroad is false or distorted, it may submit its version of the facts (hereinafter called "communiqué") to the Contracting States within whose territories such dispatch has been published or disseminated.

A copy of the communiqué shall be forwarded at the same time to the correspondent or information agency concerned to enable that correspondent or information agency to correct the news dispatch in question.

2. A communiqué may be issued only with respect to news dispatches and must be without comment or expression of opinion. It should not be longer than is necessary to correct the alleged inaccuracy or distortion and must be accompanied by a verbatim text of the dispatch as published or disseminated, and by evidence that the dispatch has been transmitted from abroad by a correspondent or an information agency.

Article III

1. With the least possible delay and in any case not later than five clear days from the date of receiving a communiqué transmitted in accordance with provisions of article II, a Contracting State, whatever be its opinion concerning the facts in question, shall:

(a) Release the communiqué to the correspondents and information agencies operating in its territory through the channels customarily used for the release of news concerning international affairs for publications; and

(b) Transmit the communiqué to the headquarters of the information agency whose correspondent was responsible for originating the dispatch in question, if such headquarters are within its territory.

2. In the event that a Contracting State does not discharge its obligation under this article, with respect to the communiqué of another Contracting State, the latter may accord, on the basis of reciprocity, similar treatment to a communiqué thereafter submitted to it by the defaulting State.

Article IV

1. If any of the Contracting States to which a communiqué has been transmitted in accordance with article II fails to fulfil, within the prescribed

time-limit, the obligations laid down in article III, the Contracting State exercising the right of correction may submit the said communiqué, together with a verbatim text of the dispatch as published or disseminated, to the Secretary-General of the United Nations and shall at the same time notify the State complained against that it is doing so. The latter State, may, within five clear days after receiving such notice, submit its comments to the Secretary-General, which shall relate only to the allegation that it has not discharged its obligations under article III.

2.   The Secretary-General shall in any event, within ten clear days after receiving the communiqué, give appropriate publicity through the information channels at his disposal to the communiqué, together with the dispatch and the comments, if any, submitted to him by the State complained against.

Article V

Any dispute betwen any two or more Contracting States concerning the interpretation or application of the present Convention which is not settled by negotiations shall be referred to the International Court of Justice for decision unless the Contracting States agree to another mode of settlement.

Article VI

1.   The present Convention shall be open for signature to all States Members of the United Nations, to every State invited to the United Nations Conference on Freedom of Information held at Geneva in 1948, and to every other State which the General Assembly may, by resolution, declare to be eligible.

2.   The present Convention shall be ratified by the States signatory hereto in conformity with their respective constitutional processes. The instruments of ratification shall be deposited with the Secretary-General of the United Nations.

Article VII

1.   The present Convention shall be open for accession to the States referred to in article VI (1).

2.   Accession shall be effected by the deposit of an instrument of accession with the Secretary-General of the United Nations.

Article VIII

When any six of the States referred to in article VI (1) have deposited their instruments of ratification or accession, the present Convention shall come into force among them on the thirtieth day after the date of the deposit of the sixth instrument of ratification or accession. It shall come into force for each State which ratifies or accedes after that date on the thirtieth day after the deposit of its instrument of ratification or accession.

Article IX

The provisions of the present Convention shall extend to or be applicable equally to a contracting metropolitan State and all territories, be they Non-Self-Governing, Trust or Colonial Territories, which are being administered or governed by such metropolitan State.

Article X

Any Contracting State may denounce the present Convention by notification to the Secretary-General of the United Nations. Denunciation shall take effect six months after the date of receipt of the notification by the Secretary-General.

Article XI

The present Convention shall cease to be in force as from the date when the denunciation which reduces the number of Parties to less than six becomes effective.

Article XII

1. A request for the revision of the present Convention may be made at any time by any Contracting State by means of a notification to the Secretary-General of the United Nations.

2. The General Assembly shall decide upon the steps, if any, to be taken in respect of such request.

Article XIII

The Secretary-General of the United Nations shall notify the States referred to in article VI (1) of the following:

(a) Signatures, ratifications and accessions received in accordance with articles VI and VII;

(b) The date upon which the present Convention comes into force in accordance with article VIII;

(c) Denunciations received in accordance with article X;

(*d*) Abrogation in accordance with article XI;

(*e*) Notifications received in accordance with article XII.

Article XIV

1.   The present Convention, of which the Chinese, English, French, Russian and Spanish texts shall be equally authentic, shall be deposited in the archives of the United Nations.

2.   The Secretary-General of the United Nations shall transmit a certified copy to each State referred to in article VI (1).

3.   The present Convention shall be registered with the Secretariat of the United Nations on the date of its coming into force.

J. FREEDOM OF ASSOCIATION

55. Freedom of Association and Protection of the Right to Organise Convention

CONVENTION (No. 87) CONCERNING FREEDOM OF ASSOCIATION AND PROTECTION OF THE RIGHT TO ORGANISE

Adopted on 9 July 1948 by the General Conference of the International Labour Organisation at its thirty-first session

ENTRY INTO FORCE: 4 July 1950, in accordance with article 15

The General Conference of the International Labour Organisation,

Having been convened at San Francisco by the Governing Body of the International Labour Office, and having met in its thirty-first session on 17 June 1948,

Having decided to adopt, in the form of a Convention, certain proposals concerning freedom of association and protection of the right to organise which is the seventh item on the agenda of the session,

Considering that the Preamble to the Constitution of the International Labour Organisation declares "recognition of the principle of freedom of association" to be a means of improving conditions of labour and of establishing peace,

Considering that the Declaration of Philadelphia reaffirms that "freedom of expression and of association are essential to sustained progress",

Considering that the International Labour Conference, at its thirtieth session, unanimously adopted the principles which should form the basis for international regulation,

Considering that the General Assembly of the United Nations, at its second session, endorsed these principles and requested the International Labour Organisation to continue every effort in order that it may be possible to adopt one or several international Conventions,

Adopts this ninth day of July of the year one thousand nine hundred and forty-eight the following Convention, which may be cited as the Freedom of Association and Protection of the Right to Organise Convention, 1948:

PART I

FREEDOM OF ASSOCIATION

Article 1

Each Member of the International Labour Organisation for which this Convention is in force undertakes to give effect to the following provisions.

Article 2

Workers and employers, without distinction whatsoever, shall have the right to establish and, subject only to the rules of the organisation concerned, to join organisations of their own choosing without previous authorisation.

Article 3

1. Workers' and employers' organisations shall have the right to draw up their constitutions and rules, to elect their representatives in full freedom, to organise their administration and activities and to formulate their programmes.

2. The public authorities shall refrain from any interference which would restrict this right or impede the lawful exercise thereof.

Article 4

Workers' and employers' organisations shall not be liable to be dissolved or suspended by administrative authority.

Article 5

Workers' and employers' organisations shall have the right to establish and join federations and confederations and any such organisation, federation or confederation shall have the right to affiliate with international organisations of workers and employers.

Article 6

The provisions of articles 2, 3 and 4 hereof apply to federations and confederations of workers' and employers' organisations.

Article 7

The acquisition of legal personality by workers' and employers' organisations, federations and confederations shall not be made subject to conditions of such a character as to restrict the application of the provisions of articles 2, 3 and 4 hereof.

Article 8

1. In exercising the rights provided for in this Convention workers and employers and their respective organisations, like other persons or organised collectivities, shall respect the law of the land.

2. The law of the land shall not be such as to impair, nor shall it be so applied as to impair, the guarantees provided for in this Convention.

Article 9

1. The extent to which the guarantees provided for in this Convention shall apply to the armed forces and the police shall be determined by national laws or regulations.

2. In accordance with the principle set forth in paragraph 8 of article 19 of the Constitution of the International Labour Organisation, the ratification of this Convention by any Member shall not be deemed to affect any existing law, award, custom or agreement in virtue of which members of the armed forces or the police enjoy any right guaranteed by this Convention.

Article 10

In this Convention the term "organisation" means any organisation of workers or of employers for furthering and defending the interests of workers or of employers.

PART II

PROTECTION OF THE RIGHT TO ORGANISE

Article 11

Each Member of the International Labour Organisation for which this Convention is in force undertakes to take all necessary and appropriate measures to ensure that workers and employers may exercise freely the right to organise.

Part III

MISCELLANEOUS PROVISIONS

Article 12

1.   In respect of the territories referred to in article 35 of the Constitution of the International Labour Organisation as amended by the Constitution of the International Labour Organisation Instrument of Amendment, 1946, other than the territories referred to in paragraphs 4 and 5 of the said article as so amended, each Member of the Organisation which ratifies this Convention shall communicate to the Director-General of the International Labour Office with or as soon as possible after its ratification a declaration stating:

(*a*) The territories in respect of which it undertakes that the provisions of the Convention shall be applied without modification;

(*b*) The territories in respect of which it undertakes that the provisions of the Convention shall be applied subject to modifications, together with details of the said modifications;

(*c*) The territories in respect of which the Convention is inapplicable and in such cases the grounds on which it is inapplicable;

(*d*) The territories in respect of which it reserves its decision.

2.   The undertakings referred to in subparagraphs (*a*) and (*b*) of paragraph 1 of this article shall be deemed to be an integral part of the ratification and shall have the force of ratification.

3.   Any Member may at any time by a subsequent declaration cancel in whole or in part any reservations made in its original declaration in virtue of subparagraphs (*b*), (*c*) or (*d*) of paragraph 1 of this article.

4.   Any Member may, at any time at which this Convention is subject to denunciation in accordance with the provisions of article 16, communicate to the Director-General a declaration modifying in any other respect the terms of any former declaration and stating the present position in respect of such territories as it may specify.

Article 13

1.   Where the subject-matter of this Convention is within the self-governing powers of any non-metropolitan territory, the Member responsible for the international relations of that territory may, in agreement with the government of the territory, communicate to the Director-General of the

International Labour Office a declaration accepting on behalf of the territory the obligations of this Convention.

2. A declaration accepting the obligations of this Convention may be communicated to the Director-General of the International Labour Office:

(*a*) By two or more Members of the Organisation in respect of any territory which is under their joint authority; or

(*b*) By any international authority responsible for the administration of any territory, in virtue of the Charter of the United Nations or otherwise, in respect of any such territory.

3. Declarations communicated to the Director-General of the International Labour Office in accordance with the preceding paragraphs of this article shall indicate whether the provisions of the Convention will be applied in the territory concerned without modification or subject to modifications; when the declaration indicates that the provisions of the Convention will be applied subject to modifications it shall give details of the said modifications.

4. The Member, Members or international authority concerned may at any time by a subsequent declaration renounce in whole or in part the right to have recourse to any modification indicated in any former declaration.

5. The Member, Members or international authority concerned may, at any time at which this Convention is subject to denunciation in accordance with the provisions of article 16, communicate to the Director-General of the International Labour Office a declaration modifying in any other respect the terms of any former declaration and stating the present position in respect of the application of the Convention.

PART IV

FINAL PROVISIONS

Article 14

The formal ratifications of this Convention shall be communicated to the Director-General of the International Labour Office for registration.

Article 15

1. This Convention shall be binding only upon those Members of the International Labour Organisation whose ratifications have been registered with the Director-General.

2.   It shall come into force twelve months after the date on which the ratifications of two Members have been registered with the Director-General.

3.   Thereafter, this Convention shall come into force for any Member twelve months after the date on which its ratification has been registered.

Article 16

1.   A Member which has ratified this Convention may denounce it after the expiration of ten years from the date on which the Convention first comes into force, by an act communicated to the Director-General of the International Labour Office for registration. Such denunciation shall not take effect until one year after the date on which it is registered.

2.   Each Member which has ratified this Convention and which does not, within the year following the expiration of the period of ten years mentioned in the preceding paragraph, exercise the right of denunciation provided for in this article, will be bound for another period of ten years and, thereafter, may denounce this Convention at the expiration of each period of ten years under the terms provided for in this article.

Article 17

1.   The Director-General of the International Labour Office shall notify all Members of the International Labour Organisation of the registration of all ratifications, declarations and denunciations communicated to him by the Members of the Organisation.

2.   When notifying the Members of the Organisation of the registration of the second ratification communicated to him, the Director-General shall draw the attention of the Members of the Organisation to the date upon which the Convention will come into force.

Article 18

The Director-General of the International Labour Office shall communicate to the Secretary-General of the United Nations for registration in accordance with Article 102 of the Charter of the United Nations full particulars of all ratifications, declarations and acts of denunciation registered by him in accordance with the provisions of the preceding articles.

Article 19

At the expiration of each period of ten years after the coming into force of this Convention, the Governing Body of the International Labour Office shall present to the General Conference a report on the working of this Convention and shall consider the desirability of placing on the agenda of the Conference the question of its revision in whole or in part.

Article 20

1. Should the Conference adopt a new Convention revising this Convention in whole or in part, then, unless the new Convention otherwise provides:

(*a*) The ratification by a Member of the new revising Convention shall *ipso jure* involve the immediate denunciation of this Convention, notwithstanding the provisions of article 16 above, if and when the new revising Convention shall have come into force;

(*b*) As from the date when the new revising Convention comes into force this Convention shall cease to be open to ratification by the Members.

2. This Convention shall in any case remain in force in its actual form and content for those Members which have ratified it but have not ratified the revising Convention.

Article 21

The English and French versions of the text of this Convention are equally authoritative.

The foregoing is the authentic text of the Convention duly adopted by the General Conference of the International Labour Organisation during its thirty-first session which was held at San Francisco and declared closed the tenth day of July 1948.

IN FAITH WHEREOF we have appended our signatures this thirty-first day of August 1948.

56. Right to Organise and Collective Bargaining Convention

CONVENTION (No. 98) CONCERNING THE APPLICATION OF THE PRINCIPLES OF THE RIGHT TO ORGANISE AND TO BARGAIN COLLECTIVELY

Adopted on 1 July 1949 by the General Conference of the International Labour Organisation at its thirty-second session

ENTRY INTO FORCE: 18 July 1951, in accordance with article 8

The General Conference of the International Labour Organisation,

Having been convened at Geneva by the Governing Body of the International Labour Office, and having met in its thirty-second session on 8 June 1949, and

Having decided upon the adoption of certain proposals concerning the application of the principles of the right to organise and to bargain collectively, which is the fourth item on the agenda of the session, and

Having determined that these proposals shall take the form of an international Convention,

Adopts this first day of July of the year one thousand nine hundred and forty-nine the following Convention, which may be cited as the Right to Organise and Collective Bargaining Convention 1949:

Article 1

1. Workers shall enjoy adequate protection against acts of anti-union discrimination in respect of their employment.

2. Such protection shall apply more particularly in respect of acts calculated to:

(*a*) Make the employment of a worker subject to the condition that he shall not join a union or shall relinquish trade union membership;

(*b*) Cause the dismissal of or otherwise prejudice a worker by reason of union membership or because of participation in union activities outside working hours or, with the consent of the employer, within working hours.

Article 2

1. Workers' and employers' organisations shall enjoy adequate protection against any acts of interference by each other or each other's agents or members in their establishment, functioning or administration.

2. In particular, acts which are designed to promote the establishment of workers' organisations under the domination of employers or employers' organisations, or to support workers' organisations by financial or other means, with the object of placing such organisations under the control of employers or employers' organisations, shall be deemed to constitute acts of interference within the meaning of this article.

Article 3

Machinery appropriate to national conditions shall be established, where necessary, for the purpose of ensuring respect for the right to organise as defined in the preceding articles.

Article 4

Measures appropriate to national conditions shall be taken, where necessary, to encourage and promote the full development and utilisation of machinery for voluntary negotiation between employers or employers' organisations and workers' organisations, with a view to the regulation of terms and conditions of employment by means of collective agreements.

Article 5

1. The extent to which the guarantees provided for in this Convention shall apply to the armed forces and the police shall be determined by national laws or regulations.

2. In accordance with the principle set forth in paragraph 8 of article 19 of the Constitution of the International Labour Organisation the ratification of this Convention by any Member shall not be deemed to affect any existing law, award, custom or agreement in virtue of which members of the armed forces or the police enjoy any right guaranteed by this Convention.

Article 6

This Convention does not deal with the position of public servants engaged in the administration of the State, nor shall it be construed as prejudicing their rights or status in any way.

Article 7

The formal ratifications of this Convention shall be communicated to the Director-General of the International Labour Office for registration.

Article 8

1. This Convention shall be binding only upon those Members of the International Labour Organisation whose ratifications have been registered with the Director-General.

2. It shall come into force twelve months after the date on which the ratifications of two Members have been registered with the Director-General.

3. Thereafter, this Convention shall come into force for any Member twelve months after the date on which its ratification has been registered.

Article 9

1. Declarations communicated to the Director-General of the International Labour Office in accordance with paragraph 2 of article 35 of the Constitution of the International Labour Organisation shall indicate:

(*a*) The territories in respect of which the Member concerned undertakes that the provisions of the Convention shall be applied without modification;

(*b*) The territories in respect of which it undertakes that the provisions of the Convention shall be applied subject to modifications, together with details of the said modifications;

(*c*) The territories in respect of which the Convention is inapplicable and in such cases the grounds on which it is inapplicable;

(*d*) The territories in respect of which it reserves its decision pending further consideration of the position.

2. The undertakings referred to in subparagraphs (*a*) and (*b*) of paragraph 1 of this article shall be deemed to be an integral part of the ratification and shall have the force of ratification.

3. Any Member may at any time by a subsequent declaration cancel in whole or in part any reservation made in its original declaration in virtue of subparagraphs (*b*), (*c*) or (*d*) of paragraph 1 of this article.

4. Any Member may, at any time at which the Convention is subject to denunciation in accordance with the provisions of article 11, communicate to the Director-General a declaration modifying in any other respect the terms

of any former declaration and stating the present position in respect of such territories as it may specify.

Article 10

1.   Declarations communicated to the Director-General of the International Labour Office in accordance with paragraphs 4 and 5 of article 35 of the Constitution of the International Labour Organisation shall indicate whether the provisions of the Convention will be applied in the territory concerned without modification or subject to modifications; when the declaration indicates that the provisions of the Convention will be applied subject to modifications, it shall give details of the said modifications.

2.   The Member, Members or international authority concerned may at any time by a subsequent declaration renounce in whole or in part the right to have recourse to any modification indicated in any former declaration.

3.   The Member, Members or international authority concerned may, at any time at which this Convention is subject to denunciation in accordance with the provisions of article 11, communicate to the Director-General a declaration modifying in any other respect the terms of any former declaration and stating the present position in respect of the application of the Convention.

Article 11

1.   A Member which has ratified this Convention may denounce it after the expiration of ten years from the date on which the Convention first comes into force, by an act communicated to the Director-General of the International Labour Office for registration. Such denunciation shall not take effect until one year after the date on which it is registered.

2.   Each Member which has ratified this Convention and which does not, within the year following the expiration of the period of ten years mentioned in the preceding paragraph, exercise the right of denunciation provided for in this article, will be bound for another period of ten years and, thereafter, may denounce this Convention at the expiration of each period of ten years under the terms provided for in this article.

Article 12

1.   The Director-General of the International Labour Office shall notify all Members of the International Labour Organisation of the registration of all ratifications, delcarations and denunciations communicated to him by the Members of the Organisation.

2.   When notifying the Members of the Organisation of the registration of the second ratification communicated to him, the Director-General shall draw the attention of the Members of the Organisation to the date upon which the Convention will come into force.

Article 13

The Director-General of the International Labour Office shall communicate to the Secretary-General of the United Nations for registration in accordance with Article 102 of the Charter of the United Nations full particulars of all ratifications, declarations and acts of denunciation registered by him in accordance with the provisions of the preceding articles.

Article 14

At the expiration of each period of ten years after the coming into force of this Convention, the Governing Body of the International Labour Office shall present to the General Conference a report on the working of this Convention and shall consider the desirability of placing on the agenda of the Conference the question of its revision in whole or in part.

Article 15

1.   Should the Conference adopt a new Convention revising this Convention in whole or in part, then, unless the new Convention otherwise provides:

(*a*) The ratification by a Member of the new revising Convention shall *ipso jure* involve the immediate denunciation of this Convention, notwithstanding the provisions of article 11 above, if and when the new revising Convention shall have come into force;

(*b*) As from the date when the new revising Convention comes into force this Convention shall cease to be open to ratification by the Members.

2.   This Convention shall in any case remain in force in its actual form and content for those Members which have ratified it but have not ratified the revising Convention.

Article 16

The English and French versions of the text of this Convention are equally authoritative.

The foregoing is the authentic text of the Convention duly adopted by the General Conference of the International Labour Organisation during its thirty-second session which was held at Geneva and declared closed the second day of July 1949.

IN FAITH WHEREOF we have appended our signatures this eighteenth day of August 1949.

57. Workers' Representatives Convention

CONVENTION (No. 135) CONCERNING PROTECTION AND FACILITIES TO BE
AFFORDED TO WORKERS' REPRESENTATIVES IN THE UNDERTAKING

*Adopted on 23 June 1971 by the General Conference of the International Labour
Organisation at its fifty-sixth session*

ENTRY INTO FORCE: 30 June 1973, in accordance with article 8

The General Conference of the International Labour Organisation,

Having been convened at Geneva by the Governing Body of the International Labour Office, and having met in its fifty-sixth session on 2 June 1971, and

Noting the terms of the Right to Organise and Collective Bargaining Convention, 1949, which provides for protection of workers against acts of anti-union discrimination in respect of their employment, and

Considering that it is desirable to supplement these terms with respect to workers' representatives, and

Having decided upon the adoption of certain proposals with regard to protection and facilities afforded to workers' representatives in the undertaking, which is the fifth item on the agenda of the session, and

Having determined that these proposals shall take the form of an international Convention,

Adopts this twenty-third day of June of the year one thousand nine hundred and seventy-one the following Convention, which may be cited as the Workers' Representatives Convention, 1971:

Article 1

Workers' representatives in the undertaking shall enjoy effective protection against any act prejudicial to them, including dismissal, based on their status or activities as a workers' representative or on union membership or participation in union activities, in so far as they act in conformity with existing laws or collective agreements or other jointly agreed arrangements.

Article 2

1.   Such facilities in the undertaking shall be afforded to workers' representatives as may be appropriate in order to enable them to carry out their functions promptly and efficiently.

2.   In this connection account shall be taken of the characteristics of the industrial relations system of the country and the needs, size and capabilities of the undertaking concerned.

3.   The granting of such facilities shall not impair the efficient operation of the undertaking concerned.

Article 3

For the purpose of this Convention the term "workers' representatives" means persons who are recognised as such under national law or practice, whether they are:

(a) Trade union representatives, namely, representatives designated or elected by trade unions or by the members of such unions; or

(b) Elected representatives, namely, representatives who are freely elected by the workers of the undertaking in accordance with provisions of national laws or regulations or of collective agreements and whose functions do not include activities which are recognised as the exclusive prerogative of trade unions in the country concerned.

Article 4

National laws or regulations, collective agreements, arbitration awards or court decisions may determine the type or types of workers' representatives which shall be entitled to the protection and facilities provided for in this Convention.

Article 5

Where there exist in the same undertaking both trade union representatives and elected representatives, appropriate measures shall be taken, wherever necessary, to ensure that the existence of elected representatives is not used to undermine the position of the trade unions concerned or their representatives and to encourage co-operation on all relevant matters between the elected representatives and the trade unions concerned and their representatives.

Article 6

Effect may be given to this Convention through national laws or regulations or collective agreements, or in any other manner consistent with national practice.

Article 7

The formal ratifications of this Convention shall be communicated to the Director-General of the International Labour Office for registration.

Article 8

1.   This Convention shall be binding only upon those Members of the International Labour Organisation whose ratifications have been registered with the Director-General.

2.   It shall come into force twelve months after the date on which the ratifications of two Members have been registered with the Director-General.

3.   Thereafter, this Convention shall come into force for any Member twelve months after the date on which its ratification has been registered.

Article 9

1.   A Member which has ratified this Convention may denounce it after the expiration of ten years from the date on which the Convention first comes into force, by an act communicated to the Director-General of the International Labour Office for registration. Such denunciation shall not take effect until one year after the date on which it is registered.

2.   Each Member which has ratified this Convention and which does not, within the year following the expiration of the period of ten years mentioned in the preceding paragraph, exercise the right of denunciation provided for in this article, will be bound for another period of ten years and, thereafter, may denounce this Convention at the expiration of each period of ten years under the terms provided for in this article.

Article 10

1.   The Director-General of the International Labour Office shall notify all Members of the International Labour Organisation of the registration of all ratifications and denunciations communicated to him by the Members of the Organisation,

2.   When notifying the Members of the Organisation of the registration of the second ratification communicated to him, the Director-General shall draw the attention of the Members of the Organisation to the date upon which the Convention will come into force.

Article 11

The Director-General of the International Labour Office shall communicate to the Secretary-General of the United Nations for registration in accordance with Article 102 of the Charter of the United Nations full particulars of all ratifications and acts of denunciation registered by him in accordance with the provisions of the preceding articles.

Article 12

At such times as it may consider necessary the Governing Body of the International Labour Office shall present to the General Conference a report on the working of this Convention and shall examine the desirability of placing on the agenda of the Conference the question of its revision in whole or in part.

Article 13

1.   Should the Conference adopt a new Convention revising this Convention in whole or in part, then, unless the new Convention otherwise provides:

(*a*) The ratification by a Member of the new revising Convention shall *ipso jure* involve the immediate denunciation of this Convention, notwithstanding the provisions of article 9 above, if and when the new revising Convention shall have come into force;

(*b*) As from the date when the new revising Convention comes into force this Convention shall cease to be open to ratification by the Members.

2.   This Convention shall in any case remain in force in its actual form and content for those Members which have ratified it but have not ratified the revising Convention.

Article 14

The English and French versions of the text of this Convention are equally authoritative.

The foregoing is the authentic text of the Convention duly adopted by the General Conference of the International Labour Organisation during its fifty-sixth session which was held at Geneva and declared closed the twenty-third day of June 1971.

IN FAITH WHEREOF we have appended our signatures this thirtieth day of June 1971.

58. Labour Relations (Public Service) Convention

CONVENTION (No. 151) CONCERNING PROTECTION OF THE RIGHT TO ORGAN-
ISE AND PROCEDURES FOR DETERMINING CONDITIONS OF EMPLOYMENT
IN THE PUBLIC SERVICE

*Adopted on 27 June 1978 by the General Conference of the International Labour
Organisation at its sixty-fourth session*

ENTRY INTO FORCE: 25 February 1981, in accordance with article 11 (2)

The General Conference of the International Labour Organisation,

Having been convened at Geneva by the Governing Body of the International Labour Office, and having met in its sixty-fourth session on 7 June 1978, and

Noting the terms of the Freedom of Association and Protection of the Right to Organise Convention, 1948, the Right to Organise and Collective Bargaining Convention, 1949, and the Workers' Representatives Convention and Recommendation, 1971, and

Recalling that the Right to Organise and Collective Bargaining Convention, 1949, does not cover certain categories of public employees and that the Workers' Representatives Convention and Recommendation, 1971, apply to workers' representatives in the undertaking, and

Noting the considerable expansion of public-service activities in many countries and the need for sound labour relations between public authorities and public employees' organisations, and

Having regard to the great diversity of political, social and economic systems among Member States and the differences in practice among them (e.g. as to the respective functions of central and local government, of federal, State and provincial authorities, and of state-owned undertakings and various types of autonomous or semi-autonomous public bodies, as well as to the nature of employment relationships), and

Taking into account the particular problems arising as to the scope of, and definitions for the purpose of, any international instrument, owing to the differences in many countries between private and public employment, as well as the difficulties of interpretation which have arisen in respect of the

438

application of relevant provisions of the Right to Organise and Collective Bargaining Convention 1949, to public servants, and the observations of the supervisory bodies of the ILO on a number of occasions that some governments have applied these provisions in a manner which excludes large groups of public employees from coverage by that Convention, and

Having decided upon the adoption of certain proposals with regard to freedom of association and procedures for determining conditions of employment in the public service, which is the fifth item on the agenda of the session, and

Having determined that these proposals shall take the form of an international Convention,

Adopts this twenty-seventh day of June of the year one thousand nine hundred and seventy-eight the following Convention, which may be cited as the Labour Relations (Public Service) Convention, 1978:

PART I

SCOPE AND DEFINITIONS

Article 1

1. This Convention applies to all persons employed by public authorities, to the extent that more favourable provisions in other international labour Conventions are not applicable to them.

2. The extent to which the guarantees provided for in this Convention shall apply to high-level employees whose functions are normally considered as policy-making or managerial, or to employees whose duties are of a highly confidential nature, shall be determined by national laws or regulations.

3. The extent to which the guarantees provided for in this Convention shall apply to the armed forces and the police shall be determined by national laws or regulations.

Article 2

For the purpose of this Convention, the term "public employee" means any person covered by the Convention in accordance with article 1 thereof.

Article 3

For the purpose of this Convention, the term "public employees' organisation" means any organisation, however composed, the purpose of which is to further and defend the interests of public employees.

PART II

PROTECTION OF THE RIGHT TO ORGANISE

Article 4

1. Public employees shall enjoy adequate protection against acts of anti-union discrimination in respect of their employment.

2. Such protection shall apply more particularly in respect of acts calculated to:

(*a*) Make the employment of public employees subject to the condition that they shall not join or shall relinquish membership of a public employees' organisation;

(*b*) Cause the dismissal of or otherwise prejudice a public employee by reason of membership of a public employees' organisation or because of participation in the normal activities of such an organisation.

Article 5

1. Public employees' organisations shall enjoy complete independence from public authorities.

2. Public employees' organisations shall enjoy adequate protection against any acts of interference by a public authority in their establishment, functioning or administration.

3. In particular, acts which are designed to promote the establishment of public employees' organisations under the domination of a public authority, or to support public employees' organisations by financial or other means, with the object of placing such organisations under the control of a public authority, shall be deemed to constitute acts of interference within the meaning of this article.

Part III

FACILITIES TO BE AFFORDED TO PUBLIC EMPLOYEES' ORGANISATIONS

Article 6

1.   Such facilities shall be afforded to the representatives of recognised public employees' organisations as may be appropriate in order to enable them to carry out their functions promptly and efficiently, both during and outside their hours of work.

2.   The granting of such facilities shall not impair the efficient operation of the administration or service concerned.

3.   The nature and scope of these facilities shall be determined in accordance with the methods referred to in article 7 of this Convention, or by other appropriate means.

Part IV

PROCEDURES FOR DETERMINING TERMS AND CONDITIONS OF EMPLOYMENT

Article 7

Measures appropriate to national conditions shall be taken, where necessary, to encourage and promote the full development and utilisation of machinery for negotiation of terms and conditions of employment between the public authorities concerned and public employees' organisations, or of such other methods as will allow representatives of public employees to participate in the determination of these matters.

Part V

SETTLEMENT OF DISPUTES

Article 8

The settlement of disputes arising in connection with the determination of terms and conditions of employment shall be sought, as may be appropriate to national conditions, through negotiation between the parties or through independent and impartial machinery, such as mediation, conciliation and arbitration, established in such a manner as to ensure the confidence of the parties involved.

PART VI

CIVIL AND POLITICAL RIGHTS

Article 9

Public employees shall have, as other workers, the civil and political rights which are essential for the normal exercise of freedom of association, subject only to the obligations arising from their status and the nature of their functions.

PART VII

FINAL PROVISIONS

Article 10

The formal ratifications of this Convention shall be communicated to the Director-General of the International Labour Office for registration.

Article 11

1. This Convention shall be binding only upon those Members of the International Labour Organisation whose ratifications have been registered with the Director-General.

2. It shall come into force twelve months after the date on which the ratifications of two Members have been registered with the Director-General.

3. Thereafter, this Convention shall come into force for any Member, twelve months after the date on which its ratification has been registered.

Article 12

1. A Member which has ratified this Convention may denounce it after the expiration of ten years from the date on which the Convention first comes into force, by an act communicated to the Director-General of the International Labour Office for registration. Such denunciation shall not take effect until one year after the date on which it is registered.

2. Each Member which has ratified this Convention and which does not, within the year following the expiration of the period of ten years mentioned in the preceding paragraph, exercise the right of denunciation provided for in this article, will be bound for another period of ten years and, thereafter,

may denounce this Convention at the expiration of each period of ten years under the terms provided for in this article.

Article 13

1. The Director-General of the International Labour Office shall notify all Members of the International Labour Organisation of the registration of all ratifications and denunciations communicated to him by the Members of the Organisation.

2. When notifying the Members of the Organisation of the registration of the second ratification communicated to him, the Director-General shall draw the attention of the Members of the Organisation to the date upon which the Convention will come into force.

Article 14

The Director-General of the International Labour Office shall communicate to the Secretary-General of the United Nations for registration in accordance with Article 102 of the Charter of the United Nations full particulars of all ratifications and acts of denunciation registered by him in accordance with the provisions of the preceding articles.

Article 15

At such times as it may consider necessary the Governing Body of the International Labour Office shall present to the General Conference a report on the working of this Convention and shall examine the desirability of placing on the agenda of the Conference the question of its revision in whole or in part.

Article 16

1. Should the Conference adopt a new Convention revising this Convention in whole or in part, then, unless the new Convention otherwise provides:

(*a*) The ratification by a Member of the new revising Convention shall *ipso jure* involve the immediate denunciation of this Convention, notwithstanding the provisions of article 12 above, if and when the new revising Convention shall have come into force;

(*b*) As from the date when the new revising Convention comes into force this Convention shall cease to be open to ratification by the Members.

2.   This Convention shall in any case remain in force in its actual form and content for those Members which have ratified it but have not ratified the revising Convention.

Article 17

The English and French versions of the text of this Convention are equally authoritative.

K. EMPLOYMENT

59. Employment Policy Convention

CONVENTION (No. 122) CONCERNING EMPLOYMENT POLICY

Adopted on 9 July 1964 by the General Conference of the International Labour Organisation at its forty-eighth session

ENTRY INTO FORCE: 15 July 1966, in accordance with article 5

The General Conference of the International Labour Organisation,

Having been convened at Geneva by the Governing Body of the International Labour Office, and having met in its forty-eighth session on 17 June 1964, and

Considering that the Declaration of Philadelphia recognises the solemn obligation of the International Labour Organisation to further among the nations of the world programmes which will achieve full employment and the raising of standards of living, and that the Preamble to the Constitution of the International Labour Organisation provides for the prevention of unemployment and the provision of an adequate living wage, and

Considering further that under the terms of the Declaration of Philadelphia it is the responsibility of the International Labour Organisation to examine and consider the bearing of economic and financial policies upon employment policy in the light of the fundamental objective that "all human beings, irrespective of race, creed or sex, have the right to pursue both their material well-being and their spiritual development in conditions of freedom and dignity, of economic security and equal opportunity", and

Considering that the Universal Declaration of Human Rights provides that "everyone has the right to work, to free choice of employment, to just and favourable conditions of work and to protection against unemployment", and

Noting the terms of existing international labour Conventions and Recommendations of direct relevance to employment policy, and in particular of the Employment Service Convention and Recommendation, 1948, the

Vocational Guidance Recommendation, 1949, the Vocational Training Re-commendation, 1962, and the Discrimination (Employment and Occupa-tion) Convention and Recommendation, 1958, and

Considering that these instruments should be placed in the wider frame-work of an international programme for economic expansion on the basis of full, productive and freely chosen employment, and

Having decided upon the adoption of certain proposals with regard to employment policy, which are included in the eighth item on the agenda of the session, and

Having determined that these proposals shall take the form of an inter-national Convention,

Adopts this ninth day of July of the year one thousand nine hundred and sixty-four the following Convention, which may be cited as the Employment Policy Convention, 1964:

Article 1

1.   With a view to stimulating economic growth and development, rais-ing levels of living, meeting manpower requirements and overcoming unem-ployment and under-employment, each Member shall declare and pursue, as a major goal, an active policy designed to promote full, productive and freely chosen employment.

2.   The said policy shall aim at ensuring that:

(*a*) There is work for all who are available for and seeking work;

(*b*) Such work is as productive as possible;

(*c*) There is freedom of choice of employment and the fullest possible opportunity for each worker to qualify for, and to use his skills and endow-ments in, a job for which he is well suited, irrespective of race, colour, sex, religion, political opinion, national extraction or social origin.

3.   The said policy shall take due account of the stage and level of economic development and the mutual relationships between employment objectives and other economic and social objectives, and shall be pursued by methods that are appropriate to national conditions and practices.

Article 2

Each Member shall, by such methods and to such extent as may be appropriate under national conditions:

(*a*) Decide on and keep under review, within the framework of a co-ordinated economic and social policy, the measures to be adopted for attaining the objectives specified in article 1;

(*b*) Take such steps as may be needed, including when appropriate the establishment of programmes, for the application of these measures.

Article 3

In the application of this Convention, representatives of the persons affected by the measures to be taken, and in particular representatives of employers and workers, shall be consulted concerning employment policies, with a view to taking fully into account their experience and views and securing their full co-operation in formulating and enlisting support for such policies.

Article 4

The formal ratifications of this Convention shall be communicated to the Director-General of the International Labour Office for registration.

Article 5

1. This Convention shall be binding only upon those Members of the International Labour Organisation whose ratifications have been registered with the Director-General.

2. It shall come into force twelve months after the date on which the ratifications of two Members have been registered with the Director-General.

3. Thereafter, this Convention shall come into force for any Member twelve months after the date on which its ratification has been registered.

Article 6

1. A Member which has ratified this Convention may denounce it after the expiration of ten years from the date on which the Convention first comes into force, by an act communicated to the Director-General of the International Labour Office for registration. Such denunciation shall not take effect until one year after the date on which it is registered.

2. Each Member which has ratified this Convention and which does not, within the year following the expiration of the period of ten years mentioned in the preceding paragraph, exercise the right of denunciation provided for in this article, will be bound for another period of ten years and, thereafter,

may denounce this Convention at the expiration of each period of ten years under the terms provided for in this article.

Article 7

1. The Director-General of the International Labour Office shall notify all Members of the International Labour Organisation of the registration of all ratifications and denunciations communicated to him by the Members of the Organisation.

2. When notifying the Members of the Organisation of the registration of the second ratification communicated to him, the Director-General shall draw the attention of the Members of the Organisation to the date upon which the Convention will come into force.

Article 8

The Director-General of the International Labour Office shall communicate to the Secretary-General of the United Nations for registration in accordance with Article 102 of the Charter of the United Nations full particulars of all ratifications and acts of denunciation registered by him in accordance with the provisions of the preceding articles.

Article 9

At such times as it may consider necessary the Governing Body of the International Labour Office shall present to the General Conference a report on the working of this Convention and shall examine the desirability of placing on the agenda of the Conference the question of its revision in whole or in part.

Article 10

1. Should the Conference adopt a new Convention revising this Convention in whole or in part, then, unless the new Convention otherwise provides:

(*a*) The ratification by a Member of the new revising Convention shall *ipso jure* involve the immediate denunciation of this Convention, notwithstanding the provisions of article 6 above, if and when the new revising Convention shall have come into force;

(*b*) As from the date when the new revising Convention comes into force this Convention shall cease to be open to ratification by the Members.

2.   This Convention shall in any case remain in force in its actual form and content for those Members which have ratified it but have not ratified the revising Convention.

Article 11

The English and French versions of the texts of this Convention are equally authoritative.

60. Convention (No. 154) concerning the Promotion of Collective Bargaining

Adopted on 19 June 1981 by the General Conference
of the International Labour Organisation at its sixty-seventh session

ENTRY INTO FORCE: 11 August 1983, in accordance with article 11

The General Conference of the International Labour Organisation,

Having been convened at Geneva by the Governing Body of the International Labour Office, and having met in its sixty-seventh session on 3 June 1981, and

Reaffirming the provision of the Declaration of Philadelphia recognising "the solemn obligation of the International Labour Organisation to further among the nations of the world programmes which will achieve . . . the effective recognition of the right of collective bargaining", and noting that this principle is "fully applicable to all people everywhere", and

Having regard to the key importance of existing international standards contained in the Freedom of Association and Protection of the Right to Organise Convention, 1948, the Right to Organise and Collective Bargaining Convention, 1949, the Collective Agreements Recommendation, 1951, the Voluntary Conciliation and Arbitration Recommendation, 1951, the Labour Relations (Public Service) Convention and Recommendation, 1978, and the Labour Administration Convention and Recommendation, 1978, and

Considering that it is desirable to make greater efforts to achieve the objectives of these standards and, particularly, the general principles set out in Article 4 of the Right to Organise and Collective Bargaining Convention, 1949, and in Paragraph 1 of the Collective Agreements Recommendation, 1951, and

Considering accordingly that these standards should be complemented by appropriate measures based on them and aimed at promoting free and voluntary collective bargaining, and

Having decided upon the adoption of certain proposals with regard to the promotion of collective bargaining, which is the fourth item on the agenda of the session, and

Having determined that these proposals shall take the form of an international Convention,

Adopts this nineteenth day of June of the year one thousand nine hundred and eighty-one the following Convention, which may be cited as the Collective Bargaining Convention, 1981:

PART I. SCOPE AND DEFINITIONS

Article 1

1. This Convention applies to all branches of economic activity.

2. The extent to which the guarantees provided for in this Convention apply to the armed forces and the police may be determined by national laws or regulations or national practice.

3. As regards the public service, special modalities of application of this Convention may be fixed by national laws or regulations or national practice.

Article 2

For the purpose of this Convention the term "collective bargaining" extends to all negotiations which take place between an employer, a group of employers or one or more employers' organisations, on the one hand, and one or more workers' organisations, on the other, for:

(*a*) Determining working conditions and terms of employment; and/or

(*b*) Regulating relations between employers and workers; and/or

(*c*) Regulating relations between employers or their organisations and a workers' organisation or workers' organisations.

Article 3

1. Where national law or practice recognises the existence of workers' representatives as defined in Article 3, subparagraph (*b*), of the Workers' Representatives Convention, 1971, national law or practice may determine the extent to which the term "collective bargaining" shall also extend, for the purpose of this Convention, to negotiations with these representatives.

2. Where, in pursuance of paragraph 1 of this Article, the term "collective bargaining" also includes negotiations with the workers' representatives referred to in that paragraph, appropriate measures shall be taken, wherever necessary, to ensure that the existence of these representatives is not used to undermine the position of the workers' organisations concerned.

PART II. METHODS OF APPLICATION

Article 4

The provisions of this Convention shall, in so far as they are not otherwise made effective by means of collective agreements, arbitration awards or in such other manner as may be consistent with national practice, be given effect by national laws or regulations.

PART III. PROMOTION OF COLLECTIVE BARGAINING

Article 5

1. Measures adapted to national conditions shall be taken to promote collective bargaining.

2. The aims of the measures referred to in paragraph 1 of this Article shall be the following:

(*a*) Collective bargaining should be made possible for all employers and all groups of workers in the branches of activity covered by this Convention;

(*b*) Collective bargaining should be progressively extended to all matters covered by subparagraphs (*a*), (*b*) and (*c*) of Article 2 of this Convention;

(*c*) The establishment of rules of procedure agreed between employers' and workers' organisations should be encouraged;

(*d*) Collective bargaining should not be hampered by the absence of rules governing the procedure to be used or by the inadequacy or inappropriateness of such rules;

(*e*) Bodies and procedures for the settlement of labour disputes should be so conceived as to contribute to the promotion of collective bargaining.

Article 6

The provisions of this Convention do not preclude the operation of industrial relations systems in which collective bargaining takes place within the framework of conciliation and/or arbitration machinery or institutions, in which machinery or institutions the parties to the collective bargaining process voluntarily participate.

Article 7

Measures taken by public authorities to encourage and promote the development of collective bargaining shall be the subject of prior consultation and, whenever possible, agreement between public authorities and employers' and workers' organisations.

Article 8

The measures taken with a view to promoting collective bargaining shall not be so conceived or applied as to hamper the freedom of collective bargaining.

PART IV. FINAL PROVISIONS

Article 9

This Convention does not revise any existing Convention or Recommendation.

Article 10

The formal ratifications of this Convention shall be communicated to the Director-General of the International Labour Office for registration.

Article 11

1. This Convention shall be binding only upon those Members of the International Labour Organisation whose ratifications have been registered with the Director-General.

2. It shall come into force twelve months after the date on which the ratifications of two Members have been registered with the Director-General.

3. Thereafter, this Convention shall come into force for any Member twelve months after the date on which its ratification has been registered.

Article 12

1. A Member which has ratified this Convention may denounce it after the expiration of ten years from the date on which the Convention first comes into force, by an act communicated to the Director-General of the International Labour Office for registration. Such denunciation shall not take effect until one year after the date on which it is registered.

2. Each Member which has ratified this Convention and which does not, within the year following the expiration of the period of ten years mentioned in the preceding paragraph, exercise the right of denunciation provided for in this Article, will be bound for another period of ten years and,

thereafter, may denounce this Convention at the expiration of each period of ten years under the terms provided for in this Article.

Article 13

1. The Director-General of the International Labour Office shall notify all Members of the International Labour Organisation of the registration of all ratifications and denunciations communicated to him by the Members of the Organisation.

2. When notifying the Members of the Organisation of the registration of the second ratification communicated to him, the Director-General shall draw the attention of the Members of the Organisation to the date upon which the Convention will come into force.

Article 14

The Director-General of the International Labour Office shall communicate to the Secretary-General of the United Nations for registration in accordance with Article 102 of the Charter of the United Nations full particulars of all ratifications and acts of denunciation registered by him in accordance with the provisions of the preceding Articles.

Article 15

At such times as it may consider necessary the Governing Body of the International Labour Office shall present to the General Conference a report on the working of this Convention and shall examine the desirability of placing on the agenda of the Conference the question of its revision in whole or in part.

Article 16

1. Should the Conference adopt a new Convention revising this Convention in whole or in part, then, unless the new Convention otherwise provides:

(*a*) The ratification by a Member of the new revising Convention shall *ipso jure* involve the immediate denunciation of this Convention, notwithstanding the provisions of Article 12 above, if and when the new revising Convention shall have come into force;

(*b*) As from the date when the new revising Convention comes into force this Convention shall cease to be open to ratification by the Members.

2. This Convention shall in any case remain in force in its actual form and content for those Members which have ratified it but have not ratified the revising Convention.

Article 17

The English and French versions of the text of this Convention are equally authoritative.

61.   Convention (No. 168) concerning Employment Promotion and Protection against Unemployment

Adopted on 21 June 1988 by the General Conference of the International Labour Organisation at its seventy-fifth session

ENTRY INTO FORCE: 17 October 1991, in accordance with article 33

The General Conference of the International Labour Organisation,

Having been convened at Geneva by the Governing Body of the International Labour Office, and having met in its seventy-fifth session on 1 June 1988, and

Emphasising the importance of work and productive employment in any society not only because of the resources which they create for the community, but also because of the income which they bring to workers, the social role which they confer and the feeling of self-esteem which workers derive from them, and

Recalling the existing international standards in the field of employment and unemployment protection (the Unemployment Provision Convention and Recommendation, 1934, the Unemployment (Young Persons) Recommendation, 1935, the Income Security Recommendation, 1944, the Social Security (Minimum Standards) Convention, 1952, the Employment Policy Convention and Recommendation, 1964, the Human Resources Development Convention and Recommendation, 1975, the Labour Administration Convention and Recommendation, 1978, and the Employment Policy (Supplementary Provisions) Recommendation, 1984), and

Considering the widespread unemployment and underemployment affecting various countries throughout the world at all stages of development and in particular the problems of young people, many of whom are seeking their first employment, and

Considering that, since the adoption of the international instruments concerning protection against unemployment referred to above, there have been important new developments in the law and practice of many Members necessitating the revision of existing standards, in particular the Unemployment Provision Convention, 1934, and the adoption of new international standards concerning the promotion of full, productive and freely chosen employment by all appropriate means, including social security, and

Noting that the provisions concerning unemployment benefit in the Social Security (Minimum Standards) Convention, 1952, lay down a level of protection that has now been surpassed by most of the existing compensation schemes in the industrialised countries and, unlike standards concerning other benefits, have not been followed by higher standards, but that the standards in question can still constitute a target for developing countries that are in a position to set up an unemployment compensation scheme, and

Recognising that policies leading to stable, sustained, non-inflationary economic growth and a flexible response to change, as well as to creation and promotion of all forms of productive and freely chosen employment including small undertakings, co-operatives, self-employment and local initiatives for employment, even through the re-distribution of resources currently devoted to the financing of purely assistance-oriented activities towards activities which promote employment especially vocational guidance, training and rehabilitation, offer the best protection against the adverse effects of involuntary unemployment, but that involuntary unemployment nevertheless exists and that it is therefore important to ensure that social security systems should provide employment assistance and economic support to those who are involuntarily unemployed, and

Having decided upon the adoption of certain proposals with regard to employment promotion and social security which is the fifth item on the agenda of the session with a view, in particular, to revising the Unemployment Provision Convention, 1934, and

Having determined that these proposals shall take the form of an international Convention,

Adopts this twenty-first day of June of the year one thousand nine hundred and eighty-eight the following Convention, which may be cited as the Employment Promotion and Protection against Unemployment Convention, 1988:

I. General Provisions

Article 1

In this Convention:

(*a*) The term "legislation" includes any social security rules as well as laws and regulations;

(*b*) The term "prescribed" means determined by or in virtue of national legislation.

Article 2

Each Member shall take appropriate steps to co-ordinate its system of protection against unemployment and its employment policy. To this end, it shall seek to ensure that its system of protection against unemployment, and in particular the methods of providing unemployment benefit, contribute to the promotion of full, productive and freely chosen employment, and are not such as to discourage employers from offering and workers from seeking productive employment.

Article 3

The provisions of this Convention shall be implemented in consultation and co-operation with the organisations of employers and workers, in accordance with national practice.

Article 4

1. Each Member which ratifies this Convention may, by a declaration accompanying its ratification, exclude the provisions of Part VII from the obligations accepted by ratification.

2. Each Member which has made a declaration under paragraph 1 above may withdraw it at any time by a subsequent declaration.

Article 5

1. Each Member may avail itself, by a declaration accompanying its ratification, of at most two of the temporary exceptions provided for in Article 10, paragraph 4, Article 11, paragraph 3, Article 15, paragraph 2, Article 18, paragraph 2, Article 19, paragraph 4, Article 23, paragraph 2, Article 24, paragraph 2, and Article 25, paragraph 2. Such a declaration shall state the reasons which justify these exceptions.

2. Notwithstanding the provisions of paragraph 1 above, a Member, where it is justified by the extent of protection of its social security system, may avail itself, by a declaration accompanying its ratification, of the temporary exceptions provided for in Article 10, paragraph 4, Article 11, paragraph 3, Article 15, paragraph 2, Article 18, paragraph 2, Article 19, paragraph 4, Article 23, paragraph 2, Article 24, paragraph 2 and Article 25, paragraph 2. Such a declaration shall state the reasons which justify these exceptions.

3. Each Member which has made a declaration under paragraph 1 or paragraph 2 shall include in its reports on the application of this Convention submitted under Article 22 of the Constitution of the International Labour Organisation a statement in respect of each exception of which it avails itself:

(*a*) That its reason for doing so subsists; or

(*b*) That it renounces its right to avail itself of the exception in question as from a stated date.

4. Each Member which has made a declaration under paragraph 1 or paragraph 2 shall, as appropriate to the terms of such declaration and as circumstances permit:

(*a*) Cover the contingency of partial unemployment;

(*b*) Increase the number of persons protected;

(*c*) Increase the amount of the benefits;

(*d*) Reduce the length of the waiting period;

(*e*) Extend the duration of payment of benefits;

(*f*) Adapt statutory social security schemes to the occupational circumstances of part-time workers;

(*g*) Endeavour to ensure the provision of medical care to persons in receipt of unemployment benefit and their dependants;

(*h*) Endeavour to guarantee that the periods during which such benefit is paid will be taken into account for the acquisition of the right to social security benefits and, where appropriate, the calculation of disability, old-age and survivors' benefit.

Article 6

1. Each Member shall ensure equality of treatment for all persons protected, without discrimination on the basis of race, colour, sex, religion, political opinion, national extraction, nationality, ethnic or social origin, disability or age.

2. The provisions of paragraph 1 shall not prevent the adoption of special measures which are justified by the circumstances of identified groups under the schemes referred to in Article 12, paragraph 2, or are designed to meet the specific needs of categories of persons who have particular problems in the labour market, in particular disadvantaged groups, or the conclusion between States of bilateral or multilateral agreements relating to unemployment benefits on the basis of reciprocity.

II. PROMOTION OF PRODUCTIVE EMPLOYMENT

Article 7

Each Member shall declare as a priority objective a policy designed to promote full, productive and freely chosen employment by all appropriate means, including social security. Such means should include, *inter alia*, employment services, vocational training and vocational guidance.

Article 8

1.   Each Member shall endeavour to establish, subject to national law and practice, special programmes to promote additional job opportunities and employment assistance and to encourage freely chosen and productive employment for identified categories of disadvantaged persons having or liable to have difficulties in finding lasting employment such as women, young workers, disabled persons, older workers, the long-term unemployed, migrant workers lawfully resident in the country and workers affected by structural change.

2.   Each Member shall specify, in its reports under article 22 of the Constitution of the International Labour Organisation, the categories of persons for whom it undertakes to promote employment programmes.

3.   Each Member shall endeavour to extend the promotion of productive employment progressively to a greater number of categories than the number initially covered.

Article 9

The measures envisaged in this Part shall be taken in the light of the Human Resources Development Convention and Recommendation, 1975, and the Employment Policy (Supplementary Provisions) Recommendation, 1984.

III.   CONTINGENCIES COVERED

Article 10

1.   The contingencies covered shall include, under prescribed conditions, full unemployment defined as the loss of earnings due to inability to obtain suitable employment with due regard to the provisions of Article 21, paragraph 2, in the case of a person capable of working, available for work and actually seeking work.

2.   Each Member shall endeavour to extend the protection of the Convention, under prescribed conditions, to the following contingencies:

(*a*)   Loss of earnings due to partial unemployment, defined as a temporary reduction in the normal or statutory hours of work; and

(*b*)   Suspension or reduction of earnings due to a temporary suspension of work, without any break in the employment relationship for reasons of, in particular, an economic, technological, structural or similar nature.

3.   Each Member shall in addition endeavour to provide the payment of benefits to part-time workers who are actually seeking full-time work.

The total of benefits and earnings from their part-time work may be such as to maintain incentives to take up full-time work.

4.   Where a declaration made in virtue of Article 5 is in force, the implementation of paragraphs 2 and 3 above may be deferred.

IV. PERSONS PROTECTED

Article 11

1.   The persons protected shall comprise prescribed classes of employees, constituting not less than 85 per cent of all employees, including public employees and apprentices.

2.   Notwithstanding the provisions of paragraph 1 above, public employees whose employment up to normal retiring age is guaranteed by national laws or regulations may be excluded from protection.

3.   Where a declaration made in virtue of Article 5 is in force, the persons protected shall comprise:

(*a*) Prescribed classes of employees constituting not less than 50 per cent of all employees; or

(*b*) Where specifically justified by the level of development, prescribed classes of employees constituting not less than 50 per cent of all employees in industrial workplaces employing 20 persons or more.

V. METHODS OF PROTECTION

Article 12

1.   Unless it is otherwise provided in this Convention, each Member may determine the method or methods of protection by which it chooses to put into effect the provisions of the Convention, whether by a contributory or non-contributory system, or by a combination of such systems.

2.   Nevertheless, if the legislation of a Member protects all residents whose resources, during the contingency, do not exceed prescribed limits, the protection afforded may be limited, in the light of the resources of the beneficiary and his or her family, in accordance with the provisions of Article 16.

VI. BENEFIT TO BE PROVIDED

Article 13

Benefits provided in the form of periodical payments to the unemployed may be related to the methods of protection.

Article 14

In cases of full unemployment, benefits shall be provided in the form of periodical payments calculated in such a way as to provide the beneficiary with partial and transitional wage replacement and, at the same time, to avoid creating disincentives either to work or to employment creation.

Article 15

1.   In cases of full unemployment and suspension of earnings due to a temporary suspension of work without any break in the employment relationship, when this contingency is covered, benefits shall be provided in the form of periodical payments, calculated as follows:

(*a*) Where these benefits are based on the contributions of or on behalf of the person protected or on previous earnings, they shall be fixed at not less than 50 per cent of previous earnings, it being permitted to fix a maximum for the amount of the benefit or for the earnings to be taken into account, which may be related, for example, to the wage of a skilled manual employee or to the average wage of workers in the region concerned;

(*b*) Where such benefits are not based on contributions or previous earnings, they shall be fixed at not less than 50 per cent of the statutory minimum wage or of the wage of an ordinary labourer, or at a level which provides the minimum essential for basic living expenses, whichever is the highest;

2.   Where a declaration made in virtue of Article 5 is in force, the amount of the benefits shall be equal:

(*a*) To not less than 45 per cent of the previous earnings; or

(*b*) To not less than 45 per cent of the statutory minimum wage or of the wage of an ordinary labourer but no less than a level which provides the minimum essential for basic living expenses.

3.   If appropriate, the percentages specified in paragraphs 1 and 2 may be reached by comparing net periodical payments after tax and contributions with net earnings after tax and contributions.

Article 16

Notwithstanding the provisions of Article 15, the benefit provided beyond the initial period specified in Article 19, paragraph 2 (*a*), as well as benefits paid by a Member in accordance with Article 12, paragraph 2, may be fixed after taking account of other resources, beyond a prescribed limit, available to the beneficiary and his or her family, in accordance with a prescribed scale. In any case, these benefits, in combination with any other benefits to which they may be entitled, shall guarantee them healthy and reasonable living conditions in accordance with national standards.

Article 17

1.   Where the legislation of a Member makes the right to unemployment benefit conditional upon the completion of a qualifying period, this period shall not exceed the length deemed necessary to prevent abuse.

2.   Each Member shall endeavour to adapt the qualifying period to the occupational circumstances of seasonal workers.

Article 18

1.   If the legislation of a Member provides that the payment of benefit in cases of full employment should begin only after the expiry of a waiting period, such period shall not exceed seven days.

2.   Where a declaration made in virtue of Article 5 is in force, the length of the waiting period shall not exceed ten days.

3.   In the case of seasonal workers the waiting period specified in paragraph 1 above may be adapted to their occupational circumstances.

Article 19

1.   The benefits provided in cases of full unemployment and suspension of earnings due to a temporary suspension of work without any break in the employment relationship shall be paid throughout these contingencies.

2.   Nevertheless, in the case of full unemployment:

(*a*) The initial duration of payment of the benefit provided for in Article 15 may be limited to 26 weeks in each spell of unemployment, or to 39 weeks over any period of 24 months;

(*b*) In the event of unemployment continuing beyond this initial period of benefit, the duration of payment of benefit, which may be calculated in the light of the resources of the beneficiary and his or her family in accordance with the provisions of Article 16, may be limited to a prescribed period.

3.   If the legislation of a Member provides that the initial duration of payment of the benefit provided for in Article 15 shall vary with the length of the qualifying period, the average duration fixed for the payment of benefits shall be at least 26 weeks.

4.   Where a declaration made in virtue of Article 5 is in force, the duration of payment of benefit may be limited to 13 weeks over any period of 12 months or to an average of 13 weeks if the legislation provides that the initial duration of payment shall vary with the length of the qualifying period.

5.   In the cases envisaged in paragraph 2 (*b*) above, each Member shall endeavour to grant appropriate additional assistance to the persons concerned with a view to permitting them to find productive and freely chosen employment, having recourse in particular to the measures specified in Part II.

6.   The duration of payment of benefit to seasonal workers may be adapted to their occupational circumstances, without prejudice to the provisions of paragraph 2 (*b*) above.

Article 20

The benefit to which a protected person would have been entitled in the cases of full or partial unemployment or suspension of earnings due to a temporary suspension of work without any break in the employment relationship may be refused, withdrawn, suspended or reduced to the extent prescribed:

(*a*) For as long as the person concerned is absent from the territory of the Member;

(*b*) When it has been determined by the competent authority that the person concerned had deliberately contributed to his or her own dismissal;

(*c*) When it has been determined by the competent authority that the person concerned has left employment voluntarily without just cause;

(*d*) During the period of a labour dispute, when the person concerned has stopped work to take part in a labour dispute or when he or she is prevented from working as a direct result of a stoppage of work due to this labour dispute;

(*e*) When the person concerned has attempted to obtain or has obtained benefits fraudulently;

(*f*) When the person concerned has failed without just cause to use the facilities available for placement, vocational guidance, training, retraining or redeployment in suitable work;

(*g*) As long as the person concerned is in receipt of another income maintenance benefit provided for in the legislation of the Member concerned, except a family benefit, provided that the part of the benefit which is suspended does not exceed that other benefit.

Article 21

1. The benefit to which a protected person would have been entitled in the case of full unemployment may be refused, withdrawn, suspended or reduced, to the extent prescribed, when the person concerned refuses to accept suitable employment.

2. In assessing the suitability of employment, account shall be taken, in particular, under prescribed conditions and to an appropriate extent, of the age of unemployed persons, their length of service in their former occupation, their acquired experience, the length of their period of unemployment, the labour market situation, the impact of the employment in question on their personal and family situation and whether the employment is vacant as a direct result of a stoppage of work due to an on-going labour dispute.

Article 22

When protected persons have received directly from their employer or from any other source under national laws or regulations or collective agreements, severance pay, the principal purpose of which is to contribute towards compensating them for the loss of earnings suffered in the event of full unemployment:

(*a*) The unemployment benefit to which the persons concerned would be entitled may be suspended for a period corresponding to that during which the severance pay compensates for the loss of earnings suffered; or

(*b*) The severance pay may be reduced by an amount corresponding to the value converted into a lump sum of the unemployment benefit to which the persons concerned are entitled for a period corresponding to that during which the severance pay compensates for the loss of earnings suffered,

as each Member may decide.

Article 23

1. Each Member whose legislation provides for the right to medical care and makes it directly or indirectly conditional upon occupational activity shall endeavour to ensure, under prescribed conditions, the provision of medical care to persons in receipt of unemployment benefit and to their dependants.

2. Where a declaration made in virtue of Article 5 is in force, the implementation of paragraph 1 above may be deferred.

Article 24

1. Each Member shall endeavour to guarantee to persons in receipt of unemployment benefit, under prescribed conditions, that the periods during which benefits are paid will be taken into consideration:

(*a*) For acquisition of the right to and, where appropriate, calculation of disability, old-age and survivors' benefit, and

(*b*) For acquisition of the right to medical care and sickness, maternity and family benefit after the end of unemployment,

when the legislation of the Member concerned provides for such benefits and makes them directly or indirectly conditional upon occupational activity.

2. Where a declaration made in virtue of Article 5 is in force, the implementation of paragraph 1 above may be deferred.

Article 25

1. Each Member shall ensure that statutory social security schemes which are based on occupational activity are adjusted to the occupational circumstances of part-time workers, unless their hours of work or earnings can be considered, under prescribed conditions, as negligible.

2. Where a declaration made in virtue of Article 5 is in force, the implementation of paragraph 1 above may be deferred.

VII. SPECIAL PROVISIONS FOR NEW APPLICANTS FOR EMPLOYMENT

Article 26

1. Members shall take account of the fact that there are many categories of persons seeking work who have never been, or have ceased to be, recognised as unemployed or have never been, or have ceased to be, covered by schemes for the protection of the unemployed. Consequently, at least three of the following ten categories of persons seeking work shall receive social benefits, in accordance with prescribed terms and conditions:

(*a*) Young persons who have completed their vocational training;

(*b*) Young persons who have completed their studies;

(*c*) Young persons who have completed their compulsory military service;

(*d*) Persons after a period devoted to bringing up a child or caring for someone who is sick, disabled or elderly;

(*e*) Persons whose spouse had died, when they are not entitled to a survivor's benefit;

(*f*) Divorced or separated persons;

(*g*) Released prisoners;

(*h*) Adults, including disabled persons, who have completed a period of training;

(*i*) Migrant workers on return to their home country, except in so far as they have acquired rights under the legislation of the country where they last worked;

(*j*) Previously self-employed persons.

2. Each Member shall specify, in its reports under article 22 of the Constitution of the International Labour Organisation, the categories of persons listed in paragraph 1 above which it undertakes to protect.

3. Each Member shall endeavour to extend protection progressively to a greater number of categories than the number initially protected.

VIII. Legal, administrative and financial guarantees

Article 27

1. In the event of refusal, withdrawal, suspension or reduction of benefit or dispute as to its amount, claimants shall have the right to present a complaint to the body administering the benefit scheme and to appeal thereafter to an independent body. They shall be informed in writing of the procedures available, which shall be simple and rapid.

2. The appeal procedure shall enable the claimant, in accordance with national law and practice, to be represented or assisted by a qualified person of the claimant's choice or by a delegate of a representative workers' organisation or by a delegate of an organisation representative of protected persons.

Article 28

Each Member shall assume general responsibility for the sound administration of the institutions and services entrusted with the application of the Convention.

Article 29

1. When the administration is directly entrusted to a government department responsible to Parliament, representatives of the protected persons and of the employers shall be associated in the administration in an advisory capacity, under prescribed conditions.

2. When the administration is not entrusted to a government department responsible to Parliament:

(*a*) Representatives of the protected persons shall participate in the administration or be associated therewith in an advisory capacity under prescribed conditions;

(*b*) National laws or regulations may also provide for the participation of employers' representatives;

(*c*) The laws or regulations may further provide for the participation of representatives of the public authorities.

Article 30

In cases where subsidies are granted by the State or the social security system in order to safeguard employment, Members shall take the necessary steps to ensure that the payments are expended only for the intended purpose and to prevent fraud or abuse by those who receive such payments.

Article 31

This Convention revises the Unemployment Provision Convention, 1934.

Article 32

The formal ratifications of this Convention shall be communicated to the Director-General of the International Labour Office for registration.

Article 33

1. This Convention shall be binding only upon those Members of the International Labour Organisation whose ratifications have been registered with the Director-General.

2. It shall come into force twelve months after the date on which the ratification of two Members have been registered with the Director-General.

3. Thereafter, this Convention shall come into force for any Member twelve months after the date on which its ratification has been registered.

Article 34

1. A Member which has ratified this Convention may denounce it after the expiration of ten years from the date on which the Convention first comes into force, by an act communicated to the Director-General of the International Labour Office for registration. Such denunciation shall not take effect until one year after the date on which it is registered.

2.   Each Member which has ratified this Convention and which does not, within the year following the expiration of the period of ten years mentioned in the preceding paragraph, exercise the right of denunciation provided for in this Article, will be bound for another period of ten years and, thereafter, may denounce this Convention at the expiration of each period of ten years under the terms provided for in this Article.

Article 35

1.   The Director-General of the International Labour Office shall notify all Members of the International Labour Organisation of the registration of all ratifications and denunciations communicated to him by the Members of the Organisation.

2.   When notifying the members of the Organisation of the registration of the second ratification communicated to him, the Director-General shall draw the attention of the Members of the Organisation to the date upon which the Convention will come into force.

Article 36

The Director-General of the International Labour Office shall communicate to the Secretary-General of the United Nations for registration in accordance with Article 102 of the Charter of the United Nations full particulars of all ratifications and acts of denunciation registered by him in accordance with the provisions of the preceding Articles.

Article 37

At such times as it may consider necessary the Governing Body of the International Labour Office shall present to the General Conference a report on the working of this Convention and shall examine the desirability of placing on the agenda of the Conference the question of its revision in whole or in part.

Article 38

1.   Should the Conference adopt a new Convention revising this Convention in whole or in part, then, unless the new Convention otherwise provides:

(a) The ratification by a Member of the new revising Convention shall *ipso jure* involve the immediate denunciation of this Convention, notwithstanding the provisions of Article 34 above, if and when the new revising Convention shall have come into force;

(b) As from the date when the new revising Convention comes into force this Convention shall cease to be open to ratification by the Members.

2. This Convention shall in any case remain in force in its actual form and content for those Members which have ratified it but have not ratified the revising Convention.

Article 39

The English and French versions of the text of this Convention are equally authoritative.

62. Convention (No. 169) concerning Indigenous and Tribal Peoples in Independent Countries

Adopted on 27 June 1989 by the General Conference of the International Labour Organisation at its seventy-sixth session

ENTRY INTO FORCE: 5 September 1991

The General Conference of the International Labour Organisation,

Having been convened at Geneva by the Governing Body of the International Labour Office, and having met in its seventy-sixth session on 7 June 1989, and

Noting the international standards contained in the Indigenous and Tribal Populations Convention and Recommendation, 1957, and

Recalling the terms of the Universal Declaration of Human Rights, the International Covenant on Economic, Social and Cultural Rights, the International Covenant on Civil and Political Rights, and the many international instruments on the prevention of discrimination, and

Considering that the developments which have taken place in international law since 1957, as well as developments in the situation of indigenous and tribal peoples in all regions of the world, have made it appropriate to adopt new international standards on the subject with a view to removing the assimilationist orientation of the earlier standards, and

Recognising the aspirations of these peoples to exercise control over their own institutions, ways of life and economic development and to maintain and develop their identities, languages and religions, within the framework of the States in which they live, and

Noting that in many parts of the world these peoples are unable to enjoy their fundamental human rights to the same degree as the rest of the population of the States within which they live, and that their laws, values, customs and perspectives have often been eroded, and

Calling attention to the distinctive contributions of indigenous and tribal peoples to the cultural diversity and social and ecological harmony of humankind and to international co-operation and understanding, and

Noting that the following provisions have been framed with the co-operation of the United Nations, the Food and Agriculture Organization of the United Nations, the United Nations Educational, Scientific and Cultural

471

Organization and the World Health Organization, as well as of the Inter-American Indian Institute, at appropriate levels and in their respective fields, and that it is proposed to continue this co-operation in promoting and securing the application of these provisions, and

Having decided upon the adoption of certain proposals with regard to the partial revision of the Indigenous and Tribal Populations Convention, 1957 (No. 107), which is the fourth item on the agenda of the session, and

Having determined that these proposals shall take the form of an international Convention revising the Indigenous and Tribal Populations Convention, 1957;

Adopts this twenty-seventh day of June of the year one thousand nine hundred and eighty-nine the following Convention, which may be cited as the Indigenous and Tribal Peoples Convention, 1989;

PART I. GENERAL POLICY

Article 1

1. This Convention applies to:

(*a*) Tribal peoples in independent countries whose social, cultural and economic conditions distinguish them from other sections of the national community, and whose status is regulated wholly or partially by their own customs or traditions or by special laws or regulations;

(*b*) Peoples in independent countries who are regarded as indigenous on account of their descent from the populations which inhabited the country, or a geographical region to which the country belongs, at the time of conquest or colonisation or the establishment of present State boundaries and who, irrespective of their legal status, retain some or all of their own social, economic, cultural and political institutions.

2. Self-identification as indigenous or tribal shall be regarded as a fundamental criterion for determining the groups to which the provisions of this Convention apply.

3. The use of the term "peoples" in this Convention shall not be construed as having any implications as regards the rights which may attach to the term under international law.

Article 2

1. Governments shall have the responsibility for developing, with the participation of the peoples concerned, co-ordinated and systematic action to protect the rights of these peoples and to guarantee respect for their integrity.

2. Such action shall include measures for:

(*a*) Ensuring that members of these peoples benefit on an equal footing from the rights and opportunities which national laws and regulations grant to other members of the population;

(*b*) Promoting the full realisation of the social, economic and cultural rights of these peoples with respect for their social and cultural identity, their customs and traditions and their institutions;

(*c*) Assisting the members of the peoples concerned to eliminate socio-economic gaps that may exist between indigenous and other members of the national community, in a manner compatible with their aspirations and ways of life.

Article 3

1. Indigenous and tribal peoples shall enjoy the full measure of human rights and fundamental freedoms without hindrance or discrimination. The provisions of the Convention shall be applied without discrimination to male and female members of these peoples.

2. No form of force or coercion shall be used in violation of the human rights and fundamental freedoms of the peoples concerned, including the rights contained in this Convention.

Article 4

1. Special measures shall be adopted as appropriate for safeguarding the persons, institutions, property, labour, cultures and environment of the peoples concerned.

2. Such special measures shall not be contrary to the freely-expressed wishes of the peoples concerned.

3. Enjoyment of the general rights of citizenship, without discrimination, shall not be prejudiced in any way by such special measures.

Article 5

In applying the provisions of this Convention:

(*a*) The social, cultural, religious and spiritual values and practices of these peoples shall be recognised and protected, and due account shall be taken of the nature of the problems which face them both as groups and as individuals;

(*b*) The integrity of the values, practices and institutions of these peoples shall be respected;

(*c*) Policies aimed at mitigating the difficulties experienced by these peoples in facing new conditions of life and work shall be adopted, with the participation and co-operation of the peoples affected.

Article 6

1. In applying the provisions of this Convention, Governments shall:

(*a*) Consult the peoples concerned, through appropriate procedures and in particular through their representative institutions, whenever consideration is being given to legislative or administrative measures which may affect them directly;

(*b*) Establish means by which these peoples can freely participate, to at least the same extent as other sectors of the population, at all levels of decision-making in elective institutions and administrative and other bodies responsible for policies and programmes which concern them;

(*c*) Establish means for the full development of these peoples' own institutions and initiatives, and in appropriate cases provide the resources necessary for this purpose.

2. The consultations carried out in application of this Convention shall be undertaken, in good faith and in a form appropriate to the circumstances, with the objective of achieving agreement or consent to the proposed measures.

Article 7

1. The peoples concerned shall have the right to decide their own priorities for the process of development as it affects their lives, beliefs, institutions and spiritual well-being and the lands they occupy or otherwise use, and to exercise control, to the extent possible, over their own economic, social and cultural development. In addition, they shall participate in the formulation, implementation and evaluation of plans and programmes for national and regional development which may affect them directly.

2. The improvement of the conditions of life and work and levels of health and education of the peoples concerned, with their participation and co-operation, shall be a matter of priority in plans for the overall economic development of areas they inhabit. Special projects for development of the areas in question shall also be so designed as to promote such improvement.

3. Governments shall ensure that, whenever appropriate, studies are carried out, in co-operation with the peoples concerned, to assess the social, spiritual, cultural and environmental impact on them of planned development activities. The results of these studies shall be considered as fundamental criteria for the implementation of these activities.

4. Governments shall take measures, in co-operation with the peoples concerned, to protect and preserve the environment of the territories they inhabit.

Article 8

1. In applying national laws and regulations to the peoples concerned, due regard shall be had to their customs or customary laws.

2. These peoples shall have the right to retain their own customs and institutions, where these are not incompatible with fundamental rights defined by the national legal system and with internationally recognized human rights. Procedures shall be established, whenever necessary, to resolve conflicts which may arise in the application of this principle.

3. The application of paragraphs 1 and 2 of this Article shall not prevent members of these peoples from exercising the rights granted to all citizens and from assuming the corresponding duties.

Article 9

1. To the extent compatible with the national legal system and internationally recognised human rights, the methods customarily practised by the peoples concerned for dealing with offences committed by their members shall be respected.

2. The customs of these peoples in regard to penal matters shall be taken into consideration by the authorities and courts dealing with such cases.

Article 10

1. In imposing penalties laid down by general law on members of these peoples account shall be taken of their economic, social and cultural characteristics.

2. Preference shall be given to methods of punishment other than confinement in prison.

Article 11

The exaction from members of the peoples concerned of compulsory personal services in any form, whether paid or unpaid, shall be prohibited and punishable by law, except in cases prescribed by law for all citizens.

Article 12

The peoples concerned shall be safeguarded against the abuse of their rights and shall be able to take legal proceedings, either individually or through their representative bodies, for the effective protection of these rights. Measures shall be taken to ensure that members of these peoples can understand and be understood in legal proceedings, where necessary through the provision of interpretation or by other effective means.

Part II. Land

Article 13

1.   In applying the provisions of this Part of the Convention governments shall respect the special importance for the cultures and spiritual values of the peoples concerned of their relationship with the lands or territories, or both as applicable, which they occupy or otherwise use, and in particular the collective aspects of this relationship.

2.   The use of the term "lands" in Articles 15 and 16 shall include the concept of territories, which covers the total environment of the areas which the peoples concerned occupy or otherwise use.

Article 14

1.   The rights of ownership and possession of the peoples concerned over the lands which they traditionally occupy shall be recognised. In addition, measures shall be taken in appropriate cases to safeguard the right of the peoples concerned to use lands not exclusively occupied by them, but to which they have traditionally had access for their subsistence and traditional activities. Particular attention shall be paid to the situation of nomadic peoples and shifting cultivators in this respect.

2.   Governments shall take steps as necessary to identify the lands which the peoples concerned traditionally occupy, and to guarantee effective protection of their rights of ownership and possession.

3.   Adequate procedures shall be established within the national legal system to resolve land claims by the peoples concerned.

Article 15

1.   The rights of the peoples concerned to the natural resources pertaining to their lands shall be specially safeguarded. These rights include the right of these peoples to participate in the use, management and conservation of these resources.

2.   In cases in which the State retains the ownership of mineral or sub-surface resources or rights to other resources pertaining to lands, governments shall establish or maintain procedures through which they shall consult these peoples, with a view to ascertaining whether and to what de-

gree their interests would be prejudiced, before undertaking or permitting any programmes for the exploration or exploitation of such resources pertaining to their lands. The peoples concerned shall wherever possible participate in the benefits of such activities, and shall receive fair compensation for any damages which they may sustain as a result of such activities.

Article 16

1.   Subject to the following paragraphs of this Article, the peoples concerned shall not be removed from the lands which they occupy.

2.   Where the relocation of these peoples is considered necessary as an exceptional measure, such relocation shall take place only with their free and informed consent. Where their consent cannot be obtained, such relocation shall take place only following appropriate procedures established by national laws and regulations, including public inquiries where appropriate, which provide the opportunity for effective representation of the peoples concerned.

3.   Whenever possible, these peoples shall have the right to return to their traditional lands, as soon as the grounds for relocation cease to exist.

4.   When such return is not possible, as determined by agreement or, in the absence of such agreement, through appropriate procedures, these peoples shall be provided in all possible cases with lands of quality and legal status at least equal to that of the lands previously occupied by them, suitable to provide for their present needs and future development. Where the peoples concerned express a preference for compensation in money or in kind, they shall be so compensated under appropriate guarantees.

5.   Persons thus relocated shall be fully compensated for any resulting loss or injury.

Article 17

1.   Procedures established by the peoples concerned for the transmission of land rights among members of these peoples shall be respected.

2.   The peoples concerned shall be consulted whenever consideration is being given to their capacity to alienate their lands or otherwise transmit their rights outside their own community.

3.   Persons not belonging to these peoples shall be prevented from taking advantage of their customs or of lack of understanding of the laws on the part of their members to secure the ownership, possession or use of land belonging to them.

Article 18

Adequate penalties shall be established by law for unauthorised intrusion upon, or use of, the lands of the peoples concerned, and governments shall take measures to prevent such offences.

Article 19

National agrarian programmes shall secure to the peoples concerned treatment equivalent to that accorded to other sectors of the population with regard to:

(a) The provision of more land for these peoples when they have not the area necessary for providing the essentials of a normal existence, or for any possible increase in their numbers;

(b) The provision of the means required to promote the development of the lands which these peoples already possess.

PART III. RECRUITMENT AND CONDITIONS OF EMPLOYMENT

Article 20

1. Governments shall, within the framework of national laws and regulations, and in co-operation with the peoples concerned, adopt special measures to ensure the effective protection with regard to recruitment and conditions of employment of workers belonging to these peoples, to the extent that they are not effectively protected by laws applicable to workers in general.

2. Governments shall do everything possible to prevent any discrimination between workers belonging to the peoples concerned and other workers, in particular as regards:

(a) Admission to employment, including skilled employment, as well as measures for promotion and advancement;

(b) Equal remuneration for work of equal value;

(c) Medical and social assistance, occupational safety and health, all social security benefits and any other occupationally related benefits, and housing;

(d) The right of association and freedom for all lawful trade union activities, and the right to conclude collective agreements with employers or employers' organisations.

3. The measures taken shall include measures to ensure:

(a) That workers belonging to the peoples concerned, including seasonal, casual and migrant workers in agricultural and other employment, as well as those employed by labour contractors, enjoy the protection afforded by national law and practice to other such workers in the same sectors, and that they are fully informed of their rights under labour legislation and of the means of redress available to them;

(b) That workers belonging to these peoples are not subjected to working conditions hazardous to their health, in particular through exposure to pesticides or other toxic substances;

(c) That workers belonging to these peoples are not subjected to coercive recruitment systems, including bonded labour and other forms of debt servitude;

(d) That workers belonging to these peoples enjoy equal opportunities and equal treatment in employment for men and women, and protection from sexual harassment.

4.   Particular attention shall be paid to the establishment of adequate labour inspection services in areas where workers belonging to the peoples concerned undertake wage employment, in order to ensure compliance with the provisions of this Part of this Convention.

PART IV.   VOCATIONAL TRAINING, HANDICRAFTS AND RURAL INDUSTRIES

Article 21

Members of the peoples concerned shall enjoy opportunities at least equal to those of other citizens in respect of vocational training measures.

Article 22

1.   Measures shall be taken to promote the voluntary participation of members of the peoples concerned in vocational training programmes of general application.

2.   Whenever existing programmes of vocational training of general application do not meet the special needs of the peoples concerned, governments shall, with the participation of these peoples, ensure the provision of special training programmes and facilities.

3.   Any special training programmes shall be based on the economic environment, social and cultural conditions and practical needs of the peoples concerned. Any studies made in this connection shall be carried out in co-operation with these peoples, who shall be consulted on the organisation and operation of such programmes. Where feasible, these peoples shall progressively assume responsibility for the organisation and operation of such special training programmes, if they so decide.

Article 23

1.   Handicrafts, rural and community-based industries, and subsistence economy and traditional activities of the peoples concerned, such as hunting, fishing, trapping and gathering, shall be recognised as important factors in the maintenance of their cultures and in their economic self-reliance and development. Governments shall, with the participation of these peoples and whenever appropriate, ensure that these activities are strengthened and promoted.

2.   Upon the request of the peoples concerned, appropriate technical and financial assistance shall be provided wherever possible, taking into account the traditional technologies and cultural characteristics of these peoples, as well as the importance of sustainable and equitable development.

PART V. SOCIAL SECURITY AND HEALTH

Article 24

Social security schemes shall be extended progressively to cover the peoples concerned, and applied without discrimination against them.

Article 25

1.   Governments shall ensure that adequate health services are made available to the peoples concerned, or shall provide them with resources to allow them to design and deliver such services under their own responsibility and control, so that they may enjoy the highest attainable standard of physical and mental health.

2.   Health services shall, to the extent possible, be community-based. These services shall be planned and administered in co-operation with the peoples concerned and take into account their economic, geographic, social and cultural conditions as well as their traditional preventive care, healing practices and medicines.

3.   The health care system shall give preference to the training and employment of local community health workers, and focus on primary health care while maintaining strong links with other levels of health care services.

4.   The provision of such health services shall be co-ordinated with other social, economic and cultural measures in the country.

PART VI. EDUCATION AND MEANS OF COMMUNICATION

Article 26

Measures shall be taken to ensure that members of the peoples concerned have the opportunity to acquire education at all levels on at least an equal footing with the rest of the national community.

Article 27

1. Education programmes and services for the peoples concerned shall be developed and implemented in co-operation with them to address their special needs, and shall incorporate their histories, their knowledge and technologies, their value systems and their further social, economic and cultural aspirations.

2. The competent authority shall ensure the training of members of these peoples and their involvement in the formulation and implementation of education programmes, with a view to the progressive transfer of responsibility for the conduct of these programmes to these peoples as appropriate.

3. In addition, governments shall recognise the right of these peoples to establish their own educational institutions and facilities, provided that such institutions meet minimum standards established by the competent authority in consultation with these peoples. Appropriate resources shall be provided for this purpose.

Article 28

1. Children belonging to the peoples concerned shall, wherever practicable, be taught to read and write in their own indigenous language or in the language most commonly used by the group to which they belong. When this is not practicable, the competent authorities shall undertake consultations with these peoples with a view to the adoption of measures to achieve this objective.

2. Adequate measures shall be taken to ensure that these peoples have the opportunity to attain fluency in the national language or in one of the official languages of the country.

3. Measures shall be taken to preserve and promote the development and practice of the indigenous languages of the peoples concerned.

Article 29

The imparting of general knowledge and skills that will help children belonging to the peoples concerned to participate fully and on an equal footing in their own community and in the national community shall be an aim of education for these peoples.

Article 30

1. Governments shall adopt measures appropriate to the traditions and cultures of the peoples concerned, to make known to them their rights and duties, especially in regard to labour, economic opportunities, education and health matters, social welfare and their rights deriving from this Convention.

2. If necessary, this shall be done by means of written translations and through the use of mass communications in the languages of these peoples.

Article 31

Educational measures shall be taken among all sections of the national community, and particularly among those that are in most direct contact with the peoples concerned, with the object of eliminating prejudices that they may harbour in respect of these peoples. To this end, efforts shall be made to ensure that history textbooks and other educational materials provide a fair, accurate and informative portrayal of the societies and cultures of these peoples.

PART VII. CONTACTS AND CO-OPERATION ACROSS BORDERS

Article 32

Governments shall take appropriate measures, including by means of international agreements, to facilitate contacts and co-operation between indigenous and tribal peoples across borders, including activities in the economic, social, cultural, spiritual and environmental fields.

PART VIII. ADMINISTRATION

Article 33

1. The governmental authority responsible for the matters covered in this Convention shall ensure that agencies or other appropriate mechanisms exist to administer the programmes affecting the peoples concerned, and shall ensure that they have the means necessary for the proper fulfilment of the functions assigned to them.

2. These programmes shall include:

(*a*) The planning, co-ordination, execution and evaluation, in co-operation with the peoples concerned, of the measures provided for in this Convention;

(*b*) The proposing of legislative and other measures to the competent authorities and supervision of the application of the measures taken, in co-operation with the peoples concerned.

PART IX. GENERAL PROVISIONS

Article 34

The nature and scope of the measures to be taken to give effect to this Convention shall be determined in a flexible manner, having regard to the conditions characteristic of each country.

Article 35

The application of the provisions of this Convention shall not adversely affect rights and benefits of the peoples concerned pursuant to other Conventions and Recommendations, international instruments, treaties, or national laws, awards, custom or agreements.

PART X. FINAL PROVISIONS

Article 36

This Convention revises the Indigenous and Tribal Populations Convention, 1957.

Article 37

The formal ratifications of this Convention shall be communicated to the Director-General of the International Labour Office for registration.

Article 38

1. This Convention shall be binding only upon those Members of the International Labour Organisation whose ratifications have been registered with the Director-General.

2. It shall come into force twelve months after the date on which the ratifications of two Members have been registered with the Director-General.

3. Thereafter, this Convention shall come into force for any Member twelve months after the date on which its ratification has been registered.

Article 39

1. A Member which has ratified this Convention may denounce it after the expiration of ten years from the date on which the Convention first comes into force, by an act communicated to the Director-General of the International Labour Office for registration. Such denunciation shall not take effect until one year after the date on which it is registered.

2. Each Member which has ratified this Convention and which does not, within the year following the expiration of the period of ten years mentioned in the preceding paragraph, exercise the right of denunciation provided for in this Article, will be bound for another period of ten years and, thereafter, may denounce this Convention at the expiration of each period of ten years under the terms provided for in this Article.

Article 40

1. The Director-General of the International Labour Office shall notify all Members of the International Labour Organisation of the registration of all ratifications and denunciations communicated to him by the Members of the Organisation.

2. When notifying the Members of the Organisation of the registration of the second ratification communicated to him, the Director-General shall draw the attention of the Members of the Organisation to the date upon which the Convention will come into force.

Article 41

The Director-General of the International Labour Office shall communicate to the Secretary-General of the United Nations for registration in accordance with Article 102 of the Charter of the United Nations full particulars of all ratifications and acts of denunciation registered by him in accordance with the provisions of the preceding Articles.

Article 42

At such times as it may consider necessary the Governing Body of the International Labour Office shall present to the General Conference a report on the working of this Convention and shall examine the desirability of placing on the agenda of the Conference the question of its revision in whole or in part.

Article 43

1.　Should the Conference adopt a new Convention revising this Convention in whole or in part, then, unless the new Convention otherwise provides:

(*a*) The ratification by a Member of the new revising Convention shall *ipso jure* involve the immediate denunciation of this Convention, notwithstanding the provisions of Article 39 above, if and when the new revising Convention shall have come into force:

(*b*) As from the date when the new revising Convention comes into force this Convention shall cease to be open to ratification by the Members.

2.　This Convention shall in any case remain in force in its actual form and content for those Members which have ratified it but have not ratified the revising Convention.

Article 44

The English and French versions of the text of this Convention are equally authoritative.

L. MARRIAGE, FAMILY AND YOUTH

63. Convention on Consent to Marriage, Minimum Age for Marriage and Registration of Marriages

Opened for signature and ratification by General Assembly resolution 1763 A (XVII) of 7 November 1962

ENTRY INTO FORCE: 9 December 1964, in accordance with article 6

The Contracting States,

Desiring, in conformity with the Charter of the United Nations, to promote universal respect for, and observance of, human rights and fundamental freedoms for all, without distinction as to race, sex, language or religion,

Recalling that article 16 of the Universal Declaration of Human Rights states that:

> "(1) Men and women of full age, without any limitation due to race, nationality or religion, have the right to marry and to found a family. They are entitled to equal rights as to marriage, during marriage and at its dissolution.

> "(2) Marriage shall be entered into only with the free and full consent of the intending spouses.",

Recalling further that the General Assembly of the United Nations declared, by resolution 843 (IX) of 17 December 1954, that certain customs, ancient laws and practices relating to marriage and the family were inconsistent with the principles set forth in the Charter of the United Nations and in the Universal Declaration of Human Rights,

Reaffirming that all States, including those which have or assume responsibility for the administration of Non-Self-Governing and Trust Territories until their achievement of independence, should take all appropriate measures with a view to abolishing such customs, ancient laws and practices by ensuring, *inter alia,* complete freedom in the choice of a spouse, eliminating completely child marriages and the betrothal of young girls before the age of puberty, establishing appropriate penalties where necessary and establishing a civil or other register in which all marriages will be recorded,

Hereby agree as hereinafter provided:

Article 1

1.   No marriage shall be legally entered into without the full and free consent of both parties, such consent to be expressed by them in person after due publicity and in the presence of the authority competent to solemnize the marriage and of witnesses, as prescribed by law.

2.   Notwithstanding anything in paragraph 1 above, it shall not be necessary for one of the parties to be present when the competent authority is satisfied that the circumstances are exceptional and that the party has, before a competent authority and in such manner as may be prescribed by law, expressed and not withdrawn consent.

Article 2

States Parties to the present Convention shall take legislative action to specify a minimum age for marriage. No marriage shall be legally entered into by any person under this age, except where a competent authority has granted a dispensation as to age, for serious reasons, in the interest of the intending spouses.

Article 3

All marriages shall be registered in an appropriate official register by the competent authority.

Article 4

1.   The present Convention shall, until 31 December 1963, be open for signature on behalf of all States Members of the United Nations or members of any of the specialized agencies, and of any other State invited by the General Assembly of the United Nations to become a Party to the Convention.

2.   The present Convention is subject to ratification. The instruments of ratification shall be deposited with the Secretary-General of the United Nations.

Article 5

1.   The present Convention shall be open for accession to all States referred to in article 4, paragraph 1.

2.   Accession shall be effected by the deposit of an instrument of accession with the Secretary-General of the United Nations.

Article 6

1. The present Convention shall come into force on the ninetieth day following the date of deposit of the eighth instrument of ratification or accession.

2. For each State ratifying or acceding to the Convention after the deposit of the eighth instrument of ratification or accession, the Convention shall enter into force on the ninetieth day after deposit by such State of its instrument of ratification or accession.

Article 7

1. Any Contracting State may denounce the present Convention by written notification to the Secretary-General of the United Nations. Denunciation shall take effect one year after the date of receipt of the notification by the Secretary-General.

2. The present Convention shall cease to be in force as from the date when the denunciation which reduces the number of Parties to less than eight becomes effective.

Article 8

Any dispute which may arise between any two or more Contracting States concerning the interpretation or application of the present Convention which is not settled by negotiation shall, at the request of all the parties to the dispute, be referred to the International Court of Justice for decision, unless the parties agree to another mode of settlement.

Article 9

The Secretary-General of the United Nations shall notify all States Members of the United Nations and the non-member States contemplated in article 4, paragraph 1, of the present Convention of the following:

(*a*) Signatures and instruments of ratification received in accordance with article 4;

(*b*) Instruments of accession received in accordance with article 5;

(*c*) The date upon which the Convention enters into force in accordance with article 6;

(*d*) Notifications of denunciation received in accordance with article 7, paragraph 1;

(*e*) Abrogation in accordance with article 7, paragraph 2.

Article 10

1.   The present Convention, of which the Chinese, English, French, Russian and Spanish texts shall be equally authentic, shall be deposited in the archives of the United Nations.

2.   The Secretary-General of the United Nations shall transmit a certified copy of the Convention to all States Members of the United Nations and to the non-member States contemplated in article 4, paragraph 1.

64. Recommendation on Consent to Marriage, Minimum Age for Marriage and Registration of Marriages

General Assembly resolution 2018 (XX) of 1 November 1965

The General Assembly,

Recognizing that the family group should be strengthened because it is the basic unit of every society, and that men and women of full age have the right to marry and to found a family, that they are entitled to equal rights as to marriage and that marriage shall be entered into only with the free and full consent of the intending spouses, in accordance with the provisions of article 16 of the Universal Declaration of Human Rights,

Recalling its resolution 843 (IX) of 17 December 1954,

Recalling further article 2 of the Supplementary Convention on the Abolition of Slavery, the Slave Trade, and Institutions and Practices Similar to Slavery of 1956, which makes certain provisions concerning the age of marriage, consent to marriage and registration of marriages,

Recalling also that Article 13, paragraph 1 b, of the Charter of the United Nations provides that the General Assembly shall make recommendations for the purpose of assisting in the realization of human rights and fundamental freedoms for all without distinction as to race, sex, language or religion,

Recalling likewise that, under Article 64 of the Charter, the Economic and Social Council may make arrangements with the Members of the United Nations to obtain reports on the steps taken to give effect to its own recommendations and to recommendations on matters falling within its competence made by the General Assembly,

1. *Recommends,* that, where not already provided by existing legislative or other measures, each Member State should take the necessary steps, in accordance with its constitutional processes and its traditional and religious practices, to adopt such legislative or other measures as may be appropriate to give effect to the following principles:

Principle 1

(*a*) No marriage shall be legally entered into without the full and free consent of both parties, such consent to be expressed by them in person, after due publicity and in the presence of the authority competent to solemnize the marriage and of witnesses, as prescribed by law.

(*b*) Marriage by proxy shall be permitted only when the competent authorities are satisfied that each party has, before a competent authority and in such manner as may be prescribed by law, fully and freely expressed consent before witnesses and not withdrawn such consent.

Principle II

Member States shall take legislative action to specify a minimum age for marriage, which in any case shall not be less than fifteen years of age; no marriage shall be legally entered into by any person under this age, except where a competent authority has granted a dispensation as to age, for serious reasons, in the interest of the intending spouses.

Principle III

All marriages shall be registered in an appropriate official register by the competent authority.

2. *Recommends* that each Member State should bring the Recommendation on Consent to Marriage, Minimum Age for Marriage and Registration of Marriages contained in the present resolution before the authorities competent to enact legislation or to take other action at the earliest practicable moment and, if possible, no later than eighteen months after the adoption of the Recommendation;

3. *Recommends* that Member States should inform the Secretary-General, as soon as possible after the action referred to in paragraph 2 above, of the measures taken under the present Recommendation to bring it before the competent authority or authorities, with particulars regarding the authority or authorities considered as competent;

4. *Recommends further* that Member States should report to the Secretary-General at the end of three years, and thereafter at intervals of five years, on their law and practice with regard to the matters dealt with in the present Recommendation, showing the extent to which effect has been given or is proposed to be given to the provisions of the Recommendation and such modifications as have been found or may be found necessary in adapting or applying it;

5. *Requests* the Secretary-General to prepare for the Commission on the Status of Women a document containing the reports received from Governments concerning methods of implementing the three basic principles of the present Recommendation;

6. *Invites* the Commission on the Status of Women to examine the reports received from Member States pursuant to the present Recommendation and to report thereon to the Economic and Social Council with such recommendations as it may deem fitting.

65. Declaration on the Promotion among Youth of the Ideals of Peace, Mutual Respect and Understanding between Peoples

Proclaimed by General Assembly resolution 2037 (XX) of 7 December 1965

The General Assembly,

Recalling that under the terms of the Charter of the United Nations the peoples have declared themselves determined to save succeeding generations from the scourge of war,

Recalling further that in the Charter the United Nations has affirmed its faith in fundamental human rights, in the dignity of the human person and in the equal rights of men and nations,

Reaffirming the principles embodied in the Universal Declaration of Human Rights, the Declaration on the Granting of Independence to Colonial Countries and Peoples, the United Nations Declaration on the Elimination of All Forms of Racial Discrimination, General Assembly resolution 110 (II) of 3 November 1947 condemning all forms of propaganda designed or likely to provoke or encourage any threat to the peace, the Declaration of the Rights of the Child, and General Assembly resolution 1572 (XV) of 18 December 1960, which have a particular bearing upon the upbringing of young people in a spirit of peace, mutual respect and understanding among peoples,

Recalling that the purpose of the United Nations Educational, Scientific and Cultural Organization is to contribute to peace and security by promoting collaboration among nations through education, science and culture, and recognizing the role and contributions of that organization towards the education of young people in the spirit of international understanding, co-operation and peace,

Taking into consideration the fact that in the conflagrations which have afflicted mankind it is the young people who have had to suffer most and who have had the greatest number of victims,

Convinced that young people wish to have an assured future and that peace, freedom and justice are among the chief guarantees that their desire for happiness will be fulfilled,

Bearing in mind the important part being played by young people in every field of human endeavour and the fact that they are destined to guide the fortunes of mankind,

Bearing in mind furthermore that, in this age of great scientific, technological and cultural achievements, the energies, enthusiasm and creative abilities of the young should be devoted to the material and spiritual advancement of all peoples,

Convinced that the young should know, respect and develop the cultural heritage of their own country and that of all mankind,

Convinced furthermore that the education of the young and exchanges of young people and of ideas in a spirit of peace, mutual respect and understanding between peoples can help to improve international relations and to strengthen peace and security,

Proclaims this Declaration on the Promotion among Youth of the Ideals of Peace, Mutual Respect and Understanding between Peoples and calls upon Governments, non-governmental organizations and youth movements to recognize the principles set forth therein and to ensure their observance by means of appropriate measures:

Principle I

Young people shall be brought up in the spirit of peace, justice, freedom, mutual respect and understanding in order to promote equal rights for all human beings and all nations, economic and social progress, disarmament and the maintenance of international peace and security.

Principle II

All means of education, including as of major importance the guidance given by parents or family, instruction and information intended for the young should foster among them the ideals of peace, humanity, liberty and international solidarity and all other ideals which help to bring peoples closer together, and acquaint them with the role entrusted to the United Nations as a means of preserving and maintaining peace and promoting international understanding and co-operation.

Principle III

Young people shall be brought up in the knowledge of the dignity and equality of all men, without distinction as to race, colour, ethnic origins or beliefs, and in respect for fundamental human rights and for the right of peoples to self-determination.

Principle IV

Exchanges, travel, tourism, meetings, the study of foreign languages, the twinning of towns and universities without discrimination and similar activities should be encouraged and facilitated among young people of all countries in order to bring them together in educational, cultural and sporting activities in the spirit of this Declaration.

Principle V

National and international associations of young people should be encouraged to promote the purposes of the United Nations, particularly international peace and security, friendly relations among nations based on respect for the equal sovereignty of States, the final abolition of colonialism and of racial discrimination and other violations of human rights.

Youth organizations in accordance with this Declaration should take all appropriate measures within their respective fields of activity in order to make their contribution without any discrimination to the work of educating the young generation in accordance with these ideals.

Such organizations, in conformity with the principle of freedom of association, should promote the free exchange of ideas in the spirit of the principles of this Declaration and of the purposes of the United Nations set forth in the Charter.

All youth organizations should conform to the principles set forth in this Declaration.

Principle VI

A major aim in educating the young shall be to develop all their faculties and to train them to acquire higher moral qualities, to be deeply attached to be noble ideals of peace, liberty, the dignity and equality of all men, and imbued with respect and love for humanity and its creative achievements. To this end the family has an important role to play.

Young people must become conscious of their responsibilities in the world they will be called upon to manage and should be inspired with confidence in a future of happiness for mankind.

M. SOCIAL WELFARE, PROGRESS
AND DEVELOPMENT

66. Declaration on Social Progress and Development

Proclaimed by General Assembly resolution 2542 (XXIV) of 11 December 1969

The General Assembly,

Mindful of the pledge of Members of the United Nations under the Charter to take joint and separate action in co-operation with the Organization to promote higher standards of living, full employment and conditions of economic and social progress and development,

Reaffirming faith in human rights and fundamental freedoms and in the principles of peace, of the dignity and worth of the human person, and of social justice proclaimed in the Charter,

Recalling the principles of the Universal Declaration of Human Rights, the International Covenants on Human Rights, the Declaration of the Rights of the Child, the Declaration on the Granting of Independence to Colonial Countries and Peoples, the International Convention on the Elimination of All Forms of Racial Discrimination, the United Nations Declaration on the Elimination of All Forms of Racial Discrimination, the Declaration on the Promotion among Youth of the Ideals of Peace, Mutual Respect and Understanding between Peoples, the Declaration on the Elimination of Discrimination against Women and of resolutions of the United Nations,

Bearing in mind the standards already set for social progress in the constitutions, conventions, recommendations and resolutions of the International Labour Organisation, the Food and Agriculture Organization of the United Nations, the United Nations Educational, Scientific and Cultural Organization, the World Health Organization, the United Nations Children's Fund and of other organizations concerned,

Convinced that man can achieve complete fulfilment of his aspirations only within a just social order and that it is consequently of cardinal importance to accelerate social and economic progress everywhere, thus contributing to international peace and solidarity,

Convinced that international peace and security on the one hand, and social progress and economic development on the other, are closely interdependent and influence each other,

Persuaded that social development can be promoted by peaceful co-existence, friendly relations and co-operation among States with different social, economic or political systems,

Emphasizing the interdependence of economic and social development in the wider process of growth and change, as well as the importance of a strategy of integrated development which takes full account at all stages of its social aspects,

Regretting the inadequate progress achieved in the world social situation despite the efforts of States and the international community,

Recognizing that the primary responsibility for the development of the developing countries rests on those countries themselves and acknowledging the pressing need to narrow and eventually close the gap in the standards of living between economically more advanced and developing countries and, to that end, that Member States shall have the responsibility to pursue internal and external policies designed to promote social development throughout the world, and in particular to assist developing countries to accelerate their economic growth,

Recognizing the urgency of devoting to works of peace and social progress resources being expended on armaments and wasted on conflict and destruction,

Conscious of the contribution that science and technology can render towards meeting the needs common to all humanity,

Believing that the primary task of all States and international organizations is to eliminate from the life of society all evils and obstacles to social progress, particularly such evils as inequality, exploitation, war, colonialism and racism,

Desirous of promoting the progress of all mankind towards these goals and of overcoming all obstacles to their realization,

Solemnly proclaims this Declaration on Social Progress and Development and calls for national and international action for its use as a common basis for social development policies:

PART I

PRINCIPLES

Article 1

All peoples and all human beings, without distinction as to race, colour, sex, language, religion, nationality, ethnic origin, family or social status, or political or other conviction, shall have the right to live in dignity and freedom and to enjoy the fruits of social progress and should, on their part, contribute to it.

Article 2

Social progress and development shall be founded on respect for the dignity and value of the human person and shall ensure the promotion of human rights and social justice, which requires:

(*a*) The immediate and final elimination of all forms of inequality, exploitation of peoples and individuals, colonialism and racism, including nazism and *apartheid,* and all other policies and ideologies opposed to the purposes and principles of the United Nations;

(*b*) The recognition and effective implementation of civil and political rights as well as of economic, social and cultural rights without any discrimination.

Article 3

The following are considered primary conditions of social progress and development:

(*a*) National independence based on the right of peoples to self-determination;

(*b*) The principle of non-interference in the internal affairs of States;

(*c*) Respect for the sovereignty and territorial integrity of States;

(*d*) Permanent sovereignty of each nation over its natural wealth and resources;

(*e*) The right and responsibility of each State and, as far as they are concerned, each nation and people to determine freely its own objectives of social development, to set its own priorities and to decide in conformity with the principles of the Charter of the United Nations the means and methods of their achievement without any external interference;

(*f*) Peaceful coexistence, peace, friendly relations and co-operation among States irrespective of differences in their social, economic or political systems.

Article 4

The family as a basic unit of society and the natural environment for the growth and well-being of all its members, particularly children and youth, should be assisted and protected so that it may fully assume its responsibilities within the community. Parents have the exclusive right to determine freely and responsibly the number and spacing of their children.

Article 5

Social progress and development require the full utilization of human resources, including, in particular:

(*a*) The encouragement of creative initiative under conditions of enlightened public opinion;

(*b*) The dissemination of national and international information for the purpose of making individuals aware of changes occurring in society as a whole;

(*c*) The active participation of all elements of society, individually or through associations, in defining and in achieving the common goals of development with full respect for the fundamental freedoms embodied in the Universal Declaration of Human Rights;

(*d*) The assurance to disadvantaged or marginal sectors of the population of equal opportunities for social and economic advancement in order to achieve an effectively integrated society.

Article 6

Social development requires the assurance to everyone of the right to work and the free choice of employment.

Social progress and development require the participation of all members of society in productive and socially useful labour and the establishment, in conformity with human rights and fundamental freedoms and with the principles of justice and the social function of property, of forms of ownership of land and of the means of production which preclude any kind of exploitation of man, ensure equal rights to property for all and create conditions leading to genuine equality among people.

Article 7

The rapid expansion of national income and wealth and their equitable distribution among all members of society are fundamental to all social progress, and they should therefore be in the forefront of the preoccupations of every State and Government.

The improvement in the position of the developing countries in international trade resulting among other things from the achievement of favourable terms of trade and of equitable and remunerative prices at which developing countries market their products is necessary in order to make it possible to increase national income and in order to advance social development.

Article 8

Each Government has the primary role and ultimate responsibility of ensuring the social progress and well-being of its people, of planning social development measures as part of comprehensive development plans, of encouraging and co-ordinating or integrating all national efforts towards this end and of introducing necessary changes in the social structure. In planning social development measures, the diversity of the needs of developing and developed areas, and of urban and rural areas, within each country, shall be taken into due account.

Article 9

Social progress and development are the common concerns of the international community, which shall supplement, by concerted international action, national efforts to raise the living standards of peoples.

Social progress and economic growth require recognition of the common interest of all nations in the exploration, conservation, use and exploitation, exclusively for peaceful purposes and in the interests of all mankind, of those areas of the environment such as outer space and the sea-bed and ocean floor and the subsoil thereof, beyond the limits of national jurisdiction, in accordance with the purposes and principles of the Charter of the United Nations.

PART II

OBJECTIVES

Social progress and development shall aim at the continuous raising of the material and spiritual standards of living of all members of society, with respect for and in compliance with human rights and fundamental freedoms, through the attainment of the following main goals:

Article 10

(*a*) The assurance at all levels of the right to work and the right of everyone to form trade unions and workers' associations and to bargain collectively; promotion of full productive employment and elimination of unemployment and under-employment; establishment of equitable and favourable conditions of work for all, including the improvement of health and safety conditions; assurance of just remuneration for labour without any discrimination as well as a sufficiently high minimum wage to ensure a decent standard of living; the protection of the consumer;

(*b*) The elimination of hunger and malnutrition and the guarantee of the right to proper nutrition;

(*c*) The elimination of poverty; the assurance of a steady improvement in levels of living and of a just and equitable distribution of income;

(*d*) The achievement of the highest standards of health and the provision of health protection for the entire population, if possibe free of charge;

(*e*) The eradication of illiteracy and the assurance of the right to universal access to culture, to free compulsory education at the elementary level and to free education at all levels; the raising of the general level of life-long education;

(*f*) The provision for all, particularly persons in low income groups and large families, of adequate housing and community services.

Social progress and development shall aim equally at the progressive attainment of the following main goals:

Article 11

(*a*) The provision of comprehensive social security schemes and social welfare services; the establishment and improvement of social security and insurance schemes for all persons who, because of illness, disability or old age, are temporarily or permanently unable to earn a living, with a view to ensuring a proper standard of living for such persons and for their families and dependants;

(*b*) The protection of the rights of the mother and child; concern for the upbringing and health of children; the provision of measures to safeguard the health and welfare of women and particularly of working mothers during pregnancy and the infancy of their children, as well as of mothers whose earnings are the sole source of livelihood for the family; the granting to women of pregnancy and maternity leave and allowances without loss of employment or wages;

(c) The protection of the rights and the assuring of the welfare of children, the aged and the disabled; the provision of protection for the physically or mentally disadvantaged;

(d) The education of youth in, and promotion among them of, the ideals of justice and peace, mutual respect and understanding among peoples; the promotion of full participation of youth in the process of national development;

(e) The provision of social defence measures and the elimination of conditions leading to crime and delinquency especially juvenile delinquency;

(f) The guarantee that all individuals, without discrimination of any kind, are made aware of their rights and obligations and receive the necessary aid in the exercise and safeguarding of their rights.

Social progress and development shall further aim at achieving the following main objectives:

Article 12

(a) The creation of conditions for rapid and sustained social and economic development, particularly in the developing countries; change in international economic relations; new and effective methods of international co-operation in which equality of opportunity should be as much a prerogative of nations as of individuals within a nation;

(b) The elimination of all forms of discrimination and exploitation and all other practices and ideologies contrary to the purposes and principles of the Charter of the United Nations;

(c) The elimination of all forms of foreign economic exploitation, particularly that practised by international monopolies, in order to enable the people of every country to enjoy in full the benefits of their national resources.

Social progress and development shall finally aim at the attainment of the following main goals:

Article 13

(a) Equitable sharing of scientific and technological advances by developed and developing countries, and a steady increase in the use of science and technology for the benefit of the social development of society;

(*b*) The establishment of a harmonious balance between scientific, technological and material progress and the intellectual, spiritual, cultural and moral advancement of humanity;

(*c*) The protection and improvement of the human environment.

PART III

MEANS AND METHODS

On the basis of the principles set forth in this Declaration, the achievement of the objectives of social progress and development requires the mobilization of the necessary resources by national and international action, with particular attention to such means and methods as:

Article 14

(*a*) Planning for social progress and development as an integrated part of balanced overall development planning;

(*b*) The establishment, where necessary, of national systems for framing and carrying out social policies and programmes, and the promotion by the countries concerned of planned regional development, taking into account differing regional conditions and needs, particularly the development of regions which are less favoured or under-developed by comparison with the rest of the country;

(*c*) The promotion of basic and applied social research, particularly comparative international research applied to the planning and execution of social development programmes.

Article 15

(*a*) The adoption of measures, to ensure the effective participation, as appropriate, of all the elements of society in the preparation and execution of national plans and programmes of economic and social development;

(*b*) The adoption of measures for an increasing rate of popular participation in the economic, social, cultural and political life of countries through national governmental bodies, non-governmental organizations, co-operatives, rural associations, workers' and employers' organizations and women's and youth organizations, by such methods as national and regional plans for social and economic progress and community development, with a view to achieving a fully integrated national society, accelerating the process of social mobility and consolidating the democratic system;

(c) Mobilization of public opinion, at both national and international levels, in support of the principles and objectives of social progress and development;

(d) The dissemination of social information, at the national and the international level, to make people aware of changing circumstances in society as a whole, and to educate the consumer.

Article 16

(a) Maximum mobilization of all national resources and their rational and efficient utilization; promotion of increased and accelerated productive investment in social and economic fields and of employment; orientation of society towards the development process;

(b) Progressively increasing provision of the necessary budgetary and other resources required for financing the social aspects of development;

(c) Achievement of equitable distribution of national income, utilizing, *inter alia,* the fiscal system and government spending as an instrument for the equitable distribution and redistribution of income in order to promote social progress;

(d) The adoption of measures aimed at prevention of such an outflow of capital from developing countries as would be detrimental to their economic and social development.

Article 17

(a) The adoption of measures to accelerate the process of industrialization, especially in developing countries, with due regard for its social aspects, in the interests of the entire population; development of an adequate organization and legal framework conducive to an uninterrupted and diversified growth of the industrial sector; measures to overcome the adverse social effects which may result from urban development and industrialization, including automation; maintenance of a proper balance between rural and urban development, and in particular, measures designed to ensure healthier living conditions, especially in large industrial centres;

(b) Integrated planning to meet the problems of urbanization and urban development;

(c) Comprehensive rural development schemes to raise the levels of living of the rural populations and to facilitate such urban-rural relationships and population distribution as will promote balanced national development and social progress;

(*d*) Measures for appropriate supervision of the utilization of land in the interests of society.

The achievement of the objectives of social progress and development equally requires the implementation of the following means and methods:

Article 18

(*a*) The adoption of appropriate legislative, administrative and other measures ensuring to everyone not only political and civil rights, but also the full realization of economic, social and cultural rights without any discrimination;

(*b*) The promotion of democratically based social and institutional reforms and motivation for change basic to the elimination of all forms of discrimination and exploitation and conducive to high rates of economic and social progress, to include land reform, in which the ownership and use of land will be made to serve best the objectives of social justice and economic development;

(*c*) The adoption of measures to boost and diversify agricultural production through, *inter alia,* the implementation of democratic agrarian reforms, to ensure an adequate and well-balanced supply of food, its equitable distribution among the whole population and the improvement of nutritional standards;

(*d*) The adoption of measures to introduce, with the participation of the Government, low-cost housing programmes in both rural and urban areas;

(*e*) Development and expansion of the system of transportation and communications, particularly in developing countries.

Article 19

(*a*) The provision of free health services to the whole population and of adequate preventive and curative facilities and welfare medical services accessible to all;

(*b*) The enactment and establishment of legislative measures and administrative regulations with a view to the implementation of comprehensive programmes of social security schemes and social welfare services and to the improvement and co-ordination of existing services;

(*c*) The adoption of measures and the provision of social welfare services to migrant workers and their families, in conformity with the provisions of

Convention No. 97 of the International Labour Organisation and other international instruments relating to migrant workers;

(*d*) The institution of appropriate measures for the rehabilitation of mentally or physically disabled persons, especially children and youth, so as to enable them to the fullest possible extent to be useful members of society— these measures shall include the provision of treatment and technical appliances, education, vocational and social guidance, training and selective. placement, and other assistance required—and the creation of social conditions in which the handicapped are not discriminated against because of their disabilities.

Article 20

(*a*) The provision of full democratic freedoms to trade unions; freedom of association for all workers, including the right to bargain collectively and to strike; recognition of the right to form other organizations of working people; the provision for the growing participation of trade unions in economic and social development; effective participation of all members in trade unions in the deciding of economic and social issues which affect their interests;

(*b*) The improvement of health and safety conditions for workers, by means of appropriate technological and legislative measures and the provision of the material prerequisites for the implementation of those measures, including the limitation of working hours;

(*c*) The adoption of appropriate measures for the development of harmonious industrial relations.

Article 21

(*a*) The training of national personnel and cadres, including administrative, executive, professional and technical personnel needed for social development and for overall development plans and policies;

(*b*) The adoption of measures to accelerate the extension and improvement of general, vocational and technical education and of training and retraining, which should be provided free at all levels;

(*c*) Raising the general level of education; development and expansion of national information media, and their rational and full use towards continuing education of the whole population and towards encouraging its participation in social development activities; the constructive use of leisure, particularly that of children and adolescents;

(*d*) The formulation of national and international policies and measures to avoid the "brain drain" and obviate its adverse effects.

Article 22

(*a*) The development and co-ordination of policies and measures designed to strengthen the essential functions of the family as a basic unit of society;

(*b*) The formulation and establishment, as needed, of programmes in the field of population, within the framework of national demographic policies and as part of the welfare medical services, including education, training of personnel and the provision to families of the knowledge and means necessary to enable them to exercise their right to determine freely and responsibly the number and spacing of their children;

(*c*) The establishment of appropriate child-care facilities in the interest of children and working parents.

The achievement of the objectives of social progress and development finally requires the implementation of the following means and methods:

Article 23

(*a*) The laying down of economic growth rate targets for the developing countries within the United Nations policy for development, high enough to lead to a substantial acceleration of their rates of growth;

(*b*) The provision of greater assistance on better terms; the implementation of the aid volume target of a minimum of 1 per cent of the gross national product at market prices of economically advanced countries; the general easing of the terms of lending to the developing countries through low interest rates on loans and long grace periods for the repayment of loans, and the assurance that the allocation of such loans will be based strictly on socio-economic criteria free of any political considerations;

(*c*) The provision of technical, financial and material assistance, both bilateral and multilateral, to the fullest possible extent and on favourable terms, and improved co-ordination of international assistance for the achievement of the social objectives of national development plans;

(*d*) The provision to the developing countries of technical, financial and material assistance and of favourable conditions to facilitate the direct exploitation of their national resources and natural wealth by those countries with a view to enabling the peoples of those countries to benefit fully from their national resources;

(*e*) The expansion of international trade based on principles of equality and non-discrimination, the rectification of the position of developing countries in international trade by equitable terms of trade, a general non-reciprocal and non-discriminatory system of preferences for the exports of developing countries to the developed countries, the establishment and implementation of general and comprehensive commodity agreements, and the financing of reasonable buffer stocks by international institutions.

Article 24

(*a*) Intensification of international co-operation with a view to ensuring the international exchange of information, knowledge and experience concerning social progress and development;

(*b*) The broadest possible international technical, scientific and cultural co-operation and reciprocal utilization of the experience of countries with different economic and social systems and different levels of development, on the basis of mutual advantage and strict observance of and respect for national sovereignty;

(*c*) Increased utilization of science and technology for social and economic development; arrangements for the transfer and exchange of technology, including know-how and patents, to the developing countries.

Article 25

(*a*) The establishment of legal and administrative measures for the protection and improvement of the human environment, at both national and international level;

(*b*) The use and exploitation, in accordance with the appropriate international régimes, of the resources of areas of the environment such as outer space and the sea-bed and ocean floor and the subsoil thereof, beyond the limits of national jurisdiction, in order to supplement national resources available for the achievement of economic and social progress and development in every country, irrespective of its geographical location, special consideration being given to the interests and needs of the developing countries.

Article 26

Compensation for damages, be they social or economic in nature—including restitution and reparations—caused as a result of aggression and of illegal occupation of territory by the aggressor.

Article 27

(*a*) The achievement of general and complete disarmament and the channelling of the progressively released resources to be used for economic and social progress for the welfare of people everywhere and, in particular, for the benefit of developing countries;

(*b*) The adoption of measures contributing to disarmament, including, *inter alia,* the complete prohibition of tests of nuclear weapons, the prohibition of the development, production and stockpiling of chemical and bacteriological (biological) weapons and the prevention of the pollution of oceans and inland waters by nuclear wastes.

67. Declaration on the Rights of Mentally Retarded Persons

Proclaimed by General Assembly resolution 2856 (XXVI) of 20 December 1971

The General Assembly,

Mindful of the pledge of the States Members of the United Nations under the Charter to take joint and separate action in co-operation with the Organization to promote higher standards of living, full employment and conditions of economic and social progress and development,

Reaffirming faith in human rights and fundamental freedoms and in the principles of peace, of the dignity and worth of the human person and of social justice proclaimed in the Charter,

Recalling the principles of the Universal Declaration of Human Rights, the International Covenants on Human Rights, the Declaration of the Rights of the Child and the standards already set for social progress in the constitutions, conventions, recommendations and resolutions of the International Labour Organisation, the United Nations Educational, Scientific and Cultural Organization, the World Health Organization, the United Nations Children's Fund and other organizations concerned,

Emphasizing that the Declaration on Social Progress and Development has proclaimed the necessity of protecting the rights and assuring the welfare and rehabilitation of the physically and mentally disadvantaged,

Bearing in mind the necessity of assisting mentally retarded persons to develop their abilities in various fields of activities and of promoting their integration as far as possible in normal life,

Aware that certain countries, at their present stage of development, can devote only limited efforts to this end,

Proclaims this Declaration on the Rights of Mentally Retarded Persons and calls for national and international action to ensure that it will be used as a common basis and frame of reference for the protection of these rights:

1. The mentally retarded person has, to the maximum degree of feasibility, the same rights as other human beings.

2. The mentally retarded person has a right to proper medical care and physical therapy and to such education, training, rehabilitation and guidance as will enable him to develop his ability and maximum potential.

511

3. The mentally retarded person has a right to economic security and to a decent standard of living. He has a right to perform productive work or to engage in any other meaningful occupation to the fullest possible extent of his capabilities.

4. Whenever possible, the mentally retarded person should live with his own family or with foster parents and participate in different forms of community life. The family with which he lives should receive assistance. If care in an institution becomes necessary, it should be provided in surroundings and other circumstances as close as possible to those of normal life.

5. The mentally retarded person has a right to a qualified guardian when this is required to protect his personal well-being and interests.

6. The mentally retarded person has a right to protection from exploitation, abuse and degrading treatment. If prosecuted for any offence, he shall have a right to due process of law with full recognition being given to his degree of mental responsibility.

7. Whenever mentally retarded persons are unable, because of the severity of their handicap, to exercise all their rights in a meaningful way or it should become necessary to restrict or deny some or all of these rights, the procedure used for that restriction or denial of rights must contain proper legal safeguards against every form of abuse. This procedure must be based on an evaluation of the social capability of the mentally retarded person by qualified experts and must be subject to periodic review and to the right of appeal to higher authorities.

68. Principles for the protection of persons with mental illness and the improvement of mental health care

Adopted by General Assembly resolution 46/119 of 17 December 1991

Application

These Principles shall be applied without discrimination of any kind such as on grounds of disability, race, colour, sex, language, religion, political or other opinion, national, ethnic or social origin, legal or social status, age, property or birth.

Definitions

In these Principles:

"Counsel" means a legal or other qualified representative;

"Independent authority" means a competent and independent authority prescribed by domestic law;

"Mental health care" includes analysis and diagnosis of a person's mental condition, and treatment, care and rehabilitation for a mental illness or suspected mental illness;

"Mental health facility" means any establishment, or any unit of an establishment, which as its primary function provides mental health care;

"Mental health practitioner" means a medical doctor, clinical psychologist, nurse, social worker or other appropriately trained and qualified person with specific skills relevant to mental health care;

"Patient" means a person receiving mental health care and includes all persons who are admitted to a mental health facility;

"Personal representative" means a person charged by law with the duty of representing a patient's interests in any specified respect or of exercising specified rights on the patient's behalf, and includes the parent or legal guardian of a minor unless otherwise provided by domestic law;

"The review body" means the body established in accordance with Principle 17 to review the involuntary admission or retention of a patient in a mental health facility.

General limitation clause

The exercise of the rights set forth in these Principles may be subject only to such limitations as are prescribed by law and are necessary to protect the health or safety of the person concerned or of others, or otherwise to protect public safety, order, health or morals or the fundamental rights and freedoms of others.

Principle 1

Fundamental freedoms and basic rights

1.   All persons have the right to the best available mental health care, which shall be part of the health and social care system.

2.   All persons with a mental illness, or who are being treated as such persons, shall be treated with humanity and respect for the inherent dignity of the human person.

3.   All persons with a mental illness, or who are being treated as such persons, have the right to protection from economic, sexual and other forms of exploitation, physical or other abuse and degrading treatment.

4.   There shall be no discrimination on the grounds of mental illness. "Discrimination" means any distinction, exclusion or preference that has the effect of nullifying or impairing equal enjoyment of rights. Special measures solely to protect the rights, or secure the advancement, of persons with mental illness shall not be deemed to be discriminatory. Discrimination does not include any distinction, exclusion or preference undertaken in accordance with the provisions of these Principles and necessary to protect the human rights of a person with a mental illness or of other individuals.

5.   Every person with a mental illness shall have the right to exercise all civil, political, economic, social and cultural rights as recognized in the Universal Declaration of Human Rights, the International Covenant on Economic, Social and Cultural Rights, the International Covenant on Civil and Political Rights, and in other relevant instruments, such as the Declaration on the Rights of Disabled Persons and the Body of Principles for the Protection of All Persons under Any Form of Detention or Imprisonment.

6.   Any decision that, by reason of his or her mental illness, a person lacks legal capacity, and any decision that, in consequence of such incapacity, a personal representative shall be appointed, shall be made only after a fair hearing by an independent and impartial tribunal established by domestic law. The person whose capacity is at issue shall be entitled to be represented by a counsel. If the person whose capacity is at issue does not himself or herself secure such representation, it shall be made available without payment by that person to the extent that he or she does not have sufficient means to pay for it. The counsel shall not in the same proceedings represent

a mental health facility or its personnel and shall not also represent a member of the family of the person whose capacity is at issue unless the tribunal is satisfied that there is no conflict of interest. Decisions regarding capacity and the need for a personal representative shall be reviewed at reasonable intervals prescribed by domestic law. The person whose capacity is at issue, his or her personal representative, if any, and any other interested person shall have the right to appeal to a higher court against any such decision.

7.   Where a court or other competent tribunal finds that a person with mental illness is unable to manage his or her own affairs, measures shall be taken, so far as is necessary and appropriate to that person's condition, to ensure the protection of his or her interest

Principle 2

Protection of minors

Special care should be given within the purposes of these Principles and within the context of domestic law relating to the protection of minors to protect the rights of minors, including, if necessary, the appointment of a personal representative other than a family member.

Principle 3

Life in the community

Every person with a mental illness shall have the right to live and work, as far as possible, in the community.

Principle 4

Determination of mental illness

1.   A determination that a person has a mental illness shall be made in accordance with internationally accepted medical standards.

2.   A determination of mental illness shall never be made on the basis of political, economic or social status, or membership of a cultural, racial or religious group, or any other reason not directly relevant to mental health status.

3.   Family or professional conflict, or non-conformity with moral, social, cultural or political values or religious beliefs prevailing in a person's community, shall never be a determining factor in diagnosing mental illness.

4.   A background of past treatment or hospitalization as a patient shall not of itself justify any present or future determination of mental illness.

5.   No person or authority shall classify a person as having, or otherwise indicate that a person has, a mental illness except for purposes directly relating to mental illness or the consequences of mental illness.

Principle 5

Medical examination

No person shall be compelled to undergo medical examination with a view to determining whether or not he or she has a mental illness except in accordance with a procedure authorized by domestic law.

Principle 6

Confidentiality

The right of confidentiality of information concerning all persons to whom these Principles apply shall be respected.

Principle 7

Role of community and culture

1.   Every patient shall have the right to be treated and cared for, as far as possible, in the community in which he or she lives.

2.   Where treatment takes place in a mental health facility, a patient shall have the right, whenever possible, to be treated near his or her home or the home of his or her relatives or friends and shall have the right to return to the community as soon as possible.

3.   Every patient shall have the right to treatment suited to his or her cultural background.

Principle 8

Standards of care

1.   Every patient shall have the right to receive such health and social care as is appropriate to his or her health needs, and is entitled to care and treatment in accordance with the same standards as other ill persons.

2.   Every patient shall be protected from harm, including unjustified medication, abuse by other patients, staff or others or other acts causing mental distress or physical discomfort.

Principle 9

Treatment

1.   Every patient shall have the right to be treated in the least restrictive environment and with the least restrictive or intrusive treatment appropriate to the patient's health needs and the need to protect the physical safety of others.

2.   The treatment and care of every patient shall be based on an individually prescribed plan, discussed with the patient, reviewed regularly, revised as necessary and provided by qualified professional staff.

3.   Mental health care shall always be provided in accordance with applicable standards of ethics for mental health practitioners, including internationally accepted standards such as the Principles of Medical Ethics adopted by the United Nations General Assembly. Mental health knowledge and skills shall never be abused.

4.   The treatment of every patient shall be directed towards preserving and enhancing personal autonomy.

Principle 10

Medication

1.   Medication shall meet the best health needs of the patient, shall be given to a patient only for therapeutic or diagnostic purposes and shall never be administered as a punishment or for the convenience of others. Subject to the provisions of paragraph 15 of Principle 11, mental health practitioners shall only administer medication of known or demonstrated efficacy.

2.   All medication shall be prescribed by a mental health practitioner authorized by law and shall be recorded in the patient's records.

Principle 11

Consent to treatment

1.   No treatment shall be given to a patient without his or her informed consent, except as provided for in paragraphs 6, 7, 8, 13 and 15 below.

2.   Informed consent is consent obtained freely, without threats or improper inducements, after appropriate disclosure to the patient of adequate and understandable information in a form and language understood by the patient on:

(*a*) The diagnostic assessment;

(*b*) The purpose, method, likely duration and expected benefit of the proposed treatment;

(*c*) Alternative modes of treatment, including those less intrusive; and

(*d*) Possible pain or discomfort, risks and side-effects of the proposed treatment.

3.   A patient may request the presence of a person or persons of the patient's choosing during the procedure for granting consent.

4.   A patient has the right to refuse or stop treatment, except as provided for in paragraphs 6, 7, 8, 13 and 15 below. The consequences of refusing or stopping treatment must be explained to the patient.

5.   A patient shall never be invited or induced to waive the right to informed consent. If the patient should seek to do so, it shall be explained to the patient that the treatment cannot be given without informed consent.

6.   Except as provided in paragraphs 7, 8, 12, 13, 14 and 15 below, a proposed plan of treatment may be given to a patient without a patient's informed consent if the following conditions are satisfied:

(*a*) The patient is, at the relevant time, held as an involuntary patient;

(*b*) An independent authority, having in its possession all relevant information, including the information specified in paragraph 2 above, is satisfied that, at the relevant time, the patient lacks the capacity to give or withhold informed consent to the proposed plan of treatment or, if domestic legislation so provides, that, having regard to the patient's own safety or the safety of others, the patient unreasonably withholds such consent; and

(*c*) The independent authority is satisfied that the proposed plan of treatment is in the best interest of the patient's health needs.

7.   Paragraph 6 above does not apply to a patient with a personal representative empowered by law to consent to treatment for the patient; but, except as provided in paragraphs 12, 13, 14 and 15 below, treatment may be given to such a patient without his or her informed consent if the personal representative, having been given the information described in paragraph 2 above, consents on the patient's behalf.

8.   Except as provided in paragraphs 12, 13, 14 and 15 below, treatment may also be given to any patient without the patient's informed consent if a qualified mental health practitioner authorized by law determines that it is urgently necessary in order to prevent immediate or imminent harm to the patient or to other persons. Such treatment shall not be prolonged beyond the period that is strictly necessary for this purpose.

9.   Where any treatment is authorized without the patient's informed consent, every effort shall nevertheless be made to inform the patient about

the nature of the treatment and any possible alternatives and to involve the patient as far as practicable in the development of the treatment plan.

10.   All treatment shall be immediately recorded in the patient's medical records, with an indication of whether involuntary or voluntary.

11.   Physical restraint or involuntary seclusion of a patient shall not be employed except in accordance with the officially approved procedures of the mental health facility and only when it is the only means available to prevent immediate or imminent harm to the patient or others. It shall not be prolonged beyond the period which is strictly necessary for this purpose. All instances of physical restraint or involuntary seclusion, the reasons for them and their nature and extent shall be recorded in the patient's medical record. A patient who is restrained or secluded shall be kept under humane conditions and be under the care and close and regular supervision of qualified members of the staff. A personal representative, if any and if relevant, shall be given prompt notice of any physical restraint or involuntary seclusion of the patient.

12.   Sterilization shall never be carried out as a treatment for mental illness.

13.   A major medical or surgical procedure may be carried out on a person with mental illness only where it is permitted by domestic law, where it is considered that it would best serve the health needs of the patient and where the patient gives informed consent, except that, where the patient is unable to give informed consent, the procedure shall be authorized only after independent review.

14.   Psychosurgery and other intrusive and irreversible treatments for mental illness shall never be carried out on a patient who is an involuntary patient in a mental health facility and, to the extent that domestic law permits them to be carried out, they may be carried out on any other patient only where the patient has given informed consent and an independent external body has satisfied itself that there is genuine informed consent and that the treatment best serves the health needs of the patient.

15.   Clinical trials and experimental treatment shall never be carried out on any patient without informed consent, except that a patient who is unable to give informed consent may be admitted to a clinical trial or given experimental treatment, but only with the approval of a competent, independent review body specifically constituted for this purpose.

16.   In the cases specified in paragraphs 6, 7, 8, 13, 14 and 15 above, the patient or his or her personal representative, or any interested person, shall have the right to appeal to a judicial or other independent authority concerning any treatment given to him or her.

Principle 12

Notice of rights

1.   A patient in a mental health facility shall be informed as soon as possible after admission, in a form and a language which the patient understands, of all his or her rights in accordance with these Principles and under domestic law, which information shall include an explanation of those rights and how to exercise them.

2.   If and for so long as a patient is unable to understand such information, the rights of the patient shall be communicated to the personal representative, if any and if appropriate, and to the person or persons best able to represent the patient's interests and willing to do so.

3.   A patient who has the necessary capacity has the right to nominate a person who should be informed on his or her behalf, as well as a person to represent his or her interests to the authorities of the facility.

Principle 13

Rights and conditions in mental health facilities

1.   Every patient in a mental health facility shall, in particular, have the right to full respect for his or her:

(*a*) Recognition everywhere as a person before the law;

(*b*) Privacy;

(*c*) Freedom of communication, which includes freedom to communicate with other persons in the facility; freedom to send and receive uncensored private communications; freedom to receive, in private, visits from a counsel or personal representative and, at all reasonable times, from other visitors; and freedom of access to postal and telephone services and to newspapers, radio and television;

(*d*) Freedom of religion or belief.

2.   The environment and living conditions in mental health facilities shall be as close as possible to those of the normal life of persons of similar age and in particular shall include:

(*a*) Facilities for recreational and leisure activities;

(*b*) Facilities for education;

(*c*) Facilities to purchase or receive items for daily living, recreation and communication;

(*d*) Facilities, and encouragement to use such facilities, for a patient's engagement in active occupation suited to his or her social and cultural background, and for appropriate vocational rehabilitation measures to promote reintegration in the community. These measures should include vocational guidance, vocational training and placement services to enable patients to secure or retain employment in the community.

3. In no circumstances shall a patient be subject to forced labour. Within the limits compatible with the needs of the patient and with the requirements of institutional administration, a patient shall be able to choose the type of work he or she wishes to perform.

4. The labour of a patient in a mental health facility shall not be exploited. Every such patient shall have the right to receive the same remuneration for any work which he or she does as would, according to domestic law or custom, be paid for such work to a non-patient. Every such patient shall, in any event, have the right to receive a fair share of any remuneration which is paid to the mental health facility for his or her work.

Principle 14

Resources for mental health facilities

1. A mental health facility shall have access to the same level of resources as any other health establishment, and in particular:

(*a*) Qualified medical and other appropriate professional staff in sufficient numbers and with adequate space to provide each patient with privacy and a programme of appropriate and active therapy;

(*b*) Diagnostic and therapeutic equipment for the patient;

(*c*) Appropriate professional care; and

(*d*) Adequate, regular and comprehensive treatment, including supplies of medication.

2. Every mental health facility shall be inspected by the competent authorities with sufficient frequency to ensure that the conditions, treatment and care of patients comply with these Principles.

Principle 15

Admission principles

1. Where a person needs treatment in a mental health facility, every effort shall be made to avoid involuntary admission.

2. Access to a mental health facility shall be administered in the same way as access to any other facility for any other illness.

3. Every patient not admitted involuntarily shall have the right to leave the mental health facility at any time unless the criteria for his or her retention as an involuntary patient, as set forth in Principle 16, apply, and he or she shall be informed of that right.

Principle 16

Involuntary admission

1.   A person may (*a*) be admitted involuntarily to a mental health facility as a patient; or (*b*) having already been admitted voluntarily as a patient, be retained as an involuntary patient in the mental health facility if, and only if, a qualified mental health practitioner authorized by law for that purpose determines, in accordance with Principle 4, that that person has a mental illness and considers:

(*a*)   That, because of that mental illness, there is a serious likelihood of immediate or imminent harm to that person or to other persons; or

(*b*)   That, in the case of a person whose mental illness is severe and whose judgement is impaired, failure to admit or retain that person is likely to lead to a serious deterioration in his or her condition or will prevent the giving of appropriate treatment that can only be given by admission to a mental health facility in accordance with the principle of the least restrictive alternative.

In the case referred to in subparagraph (*b*), a second such mental health practitioner, independent of the first, should be consulted where possible. If such consultation takes place, the involuntary admission or retention may not take place unless the second mental health practitioner concurs.

2.   Involuntary admission or retention shall initially be for a short period as specified by domestic law for observation and preliminary treatment pending review of the admission or retention by the review body. The grounds of the admission shall be communicated to the patient without delay and the fact of the admission and the grounds for it shall also be communicated promptly and in detail to the review body, to the patient's personal representative, if any, and, unless the patient objects, to the patient's family.

3.   A mental health facility may receive involuntarily admitted patients only if the facility has been designated to do so by a competent authority prescribed by domestic law.

Principle 17

Review body

1.   The review body shall be a judicial or other independent and impartial body established by domestic law and functioning in accordance with procedures laid down by domestic law. It shall, in formulating its decisions, have the assistance of one or more qualified and independent mental health practitioners and take their advice into account.

2.   The review body's initial review, as required by paragraph 2 of Principle 16, of a decision to admit or retain a person as an involuntary pa-

tient shall take place as soon as possible after that decision and shall be conducted in accordance with simple and expeditious procedures as specified by domestic law.

3. The review body shall periodically review the cases of involuntary patients at reasonable intervals as specified by domestic law.

4. An involuntary patient may apply to the review body for release or voluntary status, at reasonable intervals as specified by domestic law.

5. At each review, the review body shall consider whether the criteria for involuntary admission set out in paragraph 1 of Principle 16 are still satisfied, and, if not, the patient shall be discharged as an involuntary patient.

6. If at any time the mental health practitioner responsible for the case is satisfied that the conditions for the retention of a person as an involuntary patient are no longer satisfied, he or she shall order the discharge of that person as such a patient.

7. A patient or his personal representative or any interested person shall have the right to appeal to a higher court against a decision that the patient be admitted to, or be retained in, a mental health facility.

Principle 18

Procedural safeguards

1. The patient shall be entitled to choose and appoint a counsel to represent the patient as such, including representation in any complaint procedure or appeal. If the patient does not secure such services, a counsel shall be made available without payment by the patient to the extent that the patient lacks sufficient means to pay.

2. The patient shall also be entitled to the assistance, if necessary, of the services of an interpreter. Where such services are necessary and the patient does not secure them, they shall be made available without payment by the patient to the extent that the patient lacks sufficient means to pay.

3. The patient and the patient's counsel may request and produce at any hearing an independent mental health report and any other reports and oral, written and other evidence that are relevant and admissible.

4. Copies of the patient's records and any reports and documents to be submitted shall be given to the patient and to the patient's counsel, except in special cases where it is determined that a specific disclosure to the patient would cause serious harm to the patient's health or put at risk the safety of others. As domestic law may provide, any document not given to the patient should, when this can be done in confidence, be given to the patient's personal representative and counsel. When any part of a document is with-

held from a patient, the patient or the patient's counsel, if any, shall receive notice of the withholding and the reasons for it and shall be subject to judicial review.

5.   The patient and the patient's personal representative and counsel shall be entitled to attend, participate and be heard personally in any hearing.

6.   If the patient or the patient's personal representative or counsel requests that a particular person be present at a hearing, that person shall be admitted unless it is determined that the person's presence could cause serious harm to the patient's health or put at risk the safety of others.

7.   Any decision whether the hearing or any part of it shall be in public or in private and may be publicly reported shall give full consideration to the patient's own wishes, to the need to respect the privacy of the patient and of other persons and to the need to prevent serious harm to the patient's health or to avoid putting at risk the safety of others.

8.   The decision arising out of the hearing and the reasons for it shall be expressed in writing. Copies shall be given to the patient and his or her personal representative and counsel. In deciding whether the decision shall be published in whole or in part, full consideration shall be given to the patient's own wishes, to the need to respect his or her privacy and that of other persons, to the public interest in the open administration of justice and to the need to prevent serious harm to the patient's health or to avoid putting at risk the safety of others.

Principle 19

Access to information

1.   A patient (which term in this Principle includes a former patient) shall be entitled to have access to the information concerning the patient in his or her health and personal records maintained by a mental health facility. This right may be subject to restrictions in order to prevent serious harm to the patient's health and avoid putting at risk the safety of others. As domestic law may provide, any such information not given to the patient should, when this can be done in confidence, be given to the patient's personal representative and counsel. When any of the information is withheld from a patient, the patient or the patient's counsel, if any, shall receive notice of the withholding and the reasons for it and it shall be subject to judicial review.

2.   Any written comments by the patient or the patient's personal representative or counsel shall, on request, be inserted in the patient's file.

Principle 20

Criminal offenders

1.   This Principle applies to persons serving sentences of imprisonment for criminal offences, or who are otherwise detained in the course of criminal proceedings or investigations against them, and who are determined to have a mental illness or who it is believed may have such an illness.

2.   All such persons should receive the best available mental health care as provided in Principle 1. These Principles shall apply to them to the fullest extent possible, with only such limited modifications and exceptions as are necessary in the circumstances. No such modifications and exceptions shall prejudice the persons' rights under the instruments noted in paragraph 5 of Principle 1.

3.   Domestic law may authorize a court or other competent authority, acting on the basis of competent and independent medical advice, to order that such persons be admitted to a mental health facility.

4.   Treatment of persons determined to have a mental illness shall in all circumstances be consistent with Principle 11.

Principle 21

Complaints

Every patient and former patient shall have the right to make a complaint through procedures as specified by domestic law.

Principle 22

Monitoring and remedies

States shall ensure that appropriate mechanisms are in force to promote compliance with these Principles, for the inspection of mental health facilities, for the submission, investigation and resolution of complaints and for the institution of appropriate disciplinary or judicial proceedings for professional misconduct or violation of the rights of a patient.

Principle 23

Implementation

1.   States should implement these Principles through appropriate legislative, judicial, administrative, educational and other measures, which they shall review periodically.

2.   States shall make these Principles widely known by appropriate and active means.

Principle 24

Scope of principles relating to mental health facilities

These Principles apply to all persons who are admitted to a mental health facility.

Principle 25

Saving of existing rights

There shall be no restriction upon or derogation from any existing rights of patients, including rights recognized in applicable international or domestic law, on the pretext that these Principles do not recognize such rights or that they recognize them to a lesser extent.

69. Universal Declaration on the Eradication of Hunger and Malnutrition

Adopted on 16 November 1974 by the World Food Conference convened under General Assembly resolution 3180 (XXVIII) of 17 December 1973; and endorsed by General Assembly resolution 3348 (XXIX) of 17 December 1974

The World Food Conference,

Convened by the General Assembly of the United Nations and entrusted with developing ways and means whereby the international community, as a whole, could take specific action to resolve the world food problem within the broader context of development and international economic co-operation,

Adopts the following Declaration:

UNIVERSAL DECLARATION ON THE ERADICATION OF HUNGER AND MALNUTRITION

Recognizing that:

(*a*) The grave food crisis that is afflicting the peoples of the developing countries where most of the world's hungry and ill-nourished live and where more than two thirds of the world's population produce about one third of the world's food—an imbalance which threatens to increase in the next 10 years— is not only fraught with grave economic and social implications, but also acutely jeopardizes the most fundamental principles and values associated with the right to life and human dignity as enshrined in the Universal Declaration of Human Rights;

(*b*) The elimination of hunger and malnutrition, included as one of the objectives in the United Nations Declaration on Social Progress and Development, and the elimination of the causes that determine this situation are the common objectives of all nations;

(*c*) The situation of the peoples afflicted by hunger and malnutrition arises from their historical circumstances, especially social inequalities, including in many cases alien and colonial domination, foreign occupation, racial discrimination, *apartheid* and neo-colonialism in all its forms, which continue to be among the greatest obstacles to the full emancipation and progress of the developing countries and all the peoples involved;

(*d*) This situation has been aggravated in recent years by a series of crises to which the world economy has been subjected, such as the deterioration in the international monetary system, the inflationary increase in import costs, the heavy burdens imposed by external debt on the balance of payments of many developing countries, a rising food demand partly due to demographic pressure, speculation, and a shortage of, and increased costs for, essential agricultural inputs;

(*e*) These phenomena should be considered within the framework of the on-going negotiations on the Charter of Economic Rights and Duties of States, and the General Assembly of the United Nations should be urged unanimously to agree upon, and to adopt, a Charter that will be an effective instrument for the establishment of new international economic relations based on principles of equity and justice;

(*f*) All countries, big or small, rich or poor, are equal. All countries have the full right to participate in the decisions on the food problem;

(*g*) The well-being of the peoples of the world largely depends on the adequate production and distribution of food as well as the establishment of a world food security system which would ensure adequate availability of, and reasonable prices for, food at all times, irrespective of periodic fluctuations and vagaries of weather and free of political and economic pressures, and should thus facilitate, amongst other things, the development process of developing countries;

(*h*) Peace and justice encompass an economic dimension helping the solution of the world economic problems, the liquidation of under-development, offering a lasting and definitive solution of the food problem for all peoples and guaranteeing to all countries the right to implement freely and effectively their development programmes. To this effect, it is necessary to eliminate threats and resort to force and to promote peaceful co-operation between States to the fullest extent possible, to apply the principles of non-interference in the internal affairs of other States, full equality of rights and respect of national independence and sovereignty, as well as to encourage the peaceful co-operation between all States, irrespective of their political, social and economic systems. The further improvement of international relations will create better conditions for international co-operation in all fields which should make possible large financial and material resources to be used, *inter alia,* for developing agricultural production and substantially improving world food security;

(*i*) For a lasting solution of the food problem all efforts should be made to eliminate the widening gaps which today separate developed and developing countries and to bring about a new international economic order. It should be possible for all countries to participate actively and effectively in the new international economic relations by the establishment of suitable international systems, where appropriate, capable of producing adequate action in order to establish just and equitable relations in international economic co-operation;

(*j*) Developing countries reaffirm their belief that the primary responsibility for ensuring their own rapid development rests with themselves. They declare, therefore, their readiness to continue to intensify their individual and collective efforts with a view to expanding their mutual co-operation in the field of agricultural development and food production, including the eradication of hunger and malnutrition;

(*k*) Since, for various reasons, many developing countries are not yet always able to meet their own food needs, urgent and effective international action should be taken to assist them, free of political pressures,

Consistent with the aims and objectives of the Declaration on the Establishment of a New International Economic Order and the Programme of Action adopted by the General Assembly at its sixth special session,

The Conference consequently solemnly proclaims:

1.   Every man, woman and child has the inalienable right to be free from hunger and malnutrition in order to develop fully and maintain their physical and mental faculties. Society today already possesses sufficient resources, organizational ability and technology and hence the competence to achieve this objective. Accordingly, the eradication of hunger is a common objective of all the countries of the international community, especially of the developed countries and others in a position to help.

2.   It is a fundamental responsibility of Governments to work together for higher food production and a more equitable and efficient distribution of food between countries and within countries. Governments should initiate immediately a greater concerted attack on chronic malnutrition and deficiency diseases among the vulnerable and lower income groups. In order to ensure adequate nutrition for all, Governments should formulate appropriate food and nutrition policies integrated in overall socio-economic and agricultural development plans based on adequate knowledge of available as well as potential food resources. The importance of human milk in this connection should be stressed on nutritional grounds.

3.   Food problems must be tackled during the preparation and implementation of national plans and programmes for economic and social development, with emphasis on their humanitarian aspects.

4.   It is a responsibility of each State concerned, in accordance with its sovereign judgement and internal legislation, to remove the obstacles to food production and to provide proper incentives to agricultural producers. Of prime importance for the attainment of these objectives are effective measures of socio-economic transformation by agrarian, tax, credit and investment policy reform and the reorganization of rural structures, such as the reform of the conditions of ownership, the encouragement of producer and consumer co-operatives, the mobilization of the full potential of human resources, both male and female, in the developing countries for an integrated rural development and the involvement of small farmers, fishermen and landless workers in attaining the required food production and employment targets. Moreover, it is necessary to recognize the key role of women in agricultural production and rural economy in many countries, and to ensure that appropriate education, extension programmes and financial facilities are made available to women on equal terms with men.

5.   Marine and inland water resources are today becoming more important than ever as a source of food and economic prosperity. Accordingly, action should be taken to promote a rational exploitation of these resources, preferably for direct consumption, in order to contribute to meeting the food requirements of all peoples.

6.   The efforts to increase food production should be complemented by every endeavour to prevent wastage of food in all its forms.

7.   To give impetus to food production in developing countries and in particular in the least developed and most seriously affected among them, urgent and effective international action should be taken, by the developed countries and other countries in a position to do so, to provide them with sustained additional technical and financial assistance on favourable terms and in a volume sufficient to their needs on the basis of bilateral and multilateral arrangements. This assistance must be free of conditions inconsistent with the sovereignty of the receiving States.

8.   All countries, and primarily the highly industrialized countries, should promote the advancement of food production technology and should make all efforts to promote the transfer, adaptation and dissemination of appropriate food production technology for the benefit of the developing countries and, to that end, they should *inter alia* make all efforts to disseminate the results of their research work to Governments and scientific insti-

tutions of developing countries in order to enable them to promote a sustained agricultural development.

9.   To assure the proper conservation of natural resources being utilized, or which might be utilized, for food production, all countries must collaborate in order to facilitate the preservation of the environment, including the marine environment.

10.   All developed countries and others able to do so should collaborate technically and financially with the developing countries in their efforts to expand land and water resources for agricultural production and to assure a rapid increase in the availability, at fair costs, of agricultural inputs such as fertilizers and other chemicals, high-quality seeds, credit and technology. Co-operation among developing countries, in this connection, is also important.

11.   All States should strive to the utmost to readjust, where appropriate, their agricultural policies to give priority to food production, recognizing, in this connection the interrelationship between the world food problem and international trade. In the determination of attitudes towards farm support programmes for domestic food production, developed countries should take into account, as far as possible, the interest of the food-exporting developing countries, in order to avoid detrimental effect on their exports. Moreover, all countries should co-operate to devise effective steps to deal with the problem of stabilizing world markets and promoting equitable and remunerative prices, where appropriate through international arrangements, to improve access to markets through reduction or elimination of tariff and non-tariff barriers on the products of interest to the developing countries, to substantially increase the export earnings of these countries, to contribute to the diversification of their exports, and apply to them, in the multilateral trade negotiations, the principles as agreed upon in the Tokyo Declaration, including the concept of non-reciprocity and more favourable treatment.

12.   As it is the common responsibility of the entire international community to ensure the availability at all times of adequate world supplies of basic food-stuffs by way of appropriate reserves, including emergency reserves, all countries should co-operate in the establishment of an effective system of world food security by:

Participating in and supporting the operation of the Global Information and
Early Warning System on Food and Agriculture;

Adhering to the objectives, policies and guidelines of the proposed International Undertaking on World Food Security as endorsed by the World Food Conference;

Earmarking, where possible, stocks or funds for meeting international emergency food requirements as envisaged in the proposed International Undertaking on World Food Security and developing international guidelines to provide for the co-ordination and the utilization of such stocks;

Co-operating in the provision of food aid for meeting emergency and nutritional needs as well as for stimulating rural employment through development projects.

All donor countries should accept and implement the concept of forward planning of food aid and make all efforts to provide commodities and/or financial assistance that will ensure adequate quantities of grains and other food commodities.

Time is short. Urgent and sustained action is vital. The Conference, therefore, calls upon all peoples expressing their will as individuals, and through their Governments, and non-governmental organizations, to work together to bring about the end of the age-old scourge of hunger.

The Conference affirms:

The determination of the participating States to make full use of the United Nations system in the implementation of this Declaration and the other decisions adopted by the Conference.

70. Declaration on the Use of Scientific and Technological Progress in the Interests of Peace and for the Benefit of Mankind

Proclaimed by General Assembly resolution 3384 (XXX) of 10 November 1975

The General Assembly,

Noting that scientific and technological progress has become one of the most important factors in the development of human society,

Taking into consideration that, while scientific and technological developments provide ever increasing opportunities to better the conditions of life of peoples and nations, in a number of instances they can give rise to social problems, as well as threaten the human rights and fundamental freedoms of the individual,

Noting with concern that scientific and technological achievements can be used to intensify the arms race, suppress national liberation movements and deprive individuals and peoples of their human rights and fundamental freedoms,

Also noting with concern that scientific and technological achievements can entail dangers for the civil and political rights of the individual or of the group and for human dignity,

Noting the urgent need to make full use of scientific and technological developments for the welfare of man and to neutralize the present and possible future harmful consequences of certain scientific and technological achievements,

Recognizing that scientific and technological progress is of great importance in accelerating the social and economic development of developing countries,

Aware that the transfer of science and technology is one of the principal ways of accelerating the economic development of developing countries,

Reaffirming the right of peoples to self-determination and the need to respect human rights and freedoms and the dignity of the human person in the conditions of scientific and technological progress,

Desiring to promote the realization of the principles which form the basis of the Charter of the United Nations, the Universal Declaration of Human

Rights, the International Covenants on Human Rights, the Declaration on the Granting of Independence to Colonial Countries and Peoples, the Declaration on Principles of International Law concerning Friendly Relations and Co-operation among States in accordance with the Charter of the United Nations, the Declaration on Social Progress and Development, and the Charter of Economic Rights and Duties of States;

Solemnly proclaims that:

1.   All States shall promote international co-operation to ensure that the results of scientific and technological developments are used in the interests of strengthening international peace and security, freedom and independence, and also for the purpose of the economic and social development of peoples and the realization of human rights and freedoms in accordance with the Charter of the United Nations.

2.   All States shall take appropriate measures to prevent the use of scientific and technological developments, particularly by the State organs, to limit or interfere with the enjoyment of the human rights and fundamental freedoms of the individual as enshrined in the Universal Declaration of Human Rights, the International Covenants on Human Rights and other relevant international instruments.

3.   All States shall take measures to ensure that scientific and technological achievements satisfy the material and spiritual needs for all sectors of the population.

4.   All States shall refrain from any acts involving the use of scientific and technological achievements for the purposes of violating the sovereignty and territorial integrity of other States, interfering in their internal affairs, waging aggressive wars, suppressing national liberation movements or pursuing a policy of racial discrimination. Such acts are not only a flagrant violation of the Charter of the United Nations and principles of international law, but constitute an inadmissible distortion of the purposes that should guide scientific and technological developments for the benefit of mankind.

5.   All States shall co-operate in the establishment, strengthening and development of the scientific and technological capacity of developing countries with a view to accelerating the realization of the social and economic rights of the peoples of those countries.

6.   All States shall take measures to extend the benefits of science and technology to all strata of the population and to protect them, both socially and materially, from possible harmful effects of the misuse of scientific and technological developments, including their misuse to infringe upon the

rights of the individual or of the group, particularly with regard to respect for privacy and the protection of the human personality and its physical and intellectual integrity.

7. All States shall take the necessary measures, including legislative measures, to ensure that the utilization of scientific and technological achievements promotes the fullest realization of human rights and fundamental freedoms without any discrimination whatsoever on grounds of race, sex, language or religious beliefs.

8. All States shall take effective measures, including legislative measures, to prevent and preclude the utilization of scientific and technological achievements to the detriment of human rights and fundamental freedoms and the dignity of the human person.

9. All States shall, whenever necessary, take action to ensure compliance with legislation guaranteeing human rights and freedoms in the conditions of scientific and technological developments.

71. Guidelines for the Regulation of Computerized Personal Data Files

Adopted by General Assembly resolution 45/95 of 14 December 1990

The procedures for implementing regulations concerning computerized personal data files are left to the initiative of each State subject to the following orientations:

A. PRINCIPLES CONCERNING THE MINIMUM GUARANTEES THAT SHOULD BE PROVIDED IN NATIONAL LEGISLATIONS

1. *Principle of lawfulness and fairness*

Information about persons should not be collected or processed in unfair or unlawful ways, nor should it be used for ends contrary to the purposes and principles of the Charter of the United Nations.

2. *Principle of accuracy*

Persons responsible for the compilation of files or those responsible for keeping them have an obligation to conduct regular checks on the accuracy and relevance of the data recorded and to ensure that they are kept as complete as possible in order to avoid errors of omission and that they are kept up to date regularly or when the information contained in a file is used, as long as they are being processed.

3. *Principle of the purpose-specification*

The purpose which a file is to serve and its utilization in terms of that purpose should be specified, legitimate and, when it is established, receive a certain amount of publicity or be brought to the attention of the person concerned, in order to make it possible subsequently to ensure that:

(*a*) All the personal data collected and recorded remain relevant and adequate to the purposes so specified;

(*b*) None of the said personal data is used or disclosed, except with the consent of the person concerned, for purposes incompatible with those specified;

(*c*) The period for which the personal data are kept does not exceed that which would enable the achievement of the purposes so specified.

4. *Principle of interested-person access*

Everyone who offers proof of identity has the right to know whether information concerning him is being processed and to obtain it in an intelligible form, without undue delay or expense, and to have appropriate rectifications or erasures made in the case of unlawful, unnecessary or inaccurate entries and, when it is being communicated, to be informed of the addressees. Provision should be made for a remedy, if need be with the supervisory authority specified in principle 8 below. The cost of any rectification shall be borne by the person responsible for the file. It is desirable that the provisions of this principle should apply to everyone, irrespective of nationality or place of residence.

5. *Principle of non-discrimination*

Subject to cases of exceptions restrictively envisaged under principle 6, data likely to give rise to unlawful or arbitrary discrimination, including information on racial or ethnic origin, colour, sex life, political opinions, religious, philosophical and other beliefs as well as membership of an association or trade union, should not be compiled.

6. *Power to make exceptions*

Departures from principles 1 to 4 may be authorized only if they are necessary to protect national security, public order, public health or morality, as well as, *inter alia*, the rights and freedoms of others, especially persons being persecuted (humanitarian clause) provided that such departures are expressly specified in a law or equivalent regulation promulgated in accordance with the internal legal system which expressly states their limits and sets forth appropriate safeguards.

Exceptions to principle 5 relating to the prohibition of discrimination, in addition to being subject to the same safeguards as those prescribed for exceptions to principles 1 and 4, may be authorized only within the limits prescribed by the International Bill of Human Rights and the other relevant instruments in the field of protection of human rights and the prevention of discrimination.

7. *Principle of security*

Appropriate measures should be taken to protect the files against both natural dangers, such as accidental loss or destruction and human dangers, such as unauthorized access, fraudulent misuse of date or contamination by computer viruses.

8. *Supervision and sanctions*

The law of every country shall designate the authority which, in accordance with its domestic legal system, is to be responsible for supervising observance of the principles set forth above. This authority shall offer guarantees of impartiality, independence *vis-à-vis* persons or agencies responsible for processing and establishing data, and technical competence. In the event of violation of the provisions of the national law implementing the aforementioned principles, criminal or other penalties should be envisaged together with the appropriate individual remedies.

9. *Transborder data flows*

When the legislation of two or more countries concerned by a transborder data flow offers comparable safeguards for the protection of privacy, information should be able to circulate as freely as inside each of the territories concerned. If there are no reciprocal safeguards, limitations on such circulation may not be imposed unduly and only in so far as the protection of privacy demands.

10. *Field of application*

The present principles should be made applicable, in the first instance, to all public and private computerized files as well as, by means of optional extension and subject to appropriate adjustments, to manual files. Special provision, also optional, might be made to extend all or part of the principles to files on legal persons particularly when they contain some information on individuals.

B. APPLICATION OF THE GUIDELINES TO PERSONAL DATA FILES KEPT BY GOVERNMENTAL INTERNATIONAL ORGANIZATIONS

The present guidelines should apply to personal data files kept by governmental international organizations, subject to any adjustments required to take account of any differences that might exist between files for internal purposes such as those that concern personnel management and files for external purposes concerning third parties having relations with the organization.

Each organization should designate the authority statutorily competent to supervise the observance of these guidelines.

Humanitarian clause: a derogation from these principles may be specifically provided for when the purpose of the file is the protection of human rights and fundamental freedoms of the individual concerned or humanitarian assistance.

rights and fundamental freedoms of the individual concerned or humanitarian assistance.

A similar derogation should be provided in national legislation for governmental international organizations whose headquarters agreement does not preclude the implementation of the said national legislation as well as for non-governmental international organizations to which this law is applicable.

72. Declaration on the Rights of Disabled Persons

Proclaimed by General Assembly resolution 3447 (XXX) of 9 December 1975

The General Assembly,

Mindful of the pledge made by Member States, under the Charter of the United Nations to take joint and separate action in co-operation with the Organization to promote higher standards of living, full employment and conditions of economic and social progress and development,

Reaffirming its faith in human rights and fundamental freedoms and in the principles of peace, of the dignity and worth of the human person and of social justice proclaimed in the Charter,

Recalling the principles of the Universal Declaration of Human Rights, the International Covenants on Human Rights, the Declaration of the Rights of the Child and the Declaration on the Rights of Mentally Retarded Persons, as well as the standards already set for social progress in the constitutions, conventions, recommendations and resolutions of the International Labour Organisation, the United Nations Educational, Scientific and Cultural Organization, the World Health Organization, the United Nations Children's Fund and other organizations concerned,

Recalling also Economic and Social Council resolution 1921 (LVIII) of 6 May 1975 on the prevention of disability and the rehabilitation of disabled persons,

Emphasizing that the Declaration on Social Progress and Development has proclaimed the necessity of protecting the rights and assuring the welfare and rehabilitation of the physically and mentally disadvantaged,

Bearing in mind the necessity of preventing physical and mental disabilities and of assisting disabled persons to develop their abilities in the most varied fields of activities and of promoting their integration as far as possible in normal life,

Aware that certain countries, at their present stage of development, can devote only limited efforts to this end,

Proclaims this Declaration on the Rights of Disabled Persons and calls for national and international action to ensure that it will be used as a common basis and frame of reference for the protection of these rights:

1. The term "disabled person" means any person unable to ensure by himself or herself, wholly or partly, the necessities of a normal individual and/or social life, as a result of deficiency, either congenital or not, in his or her physical or mental capabilities.

2. Disabled persons shall enjoy all the rights set forth in this Declaration. These rights shall be granted to all disabled persons without any exception whatsoever and without distinction or discrimination on the basis of race, colour, sex, language, religion, political or other opinions, national or social origin, state of wealth, birth or any other situation applying either to the disabled person himself or herself or to his or her family.

3. Disabled persons have the inherent right to respect for their human dignity. Disabled persons, whatever the origin, nature and seriousness of their handicaps and disabilities, have the same fundamental rights as their fellow-citizens of the same age, which implies first and foremost the right to enjoy a decent life, as normal and full as possible.

4. Disabled persons have the same civil and political rights as other human beings; paragraph 7 of the Declaration on the Rights of Mentally Retarded Persons applies to any possible limitation or suppression of those rights for mentally disabled persons.

5. Disabled persons are entitled to the measures designed to enable them to become as self-reliant as possible.

6. Disabled persons have the right to medical, psychological and functional treatment, including prosthetic and orthetic appliances, to medical and social rehabilitation, education, vocational training and rehabilitation, aid, counselling, placement services and other services which will enable them to develop their capabilities and skills to the maximum and will hasten the processes of their social integration or reintegration.

7. Disabled persons have the right to economic and social security and to a decent level of living. They have the right, according to their capabilities, to secure and retain employment or to engage in a useful, productive and remunerative occupation and to join trade unions.

8. Disabled persons are entitled to have their special needs taken into consideration at all stages of economic and social planning.

9. Disabled persons have the right to live with their families or with foster parents and to participate in all social, creative or recreational activities. No disabled person shall be subjected, as far as his or her residence is concerned, to differential treatment other than that required by his or her

condition or by the improvement which he or she may derive therefrom. If the stay of a disabled person in a specialized establishment is indispensable, the environment and living conditions therein shall be as close as possible to those of the normal life of a person of his or her age.

10.   Disabled persons shall be protected against all exploitation, all regulations and all treatment of a discriminatory, abusive or degrading nature.

11.   Disabled persons shall be able to avail themselves of qualified legal aid when such aid proves indispensable for the protection of their persons and property. If judicial proceedings are instituted against them, the legal procedure applied shall take their physical and mental condition fully into account.

12.   Organizations of disabled persons may be usefully consulted in all matters regarding the rights of disabled persons.

13.   Disabled persons, their families and communities shall be fully informed, by all appropriate means, of the rights contained in this Declaration.

73. Declaration on the Right of Peoples to Peace

Approved by General Assembly resolution 39/11 of 12 November 1984

The General Assembly,

Reaffirming that the principal aim of the United Nations is the maintenance of international peace and security,

Bearing in mind the fundamental principles of international law set forth in the Charter of the United Nations,

Expressing the will and the aspirations of all peoples to eradicate war from the life of mankind and, above all, to avert a world-wide nuclear catastrophe,

Convinced that life without war serves as the primary international prerequisite for the material well-being, development and progress of countries, and for the full implementation of the rights and fundamental human freedoms proclaimed by the United Nations,

Aware that in the nuclear age the establishment of a lasting peace on Earth represents the primary condition for the preservation of human civilization and the survival of mankind,

Recognizing that the maintenance of a peaceful life for peoples is the sacred duty of each State,

1. *Solemnly proclaims* that the peoples of our planet have a sacred right to peace;

2. *Solemnly declares* that the preservation of the right of peoples to peace and the promotion of its implementation constitute a fundamental obligation of each State;

3. *Emphasizes* that ensuring the exercise of the right of peoples to peace demands that the policies of States be directed towards the elimination of the threat of war, particularly nuclear war, the renunciation of the use of force in international relations and the settlement of international disputes by peaceful means on the basis of the Charter of the United Nations;

4. *Appeals* to all States and international organizations to do their utmost to assist in implementing the right of peoples to peace through the adoption of appropriate measures at both the national and the international level.

74. Declaration on the Right to Development

Adopted by General Assembly resolution 41/128 of 4 December 1986

The General Assembly,

Bearing in mind the purposes and principles of the Charter of the United Nations relating to the achievement of international co-operation in solving international problems of an economic, social, cultural or humanitarian nature, and in promoting and encouraging respect for human rights and fundamental freedoms for all without distinction as to race, sex, language or religion,

Recognizing that development is a comprehensive economic, social, cultural and political process, which aims at the constant improvement of the well-being of the entire population and of all individuals on the basis of their active, free and meaningful participation in development and in the fair distribution of benefits resulting therefrom,

Considering that under the provisions of the Universal Declaration of Human Rights everyone is entitled to a social and international order in which the rights and freedoms set forth in that Declaration can be fully realized,

Recalling the provisions of the International Covenant on Economic, Social and Cultural Rights and of the International Covenant on Civil and Political Rights,

Recalling further the relevant agreements, conventions, resolutions, recommendations and other instruments of the United Nations and its specialized agencies concerning the integral development of the human being, economic and social progress and development of all peoples, including those instruments concerning decolonization, the prevention of discrimination, respect for and observance of, human rights and fundamental freedoms, the maintenance of international peace and security and the further promotion of friendly relations and co-operation among States in accordance with the Charter,

Recalling the right of peoples to self-determination, by virtue of which they have the right freely to determine their political status and to pursue their economic, social and cultural development,

Recalling also the right of peoples to exercise, subject to the relevant provisions of both International Covenants on Human Rights, full and complete sovereignty over all their natural wealth and resources,

Mindful of the obligation of States under the Charter to promote universal respect for and observance of human rights and fundamental freedoms for all without distinction of any kind such as race, colour, sex, language, religion, political or other opinion, national or social origin, property, birth or other status,

Considering that the elimination of the massive and flagrant violations of the human rights of the peoples and individuals affected by situations such as those resulting from colonialism, neo-colonialism, *apartheid,* all forms of racism and racial discrimination, foreign domination and occupation, aggression and threats against national sovereignty, national unity and territorial integrity and threats of war would contribute to the establishment of circumstances propitious to the development of a great part of mankind,

Concerned at the existence of serious obstacles to development, as well as to the complete fulfilment of human beings and of peoples, constituted, *inter alia,* by the denial of civil, political, economic, social and cultural rights, and considering that all human rights and fundamental freedoms are indivisible and interdependent and that, in order to promote development, equal attention and urgent consideration should be given to the implementation, promotion and protection of civil, political, economic, social and cultural rights and that, accordingly, the promotion of, respect for and enjoyment of certain human rights and fundamental freedoms cannot justify the denial of other human rights and fundamental freedoms,

Considering that international peace and security are essential elements for the realization of the right to development,

Reaffirming that there is a close relationship between disarmament and development and that progress in the field of disarmament would considerably promote progress in the field of development and that resources released through disarmament measures should be devoted to the economic and social development and well-being of all peoples and, in particular, those of the developing countries,

Recognizing that the human person is the central subject of the development process and that development policy should therefore make the human being the main participant and beneficiary of development,

Recognizing that the creation of conditions favourable to the development of peoples and individuals is the primary responsibility of their States,

Aware that efforts at the international level to promote and protect human rights should be accompanied by efforts to establish a new international economic order,

Confirming that the right to development is an inalienable human right and that equality of opportunity for development is a prerogative both of nations and of individuals who make up nations,

Proclaims the following Declaration on the Right to Development:

Article 1

1. The right to development is an inalienable human right by virtue of which every human person and all peoples are entitled to participate in, contribute to, and enjoy economic, social, cultural and political development, in which all human rights and fundamental freedoms can be fully realized.

2. The human right to development also implies the full realization of the right of peoples to self-determination, which includes, subject to the relevant provisions of both International Covenants on Human Rights, the exercise of their inalienable right to full sovereignty over all their natural wealth and resources.

Article 2

1. The human person is the central subject of development and should be the active participant and beneficiary of the right to development.

2. All human beings have a responsibility for development, individually and collectively, taking into account the need for full respect for their human rights and fundamental freedoms as well as their duties to the community, which alone can ensure the free and complete fulfilment of the human being, and they should therefore promote and protect an appropriate political, social and economic order for development.

3. States have the right and the duty to formulate appropriate national development policies that aim at the constant improvement of the well-being of the entire population and of all individuals, on the basis of their active, free and meaningful participation in development and in the fair distribution of the benefits resulting therefrom.

Article 3

1. States have the primary responsibility for the creation of national and international conditions favourable to the realization of the right to development.

2. The realization of the right to development requires full respect for the principles of international law concerning friendly relations and co-operation among States in accordance with the Charter of the United Nations.

3. States have the duty to co-operate with each other in ensuring development and eliminating obstacles to development. States should realize their rights and fulfil their duties in such a manner as to promote a new international economic order based on sovereign equality, interdependence, mutual interest and co-operation among all States, as well as to encourage the observance and realization of human rights.

Article 4

1. States have the duty to take steps, individually and collectively, to formulate international development policies with a view to facilitating the full realization of the right to development.

2. Sustained action is required to promote more rapid development of developing countries. As a complement to the efforts of developing countries, effective international co-operation is essential in providing these countries with appropriate means and facilities to foster their comprehensive development.

Article 5

States shall take resolute steps to eliminate the massive and flagrant violations of the human rights of peoples and human beings affected by situations such as those resulting from *apartheid,* all forms of racism and racial discrimination, colonialism, foreign domination and occupation, aggression, foreign interference and threats against national sovereignty, national unity and territorial integrity, threats of war and refusal to recognize the fundamental right of peoples to self-determination.

Article 6

1. All States should co-operate with a view to promoting, encouraging and strengthening universal respect for and observance of all human rights and fundamental freedoms for all without any distinction as to race, sex, language or religion.

2. All human rights and fundamental freedoms are indivisible and interdependent; equal attention and urgent consideration should be given to the implementation, promotion and protection of civil, political, economic, social and cultural rights.

3.   States should take steps to eliminate obstacles to development result-ing from failure to observe civil and political rights, as well as economic, social and cultural rights.

Article 7

All States should promote the establishment, maintenance and strength-ening of international peace and security and, to that end, should do their utmost to achieve general and complete disarmament under effective inter-national control, as well as to ensure that the resources released by effective disarmament measures are used for comprehensive development, in particu-lar that of the developing countries.

Article 8

1.   States should undertake, at the national level, all necessary measures for the realization of the right to development and shall ensure, *inter alia,* equality of opportunity for all in their access to basic resources, education, health services, food, housing, employment and the fair distribution of income. Effective measures should be undertaken to ensure that women have an active role in the development process. Appropriate economic and social reforms should be carried out with a view to eradicating all social injustices.

2.   States should encourage popular participation in all spheres as an important factor in development and in the full realization of all human rights.

Article 9

1.   All the aspects of the right to development set forth in the present Declaration are indivisible and interdependent and each of them should be considered in the context of the whole.

2.   Nothing in the present Declaration shall be construed as being con-trary to the purposes and principles of the United Nations, or as implying that any State, group or person has a right to engage in any activity or to perform any act aimed at the violation of the rights set forth in the Universal Dec-laration of Human Rights and in the International Covenants on Human Rights.

Article 10

Steps should be taken to ensure the full exercise and progressive enhancement of the right to development, including the formulation, adoption and implementation of policy, legislative and other measures at the national and international levels.

75. International Convention on the Protection of the Rights of All Migrant Workers and Members of Their Families

Adopted by General Assembly resolution 45/158 of 18 December 1990 (not in force)

PREAMBLE

The States Parties to the present Convention,

Taking into account the principles embodied in the basic instruments of the United Nations concerning human rights, in particular the Universal Declaration of Human Rights, the International Covenant on Economic, Social and Cultural Rights, the International Covenant on Civil and Political Rights, the International Convention on the Elimination of All Forms of Racial Discrimination, the Convention on the Elimination of All Forms of Discrimination against Women and the Convention on the Rights of the Child,

Taking into account also the principles and standards set forth in the relevant instruments elaborated within the framework of the International Labour Organisation, especially the Convention concerning Migration for Employment (No. 97), the Convention concerning Migrations in Abusive Conditions and the Promotion of Equality of Opportunity and Treatment of Migrant Workers (No. 143), the Recommendation concerning Migration for Employment (No. 86), the Recommendation concerning Migrant Workers (No. 151), the Convention concerning Forced or Compulsory Labour (No. 29) and the Convention concerning Abolition of Forced Labour (No. 105),

Reaffirming the importance of the principles contained in the Convention against Discrimination in Education of the United Nations Educational, Scientific and Cultural Organization,

Recalling the Convention against Torture and Other Cruel, Inhuman or Degrading Treatment or Punishment, the Declaration of the Fourth United Nations Congress on the Prevention of Crime and the Treatment of Offenders, the Code of Conduct for Law Enforcement Officials, and the Slavery Conventions,

Recalling that one of the objectives of the International Labour Organisation, as stated in its Constitution, is the protection of the interests of workers when employed in countries other than their own, and bearing in mind the expertise and experience of that organization in matters related to migrant workers and members of their families,

Recognizing the importance of the work done in connection with migrant workers and members of their families in various organs of the United Nations, in particular in the Commission on Human Rights and the Commission for Social Development, and in the Food and Agriculture Organization of the United Nations, the United Nations Educational, Scientific and Cultural Organization and the World Health Organization, as well as in other international organizations,

Recognizing also the progress made by certain States on a regional or bilateral basis towards the protection of the rights of migrant workers and members of their families, as well as the importance and usefulness of bilateral and multilateral agreements in this field,

Realizing the importance and extent of the migration phenomenon, which involves millions of people and affects a large number of States in the international community,

Aware of the impact of the flows of migrant workers on States and people concerned, and desiring to establish norms which may contribute to the harmonization of the attitudes of States through the acceptance of basic principles concerning the treatment of migrant workers and members of their families,

Considering the situation of vulnerability in which migrant workers and members of their families frequently find themselves owing, among other things, to their absence from their State of origin and to the difficulties they may encounter arising from their presence in the State of employment,

Convinced that the rights of migrant workers and members of their families have not been sufficiently recognized everywhere and therefore require appropriate international protection,

Taking into account the fact that migration is often the cause of serious problems for the members of the families of migrant workers as well as for the workers themselves, in particular because of the scattering of the family,

Bearing in mind that the human problems involved in migration are even more serious in the case of irregular migration and convinced therefore that appropriate action should be encouraged in order to prevent and eliminate clandestine movements and trafficking in migrant workers, while at the same time assuring the protection of their fundamental human rights,

Considering that workers who are non-documented or in an irregular situation are frequently employed under less favourable conditions of work than other workers and that certain employers find this an inducement to seek such labour in order to reap the benefits of unfair competition,

Considering also that recourse to the employment of migrant workers who are in an irregular situation will be discouraged if the fundamental human rights of all migrant workers are more widely recognized and, moreover, that granting certain additional rights to migrant workers and members of their families in a regular situation will encourage all migrants and employers to respect and comply with the laws and procedures established by the States concerned,

Convinced, therefore, of the need to bring about the international protection of the rights of all migrant workers and members of their families, reaffirming and establishing basic norms in a comprehensive convention which could be applied universally,

Have agreed as follows:

PART I

SCOPE AND DEFINITIONS

Article 1

1. The present Convention is applicable, except as otherwise provided hereafter, to all migrant workers and members of their families without distinction of any kind such as sex, race, colour, language, religion or conviction, political or other opinion, national, ethnic or social origin, nationality, age, economic position, property, marital status, birth or other status.

2. The present Convention shall apply during the entire migration process of migrant workers and members of their families, which comprises preparation for migration, departure, transit and the entire period of stay and remunerated activity in the State of employment as well as return to the State of origin or the State of habitual residence.

Article 2

For the purposes of the present Convention:

1. The term "migrant worker" refers to a person who is to be engaged, is engaged or has been engaged in a remunerated activity in a State of which he or she is not a national.

2. (*a*) The term "frontier worker" refers to a migrant worker who retains his or her habitual residence in a neighbouring State to which he or she normally returns every day or at least once a week;

(*b*) The term "seasonal worker" refers to a migrant worker whose work by its character is dependent on seasonal conditions and is performed only during part of the year;

(*c*) The term "seafarer", which includes a fisherman, refers to a migrant worker employed on board a vessel registered in a State of which he or she is not a national;

(*d*) The term "worker on an offshore installation" refers to a migrant worker employed on an offshore installation that is under the jurisdiction of a State of which he or she is not a national;

(*e*) The term "itinerant worker" refers to a migrant worker who, having his or her habitual residence in one State, has to travel to another State or States for short periods, owing to the nature of his or her occupation;

(*f*) The term "project-tied worker" refers to a migrant worker admitted to a State of employment for a defined period to work solely on a specific project being carried out in that State by his or her employer;

(*g*) The term "specified-employment worker" refers to a migrant worker:

(i) Who has been sent by his or her employer for a restricted and defined period of time to a State of employment to undertake a specific assignment or duty; or

(ii) Who engages for a restricted and defined period of time in work that requires professional, commercial, technical or other highly specialized skill; or

(iii) Who, upon the request of his or her employer in the State of employment, engages for a restricted and defined period of time in work whose nature is transitory or brief;

and who is required to depart from the State of employment either at the expiration of his or her authorized period of stay, or earlier if he or she no longer undertakes that specific assignment or duty or engages in that work;

(*h*) The term "self-employed worker" refers to a migrant worker who is engaged in a remunerated activity otherwise than under a contract of employment and who earns his or her living through this activity normally working alone or together with members of his or her family, and to any other migrant worker recognized as self-employed by applicable legislation of the State of employment or bilateral or multilateral agreements.

Article 3

The present Convention shall not apply to:

(*a*) Persons sent or employed by international organizations and agencies or persons sent or employed by a State outside its territory to perform official functions, whose admission and status are regulated by general international law or by specific international agreements or conventions;

(*b*) Persons sent or employed by a State or on its behalf outside its territory who participate in development programmes and other co-operation programmes, whose admission and status are regulated by agreement with the State of employment and who, in accordance with that agreement, are not considered migrant workers;

(*c*) Persons taking up residence in a State different from their State of origin as investors;

(*d*) Refugees and stateless persons, unless such application is provided for in the relevant national legislation of, or international instruments in force for, the State Party concerned;

(*e*) Students and trainees;

(*f*) Seafarers and workers on an offshore installation who have not been admitted to take up residence and engage in a remunerated activity in the State of employment.

Article 4

For the purposes of the present Convention the term "members of the family" refers to persons married to migrant workers or having with them a relationship that, according to applicable law, produces effects equivalent to marriage, as well as their dependent children and other dependent persons who are recognized as members of the family by applicable legislation or applicable bilateral or multilateral agreements between the States concerned.

Article 5

For the purposes of the present Convention, migrant workers and members of their families:

(*a*) Are considered as documented or in a regular situation if they are authorized to enter, to stay and to engage in a remunerated activity in the State of employment pursuant to the law of that State and to international agreements to which that State is a party;

(*b*) Are considered as non-documented or in an irregular situation if they do not comply with the conditions provided for in subparagraph (*a*) of the present article.

Article 6

For the purposes of the present Convention:

(*a*) The term "State of origin" means the State of which the person concerned is a national;

(*b*) The term "State of employment" means a State where the migrant worker is to be engaged, is engaged or has been engaged in a remunerated activity, as the case may be;

(*c*) The term "State of transit" means any State through which the person concerned passes on any journey to the State of employment or from the State of employment to the State of origin or the State of habitual residence.

PART II

NON-DISCRIMINATION WITH RESPECT TO RIGHTS

Article 7

States Parties undertake, in accordance with the international instruments concerning human rights, to respect and to ensure to all migrant workers and members of their families within their territory or subject to their jurisdiction the rights provided for in the present Convention without distinction of any kind such as to sex, race, colour, language, religion or conviction, political or other opinion, national, ethnic or social origin, nationality, age, economic position, property, marital status, birth or other status.

PART III

HUMAN RIGHTS OF ALL MIGRANT WORKERS AND MEMBERS OF THEIR FAMILIES

Article 8

1.   Migrant workers and members of their families shall be free to leave any State, including their State of origin. This right shall not be subject to any restrictions except those that are provided by law, are necessary to protect national security, public order (*ordre public*), public health or morals or the rights and freedoms of others and are consistent with the other rights recognized in the present part of the Convention.

2.   Migrant workers and members of their families shall have the right at any time to enter and remain in their State of origin.

Article 9

The right to life of migrant workers and members of their families shall be protected by law.

Article 10

No migrant worker or member of his or her family shall be subjected to torture or to cruel, inhuman or degrading treatment or punishment.

Article 11

1.   No migrant worker or member of his or her family shall be held in slavery or servitude.

2.   No migrant worker or member of his or her family shall be required to perform forced or compulsory labour.

3.   Paragraph 2 of the present article shall not be held to preclude, in States where imprisonment with hard labour may be imposed as a punishment for a crime, the performance of hard labour in pursuance of a sentence to such punishment by a competent court.

4.   For the purpose of the present article the term ''forced or compulsory labour'' shall not include:

(*a*) Any work or service not referred to in paragraph 3 of the present article normally required of a person who is under detention in consequence of a lawful order of a court or of a person during conditional release from such detention;

(*b*) Any service exacted in cases of emergency or clamity threatening the life or well-being of the community;

(*c*) Any work or service that forms part of normal civil obligations so far as it is imposed also on citizens of the State concerned.

Article 12

1.   Migrant workers and members of their families shall have the right to freedom of thought, conscience and religion. This right shall include freedom to have or to adopt a religion or belief of their choice and freedom either individually or in community with others and in public or private to manifest their religion or belief in worship, observance, practice and teaching.

2.   Migrant workers and members of their families shall not be subject to coercion that would impair their freedom to have or to adopt a religion or belief of their choice.

3.   Freedom to manifest one's religion or belief may be subject only to such limitations as are prescribed by law and are necessary to protect public safety, order, health or morals or the fundamental rights and freedoms of others.

4.   States Parties to the present Convention undertake to have respect for the liberty of parents, at least one of whom is a migrant worker, and,

when applicable, legal guardians to ensure the religious and moral education of their children in conformity with their own convictions.

Article 13

1.   Migrant workers and members of their families shall have the right to hold opinions without interference.

2.   Migrant workers and members of their families shall have the right to freedom of expression; this right shall include freedom to seek, receive and impart information and ideas of all kinds, regardless of frontiers, either orally, in writing or in print, in the form of art or through any other media of their choice.

3.   The exercise of the right provided for in paragraph 2 of the present article carries with it special duties and responsibilities. It may therefore be subject to certain restrictions, but these shall only be such as are provided by law and are necessary:

(*a*)   For respect of the rights or reputation of others;

(*b*)   For the protection of the national security of the States concerned or of public order (*ordre public*) or of public health or morals;

(*c*)   For the purpose of preventing any propaganda for war;

(*d*)   For the purpose of preventing any advocacy of national, racial or religious hatred that constitutes incitement to discrimination, hostility or violence.

Article 14

No migrant worker or member of his or her family shall be subjected to arbitrary or unlawful interference with his or her privacy, family, home, correspondence or other communications, or to unlawful attacks on his or her honour and reputation. Each migrant worker and member of his or her family shall have the right to the protection of the law against such interference or attacks.

Article 15

No migrant worker or member of his or her family shall be arbitrarily deprived of property, whether owned individually or in association with others. Where, under the legislation in force in the State of employment, the assets of a migrant worker or a member of his or her family are expropriated in whole or in part, the person concerned shall have the right to fair and adequate compensation.

Article 16

1. Migrant workers and members of their families shall have the right to liberty and security of person.

2. Migrant workers and members of their families shall be entitled to effective protection by the State against violence, physical injury, threats and intimidation, whether by public officials or by private individuals, groups or institutions.

3. Any verification by law enforcement officials of the identity of migrant workers or members of their families shall be carried out in accordance with procedure established by law.

4. Migrant workers and members of their families shall not be subjected individually or collectively to arbitrary arrest or detention; they shall not be deprived o their liberty except on such grounds and in accordance with such procedures as are established by law.

5. Migrant workers and members of their families who are arrested shall be informed at the time of arrest as far as possible in a language they understand of the reasons for their arrest and they shall be promptly informed in a language they understand of any charges against them.

6. Migrant workers and members of their families who are arrested or detained on a criminal charge shall be brought promptly before a judge or other officer authorized by law to exercise judicial power and shall be entitled to trial within a reasonable time or to release. It shall not be the general rule that while awaiting trial they shall be detained in custody, but release may be subject to guarantees to appear for trial, at any other stage of the judicial proceedings and, should the occasion arise, for the execution of the judgement.

7. When a migrant worker or a member of his or her family is arrested or committed to prison or custody pending trial or is detained in any other manner:

(*a*) The consular or diplomatic authorities of his or her State of origin or of a State representing the interests of that State shall, if he or she so requests, be informed without delay of his or her arrest or detention and of the reasons therefor;

(*b*) The person concerned shall have the right to communicate with the said authorities. Any communication by the person concerned to the said authorities shall be forwarded without delay, and he or she shall also have the right to receive communications sent by the said authorities without delay;

(*c*) The person concerned shall be informed without delay of this right and of rights deriving from relevant treaties, if any, applicable between the States concerned, to correspond and to meet with representatives of the said authorities and to make arrangements with them for his or her legal representation.

8. Migrant workers and members of their families who are deprived of their liberty by arrest or detention shall be entitled to take proceedings before a court, in order that that court may decide without delay on the lawfulness of their detention and order their release if the detention is not lawful. When they attend such proceedings, they shall have the assistance, if necessary without cost to them, of an interpreter, if they cannot understand or speak the language used.

9. Migrant workers and members of their families who have been victims of unlawful arrest or detention shall have an enforceable right to compensation.

Article 17

1. Migrant workers and members of their families who are deprived of their liberty shall be treated with humanity and with respect for the inherent dignity of the human person and for their cultural identity.

2. Accused migrant workers and members of their families shall, save in exceptional circumstances, be separated from convicted persons and shall be subject to separate treatment appropriate to their status as unconvicted persons. Accused juvenile persons shall be separated from adults and brought as speedily as possible for adjudication.

3. Any migrant worker or member of his or her family who is detained in a State of transit or in a State of employment for violation of provisions relating to migration shall be held, in so far as practicable, separately from convicted persons or persons detained pending trial.

4. During any period of imprisonment in pursuance of a sentence imposed by a court of law, the essential aim of the treatment of a migrant worker or a member of his or her family shall be his or her reformation and social rehabilitation. Juvenile offenders shall be separated from adults and be accorded treatment appropriate to their age and legal status.

5. During detention or imprisonment, migrant workers and members of their families shall enjoy the same rights as nationals to visits by members of their families.

6. Whenever a migrant worker is deprived of his or her liberty, the competent authorities of the State concerned shall pay attention to the problems that may be posed for members of his or her family, in particular for spouses and minor children.

7. Migrant workers and members of their families who are subjected to any form of detention or imprisonment in accordance with the law in

force in the State of employment or in the State of transit shall enjoy the same rights as nationals of those States who are in the same situation.

8. If a migrant worker or a member of his or her family is detained for the purpose of verifying any infraction of provisions related to migration, he or she shall not bear any costs arising therefrom.

Article 18

1. Migrant workers and members of their families shall have the right to equality with nationals of the State concerned before the courts and tribunals. In the determination of any criminal charge against them or of their rights and obligations in a suit of law, they shall be entitled to a fair and public hearing by a competent, independent and impartial tribunal established by law.

2. Migrant workers and members of their families who are charged with a criminal offence shall have the right to be presumed innocent until proven guilty according to law.

3. In the determination of any criminal charge against them, migrant workers and members of their families shall be entitled to the following minimum guarantees:

(a) To be informed promptly and in detail in a language they understand of the nature and cause of the charge against them;

(b) To have adequate time and facilities for the preparation of their defence and to communicate with counsel of their own choosing;

(c) To be tried without undue delay;

(d) To be tried in their presence and to defend themselves in person or through legal assistance of their own choosing; to be informed, if they do not have legal assistance, of this right; and to have legal assistance assigned to them, in any case where the interests of justice so require and without payment by them in any such case if they do not have sufficient means to pay;

(e) To examine or have examined the witnesses against them and to obtain the attendance and examination of witnesses on their behalf under the same conditions as witnesses against them;

(f) To have the free assistance of an interpreter if they cannot understand or speak the language used in court;

(g) Not to be compelled to testify against themselves or to confess guilt.

4. In the case of juvenile persons, the procedure shall be such as will take account of their age and the desirability of promoting their rehabilitation.

5. Migrant workers and members of their families convicted of a crime shall have the right to their conviction and sentence being reviewed by a higher tribunal according to law.

6. When a migrant worker or a member of his or her family has, by a final decision, been convicted of a criminal offence and when subsequently his or her conviction has been reversed or he or she has been pardoned on the ground that a new or newly discovered fact shows conclusively that there has been a miscarriage of justice, the person who has suffered punishment as a result of such conviction shall be compensated according to law, unless it is proved that the non-disclosure of the unknown fact in time is wholly or partly attributable to that person.

7. No migrant worker or member of his or her family shall be liable to be tried or punished again for an offence for which he or she has already been finally convicted or acquitted in accordance with the law and penal procedure of the State concerned.

Article 19

1. No migrant worker or member of his or her family shall be held guilty of any criminal offence on account of any act or omission that did not constitute a criminal offence under national or international law at the time when the criminal offence was committed, nor shall a heavier penalty be imposed than the one that was applicable at the time when it was committed. If, subsequent to the commission of the offence, provision is made by law for the imposition of a lighter penalty, he or she shall benefit thereby.

2. Humanitarian considerations related to the status of a migrant worker, in particular with respect to his or her right of residence or work, should be taken into account in imposing a sentence for a criminal offence committed by a migrant worker or a member of his or her family.

Article 20

1. No migrant worker or member of his or her family shall be imprisoned merely on the ground of failure to fulfil a contractual obligation.

2. No migrant worker or member of his or her family shall be deprived of his or her authorization of residence or work permit or expelled merely on the ground of failure to fulfil an obligation arising out of a work contract unless fulfilment of that obligation constitutes a condition for such authorization or permit.

Article 21

It shall be unlawful for anyone, other than a public official duly authorized by law, to confiscate, destroy or attempt to destroy identity documents, documents authorizing entry to or stay, residence or establishment in the national territory or work permits. No authorized confiscation of such documents shall take place without delivery of a detailed receipt. In no case shall it be permitted to destroy the passport or equivalent document of a migrant worker or a member of his or her family.

Article 22

1. Migrant workers and members of their families shall not be subject to measures of collective expulsion. Each case of expulsion shall be examined and decided individually.

2. Migrant workers and members of their families may be expelled from the territory of a State Party only in pursuance of a decision taken by the competent authority in accordance with law.

3. The decision shall be communicated to them in a language they understand. Upon their request where not otherwise mandatory, the decision shall be communicated to them in writing and, save in exceptional circumstances on account of national security, the reasons for the decision likewise stated. The persons concerned shall be informed of these rights before or at the latest at the time the decision is rendered.

4. Except where a final decision is pronounced by a judicial authority, the person concerned shall have the right to submit the reason he or she should not be expelled and to have his or her case reviewed by the competent authority, unless compelling reasons of national security require otherwise. Pending such review, the person concerned shall have the right to seek a stay of the decision of expulsion.

5. If a decision of expulsion that has already been executed is subsequently annulled, the person concerned shall have the right to seek compensation according to law and the earlier decision shall not be used to prevent him or her from re-entering the State concerned.

6. In case of expulsion, the person concerned shall have a reasonable opportunity before or after departure to settle any claims for wages and other entitlements due to him or her and any pending liabilities.

7. Without prejudice to the execution of a decision of expulsion, a migrant worker or a member of his or her family who is subject to such a decision may seek entry into a State other than his or her State of origin.

8. In case of expulsion of a migrant worker or a member of his or her family the costs of expulsion shall not be borne by him or her. The person concerned may be required to pay his or her own travel costs.

9. Expulsion from the State of employment shall not in itself prejudice any rights of a migrant worker or a member of his or her family ac-

quired in accordance with the law of that State, including the right to receive wages and other entitlements due to him or her.

Article 23

Migrant workers and members of their families shall have the right to have recourse to the protection and assistance of the consular or diplomatic authorities of their State of origin or of a State representing the interests of that State whenever the rights recognized in the present Convention are impaired. In particular, in case of expulsion, the person concerned shall be informed of this right without delay and the authorities of the expelling State shall facilitate the exercise of such right.

Article 24

Every migrant worker and every member of his or her family shall have the right to recognition everywhere as a person before the law.

Article 25

1. Migrant workers shall enjoy treatment not less favourable than that which applies to nationals of the State of employment in respect of remuneration and:

(*a*) Other conditions of work, that is to say, overtime, hours of work, weekly rest, holidays with pay, safety, health, termination of the employment relationship and any other conditions of work which, according to national law and practice, are covered by these terms;

(*b*) Other terms of employment, that is to say, minimum age of employment, restriction on home work and any other matters which, according to national law and practice, are considered a term of employment.

2. It shall not be lawful to derogate in private contracts of employment from the principle of equality of treatment referred to in paragraph 1 of the present article.

3. States Parties shall take all appropriate measures to ensure that migrant workers are not deprived of any rights derived from this principle by reason of any irregularity in their stay or employment. In particular, employers shall not be relieved of any legal or contractual obligations, nor shall their obligations be limited in any manner by reason of such irregularity.

Article 26

1. States Parties recognize the right of migrant workers and members of their families:

(*a*) To take part in meetings and activities of trade unions and of any other associations established in accordance with law, with a view to protecting their economic, social, cultural and other interests, subject only to the rules of the organization concerned;

(*b*) To join freely any trade union and any such association as aforesaid, subject only to the rules of the organization concerned;

(*c*) To seek the aid and assistance of any trade union and of any such association as aforesaid.

2. No restrictions may be placed on the exercise of these rights other than those that are prescribed by law and which are necessary in a democratic society in the interests of national security, public order (*ordre public*) or the protection of the rights and freedoms of others.

Article 27

1. With respect to social security, migrant workers and members of their families shall enjoy in the State of employment the same treatment granted to nationals in so far as they fulfil the requirements provided for by the applicable legislation of that State and the applicable bilateral and multilateral treaties. The competent authorities of the State of origin and the State of employment can at any time establish the necessary arrangements to determine the modalities of application of this norm.

2. Where the applicable legislation does not allow migrant workers and members of their families a benefit, the States concerned shall examine the possibility of reimbursing interested persons the amount of contributions made by them with respect to that benefit on the basis of the treatment granted to nationals who are in similar circumstances.

Article 28

Migrant workers and members of their families shall have the right to receive any medical care that is urgently required for the preservation of their life or the avoidance of irreparable harm to their health on the basis of equality of treatment with nationals of the State concerned. Such emergency medical care shall not be refused them by reason of any irregularity with regard to stay or employment.

Article 29

Each child of a migrant worker shall have the right to a name, to registration of birth and to a nationality.

Article 30

Each child of a migrant worker shall have the basic right of access to education on the basis of equality of treatment with nationals of the State concerned. Access to public pre-school educational institutions or schools shall not be refused or limited by reason of the irregular situation with respect to stay or employment of either parent or by reason of the irregularity of the child's stay in the State of employment.

Article 31

1. States Parties shall ensure respect for the cultural identity of migrant workers and members of their families and shall not prevent them from maintaining their cultural links with their State of origin.

2. States Parties may take appropriate measures to assist and encourage efforts in this respect.

Article 32

Upon the termination of their stay in the State of employment, migrant workers and members of their families shall have the right to transfer their earnings and savings and, in accordance with the applicable legislation of the States concerned, their personal effects and belongings.

Article 33

1. Migrant workers and members of their families shall have the right to be informed by the State of origin, the State of employment or the State of transit as the case may be concerning:

(*a*) Their rights arising out of the present Convention;

(*b*) The conditions of their admission, their rights and obligations under the law and practice of the State concerned and such other matters as will enable them to comply with administrative or other formalities in that State.

2. States Parties shall take all measures they deem appropriate to disseminate the said information or to ensure that it is provided by employers, trade unions or other appropriate bodies or institutions. As appropriate, they shall co-operate with other States concerned.

3. Such adequate information shall be provided upon request to migrant workers and members of their families, free of charge, and, as far as possible, in a language they are able to understand.

Article 34

Nothing in the present part of the Convention shall have the effect of relieving migrant workers and the members of their families from either the obligation to comply with the laws and regulations of any State of transit and the State of employment or the obligation to respect the cultural identity of the inhabitants of such States.

Article 35

Nothing in the present part of the Convention shall be interpreted as implying the regularization of the situation of migrant workers or members of their families who are non-documented or in an irregular situation or any right to such regularization of their situation, nor shall it prejudice the measures intended to ensure sound and equitable conditions for international migration as provided in part VI of the present Convention.

PART IV

OTHER RIGHTS OF MIGRANT WORKERS AND MEMBERS OF THEIR FAMILIES WHO ARE DOCUMENTED OR IN A REGULAR SITUATION

Article 36

Migrant workers and members of their families who are documented or in a regular situation in the State of employment shall enjoy the rights set forth in the present part of the Convention in addition to those set forth in part III.

Article 37

Before their departure, or at the latest at the time of their admission to the State of employment, migrant workers and members of their families shall have the right to be fully informed by the State of origin or the State of employment, as appropriate, of all conditions applicable to their admission and particularly those concerning their stay and the remunerated activities in which they may engage as well as of the requirements they must satisfy in the State of employment and the authority to which they must address themselves for any modification of those conditions.

Article 38

1.   States of employment shall make every effort to authorize migrant workers and members of their families to be temporarily absent without ef-

fect upon their authorization to stay or to work, as the case may be. In doing so, States of employment shall take into account the special needs and obligations of migrant workers and members of their families, in particular in their States of origin.

2. Migrant workers and members of their families shall have the right to be fully informed of the terms on which such temporary absences are authorized.

Article 39

1. Migrant workers and members of their families shall have the right to liberty of movement in the territory of the State of employment and freedom to choose their residence there.

2. The rights mentioned in paragraph 1 of the present article shall not be subject to any restrictions except those that are provided by law, are necessary to protect national security, public order (*ordre public*), public health or morals, or the rights and freedoms of others and are consistent with the other rights recognized in the present Convention.

Article 40

1. Migrant workers and members of their families shall have the right to form associations and trade unions in the State of employment for the promotion and protection of their economic, social, cultural and other interests.

2. No restrictions may be placed on the exercise of this right other than those that are prescribed by law and are necessary in a democratic society in the interests of national security, public order (*ordre public*) or the protection of the rights and freedoms of others.

Article 41

1. Migrant workers and members of their families shall have the right to participate in public affairs of their State of origin and to vote and to be elected at elections of that State, in accordance with its legislation.

2. The States concerned shall, as appropriate and in accordance with their legislation, facilitate the exercise of these rights.

Article 42

1. States Parties shall consider the establishment of procedures or institutions through which account may be taken, both in States of origin and in States of employment, of special needs, aspirations and obligations of migrant workers and members of their families and shall envisage, as appropri-

ate, the possibility for migrant workers and members of their families to have their freely chosen representatives in those institutions.

2. States of employment shall facilitate, in accordance with their national legislation, the consultation or participation of migrant workers and members of their families in decisions concerning the life and administration of local communities.

3. Migrant workers may enjoy political rights in the State of employment if that State, in the exercise of its sovereignty, grants them such rights.

Article 43

1. Migrant workers shall enjoy equality of treatment with nationals of the State of employment in relation to:

(*a*) Access to educational institutions and services subject to the admission requirements and other regulations of the institutions and services concerned;

(*b*) Access to vocational guidance and placement services;

(*c*) Access to vocational training and retraining facilities and institutions;

(*d*) Access to housing, including social housing schemes, and protection against exploitation in respect of rents;

(*e*) Access to social and health services, provided that the requirements for participation in the respective schemes are met;

(*f*) Access to co-operatives and self-managed enterprises, which shall not imply a change of their migration status and shall be subject to the rules and regulations of the bodies concerned;

(*g*) Access to and participation in cultural life.

2. States Parties shall promote conditions to ensure effective equality of treatment to enable migrant workers to enjoy the rights mentioned in paragraph 1 of the present article whenever the terms of their stay, as authorized by the State of employment, meet the appropriate requirements.

3. States of employment shall not prevent an employer of migrant workers from establishing housing or social or cultural facilities for them. Subject to article 70 of the present Convention, a State of employment may make the establishment of such facilities subject to the requirements generally applied in that State concerning their installation.

Article 44

1. States Parties, recognizing that the family is the natural and fundamental group unit of society and is entitled to protection by society and the

State, shall take appropriate measures to ensure the protection of the unity of the families of migrant workers.

2. States Parties shall take measures that they deem appropriate and that fall within their competence to facilitate the reunification of migrant workers with their spouses or persons who have with the migrant worker a relationship that, according to applicable law, produces effects equivalent to marriage, as well as with their minor dependent unmarried children.

3. States of employment, on humanitarian grounds, shall favourably consider granting equal treatment, as set forth in paragraph 2 of the present article, to other family members of migrant workers.

Article 45

1. Members of the families of migrant workers shall, in the State of employment, enjoy equality of treatment with nationals of that State in relation to:

(*a*) Access to educational institutions and services, subject to the admission requirements and other regulations of the institutions and services concerned;

(*b*) Access to vocational guidance and training institutions and services, provided that requirements for participation are met;

(*c*) Access to social and health services, provided that requirements for participation in the respective schemes are met;

(*d*) Access to and participation in cultural life.

2. States of employment shall pursue a policy, where appropriate in collaboration with the States of origin, aimed at facilitating the integration of children of migrant workers in the local school system, particularly in respect of teaching them the local language.

3. States of employment shall endeavour to facilitate for the children of migrant workers the teaching of their mother tongue and culture and, in this regard, States of origin shall collaborate whenever appropriate.

4. States of employment may provide special schemes of education in the mother tongue of children of migrant workers, if necessary in collaboration with the States of origin.

Article 46

Migrant workers and members of their families shall, subject to the applicable legislation of the States concerned, as well as relevant international agreements and the obligations of the States concerned arising out of their participation in customs unions, enjoy exemption from import and export duties and taxes in respect of their personal and household effects as well as the equipment necessary to engage in the remunerated activity for which they were admitted to the State of employment:

(*a*) Upon departure from the State of origin or State of habitual residence;

(*b*) Upon initial admission to the State of employment;

(*c*) Upon final departure from the State of employment;

(*d*) Upon final return to the State of origin or State of habitual residence.

Article 47

1.   Migrant workers shall have the right to transfer their earnings and savings, in particular those funds necessary for the support of their families, from the State of employment to their State of origin or any other State. Such transfers shall be made in conformity with procedures established by applicable legislation of the State concerned and in conformity with applicable international agreements.

2.   States concerned shall take appropriate measures to facilitate such transfers.

Article 48

1.   Without prejudice to applicable double taxation agreements, migrant workers and members of their families shall, in the matter of earnings in the State of employment:

(*a*) Not be liable to taxes, duties or charges of any description higher or more onerous than those imposed on nationals in similar circumstances;

(*b*) Be entitled to deductions or exemptions from taxes of any description and to any tax allowances applicable to nationals in similar circumstances, including tax allowances for dependent members of their families.

2.   States Parties shall endeavour to adopt appropriate measures to avoid double taxation of the earnings and savings of migrant workers and members of their families.

Article 49

1.   Where separate authorizations to reside and to engage in employment are required by national legislation, the States of employment shall issue to migrant workers authorization of residence for at least the same period of time as their authorization to engage in remunerated activity.

2.   Migrant workers who in the State of employment are allowed freely to choose their remunerated activity shall neither be regarded as in an irregular situation nor shall they lose their authorization of residence by the

mere fact of the termination of their remunerated activity prior to the expiration of their work permits or similar authorizations.

3.   In order to allow migrant workers referred to in paragraph 2 of the present article sufficient time to find alternative remunerated activities, the authorization of residence shall not be withdrawn at least for a period corresponding to that during which they may be entitled to unemployment benefits.

Article 50

1.   In the case of death of a migrant worker or dissolution of marriage, the State of employment shall favourably consider granting family members of that migrant worker residing in that State on the basis of family reunion an authorization to stay; the State of employment shall take into account the length of time they have already resided in that State.

2.   Members of the family to whom such authorization is not granted shall be allowed before departure a reasonable period of time in order to enable them to settle their affairs in the State of employment.

3.   The provisions of paragraphs 1 and 2 of the present article may not be interpreted as adversely affecting any right to stay and work otherwise granted to such family members by the legislation of the State of employment or by bilateral and multilateral treaties applicable to that State.

Article 51

Migrant workers who in the State of employment are not permitted freely to choose their remunerated activity shall neither be regarded as in an irregular situation nor shall they lose their authorization of residence by the mere fact of the termination of their remunerated activity prior to the expiration of their work permit, except where the authorization of residence is expressly dependent upon the specific remunerated activity for which they were admitted. Such migrant workers shall have the right to seek alternative employment, participation in public work schemes and retraining during the remaining period of their authorization to work, subject to such conditions and limitations as are specified in the authorization to work.

Article 52

1.   Migrant workers in the State of employment shall have the right freely to choose their remunerated activity, subject to the following restrictions or conditions.

2.   For any migrant worker a State of employment may:

(*a*) Restrict access to limited categories of employment, functions, services or activities where this is necessary in the interests of this State and provided for by national legislation;

(*b*) Restrict free choice of remunerated activity in accordance with its legislation concerning recognition of occupational qualifications acquired outside its territory. However, States Parties concerned shall endeavour to provide for recognition of such qualifications.

3.   For migrant workers whose permission to work is limited in time, a State of employment may also:

(*a*) Make the right freely to choose their remunerated activities subject to the condition that the migrant worker has resided lawfully in its territory for the purpose of remunerated activity for a period of time prescribed in its national legislation that should not exceed two years;

(*b*) Limit access by a migrant worker to remunerated activities in pursuance of a policy of granting priority to its nationals or to persons who are assimilated to them for these purposes by virtue of legislation or bilateral or multilateral agreements. Any such limitation shall cease to apply to a migrant worker who has resided lawfully in its territory for the purpose of remunerated activity for a period of time prescribed in its national legislation that should not exceed five years.

4.   States of employment shall prescribe the conditions under which a migrant worker who has been admitted to take up employment may be authorized to engage in work on his or her own account. Account shall be taken of the period during which the worker has already been lawfully in the State of employment.

Article 53

1.   Members of a migrant worker's family who have themselves an authorization of residence or admission that is without limit of time or is automatically renewable shall be permitted freely to choose their remunerated activity under the same conditions as are applicable to the said migrant worker in accordance with article 52 of the present Convention.

2.   With respect to members of a migrant worker's family who are not permitted freely to choose their remunerated activity, States Parties shall consider favourably granting them priority in obtaining permission to engage in a remunerated activity over other workers who seek admission to the State of employment, subject to applicable bilateral and multilateral agreements.

Article 54

1.   Without prejudice to the terms of their authorization of residence or their permission to work and the rights provided for in articles 25 and 27 of the present Convention, migrant workers shall enjoy equality of treatment with nationals of the State of employment in respect of:

(*a*) Protection against dismissal;

(*b*) Unemployment benefits;

(*c*) Access to public work schemes intended to combat unemployment;

(*d*) Access to alternative employment in the event of loss of work or termination of other remunerated activity, subject to article 52 of the present Convention.

2.   If a migrant worker claims that the terms of his or her work contract have been violated by his or her employer, he or she shall have the right to address his or her case to the competent authorities of the State of employment, on terms provided for in article 18, paragraph 1, of the present Convention.

Article 55

Migrant workers who have been granted permission to engage in a remunerated activity, subject to the conditions attached to such permission, shall be entitled to equality of treatment with nationals of the State of employment in the exercise of that remunerated activity.

Article 56

1.   Migrant workers and members of their families referred to in the present part of the Convention may not be expelled from a State of employment, except for reasons defined in the national legislation of that State, and subject to the safeguards established in part III.

2.   Expulsion shall not be resorted to for the purpose of depriving a migrant worker or a member of his or her family of the rights arising out of the authorization of residence and the work permit.

3.   In considering whether to expel a migrant worker or a member of his or her family, account should be taken of humanitarian considerations and of the length of time that the person concerned has already resided in the State of employment.

PART V

PROVISIONS APPLICABLE TO PARTICULAR CATEGORIES OF MIGRANT WORKERS AND MEMBERS OF THEIR FAMILIES

Article 57

The particular categories of migrant workers and members of their families specified in the present part of the Convention who are documented or in a regular situation shall enjoy the rights set forth in part III and, except as modified below, the rights set forth in part IV.

Article 58

1.   Frontier workers, as defined in article 2, paragraph 2 (*a*), of the present Convention, shall be entitled to the rights provided for in part IV that can be applied to them by reason of their presence and work in the territory of the State of employment, taking into account that they do not have their habitual residence in that State.

2.   States of employment shall consider favourably granting frontier workers the right freely to choose their remunerated activity after a specified period of time. The granting of that right shall not affect their status as frontier workers.

Article 59

1.   Seasonal workers, as defined in article 2, paragraph 2 (*b*), of the present Convention, shall be entitled to the rights provided for in part IV that can be applied to them by reason of their presence and work in the territory of the State of employment and that are compatible with their status in that State as seasonal workers, taking into account the fact that they are present in that State for only part of the year.

2.   The State of employment shall, subject to paragraph 1 of the present article, consider granting seasonal workers who have been employed in its territory for a significant period of time the possibility of taking up other remunerated activities and giving them priority over other workers who seek admission to that State, subject to applicable bilateral and multilateral agreements.

Article 60

Itinerant workers, as defined in article 2, paragraph 2 (e), of the present Convention, shall be entitled to the rights provided for in part IV that can be granted to them by reason of their presence and work in the territory of the

State of employment and that are compatible with their status as itinerant workers in that State.

Article 61

1.   Project-tied workers, as defined in article 2, paragraph 2 (*f*), of the present Convention, and members of their families shall be entitled to the rights provided for in part IV except the provisions of article 43, paragraphs 1 (*b*) and (*c*), article 43, paragraph 1 (*d*), as it pertains to social housing schemes, article 45, paragraph 1 (*b*), and articles 52 to 55.

2.   If a project-tied worker claims that the terms of his or her work contract have been violated by his or her employer, he or she shall have the right to address his or her case to the competent authorities of the State which has jurisdiction over that employer, on terms provided for in article 18, paragraph 1, of the present Convention.

3.   Subject to bilateral or multilateral agreements in force for them, the States Parties concerned shall endeavour to enable project-tied workers to remain adequately protected by the social security systems of their States of origin or habitual residence during their engagement in the project. States Parties concerned shall take appropriate measures with the aim of avoiding any denial of rights or duplication of payments in this respect.

4.   Without prejudice to the provisions of article 47 of the present Convention and to relevant bilateral or multilateral agreements, States Parties concerned shall permit payment of the earnings of project-tied workers in their State of origin or habitual residence.

Article 62

1.   Specified-employment workers as defined in article 2, paragraph 2 (*g*), of the present Convention, shall be entitled to the rights provided for in part IV, except the provisions of article 43, paragraphs 1 (*b*) and (*c*), article 43, paragraph 1 (*d*), as it pertains to social housing schemes, article 52, and article 54, paragraph 1 (*d*).

2.   Members of the families of specified-employment workers shall be entitled to the rights relating to family members of migrant workers provided for in part IV of the present Convention, except the provisions of article 53.

Article 63

1.   Self-employed workers, as defined in article 2, paragraph 2 (*h*), of the present Convention, shall be entitled to the rights provided for in part IV with the exception of those rights which are exclusively applicable to workers having a contract of employment.

2. Without prejudice to articles 52 and 79 of the present Convention, the termination of the economic activity of the self-employed workers shall not in itself imply the withdrawal of the authorization for them or for the members of their families to stay or to engage in a remunerated activity in the State of.employment except where the authorization of residence is expressly dependent upon the specific remunerated activity for which they were admitted.

PART VI

PROMOTION OF SOUND, EQUITABLE, HUMANE AND LAWFUL CONDITIONS IN CONNECTION WITH INTERNATIONAL MIGRATION OF WORKERS AND MEMBERS OF THEIR FAMILIES

Article 64

1. Without prejudice to article 79 of the present Convention, the States Parties concerned shall as appropriate consult and co-operate with a view to promoting sound, equitable and humane conditions in connection with international migration of workers and members of their families.

2. In this respect, due regard shall be paid not only to labour needs and resources, but also to the social, economic, cultural and other needs of migrant workers and members of their families involved, as well as to the consequences of such migration for the communities concerned.

Article 65

1. States Parties shall maintain appropriate services to deal with questions concerning international migration of workers and members of their families. Their functions shall include, *inter alia*:

(*a*) The formulation and implementation of policies regarding such migration;

(*b*) An exchange of information, consultation and co-operation with the competent authorities of other States Parties involved in such migration;

(*c*) The provision of appropriate information, particularly to employers, workers and their organizations on policies, laws and regulations relating to migration and employment, on agreements concluded with other States concerning migration and on other relevant matters;

(*d*) The provision of information and appropriate assistance to migrant workers and members of their families regarding requisite authorizations and formalities and arrangements for departure, travel, arrival, stay, remunerated activities, exit and return, as well as on conditions of work and life in the State of employment and on customs, currency, tax and other relevant laws and regulations.

2.   States Parties shall facilitate as appropriate the provision of adequate consular and other services that are necessary to meet the social, cultural and other needs of migrant workers and members of their families.

Article 66

1.   Subject to paragraph 2 of the present article, the right to undertake operations with a view to the recruitment of workers for employment in another State shall be restricted to:

(*a*) Public services or bodies of the State in which such operations take place;

(*b*) Public services or bodies of the State of employment on the basis of agreement between the States concerned;

(*c*) A body established by virtue of a bilateral or multilateral agreement.

2.   Subject to any authorization, approval and supervision by the public authorities of the States Parties concerned as may be established pursuant to the legislation and practice of those States, agencies, prospective employers or persons acting on their behalf may also be permitted to undertake the said operations.

Article 67

1.   States Parties concerned shall co-operate as appropriate in the adoption of measures regarding the orderly return of migrant workers and members of their families to the State of origin when they decide to return or their authorization of residence or employment expires or when they are in the State of employment in an irregular situation.

2.   Concerning migrant workers and members of their families in a regular situation, States Parties concerned shall co-operate as appropriate, on terms agreed upon by those States, with a view to promoting adequate economic conditions for their resettlement and to facilitating their durable social and cultural reintegration in the State of origin.

Article 68

1.   States Parties, including States of transit, shall collaborate with a view to preventing and eliminating illegal or clandestine movements and employment of migrant workers in an irregular situation. The measures to be

taken to this end within the jurisdiction of each State concerned shall include:

(*a*) Appropriate measures against the dissemination of misleading information relating to emigration and immigration;

(*b*) Measures to detect and eradicate illegal or clandestine movements of migrant workers and members of their families and to impose effective sanctions on persons, groups or entities which organize, operate or assist in organizing or operating such movements;

(*c*) Measures to impose effective sanctions on persons, groups or entities which use violence, threats or intimidation against migrant workers or members of their families in an irregular situation.

2.   States of employment shall take all adequate and effective measures to eliminate employment in their territory of migrant workers in an irregular situation, including, whenever appropriate, sanctions on employers of such workers. The rights of migrant workers *vis-à-vis* their employer arising from employment shall not be impaired by these measures.

Article 69

1.   States Parties shall, when there are migrant workers and members of their families within their territory in an irregular situation, take appropriate measures to ensure that such a situation does not persist.

2.   Whenever States Parties concerned consider the possibility of regularizing the situation of such persons in accordance with applicable national legislation and bilateral or multilateral agreements, appropriate account shall be taken of the circumstances of their entry, the duration of their stay in the States of employment and other relevant considerations, in particular those relating to their family situation.

Article 70

States Parties shall take measures not less favourable than those applied to nationals to ensure that working and living conditions of migrant workers and members of their families in a regular situation are in keeping with the standards of fitness, safety, health and principles of human dignity.

Article 71

1.   States Parties shall facilitate, whenever necessary, the repatriation to the State of origin of the bodies of deceased migrant workers or members of their families.

2.   As regards compensation matters relating to the death of a migrant worker or a member of his or her family, States Parties shall, as appropriate, provide assistance to the persons concerned with a view to the prompt settle-

ment of such matters. Settlement of these matters shall be carried out on the basis of applicable national law in accordance with the provisions of the present Convention and any relevant bilateral or multilateral agreements.

PART VII

APPLICATION OF THE CONVENTION

Article 72

1. (*a*) For the purpose of reviewing the application of the present Convention, there shall be established a Committee on the Protection of the Rights of All Migrant Workers and Members of Their Families (hereinafter referred to as "the Committee");

(*b*) The Committee shall consist, at the time of entry into force of the present Convention, of ten and, after the entry into force of the Convention for the forty-first State Party, of fourteen experts of high moral standing, impartiality and recognized competence in the field covered by the Convention.

2. (*a*) Members of the Committee shall be elected by secret ballot by the States Parties from a list of persons nominated by the States Parties, due consideration being given to equitable geographical distribution, including both States of origin and States of employment, and to the representation of the principal legal system. Each State Party may nominate one person from among its own nationals;

(*b*) Members shall be elected and shall serve in their personal capacity.

3. The initial election shall be held no later than six months after the date of the entry into force of the present Convention and subsequent elections every second year. At least four months before the date of each election, the Secretary-General of the United Nations shall address a letter to all States Parties inviting them to submit their nominations within two months. The Secretary-General shall prepare a list in alphabetical order of all persons thus nominated, indicating the States Parties that have nominated them, and shall submit it to the States Parties not later than one month before the date of the corresponding election, together with the curricula vitae of the persons thus nominated.

4. Elections of members of the Committee shall be held at a meeting of States Parties convened by the Secretary-General at United Nations Headquarters. At that meeting, for which two thirds of the States Parties shall constitute a quorum, the persons elected to the Committee shall be those nominees who obtain the largest number of votes and an absolute majority of the votes of the States Parties present and voting.

5.   (*a*) The members of the Committee shall serve for a term of four years. However, the terms of five of the members elected in the first election shall expire at the end of two years; immediately after the first election, the names of these five members shall be chosen by lot by the Chairman of the meeting of States Parties;

(*b*) The election of the four additional members of the Committee shall be held in accordance with the provisions of paragraphs 2, 3 and 4 of the present article, following the entry into force of the Convention for the forty-first State Party. The term of two of the additional members elected on this occasion shall expire at the end of two years; the names of these members shall be chosen by lot by the Chairman of the meeting of States Parties;

(*c*) The members of the Committee shall be eligible for re-election if renominated.

6.   If a member of the Committee dies or resigns or declares that for any other cause he or she can no longer perform the duties of the Committee, the State Party that nominated the expert shall appoint another expert from among its own nationals for the remaining part of the term. The new appointment is subject to the approval of the Committee.

7.   The Secretary-General of the United Nations shall provide the necessary staff and facilities for the effective performance of the functions of the Committee.

8.   The members of the Committee shall receive emoluments from United Nations resources on such terms and conditions as the General Assembly may decide.

9.   The members of the Committee shall be entitled to the facilities, privileges and immunities of experts on mission for the United Nations as laid down in the relevant sections of the Convention on the Privileges and Immunities of the United Nations.

Article 73

1.   States Parties undertake to submit to the Secretary-General of the United Nations for consideration by the Committee a report on the legislative, judicial, administrative and other measures they have taken to give effect to the provisions of the present Convention:

(*a*) Within one year after the entry into force of the Convention for the State Party concerned;

(*b*) Thereafter every five years and whenever the Committee so requests.

2.   Reports prepared under the present article shall also indicate factors and difficulties, if any, affecting the implementation of the Convention

and shall include information on the characteristics of migration flows in which the State Party concerned is involved.

3. The Committee shall decide any further guidelines applicable to the content of the reports.

4. States Parties shall make their reports widely available to the public in their own countries.

Article 74

1. The Committee shall examine the reports submitted by each State Party and shall transmit such comments as it may consider appropriate to the State Party concerned. This State Party may submit to the Committee observations on any comment made by the Committee in accordance with the present article. The Committee may request supplementary information from States Parties when considering these reports.

2. The Secretary-General of the United Nations shall, in due time before the opening of each regular session of the Committee, transmit to the Director-General of the International Labour Office copies of the reports submitted by States Parties concerned and information relevant to the consideration of these reports, in order to enable the Office to assist the Committee with the expertise the Office may provide regarding those matters dealt with by the present Convention that fall within the sphere of competence of the International Labour Organisation. The Committee shall consider in its deliberations such comments and materials as the Office may provide.

3. The Secretary-General of the United Nations may also, after consultation with the Committee, transmit to other specialized agencies as well as to intergovernmental organizations, copies of such parts of these reports as may fall within their competence.

4. The Committee may invite the specialized agencies and organs of the United Nations, as well as intergovernmental organizations and other concerned bodies to submit, for consideration by the Committee, written information on such matters dealt with in the present Convention as fall within the scope of their activities.

5. The International Labour Office shall be invited by the Committee to appoint representatives to participate, in a consultative capacity, in the meetings of the Committee.

6. The Committee may invite representatives of other specialized agencies and organs of the United Nations, as well as of intergovernmental organizations, to be present and to be heard in its meetings whenever matters falling within their field of competence are considered.

7.   The Committee shall present an annual report to the General Assembly of the United Nations on the implementation of the present Convention, containing its own considerations and recommendations, based, in particular, on the examination of the reports and any observations presented by States Parties.

8.   The Secretary-General of the United Nations shall transmit the annual reports of the Committee to the States Parties to the present Convention, the Economic and Social Council, the Commission on Human Rights of the United Nations, the Director-General of the International Labour Office and other relevant organizations.

Article 75

1.   The Committee shall adopt its own rules of procedure.

2.   The Committee shall elect its officers for a term of two years.

3.   The Committee shall normally meet annually.

4.   The meetings of the Committee shall normally be held at United Nations Headquarters.

Article 76

1.   A State Party to the present Convention may at any time declare under this article that it recognizes the competence of the Committee to receive and consider communications to the effect that a State Party claims that another State Party is not fulfilling its obligations under the present Convention. Communications under this article may be received and considered only if submitted by a State Party that has made a declaration recognizing in regard to itself the competence of the Committee. No communication shall be received by the Committee if it concerns a State Party which has not made such a declaration. Communications received under this article shall be dealt with in accordance with the following procedure:

(*a*) If a State Party to the present Convention considers that another State Party is not fulfilling its obligations under the present Convention, it may, by written communication, bring the matter to the attention of that State Party. The State Party may also inform the Committee of the matter. Within three months after the receipt of the communication the receiving State shall afford the State that sent the communication an explanation, or any other statement in writing clarifying the matter which should include, to the extent possible and pertinent, reference to domestic procedures and remedies taken, pending or available in the matter;

(*b*) If the matter is not adjusted to the satisfaction of both States Parties concerned within six months after the receipt by the receiving State of the initial communication, either State shall have the right to refer the matter to the Committee, by notice given to the Committee and to the other State;

(*c*) The Committee shall deal with a matter referred to it only after it has ascertained that all available domestic remedies have been invoked and exhausted in the matter, in conformity with the generally recognized principles of international law. This shall not be the rule where, in the view of the Committee, the application of the remedies is unreasonably prolonged;

(*d*) Subject to the provisions of subparagraph (*c*) of the present paragraph, the Committee shall make available its good offices to the States Parties concerned with a view to a friendly solution of the matter on the basis of the respect for the obligations set forth in the present Convention;

(*e*) The Committee shall hold closed meetings when examining communications under the present article;

(*f*) In any matter referred to it in accordance with subparagraph (*b*) of the present paragraph, the Committee may call upon the States Parties concerned, referred to in subparagraph (*b*), to supply any relevant information;

(*g*) The States Parties concerned, referred to in subparagraph (*b*) of the present paragraph, shall have the right to be represented when the matter is being considered by the Committee and to make submissions orally and/or in writing;

(*h*) The Committee shall, within twelve months after the date of receipt of notice under subparagraph (*b*) of the present paragraph, submit a report, as follows:

(i)   If a solution within the terms of subparagraph (d) of the present paragraph is reached, the Committee shall confine its report to a brief statement of the facts and of the solution reached;

(ii)   If a solution within the terms of subparagraph (d) is not reached, the Committee shall, in its report, set forth the relevant facts concerning the issue between the States Parties concerned. The written submissions and record of the oral submissions made by the States Parties concerned shall be attached to the report. The Committee may also communicate only to the States Parties concerned any views that it may consider relevant to the issue between them.

In every matter, the report shall be communicated to the States Parties concerned.

2.   The provisions of the present article shall come into force when ten States Parties to the present Convention have made a declaration under paragraph 1 of the present article. Such declarations shall be deposited by the States Parties with the Secretary-General of the United Nations, who shall transmit copies thereof to the other States Parties. A declaration may be withdrawn at any time by notification to the Secretary-General. Such a withdrawal shall not prejudice the consideration of any matter that is the subject

of a communication already transmitted under the present article; no further communication by any State Party shall be received under the present article after the notification of withdrawal of the declaration has been received by the Secretary-General, unless the State Party concerned has made a new declaration.

Article 77

1.   A State Party to the present Convention may at any time declare under the present article that it recognizes the competence of the Committee to receive and consider communications from or on behalf of individuals subject to its jurisdiction who claim that their individual rights as established by the present Convention have been violated by that State Party. No communication shall be received by the Committee if it concerns a State Party that has not made such a declaration.

2.   The Committee shall consider inadmissible any communication under the present article which is anonymous or which it considers to be an abuse of the right of submission of such communications or to be incompatible with the provisions of the present Convention.

3.   The Committee shall not consider any communication from an individual under the present article unless it has ascertained that:

(*a*) The same matter has not been, and is not being, examined under another procedure of international investigation or settlement;

(*b*) The individual has exhausted all available domestic remedies; this shall not be the rule where, in the view of the Committee, the application of the remedies is unreasonably prolonged or is unlikely to bring effective relief to that individual.

4.   Subject to the provisions of paragraph 2 of the present article, the Committee shall bring any communications submitted to it under this article to the attention of the State Party to the present Convention that has made a declaration under paragraph 1 and is alleged to be violating any provisions of the Convention. Within six months, the receiving State shall submit to the Committee written explanations or statements clarifying the matter and the remedy, if any, that may have been taken by that State.

5.   The Committee shall consider communications received under the present article in the light of all information made available to it by or on behalf of the individual and by the State Party concerned.

6.   The Committee shall hold closed meetings when examining communications under the present article.

7.   The Committee shall forward its views to the State Party concerned and to the individual.

8.   The provisions of the present article shall come into force when ten States Parties to the present Convention have made declarations under paragraph 1 of the present article. Such declarations shall be deposited by the States Parties with the Secretary-General of the United Nations, who shall transmit copies thereof to the other States Parties. A declaration may be withdrawn at any time by notification to the Secretary-General. Such a withdrawal shall not prejudice the consideration of any matter that is the subject of a communication already transmitted under the present article; no further communication by or on behalf of an individual shall be received under the present article after the notification of withdrawal of the declaration has been received by the Secretary-General, unless the State Party has made a new declaration.

Article 78

The provisions of article 76 of the present Convention shall be applied without prejudice to any procedures for settling disputes or complaints in the field covered by the present Convention laid down in the constituent instruments of, or in conventions adopted by, the United Nations and the specialized agencies and shall not prevent the States Parties from having recourse to any procedures for settling a dispute in accordance with international agreements in force between them.

PART VIII

GENERAL PROVISIONS

Article 79

Nothing in the present Convention shall affect the right of each State Party to establish the criteria governing admission of migrant workers and members of their families. Concerning other matters related to their legal situation and treatment as migrant workers and members of their families, States Parties shall be subject to the limitations set forth in the present Convention.

Article 80

Nothing in the present Convention shall be interpreted as impairing the provisions of the Charter of the United Nations and of the constitutions of the specialized agencies which define the respective responsibilities of the various organs of the United Nations and of the specialized agencies in regard to the matters dealt with in the present Convention.

Article 81

1.   Nothing in the present Convention shall affect more favourable rights or freedoms granted to migrant workers and members of their families by virtue of:

(*a*) The law or practice of a State Party; or

(*b*) Any bilateral or multilateral treaty in force for the State Party concerned.

2.   Nothing in the present Convention may be interpreted as implying for any State, group or person any right to engage in any activity or perform any act that would impair any of the rights and freedoms as set forth in the present Convention.

Article 82

The rights of migrant workers and members of their families provided for in the present Convention may not be renounced. It shall not be permissible to exert any form of pressure upon migrant workers and members of their families with a view to their relinquishing or foregoing any of the said rights. It shall not be possible to derogate by contract from rights recognized in the present Convention. States Parties shall take appropriate measures to ensure that these principles are respected.

Article 83

Each State Party to the present Convention undertakes:

(*a*) To ensure that any person whose rights or freedoms as herein recognized are violated shall have an effective remedy, notwithstanding that the violation has been committed by persons acting in an official capacity;

(*b*) To ensure that any persons seeking such a remedy shall have his or her claim reviewed and decided by competent judicial, administrative or legislative authorities, or by any other competent authority provided for by the legal system of the State, and to develop the possibilities of judicial remedy;

(*c*) To ensure that the competent authorities shall enforce such remedies when granted.

Article 84

Each State Party undertakes to adopt the legislative and other measures that are necessary to implement the provisions of the present Convention.

PART IX

FINAL PROVISIONS

Article 85

The Secretary-General of the United Nations is designated as the depositary of the present Convention.

Article 86

1.   The present Convention shall be open for signature by all States. It is subject to ratification.

2.   The present Convention shall be open to accession by any State.

3.   Instruments of ratification or accession shall be deposited with the Secretary-General of the United Nations.

Article 87

1.   The present Convention shall enter into force on the first day of the month following a period of three months after the date of the deposit of the twentieth instrument of ratification or accession.

2.   For each State ratifying or acceding to the present Convention after its entry into force, the Convention shall enter into force on the first day of the month following a period of three months after the date of the deposit of its own instrument of ratification or accession.

Article 88

A State ratifying or acceding to the present Convention may not exclude the application of any Part of it, or, without prejudice to article 3, exclude any particular category of migrant workers from its application.

Article 89

1.   Any State Party may denounce the present Convention, not earlier than five years after the Convention has entered into force for the State concerned, by means of a notification writing addressed to the Secretary-General of the United Nations.

2.   Such denunciation shall become effective on the first day of the month following the expiration of a period of twelve months after the date of the receipt of the notification by the Secretary-General of the United Nations.

3.   Such a denunciation shall not have the effect of releasing the State Party from its obligations under the present Convention in regard to any act or omission which occurs prior to the date at which the denunciation becomes effective, nor shall denunciation prejudice in any way the continued consideration of any matter which is already under consideration by the Committee prior to the date at which the denunciation becomes effective.

4.   Following the date at which the denunciation of a State Party becomes effective, the Committee shall not commence consideration of any new matter regarding that State.

Article 90

1.   After five years from the entry into force of the Convention a request for the revision of the Convention may be made at any time by any State Party by means of a notification in writing addressed to the Secretary-General of the United Nations. The Secretary-General shall thereupon communicate any proposed amendments to the States Parties with a request that they notify him whether the favour a conference of States Parties for the purpose of considering and voting upon the proposals. In the event that within four months from the date of such communication at least one third of the States Parties favours such a conference, the Secretary-General shall convene the conference under the auspices of the United Nations. Any amendment adopted by a majority of the States Parties present and voting shall be submitted to the General Assembly for approval.

2.   Amendments shall come into force when they have been approved by the General Assembly of the United Nations and accepted by a two-thirds majority of the States Parties in accordance with their respective constitutional processes.

3.   When amendments come into force, they shall be binding on those States Parties that have accepted them, other States Parties still being bound by the provisions of the present Convention and any earlier amendment that they have accepted.

Article 91

1.   The Secretary-General of the United Nations shall receive and circulate to all States the text of reservations made by States at the time of signature, ratification or accession.

2.   A reservation incompatible with the object and purpose of the present Convention shall not be permitted.

3.   Reservations may be withdrawn at any time by notification to this effect addressed to the Secretary-General of the United Nations, who shall

then inform all States thereof. Such notification shall take effect on the date on which it is received.

Article 92

1.   Any dispute between two or more States Parties concerning the interpretation or application of the present Convention that is not settled by negotiation shall, at the request of one of them, be submitted to arbitration. If within six months from the date of the request for arbitration the Parties are unable to agree on the organization of the arbitration, any one of those Parties may refer the dispute to the International Court of Justice by request in conformity with the Statute of the Court.

2.   Each State Party may at the time of signature or ratification of the present Convention or accession thereto declare that it does not consider itself bound by paragraph 1 of the present article. The other States Parties shall not be bound by that paragraph with respect to any State Party that has made such a declaration.

3.   Any State Party that has made a declaration in accordance with paragraph 2 of the present article may at any time withdraw that declaration by notification to the Secretary-General of the United Nations.

Article 93

1.   The present Convention, of which the Arabic, Chinese, English, French, Russian and Spanish texts are equally authentic, shall be deposited with the Secretary-General of the United Nations.

2.   The Secretary-General of the United Nations shall transmit certified copies of the present Convention to all States.

IN WITNESS WHEREOF the undersigned plenipotentiaries, being duly authorized thereto by their respective Governments, have signed the present Convention.

N. RIGHT TO ENJOY CULTURE; INTERNATIONAL CULTURAL DEVELOPMENT AND CO-OPERATION

76. Declaration of the Principles of International Cultural Co-operation

Proclaimed by the General Conference of the United Nations Educational, Scientific and Cultural Organization at its fourteenth session, on 4 November 1966

The General Conference of the United Nations Educational, Scientific and Cultural Organization, met in Paris for its fourteenth session, this fourth day of November 1966, being the twentieth anniversary of the foundation of the Organization,

Recalling that the Constitution of the Organization declares that "since wars begin in the minds of men, it is in the minds of men that the defences of peace must be constructed" and that the peace must be founded, if it is not to fail, upon the intellectual and moral solidarity of mankind,

Recalling that the Constitution also states that the wide diffusion of culture and the education of humanity for justice and liberty and peace are indispensable to the dignity of man and constitute a sacred duty which all the nations must fulfil in a spirit of mutual assistance and concern,

Considering that the Organization's Member States, believing in the pursuit of truth and the free exchange of ideas and knowledge, have agreed and determined to develop and to increase the means of communication between their peoples,

Considering that, despite the technical advances which facilitate the development and dissemination of knowledge and ideas, ignorance of the way of life and customs of peoples still presents an obstacle to friendship among the nations, to peaceful co-operation and to the progress of mankind,

Taking account of the Universal Declaration of Human Rights, the Declaration of the Rights of the Child, the Declaration on the Granting of Independence to Colonial Countries and Peoples, the United Nations Declaration on the Elimination of All Forms of Racial Discimination, the Declaration on the Promotion among Youth of the Ideals of Peace, Mutual Respect and Understanding between Peoples, and the Declaration on the Inadmissibility of Intervention in the Domestic Affairs of States and the Protection of their Independence and Sovereignty, proclaimed successively by the General Assembly of the United Nations,

Convinced by the experience of the Organization's first twenty years that, if international cultural co-operation is to be strengthened, its principles require to be affirmed,

Proclaims this Declaration of the principles of international cultural co-operation, to the end that governments, authorities, organizations, associations and institutions responsible for cultural activities may constantly be guided by these principles; and for the purpose, as set out in the Constitution of the Organization, of advancing, through the educational, scientific and cultural relations of the peoples of the world, the objectives of peace and welfare that are defined in the Charter of the United Nations:

Article 1

1.   Each culture has a dignity and value which must be respected and preserved.

2.   Every people has the right and the duty to develop its culture.

3.   In their rich variety and diversity, and in the reciprocal influences they exert on one another, all cultures form part of the common heritage belonging to all mankind.

Article II

Nations shall endeavour to develop the various branches of culture side by side and, as far as possible, simultaneously, so as to establish a harmonious balance between technical progress and the intellectual and moral advancement of mankind.

Article III

International cultural co-operation shall cover all aspects of intellectual and creative activities relating to education, science and culture.

Article IV

The aims of international cultural co-operation in its various forms, bilateral or multilateral, regional or universal, shall be:

1.   To spread knowledge, to stimulate talent and to enrich cultures;

2. To develop peaceful relations and friendship among the peoples and bring about a better understanding of each other's way of life;

3. To contribute to the application of the principles set out in the United Nations Declarations that are recalled in the Preamble to this Declaration;

4. To enable everyone to have access to knowledge, to enjoy the arts and literature of all peoples, to share in advances made in science in all parts of the world and in the resulting benefits, and to contribute to the enrichment of cultural life;

5. To raise the level of the spiritual and material life of man in all parts of the world.

Article V

Cultural co-operation is a right and a duty for all peoples and all nations, which should share with one another their knowledge and skills.

Article VI

International co-operation, while promoting the enrichment of all cultures through its beneficent action, shall respect the distinctive character of each.

Article VII

1. Broad dissemination of ideas and knowledge, based on the freest exchange and discussion, is essential to creative activity, the pursuit of truth and the development of the personality.

2. In cultural co-operation, stress shall be laid on ideas and values conducive to the creation of a climate of friendship and peace. Any mark of hostility in attitudes and in expression of opinion shall be avoided. Every effort shall be made, in presenting and disseminating information, to ensure its authenticity.

Article VIII

Cultural co-operation shall be carried on for the mutual benefit of all the nations practising it. Exchanges to which it gives rise shall be arranged in a spirit of broad reciprocity.

Article IX

Cultural co-operation shall contribute to the establishment of stable, long-term relations between peoples, which should be subjected as little as possible to the strains which may arise in international life.

Article X

Cultural co-operation shall be specially concerned with the moral and intellectual education of young people in a spirit of friendship, international understanding and peace and shall foster awareness among States of the need to stimulate talent and promote the training of the rising generations in the most varied sectors.

Article XI

1.   In their cultural relations, States shall bear in mind the principles of the United Nations. In seeking to achieve international co-operation, they shall respect the sovereign equality of States and shall refrain from intervention in matters which are essentially within the domestic jurisdiction of any State.

2.   The principles of this Declaration shall be applied with due regard for human rights and fundamental freedoms.

77. Recommendation concerning Education for International Understanding, Co-operation and Peace and Education relating to Human Rights and Fundamental Freedoms

Adopted by the General Conference of the UNESCO
at its 18th session on 19 November 1974

The General Conference of the United Nations Educational, Scientific and Cultural Organization, meeting in Paris from 17 October to 23 November 1974, at its eighteenth session,

Mindful of the responsibility incumbent on States to achieve through education the aims set forth in the Charter of the United Nations, the Constitution of Unesco, the Universal Declaration of Human Rights and the Geneva Conventions for the Protection of Victims of War of 12 August 1949, in order to promote international understanding, co-operation and peace and respect for human rights and fundamental freedoms,

Reaffirming the responsibility which is incumbent on Unesco to encourage and support in Member States any activity designed to ensure the education of all for the advancement of justice, freedom, human rights and peace,

Noting nevertheless that the activity of Unesco and of its Member States sometimes has an impact only on a small minority of the steadily growing numbers of schoolchildren, students, young people and adults continuing their education, and educators, and that the curricula and methods of international education are not always attuned to the needs and aspirations of the participating young people and adults,

Noting moreover that in a number of cases there is still a wide disparity between proclaimed ideals, declared intentions and the actual situation,

Having decided, at its seventeenth session, that this education should be the subject of a recommendation to Member States,

Adopts this nineteenth day of November 1974, the present recommendation.

The General Conference recommends that Member States should apply the following provisions by taking whatever legislative or other steps may be required in conformity with the constitutional practice of each State to give effect within their respective territories to the principles set forth in this recommendation.

The General Conference recommends that Member States bring this recommendation to the attention of the authorities, departments or bodies responsible for school education, higher education and out-of-school education, of the various organizations carrying out educational work among young people and adults such as student and youth movements, associations of pupils' parents, teachers' unions and other interested parties.

The General Conference recommends that Member States submit to it, by dates and in the form to be decided upon by the Conference, reports concerning the action taken by them in pursuance of this recommendation.

I. SIGNIFICANCE OF TERMS

1. For the purposes of this recommendation:

(*a*) The word "education" implies the entire process of social life by means of which individuals and social groups learn to develop consciously within, and for the benefit of, the national and international communities, the whole of their personal capacities, attitudes, aptitudes and knowledge. This process is not limited to any specific activities.

(*b*) The terms "international understanding", "co-operation" and "peace" are to be considered as an indivisible whole based on the principle of friendly relations between peoples and States having different social and political systems and on the respect for human rights and fundamental freedoms. In the text of this recommendation, the different connotations of these terms are sometimes gathered together in a concise expression, "international education".

(*c*) "Human rights" and "fundamental freedoms" are those defined in the United Nations Charter, the Universal Declaration of Human Rights and the International Covenants on Economic, Social and Cultural Rights and on Civil and Political Rights.

II. SCOPE

2. This recommendation applies to all stages and forms of education.

III. GUIDING PRINCIPLES

3. Education should be infused with the aims and purposes set forth in the Charter of the United Nations, the Constitution of Unesco and the Universal Declaration of Human Rights, particularly Article 26, paragraph 2, of the last-named, which states: "Education shall be directed to the full development of the human personality and to the strengthening of respect for human rights and fundamental freedoms. It shall promote understanding,

tolerance and friendship among all nations, racial or religious groups, and shall further the activities of the United Nations for the maintenance of peace."

4. In order to enable every person to contribute actively to the fulfilment of the aims referred to in paragraph 3, and promote international solidarity and co-operation, which are necessary in solving the world problems affecting the individuals' and communities' lives and exercise of fundamental rights and freedoms, the following objectives should be regarded as major guiding principles of educational policy:

(*a*) An international dimension and a global perspective in education at all levels and in all its forms;

(*b*) Understanding and respect for all peoples, their cultures, civilizations, values and ways of life, including domestic ethnic cultures and cultures of other nations;

(*c*) Awareness of the increasing global interdependence between peoples and nations;

(*d*) Abilities to communicate with others;

(*e*) Awareness not only of the rights but also of the duties incumbent upon individuals, social groups and nations towards each other;

(*f*) Understanding of the necessity for international solidarity and co-operation;

(*g*) Readiness on the part of the individual to participate in solving the problems of his community, his country and the world at large.

5. Combining learning, training, information and action, international education should further the appropriate intellectual and emotional development of the individual. It should develop a sense of social responsibility and of solidarity with less privileged groups and should lead to observance of the principles of equality in everyday conduct. It should also help to develop qualities, aptitudes and abilities which enable the individual to acquire a critical understanding of problems at the national and the international level; to understanding and explain facts, opinions and ideas; to work in a group; to accept and participate in free discussions; to observe the elementary rules of procedure applicable to any discussion; and to base value-judgements and decisions on a rational analysis of relevant facts and factors.

6. Education should stress the inadmissibility of recourse to war for purposes of expansion, aggression and domination, or to the use of force and violence for purposes of repression, and should bring every person to understand and assume his or her responsibilities for the maintenance of peace. It should contribute to international understanding and strengthening of world peace and to the activities in the struggle against colonialism and neo-colonialism in all their forms and manifestations, and against all forms and varieties of racialism, fascism, and apartheid as well as other ideologies

which breed national and racial hatred and which are contrary to the purposes of this recommendation.

IV. National policy, planning and administration

7. Each Member State should formulate and apply national policies aimed at increasing the efficacy of education in all its forms and strengthening its contribution to international understanding and co-operation, to the maintenance and development of a just peace, to the establishment of social justice, to respect for and application of human rights and fundamental freedoms, and to the eradication of the prejudices, misconceptions, inequalities and all forms of injustice which hinder the achievement of these aims.

8. Member States should in collaboration with the National Commissions take steps to ensure co-operation between ministries and departments and co-ordination of their efforts to plan and carry out concerted programmes of action in international education.

9. Member States should provide, consistent with their constitutional provisions, the financial, administrative, material and moral support necessary to implement this recommendation.

V. Particular aspects of learning, training and action

Ethical and civil aspects

10. Member States should take appropriate steps to strengthen and develop in the processes of learning and training, attitudes and behaviour based on recognition of the equality and necessary interdependence of nations and peoples.

11. Member States should take steps to ensure that the principles of the Universal Declaration of Human Rights and of the International Convention on the Elimination of All Forms of Racial Discrimination become an integral part of the developing personality of each child, adolescent, young person or adult by applying these principles in the daily conduct of education at each level and in all its forms, thus enabling each individual to contribute personally to the regeneration and extension of education in the direction indicated.

12. Member States should urge educators, in collaboration with pupils, parents, the organizations concerned and the community, to use methods which appeal to the creative imagination of children and adolescents and to their social activities and thereby to prepare them to exercise their rights and freedoms while recognizing and respecting the rights of others and to perform their social duties.

13.   Member States should promote, at every stage of education, an active civic training which will enable every person to gain a knowledge of the method of operation and the work of public institutions, whether local, national or international, to become acquainted with the procedures for solving fundamental problems; and to participate in the cultural life of the community and in public affairs. Wherever possible, this participation should increasingly link education and action to solve problems at the local, national and international levels.

14.   Education should include critical analysis of the historical and contemporary factors of an economic and political nature underlying the contradictions and tensions between countries, together with study of ways of overcoming these contradictions, which are the real impediments to understanding, true international co-operation and the development of world peace.

15.   Education should emphasize the true interests of peoples and their incompatibility with the interests of monopolistic groups holding economic and political power, which practise exploitation and foremen war.

16.   Student participation in the organization of studies and of the educational establishment they are attending should itself be considered a factor in civic education and an important element in international education.

Cultural aspects

17.   Member States should promote, at various stages and in various types of education, study of different cultures, their reciprocal influences, their perspectives and ways of life, in order to encourage mutual appreciation of the differences between them. Such study should, among other things, give due importance to the teaching of foreign languages, civilizations and cultural heritage as a means of promoting international and inter-cultural understanding.

Study of the major problems of mankind

18.   Education should be directed both towards the eradication of conditions which perpetuate and aggravate major problems affecting human survival and well-being—inequality, injustice, international relations based on the use of force—and towards measures of international co-operation likely to help solve them. Education which in this respect must necessarily be of an interdisciplinary nature should relate to such problems as:

(*a*) Equality of rights of peoples, and the right of peoples to self-determination;

(*b*) The maintenance of peace; different types of war and their causes and effects; disarmament; the inadmissibility of using science and technology for warlike purposes and their use for the purposes of peace and progress; the nature and effect of economic, cultural and political relations between countries and the importance of international law for these relations, particularly for the maintenance of peace;

(*c*) Action to ensure the exercise and observance of human rights, including those of refugees; racialism and its eradication; the fight against discrimination in its various forms;

(*d*) Economic growth and social development and their relation to social justice; colonialism and decolonization; ways and means of assisting developing countries; the struggle against illiteracy; the campaign against disease and famine; the fight for a better quality of life and the highest attainable standard of health; population growth and related questions;

(*e*) The use, management and conservation of natural resources, pollution of the environment;

(*f*) Preservation of the cultural heritage of mankind;

(*g*) The role and methods of action of the United Nations system in efforts to solve such problems and possibilities for strengthening and furthering its action.

19.   Steps should be taken to develop the study of those sciences and disciplines which are directly related to the exercise of the increasingly varied duties and responsibilities involved in international relations.

Other aspects

20.   Member States should encourage educational authorities and educators to give education planned in accordance with this recommendation an interdisciplinary, problem-oriented content adapted to the complexity of the issues involved in the application of human rights and in international co-operation, and in itself illustrating the ideas of reciprocal influence, mutual support and solidarity. Such programmes should be based on adequate research, experimentation and the identification of specific educational objectives.

21.   Member States should endeavour to ensure that international educational activity is granted special attention and resources when it is carried out in situations involving particularly delicate or explosive social problems in relations, for example, where there are obvious inequalities in opportunities for access to education.

VI. ACTION IN VARIOUS SECTORS OF EDUCATION

22. Increased efforts should be made to develop and infuse an international and inter-cultural dimension at all stages and in all forms of education.

23. Member States should take advantage of the experience of the Associated Schools which carry out, with Unesco's help, programmes of international education. Those concerned with Associated Schools in Member States should strengthen and renew their efforts to extend the programme to other educational institutions and work towards the general application of its results. In other Member States, similar action should be undertaken as soon as possible. The experience of other educational institutions which have carried out successful programmes of international education should also be studied and disseminated.

24. As pre-school education develops, Member States should encourage in it activities which correspond to the purposes of the recommendation because fundamental attitudes, such as, for example, attitudes on race, are often formed in the pre-school years. In this respect, the attitude of parents should be deemed to be an essential factor for the education of children, and the adult education referred to in paragraph 30 should pay special attention to the preparation of parents for their role in pre-school education. The first school should be designed and organized as a social environment having its own character and value, in which various situations, including games, will enable children to become aware of their rights, to assert themselves freely while accepting their responsibilities, and to improve and extend through direct experience their sense of belonging to larger and larger communities—the family, the school, then the local, national and world communities.

25. Member States should urge the authorities concerned, as well as teachers and students, to re-examine periodically how post-secondary and university education should be improved so that it may contribute more fully to the attainment of the objectives of this recommendation.

26. Higher education should comprise civic training and learning activities for all students that will sharpen their knowledge of the major problems which they should help to solve, provide them with possibilities for direct and continuous action aimed at the solution of those problems, and improve their sense of international co-operation.

27. As post-secondary educational establishments, particularly universities, serve growing numbers of people, they should carry out programmes of international education as part of their broadened function in lifelong education and should in all teaching adopt a global approach. Using all means of communication available to them, they should provide oppor-

tunities, facilities for learning and activities adapted to people's real interests, problems and aspirations.

28.   In order to develop the study and practice of international co-operation, post-secondary educational establishments should systematically take advantage of the forms of international action inherent in their role, such as visits from foreign professors and students and professional co-operation between professors and research teams in different countries. In particular, studies and experimental work should be carried out on the linguistic, social, emotional and cultural obstacles, tensions, attitudes and actions which affect both foreign students and host establishments.

29.   Every stage of specialized vocational training should include training to enable students to understand their role and the role of their professions in developing their society, furthering international co-operation, maintaining and developing peace, and to assume their role actively as early as possible.

30.   Whatever the aims and forms of out-of-school education, including adult education, they should be based on the following considerations:

(*a*) As far as possible a global approach should be applied in all out-of-school education programmes, which should comprise the appropriate moral, civic, cultural, scientific and technical elements of international education;

(*b*) All the parties concerned should combine efforts to adapt and use the mass media of communication, self-education, and inter-active learning, and such institutions as museums and public libraries to convey relevant knowledge to the individual, to foster in him or her favourable attitudes and a willingness to take positive action, and to spread knowledge and understanding of the educational campaigns and programmes planned in accordance with the objectives of this recommendation;

(*c*) The parties concerned, whether public or private, should endeavour to take advantage of favourable situations and opportunities, such as the social and cultural activities of youth centres and clubs, cultural centres, community centres or trade unions, youth gatherings and festivals, sporting events, contacts with foreign visitors, students or immigrants and exchanges of persons in general.

31.   Steps should be taken to assist the establishment and development of such organizations as student and teacher associations for the United Nations, international relations clubs and Unesco Clubs, which should be associated with the preparation and implementation of co-ordinated programmes of international education.

32.   Member States should endeavour to ensure that, at each stage of school and out-of-school education, activities directed towards the objectives of this recommendation be co-ordinated and form a coherent whole

within the curricula for the different levels and types of education, learning and training. The principles of co-operation and association which are inherent in this recommendation should be applied in all educational activities.

VII. TEACHER PREPARATION

33.   Member States should constantly improve the ways and means of preparing and certifying teachers and other educational personnel for their role in pursuing the objectives of this recommendation and should, to this end:

(*a*) Provide teachers with motivation for their subsequent work: commitment to the ethics of human rights and to the aim of changing society, so that human rights are applied in practice; a grasp of the fundamental unity of mankind; ability to instil appreciation of the riches which the diversity of cultures can bestow on every individual, group or nation;

(*b*) Provide basic interdisciplinary knowledge of world problems and the problems of international co-operation, through, among other means, work to solve these problems;

(*c*) Prepare teachers themselves to take an active part in devising programmes of international education and educational equipment and materials, taking into account the aspirations of pupils and working in close collaboration with them;

(*d*) Comprise experiments in the use of active methods of education and training in at least elementary techniques of evaluation, particularly those applicable to the social behaviour and attitudes of children, adolescents and adults;

(*e*) Develop aptitudes and skills such as a desire and ability to make educational innovations and to continue his or her training; experience in teamwork and in interdisciplinary studies; knowledge of group dynamics; and the ability to create favourable opportunities and take advantage of them;

(*f*) Include the study of experiments in international education, especially innovative experiments carried out in other countries, and provide those concerned, to the fullest possible extent, with opportunities for making direct contact with foreign teachers.

34.   Member States should provide those concerned with direction, supervision or guidance—for instance, inspectors, educational advisers, principals of teacher-training colleges and organizers of educational activities for young people and adults—with training, information and advice enabling them to help teachers work towards the objectives of this recommendation, taking into account the aspirations of young people with regard to international problems and new educational methods that are likely to improve prospects for fulfilling these aspirations. For these purposes, seminars

or refresher courses relating to international and inter-cultural education should be organized to bring together authorities and teachers; other seminars or courses might permit supervisory personnel and teachers to meet with other groups concerned such as parents, students, and teachers' associations. Since there must be a gradual but profound change in the role of education, the results of experiments for the remodelling of structures and hierarchical relations in educational establishments should be reflected in training, information and advice.

35.   Member States should endeavour to ensure that any programme of further training for teachers in service or for personnel responsible for direction includes components of international education and opportunities to compare the results of their experiences in international education.

36.   Member States should encourage and facilitate educational study and refresher courses abroad, particularly by awarding fellowships, and should encourage recognition of such courses as part of the regular process of initial training, appointment, refresher training and promotion of teachers.

37.   Member States should organize or assist bilateral exchanges of teachers at all levels of education.

VIII. EDUCATIONAL EQUIPMENT AND MATERIALS

38.   Member States should increase their efforts to facilitate the renewal, production, dissemination and exchange of equipment and materials for international education, giving special consideration to the fact that in many countries pupils and students receive most of their knowledge about international affairs through the mass media outside the school. To meet the needs expressed by those concerned with international education, efforts should be concentrated on overcoming the lack of teaching aids and on improving their quality. Action should be on the following lines:

(*a*) Appropriate and constructive use should be made of the entire range of equipment and aids available, from textbooks to television, and of the new educational technology;

(*b*) There should be a component of special mass media education in teaching to help the pupils to select and analyse the information conveyed by mass media;

(*c*) A global approach, comprising the introduction of international components, serving as a framework for presenting local and national aspects of different subjects and illustrating the scientific and cultural history of mankind, should be employed in textbooks and all other aids to learning, with due regard to the value of the visual arts and music as factors conducive to understanding between different cultures;

(*d*) Written and audio-visual materials of an interdisciplinary nature illustrating the major problems confronting mankind and showing in each case the need for international co-operation and its practical form should be prepared in the language or languages of instruction of the country with the aid of information supplied by the United Nations, Unesco and other Specialized Agencies;

(*e*) Documents and other materials illustrating the culture and the way of life of each country, the chief problems with which it is faced, and its participation in activities of world-wide concern should be prepared and communicated to other countries.

39.   Member States should promote appropriate measures to ensure that educational aids, especially textbooks, are free from elements liable to give rise to misunderstanding, mistrust, racialist reactions, contempt or hatred with regard to other groups or peoples. Materials should provide a broad background of knowledge which will help learners to evaluate information and ideas disseminated through the mass media that seem to run counter to the aims of this recommendation.

40.   According to its needs and possibilities, each Member State should establish or help to establish one or more documentation centres offering written and audio-visual material devised according to the objectives of this recommendation and adapted to the different forms and stages of education. These centres should be designed to foster the reform of international education, especially by developing and disseminating innovative ideas and materials, and should also organize and facilitate exchanges of information with other countries.

IX. RESEARCH AND EXPERIMENTATION

41.   Member States should stimulate and support research on the foundations, guiding principles, means of implementation and effects of international education and on innovations and experimental activities in this field, such as those taking place in the Associated Schools. This action calls for collaboration by universities, research bodies and centres, teacher-training institutions, adult education training centres and appropriate non-governmental organizations.

42.   Member States should take appropriate steps to ensure that teachers and the various authorities concerned build international education on a sound psychological and sociological basis by applying the results of research carried out in each country on the formation and development of favourable or unfavourable attitudes and behaviour, on attitude change, on the interaction of personality development and education and on the positive or negative effects of educational activity. A substantial part of this research

should be devoted to the aspirations of young people concerning international problems and relations.

X. INTERNATIONAL CO-OPERATION

43.   Member States should consider international co-operation a responsibility in developing international education. In the implementation of this recommendation they should refrain from intervening in matters which are essentially within the domestic jurisdiction of any State in accordance with the United Nations Charter. By their own actions, they should demonstrate that implementing this recommendation is itself an exercise in international understanding and co-operation. They should, for example, organize, or help the appropriate authorities and non-governmental organizations to organize, an increasing number of international meetings and study sessions on international education; strengthen their programmes for the reception of foreign students, research workers, teachers and educators belonging to workers' associations and adult education associations; promote reciprocal visits by schoolchildren, and student and teacher exchanges; extend and intensify exchanges of information on cultures and ways of life; arrange for the translation or adaptation and dissemination of information and suggestions coming from other countries.

44.   Member States should encourage the co-operation between their Associated Schools and those of other countries with the help of Unesco in order to promote mutual benefits by expanding their experiences in a wider international perspective.

45.   Member States should encourage wider exchanges of textbooks, especially history and geography textbooks, and should, where appropriate, take measures, by concluding if possible, bilateral and multilateral agreements, for the reciprocal study and revision of textbooks and other educational materials in order to ensure that they are accurate, balanced, up to date and unprejudiced and will enhance mutual knowledge and understanding between different peoples.

O. NATIONALITY, STATELESSNESS, ASYLUM AND REFUGEES

78. Convention on the Nationality of Married Women

Opened for signature and ratification by General Assembly resolution 1040 (XI) of 29 January 1957

ENTRY INTO FORCE: 11 August 1958, in accordance with article 6

The Contracting States,

Recognizing that, conflicts in law in practice with reference to nationality arise as a result of provisions concerning the loss or acquisition of nationality by women as a result of marriage, of its dissolution or of the change of nationality by the husband during marriage,

Recognizing that, in article 15 of the Universal Declaration of Human Rights, the General Assembly of the United Nations has proclaimed that "everyone has the right to a nationality" and that "no one shall be arbitrarily deprived of his nationality nor denied the right to change his nationality",

Desiring to co-operate with the United Nations in promoting universal respect for, and observance of, human rights and fundamental freedoms for all without distinction as to sex,

Hereby agree as hereinafter provided:

Article 1

Each Contracting State agrees that neither the celebration nor the dissolution of a marriage between one of its nationals and an alien, nor the change of nationality by the husband during marriage, shall automatically affect the nationality of the wife.

Article 2

Each Contracting State agrees that neither the voluntary acquisition of the nationality of another State nor the renunciation of its nationality by one of its nationals shall prevent the retention of its nationality by the wife of such national.

Article 3

1.   Each Contracting State agrees that the alien wife of one of its nationals may, at her request, acquire the nationality of her husband through specially privileged naturalization procedures; the grant of such nationality may be subject to such limitations as may be imposed in the interests of national security or public policy.

2.   Each Contracting State agrees that the present Convention shall not be construed as affecting any legislation or judicial practice by which the alien wife of one of its nationals may, at her request, acquire her husband's nationality as a matter of right.

Article 4

1.   The present Convention shall be open for signature and ratification on behalf of any State Member of the United Nations and also on behalf of any other State which is or hereafter becomes a member of any specialized agency of the United Nations, or which is or hereafter becomes a Party to the Statute of the International Court of Justice, or any other State to which an invitation has been addressed by the General Assembly of the United Nations.

2.   The present Convention shall be ratified and the instruments of ratification shall be deposited with the Secretary-General of the United Nations.

Article 5

1.   The present Convention shall be open for accession to all States referred to in paragraph 1 of article 4.

2.   Accession shall be effected by the deposit of an instrument of accession with the Secretary-General of the United Nations.

Article 6

1.   The present Convention shall come into force on the ninetieth day following the date of deposit of the sixth instrument of ratification or accession.

2. For each State ratifying or acceding to the Convention after the deposit of the sixth instrument of ratification or accession, the Convention shall enter into force on the ninetieth day after deposit by such State of its instrument of ratification or accession.

Article 7

1. The present Convention shall apply to all non-self-governing, trust, colonial and other non-metropolitan territories for the international relations of which any Contracting State is responsible; the Contracting State concerned shall, subject to the provisions of paragraph 2 of the present article, at the time of signature, ratification or accession declare the non-metropolitan territory or territories to which the Convention shall apply *ipso facto* as a result of such signature, ratification or accession.

2. In any case in which, for the purpose of nationality, a non-metropolitan territory is not treated as one with the metropolitan territory, or in any case in which the previous consent of a non-metropolitan territory is required by the constitutional laws or practices of the Contracting State or of the non-metropolitan territory for the application of the Convention to that territory, that Contracting State shall endeavour to secure the needed consent of the non-metropolitan territory within the period of twelve months from the date of signature of the Convention by that Contracting State, and when such consent has been obtained the Contracting State shall notify the Secretary-General of the United Nations. The present Convention shall apply to the territory or territories named in such notification from the date of its receipt by the Secretary-General.

3. After the expiry of the twelve-month period mentioned in paragraph 2 of the present article, the Contracting States concerned shall inform the Secretary-General of the results of the consultations with those non-metropolitan territories for whose international relations they are responsible and whose consent to the application of the present Convention may have been withheld.

Article 8

1. At the time of signature, ratification or accession, any State may make reservations to any article of the present Convention other than articles 1 and 2.

2. If any State makes a reservation in accordance with paragraph 1 of the present article, the Convention, with the exception of those provisions to which the reservation relates, shall have effect as between the reserving State and the other Parties. The Secretary-General of the United Nations shall

communicate the text of the reservation to all States which are or may become Parties to the Convention. Any State Party to the Convention or which thereafter becomes a Party may notify the Secretary-General that it does not agree to consider itself bound by the Convention with respect to the State making the reservation. This notification must be made, in the case of a State already a Party, within ninety days from the date of the communication by the Secretary-General; and, in the case of a State subsequently becoming a Party, within ninety days from the date when the instrument of ratification or accession is deposited. In the event that such a notification is made, the Convention shall not be deemed to be in effect as between the State making the notification and the State making the reservation.

3.   Any State making a reservation in accordance with paragraph 1 of the present article may at any time withdraw the reservation, in whole or in part, after it has been accepted, by a notification to this effect addressed to the Secretary-General of the United Nations. Such notification shall take effect on the date on which it is received.

Article 9

1.   Any Contracting State may denounce the present Convention by written notification to the Secretary-General of the United Nations. Denunciation shall take effect one year after the date of receipt of the notification by the Secretary-General.

2.   The present Convention shall cease to be in force as from the date when the denunciation which reduces the number of Parties to less than six becomes effective.

Article 10

Any dispute which may arise between any two or more Contracting States concerning the interpretation or application of the present Convention which is not settled by negotiation, shall, at the request of any one of the parties to the dispute, be referred to the International Court of Justice for decision, unless the parties agree to another mode of settlement.

Article 11

The Secretary-General of the United Nations shall notify all States Members of the United Nations and the non-member States contemplated in paragraph 1 of article 4 of the present Convention of the following:

(a) Signatures and instruments of ratification received in accordance with article 4;

(*b*) Instruments of accession received in accordance with article 5;

(*c*) The date upon which the present Convention enters into force in accordance with article 6;

(*d*) Communications and notifications received in accordance with article 8;

(*e*) Notifications of denunciation received in accordance with paragraph 1 of article 9;

(*f*) Abrogation in accordance with paragraph 2 of article 9.

Article 12

1. The present Convention, of which the Chinese, English, French, Russian and Spanish texts shall be equally authentic, shall be deposited in the archives of the United Nations.

2. The Secretary-General of the United Nations shall transmit a certified copy of the Convention to all States Members of the United Nations and to the non-member States contemplated in paragraph 1 of article 4.

79. Convention on the Reduction of Statelessness

*Adopted on 30 August 1961 by a Conference of Plenipotentiaries which met in 1959
and reconvened in 1961 in pursuance of General Assembly resolution 896 (IX)
of 4 December 1954*

ENTRY INTO FORCE: 13 December 1975, in accordance with article 18

The Contracting States,

Acting in pursuance of resolution 896 (IX), adopted by the General Assembly of the United Nations on 4 December 1954,

Considering it desirable to reduce statelessness by international agreement,

Have agreed as follows:

Article 1

1.   A Contracting State shall grant its nationality to a person born in its territory who would otherwise be stateless. Such nationality shall be granted:

(*a*) At birth, by operation of law, or

(*b*) Upon an application being lodged with the appropriate authority, by or on behalf of the person concerned, in the manner prescribed by the national law. Subject to the provisions of paragraph 2 of this article, no such application may be rejected.

A Contracting State which provides for the grant of its nationality in accordance with subparagraph (*b*) of this paragraph may also provide for the grant of its nationality by operation of law at such age and subject to such conditions as may be prescribed by the national law.

2.   A Contracting State may make the grant of its nationality in accordance with subparagraph (*b*) of paragraph 1 of this article subject to one or more of the following conditions:

(*a*) That the application is lodged during a period, fixed by the Contracting State, beginning not later than at the age of eighteen years and ending not earlier than at the age of twenty-one years, so, however, that the person concerned shall be allowed at least one year during which he may himself make the application without having to obtain legal authorization to do so;

(*b*) That the person concerned has habitually resided in the territory of the Contracting State for such period as may be fixed by that State, not exceeding five years immediately preceding the lodging of the application nor ten years in all;

(*c*) That the person concerned has neither been convicted of an offence against national security nor has been sentenced to imprisonment for a term of five years or more on a criminal charge;

(*d*) That the person concerned has always been stateless.

3. Notwithstanding the provisions of paragraphs 1 (*b*) and 2 of this article, a child born in wedlock in the territory of a Contracting State, whose mother has the nationality of that State, shall acquire at birth that nationality if it otherwise would be stateless.

4. A Contracting State shall grant its nationality to a person who would otherwise be stateless and who is unable to acquire the nationality of the Contracting State in whose territory he was born because he has passed the age for lodging his application or has not fulfilled the required residence conditions, if the nationality of one of his parents at the time of the person's birth was that of the Contracting State first above-mentioned. If his parents did not possess the same nationality at the time of his birth, the question whether the nationality of the person concerned should follow that of the father or that of the mother shall be determined by the national law of such Contracting State. If application for such nationality is required, the application shall be made to the appropriate authority by or on behalf of the applicant in the manner prescribed by the national law. Subject to the provisions of paragraph 5 of this article, such application shall not be refused.

5. The Contracting State may make the grant of its nationality in accordance with the provisions of paragraph 4 of this article subject to one or more of the following conditions:

(*a*) That the application is lodged before the applicant reaches an age, being not less than twenty-three years, fixed by the Contracting State;

(*b*) That the person concerned has habitually resided in the territory of the Contracting State for such period immediately preceding the lodging of the application, not exceeding three years, as may be fixed by that State;

(*c*) That the person concerned has always been stateless.

Article 2

A foundling found in the territory of a Contracting State shall, in the absence of proof to the contrary, be considered to have been born within that territory of parents possessing the nationality of that State.

Article 3

For the purpose of determining the obligations of Contracting States under this Convention, birth on a ship or in an aircraft shall be deemed to have taken place in the territory of the State whose flag the ship flies or in the territory of the State in which the aircraft is registered, as the case may be.

Article 4

1. A Contracting State shall grant its nationality to a person, not born in the territory of a Contracting State, who would otherwise be stateless, if the nationality of one of his parents at the time of the person's birth was that of that State. If his parents did not possess the same nationality at the time of his birth, the question whether the nationality of the person concerned should follow that of the father or that of the mother shall be determined by the national law of such Contracting State. Nationality granted in accordance with the provisions of this paragraph shall be granted:

(*a*) At birth, by operation of law, or

(*b*) Upon an application being lodged with the appropriate authority, by or on behalf of the person concerned, in the manner prescribed by the national law. Subject to the provisions of paragraph 2 of this article, no such application may be rejected.

2. A Contracting State may make the grant of its nationality in accordance with the provisions of paragraph 1 of this article subject to one or more of the following conditions:

(*a*) That the application is lodged before the applicant reaches an age, being not less than twenty-three years, fixed by the Contracting State;

(*b*) That the person concerned has habitually resided in the territory of the Contracting State for such period immediately preceding the lodging of the application, not exceeding three years, as may be fixed by that State;

(*c*) That the person concerned has not been convicted of an offence against national security;

(*d*) That the person concerned has always been stateless.

Article 5

1. If the law of a Contracting State entails loss of nationality as a consequence of any change in the personal status of a person such as marriage, termination of marriage, legitimation, recognition or adoption, such loss shall be conditional upon possession or acquisition of another nationality.

2. If, under the law of a Contracting State, a child born out of wedlock loses the nationality of that State in consequence of a recognition of affiliation, he shall be given an opportunity to recover that nationality by written application to the appropriate authority, and the conditions governing such application shall not be more rigorous than those laid down in paragraph 2 of article 1 of this Convention.

Article 6

If the law of a Contracting State provides for loss of its nationality by a person's spouse or children as a consequence of that person losing or being deprived of that nationality, such loss shall be conditional upon their possession or acquisition of another nationality.

Article 7

1. (*a*) If the law of a Contracting State entails loss or renunciation of nationality, such renunciation shall not result in loss of nationality unless the person concerned possesses or acquires another nationality;

(*b*) The provisions of subparagraph (*a*) of this paragraph shall not apply where their application would be inconsistent with the principles stated in articles 13 and 14 of the Universal Declaration of Human Rights approved on 10 December 1948 by the General Assembly of the United Nations.

2. A national of a Contracting State who seeks naturalization in a foreign country shall not lose his nationality unless he acquires or has been accorded assurance of acquiring the nationality of that foreign country.

3. Subject to the provisions of paragraphs 4 and 5 of this article, a national of a Contracting State shall not lose his nationality, so as to become stateless, on the ground of departure, residence abroad, failure to register or on any similar ground.

4. A naturalized person may lose his nationality on account of residence abroad for a period, not less than seven consecutive years, specified by the law of the Contracting State concerned if he fails to declare to the appropriate authority his intention to retain his nationality.

5. In the case of a national of a Contracting State, born outside its territory, the law of that State may make the retention of its nationality after

the expiry of one year from his attaining his majority conditional upon residence at that time in the territory of the State or registration with the appropriate authority.

6. Except in the circumstances mentioned in this article, a person shall not lose the nationality of a Contracting State, if such loss would render him stateless, notwithstanding that such loss is not expressly prohibited by any other provision of this Convention.

Article 8

1. A Contracting State shall not deprive a person of his nationality if such deprivation would render him stateless.

2. Notwithstanding the provisions of paragraph 1 of this article, a person may be deprived of the nationality of a Contracting State:

(a) In the circumstances in which, under paragraphs 4 and 5 of article 7, it is permissible that a person should lose his nationality;

(b) Where the nationality has been obtained by misrepresentation or fraud.

3. Notwithstanding the provisions of paragraph 1 of this article, a Contracting State may retain the right to deprive a person of his nationality, if at the time of signature, ratification or accession it specifies its retention of such right on one or more of the following grounds, being grounds existing in its national law at that time:

(a) That, inconsistently with his duty of loyalty to the Contracting State, the person:

    (i) Has, in disregard of an express prohibition by the Contracting State rendered or continued to render services to, or received or continued to receive emoluments from, another State, or

    (ii) Has conducted himself in a manner seriously prejudicial to the vital interests of the State;

(b) That the person has taken an oath, or made a formal declaration, of allegiance to another State, or given definite evidence of his determination to repudiate his allegiance to the Contracting State.

4. A Contracting State shall not exercise a power of deprivation permitted by paragraphs 2 or 3 of this article except in accordance with law, which shall provide for the person concerned the right to a fair hearing by a court or other independent body.

Article 9

A Contracting State may not deprive any person or group of persons of their nationality on racial, ethnic, religious or political grounds.

Article 10

1. Every treaty between Contracting States providing for the transfer of territory shall include provisions designed to secure that no person shall become stateless as a result of the transfer. A Contracting State shall use its best endeavours to secure that any such treaty made by it with a State which is not a Party to this Convention includes such provisions.

2. In the absence of such provisions a Contracting State to which territory is transferred or which otherwise acquires territory shall confer its nationality on such persons as would otherwise become stateless as a result of the transfer or acquisition.

Article 11

The Contracting States shall promote the establishment within the framework of the United Nations, as soon as may be after the deposit of the sixth instrument of ratification or accession, of a body to which a person claiming the benefit of this Convention may apply for the examination of his claim and for assistance in presenting it to the appropriate authority.

Article 12

1. In relation to a Contracting State which does not, in accordance with the provisions of paragraph 1 of article 1 or of article 4 of this Convention, grant its nationality at birth by operation of law, the provisions of paragraph 1 of article 1 or of article 4, as the case may be, shall apply to persons born before as well as to persons born after the entry into force of this Convention.

2. The provisions of paragraph 4 of article 1 of this Convention shall apply to persons born before as well as to persons born after its entry into force.

3. The provisions of article 2 of this Convention shall apply only to foundlings found in the territory of a Contracting State after the entry into force of the Convention for that State.

Article 13

This Convention shall not be construed as affecting any provisions more conducive to the reduction of statelessness which may be contained in the law of any Contracting State now or hereafter in force, or may be contained in any other convention, treaty or agreement now or hereafter in force between two or more Contracting States.

Article 14

Any dispute between Contracting States concerning the interpretation or application of this Convention which cannot be settled by other means shall be submitted to the International Court of Justice at the request of any one of the parties to the dispute.

Article 15

1.   This Convention shall apply to all non-self-governing, trust, colonial and other non-metropolitan territories for the international relations of which any Contracting State is responsible; the Contracting State concerned shall, subject to the provisions of paragraph 2 of this article, at the time of signature, ratification or accession, declare the non-metropolitan territory or territories to which the Convention shall apply *ipso facto* as a result of such signature, ratification or accession.

2.   In any case in which, for the purpose of nationality, a non-metropolitan territory is not treated as one with the metropolitan territory, or in any case in which the previous consent of a non-metropolitan territory is required by the constitutional laws or practices of the Contracting State or of the non-metropolitan territory for the application of the Convention to that territory, that Contracting State shall endeavour to secure the needed consent of the non-metropolitan territory within the period of twelve months from the date of signature of the Convention by that Contracting State, and when such consent has been obtained the Contracting State shall notify the Secretary-General of the United Nations. This Convention shall apply to the territory or territories named in such notification from the date of its receipt by the Secretary-General.

3.   After the expiry of the twelve-month period mentioned in paragraph 2 of this article, the Contracting States concerned shall inform the Secretary-General of the results of the consultations with those non-metropolitan territories for whose international relations they are responsible and whose consent to the application of this Convention may have been withheld.

Article 16

1.   This Convention shall be open for signature at the Headquarters of the United Nations from 30 August 1961 to 31 May 1962.

2. This Convention shall be open for signature on behalf of:

(*a*) Any State Member of the United Nations;

(*b*) Any other State invited to attend the United Nations Conference on the Elimination or Reduction of Future Statelessness;

(*c*) Any State to which an invitation to sign or to accede may be addressed by the General Assembly of the United Nations.

3. This Convention shall be ratified and the instruments of ratification shall be deposited with the Secretary-General of the United Nations.

4. This Convention shall be open for accession by the States referred to in paragraph 2 of this article. Accession shall be effected by the deposit of an instrument of accession with the Secretary-General of the United Nations.

Article 17

1. At the time of signature, ratification or accession any State may make a reservation in respect of articles 11, 14 or 15.

2. No other reservations to this Convention shall be admissible.

Article 18

1. This Convention shall enter into force two years after the date of the deposit of the sixth instrument of ratification or accession.

2. For each State ratifying or acceding to this Convention after the deposit of the sixth instrument of ratification or accession, it shall enter into force on the ninetieth day after the deposit by such State of its instrument of ratification or accession or on the date on which this Convention enters into force in accordance with the provisions of paragraph 1 of this article, whichever is the later.

Article 19

1. Any Contracting State may denounce this Convention at any time by a written notification addressed to the Secretary-General of the United Nations. Such denunciation shall take effect for the Contracting State concerned one year after the date of its receipt by the Secretary-General.

2. In cases where, in accordance with the provisions of article 15, this Convention has become applicable to a non-metropolitan territory of a Contracting State, that State may at any time thereafter, with the consent of the territory concerned, give notice to the Secretary-General of the United

Nations denouncing this Convention separately in respect to that territory. The denunciation shall take effect one year after the date of the receipt of such notice by the Secretary-General, who shall notify all other Contracting States of such notice and the date of receipt thereof.

Article 20

1. The Secretary-General of the United Nations shall notify all Members of the United Nations and the non-member States referred to in article 16 of the following particulars:

(*a*) Signatures, ratifications and accessions under article 16;

(*b*) Reservations under article 17;

(*c*) The date upon which this Convention enters into force in pursuance of article 18;

(*d*) Denunciations under article 19.

2. The Secretary-General of the United Nations shall, after the deposit of the sixth instrument of ratification or accession at the latest, bring to the attention of the General Assembly the question of the establishment, in accordance with article 11, of such a body as therein mentioned.

Article 21

This Convention shall be registered by the Secretary-General of the United Nations on the date of its entry into force.

IN WITNESS WHEREOF the undersigned Plenipotentiaries have signed this Convention.

DONE at New York, this thirtieth day of August, one thousand nine hundred and sixty-one, in a single copy, of which the Chinese, English, French, Russian and Spanish texts are equally authentic and which shall be deposited in the archives of the United Nations, and certified copies of which shall be delivered by the Secretary-General of the United Nations to all members of the United Nations and to the non-member States referred to in article 16 of this Convention.

80. Convention relating to the Status of Stateless Persons

Adopted on 28 September 1954 by a Conference of Plenipotentiaries convened by Economic and Social Council resolution 526 A (XVII) of 26 April 1954

ENTRY INTO FORCE: 6 June 1960, in accordance with article 39

PREAMBLE

The High Contracting Parties,

Considering that the Charter of the United Nations and the Universal Declaration of Human Rights approved on 10 December 1948 by the General Assembly of the United Nations have affirmed the principle that human beings shall enjoy fundamental rights and freedoms without discrimination,

Considering that the United Nations has, on various occasions, manifested its profound concern for stateless persons and endeavoured to assure stateless persons the widest possible exercise of these fundamental rights and freedoms,

Considering that only those stateless persons who are also refugees are covered by the Convention relating to the Status of Refugees of 28 July 1951, and that there are many stateless persons who are not covered by that Convention,

Considering that it is desirable to regulate and improve the status of stateless persons by an international agreement,

Have agreed as follows:

CHAPTER I

GENERAL PROVISIONS

Article 1. — Definition of the term "stateless person"

1. For the purpose of this Convention, the term "stateless person" means a person who is not considered as a national by any State under the operation of its law.

2. This Convention shall not apply:

(i) To persons who are at present receiving from organs or agencies of the United Nations other than the United Nations High Commissioner for Refugees protection or assistance so long as they are receiving such protection or assistance;

(ii) To persons who are recognized by the competent authorities of the country in which they have taken residence as having the rights and obligations which are attached to the possession of the nationality of that country;

(iii) To persons with respect to whom there are serious reasons for considering that:

(a) They have committed a crime against peace, a war crime, or a crime against humanity, as defined in the international instruments drawn up to make provisions in respect of such crimes;

(b) They have committed a serious non-political crime outside the country of their residence prior to their admission to that country;

(c) They have been guilty of acts contrary to the purposes and principles of the United Nations.

Article 2. — General obligations

Every stateless person has duties to the country in which he finds himself, which require in particular that he conform to its laws and regulations as well as to measures taken for the maintenance of public order.

Article 3. — Non-discrimination

The Contracting States shall apply the provisions of this Convention to stateless persons without discrimination as to race, religion or country of origin.

Article 4. — Religion

The Contracting States shall accord to stateless persons within their territories treatment at least as favourable as that accorded to their nationals with respect to freedom to practise their religion and freedom as regards the religious education of their children.

Article 5. — Rights granted apart from this Convention

Nothing in this Convention shall be deemed to impair any rights and benefits granted by a Contracting State to stateless persons apart from this Convention.

Article 6. — The term "in the same circumstances"

For the purpose of this Convention, the term "in the same circumstances" implies that any requirements (including requirements as to length and conditions of sojourn or residence) which the particular individual would have to fulfil for the enjoyment of the right in question, if he were not a stateless person, must be fulfilled by him, with the exception of requirements which by their nature a stateless person is incapable of fulfilling.

Article 7. — Exemption from reciprocity

1. Except where this Convention contains more favourable provisions, a Contracting State shall accord to stateless persons the same treatment as is accorded to aliens generally.

2. After a period of three years' residence, all stateless persons shall enjoy exemption from legislative reciprocity in the territory of the Contracting States.

3. Each Contracting State shall continue to accord to stateless persons the rights and benefits to which they were already entitled, in the absence of reciprocity, at the date of entry into force of this Convention for that State.

4. The Contracting States shall consider favourably the possibility of according to stateless persons, in the absence of reciprocity, rights and benefits beyond those to which they are entitled according to paragraphs 2 and 3, and to extending exemption from reciprocity to stateless persons who do not fulfil the conditions provided for in paragraphs 2 and 3.

5. The provisions of paragraphs 2 and 3 apply both to the rights and benefits referred to in articles 13, 18, 19, 21 and 22 of this Convention and to rights and benefits for which this Convention does not provide.

Article 8. — Exemption from exceptional measures

With regard to exceptional measures which may be taken against the person, property or interests of nationals or former nationals of a foreign State, the Contracting States shall not apply such measures to a stateless person solely on account of his having previously possessed the nationality of the foreign State in question. Contracting States which, under their legislation, are prevented from applying the general principle expressed in this article shall, in appropriate cases, grant exemptions in favour of such stateless persons.

Article 9. — Provisional measures

Nothing in this Convention shall prevent a Contracting State, in time of war or other grave and exceptional circumstances, from taking provisionally measures which it considers to be essential to the national security in the case of a particular person, pending a determination by the Contracting State that that person is in fact a stateless person and that the continuance of such measures is necessary in his case in the interests of national security.

Article 10. — Continuity of residence

1. Where a stateless person has been forcibly displaced during the Second World War and removed to the territory of a Contracting State, and is resident there, the period of such enforced sojourn shall be considered to have been lawful residence within that territory.

2. Where a stateless person has been forcibly displaced during the Second World War from the territory of a Contracting State and has, prior to the date of entry into force of this Convention, returned there for the purpose of taking up residence, the period of residence before and after such enforced displacement shall be regarded as one uninterrupted period for any purposes for which uninterrupted residence is required.

Article 11. — Stateless seamen

In the case of stateless persons regularly serving as crew members on board a ship flying the flag of a Contracting State, that State shall give sympathetic consideration to their establishment on its territory and the issue of travel documents to them or their temporary admission to its territory particularly with a view to facilitating their establishment in another country.

CHAPTER II

JURIDICAL STATUS

Article 12. — Personal status

1. The personal status of a stateless person shall be governed by the law of the country of his domicile or, if he has no domicile, by the law of the country of his residence.

2. Rights previously acquired by a stateless person and dependent on personal status, more particularly rights attaching to marriage, shall be

respected by a Contracting State, subject to compliance, if this be necessary, with the formalities required by the law of that State, provided that the right in question is one which would have been recognized by the law of that State had he not become stateless.

Article 13. — *Movable and immovable property*

The Contracting States shall accord to a stateless person treatment as favourable as possible and, in any event, not less favourable than that accorded to aliens generally in the same circumstances, as regards the acquisition of movable and immovable property and other rights pertaining thereto, and to leases and other contracts relating to movable and immovable property.

Article 14. — *Artistic rights and industrial property*

In respect of the protection of industrial property, such as inventions, designs or models, trade marks, trade names, and of rights in literary, artistic and scientific works, a stateless person shall be accorded in the country in which he has his habitual residence the same protection as is accorded to nationals of that country. In the territory of any other Contracting State, he shall be accorded the same protection as is accorded in that territory to nationals of the country in which he has his habitual residence.

Article 15. — *Right of association*

As regards non-political and non-profit-making associations and trade unions the Contracting States shall accord to stateless persons lawfully staying in their territory treatment as favourable as possible, and in any event, not less favourable than that accorded to aliens generally in the same circumstances.

Article 16. — *Access to courts*

1. A stateless person shall have free access to the courts of law on the territory of all Contracting States.

2. A stateless person shall enjoy in the Contracting State in which he has his habitual residence the same treatment as a national in matters pertaining to access to the courts, including legal assistance and exemption from *cautio judicatum solvi.*

3. A stateless person shall be accorded in the matters referred to in paragraph 2 in countries other than that in which he has his habitual residence the treatment granted to a national of the country of his habitual residence.

CHAPTER III

GAINFUL EMPLOYMENT

Article 17. — Wage-earning employment

1. The Contracting States shall accord to stateless persons lawfully staying in their territory treatment as favourable as possible and, in any event, not less favourable that that accorded to aliens generally in the same circumstances, as regards the right to engage in wage-earning employment.

2. The Contracting States shall give sympathetic consideration to assimilating the rights of all stateless persons with regard to wage-earning employment to those of nationals, and in particular of those stateless persons who have entered their territory pursuant to programmes of labour recruitment or under immigration schemes.

Article 18. — Self-employment

The Contracting States shall accord to a stateless person lawfully in their territory treatment as favourable as possible and, in any event, not less favourable than that accorded to aliens generally in the same circumstances, as regards the right to engage on his own account in agriculture, industry, handicrafts and commerce and to establish commercial and industrial companies.

Article 19. — Liberal professions

Each Contracting State shall accord to stateless persons lawfully staying in their territory who hold diplomas recognized by the competent authorities of that State, and who are desirous of practising a liberal profession, treatment as favourable as possible and, in any event, not less favourable than that accorded to aliens generally in the same circumstances.

CHAPTER IV

WELFARE

Article 20. — Rationing

Where a rationing system exists, which applies to the population at large and regulates the general distribution of products in short supply, stateless persons shall be accorded the same treatment as nationals.

Article 21. — Housing

As regards housing, the Contracting States, in so far as the matter is regulated by laws or regulations or is subject to the control of public authorities, shall accord to stateless persons lawfully staying in their territory treatment as favourable as possible and, in any event, not less favourable than that accorded to aliens generally in the same circumstances.

Article 22. — Public education

1. The Contracting States shall accord to stateless persons the same treatment as is accorded to nationals with respect to elementary education.

2. The Contracting States shall accord to stateless persons treatment as favourable as possible and, in any event, not less favourable than that accorded to aliens generally in the same circumstances, with respect to education other than elementary education and, in particular, as regards access to studies, the recognition of foreign school certificates, diplomas and degrees, the remission of fees and charges and the award of scholarships.

Article 23. — Public relief

The Contracting States shall accord to stateless persons lawfully staying in their territory the same treatment with respect to public relief and assistance as is accorded to their nationals.

Article 24. — Labour legislation and social security

1. The Contracting States shall accord to stateless persons lawfully staying in their territory the same treatment as is accorded to nationals in respect of the following matters:

(a) In so far as such matters are governed by laws or regulations or are subject to the control of administrative authorities; remuneration, including family allowances where these form part of remuneration, hours of work, overtime arrangements, holidays with pay, restrictions on home work, minimum age of employment, apprenticeship and training, women's work and the work of young persons, and the enjoyment of the benefits of collective bargaining;

(b) Social security (legal provisions in respect of employment injury, occupational diseases, maternity, sickness, disability, old age, death, unemployment, family responsibilities and any other contingency which, according to national laws or regulations, is covered by a social security scheme), subject to the following limitations:

(i) There may be appropriate arrangements for the maintenance of acquired rights and rights in course of acquisition;

(ii) National laws or regulations of the country of residence may prescribe special arrangements concerning benefits or portions of benefits which are payable wholly out of public funds, and concerning allowances paid to persons who do not fulfil the contribution conditions prescribed for the award of a normal pension.

2. The right to compensation for the death of a stateless person resulting from employment injury or from occupational disease shall not be affected by the fact that the residence of the beneficiary is outside the territory of the Contracting State.

3. The Contracting States shall extend to stateless persons the benefits of agreements concluded between them, or which may be concluded between them in the future, concerning the maintenance of acquired rights and rights in the process of acquisition in regard to social security, subject only to the conditions which apply to nationals of the States signatory to the agreements in question.

4. The Contracting States will give sympathetic consideration to extending to stateless persons so far as possible the benefits of similar agreements which may at any time be in force between such Contracting States and non-contracting States.

CHAPTER V

ADMINISTRATIVE MEASURES

Article 25. — Administrative assistance

1. When the exercise of a right by a stateless person would normally require the assistance of authorities of a foreign country to whom he cannot have recourse, the Contracting State in whose territory he is residing shall arrange that such assistance be afforded to him by their own authorities.

2. The authority or authorities mentioned in paragraph 1 shall deliver or cause to be delivered under their supervision to stateless persons such documents or certifications as would normally be delivered to aliens by or through their national authorities.

3. Documents or certifications so delivered shall stand in the stead of the official instruments delivered to aliens by or through their national authorities and shall be given credence in the absence of proof to the contrary.

4. Subject to such exceptional treatment as may be granted to indigent persons, fees may be charged for the services mentioned herein, but such fees shall be moderate and commensurate with those charged to nationals for similar services.

5. The provisions of this article shall be without prejudice to articles 27 and 28.

Article 26. — *Freedom of movement*

Each Contracting State shall accord to stateless persons lawfully in its territory the right to choose their place of residence and to move freely within its territory, subject to any regulations applicable to aliens generally in the same circumstances.

Article 27. — *Identity papers*

The Contracting States shall issue identity papers to any stateless person in their territory who does not possess a valid travel document.

Article 28. — *Travel documents*

The Contracting States shall issue to stateless persons lawfully staying in their territory travel documents for the purpose of travel outside their territory, unless compelling reasons of national security or public order otherwise require, and the provisions of the schedule to this Convention shall apply with respect to such documents. The Contracting States may issue such a travel document to any other stateless person in their territory; they shall in particular give sympathetic consideration to the issue of such a travel document to stateless persons in their territory who are unable to obtain a travel document from the country of their lawful residence.

Article 29. — *Fiscal charges*

1. The Contracting States shall not impose upon stateless persons duties, charges or taxes, of any description whatsoever, other or higher than those which are or may be levied on their nationals in similar situations.

2. Nothing in the above paragraph shall prevent the application to stateless persons of the laws and regulations concerning charges in respect of the issue to aliens of administrative documents including identity papers.

Article 30. — Transfer of assets

1.   A Contracting State shall, in conformity with its laws and regulations, permit stateless persons to transfer assets which they have brought into its territory, to another country where they have been admitted for the purposes of resettlement.

2.   A Contracting State shall give sympathetic consideration to the application of stateless persons for permission to transfer assets wherever they may be and which are necessary for their resettlement in another country to which they have been admitted.

Article 31. — Expulsion

1.   The Contracting States shall not expel a stateless person lawfully in their territory save on grounds of national security or public order.

2.   The expulsion of such a stateless person shall be only in pursuance of a decision reached in accordance with due process of law. Except where compelling reasons of national security otherwise require, the stateless person shall be allowed to submit evidence to clear himself, and to appeal to and be represented for the purpose before competent authority or a person or persons specially designated by the competent authority.

3.   The Contracting States shall allow such a stateless person a reasonable period within which to seek legal admission into another country. The Contracting States reserve the right to apply during that period such internal measures as they may deem necessary.

Article 32. — Naturalization

The Contracting States shall as far as possible facilitate the assimilation and naturalization of stateless persons. They shall in particular make every effort to expedite naturalization proceedings and to reduce as far as possible the charges and costs of such proceedings.

CHAPTER VI

FINAL CLAUSES

Article 33. — Information on national legislation

The Contracting States shall communicate to the Secretary-General of the United Nations the laws and regulations which they may adopt to ensure the application of this Convention.

Article 34. — Settlement of disputes

Any dispute between Parties to this Convention relating to its interpretation or application, which cannot be settled by other means, shall be referred to the International Court of Justice at the request of any one of the parties to the dispute.

Article 35. — Signature, ratification and accession

1. This Convention shall be open for signature at the Headquarters of the United Nations until 31 December 1955.

2. It shall be open for signature on behalf of:

(*a*) Any State Member of the United Nations;

(*b*) Any other State invited to attend the United Nations Conference on the Status of Stateless Persons; and

(*c*) Any State to which an invitation to sign or to accede may be addressed by the General Assembly of the United Nations.

3. It shall be ratified and the instruments of ratification shall be deposited with the Secretary-General of the United Nations.

4. It shall be open for accession by the States referred to in paragraph 2 of this article. Accession shall be effected by the deposit of an instrument of accession with the Secretary-General of the United Nations.

Article 36. — Territorial application clause

1. Any State may, at the time of signature, ratification or accession, declare that this Convention shall extend to all or any of the territories for the international relations of which it is responsible. Such a declaration shall take effect when the Convention enters into force for the State concerned.

2. At any time thereafter any such extension shall be made by notification addressed to the Secretary-General of the United Nations and shall take effect as from the ninetieth day after the day of receipt by the Secretary-General of the United Nations of this notification, or as from the date of entry into force of the Convention for the State concerned, whichever is the later.

3. With respect to those territories to which this Convention is not extended at the time of signature, ratification or accession, each State concerned shall consider the possibility of taking the necessary steps in order to extend the application of this Convention to such territories, subject, where necessary for constitutional reasons, to the consent of the Governments of such territories.

Article 37. — Federal clause

In the case of a Federal or non-unitary State, the following provisions shall apply:

(*a*) With respect to those articles of this Convention that come within the legislative jurisdiction of the federal legislative authority, the obligations of the Federal Government shall to this extent be the same as those of Parties which are not Federal States;

(*b*) With respect to those articles of this Convention that come within the legislative jurisdiction of constituent States, provinces or cantons which are not, under the constitutional system of the Federation, bound to take legislative action, the Federal Government shall bring such articles with a favourable recommendation to the notice of the appropriate authorities of States, provinces or cantons at the earliest possible moment;

(*c*) A Federal State Party to this Convention shall, at the request of any other Contracting State transmitted through the Secretary-General of the United Nations, supply a statement of the law and practice of the Federation and its constituent units in regard to any particular provision of the Convention showing the extent to which effect has been given to that provision by legislative or other action.

Article 38. — Reservations

1. At the time of signature, ratification or accession, any State may make reservations to articles of the Convention other than to articles 1, 3, 4, 16 (1) and 33 to 42 inclusive.

2. Any State making a reservation in accordance with paragraph 1 of this article may at any time withdraw the reservation by a communication to that effect addressed to the Secretary-General of the United Nations.

Article 39. — Entry into force

1. This Convention shall come into force on the ninetieth day following the day of deposit of the sixth instrument of ratification or accession.

2. For each State ratifying or acceding to the Convention after the deposit of the sixth instrument of ratification or accession, the Convention shall enter into force on the ninetieth day following the date of deposit by such State of its instrument of ratification or accession.

Article 40. — Denunciation

1. Any Contracting State may denounce this Convention at any time by a notification addressed to the Secretary-General of the United Nations.

2. Such denunciation shall take effect for the Contracting State concerned one year from the date upon which it is received by the Secretary-General of the United Nations.

3. Any State which has made a declaration or notification under article 36 may, at any time thereafter, by a notification to the Secretary-General of the United Nations, declare that the Convention shall cease to extend to such territory one year after the date of receipt of the notification by the Secretary-General.

Article 41. — Revision

1. Any Contracting State may request revision of this Convention at any time by a notification addressed to the Secretary-General of the United Nations.

2. The General Assembly of the United Nations shall recommend the steps, if any, to be taken in respect of such request.

Article 42. — Notifications by the Secretary-General of the United Nations

The Secretary-General of the United Nations shall inform all Members of the United Nations and non-member States referred to in article 35:

(*a*) Of signatures, ratifications and accessions in accordance with article 35;

(*b*) Of declarations and notifications in accordance with article 36;

(*c*) Of reservations and withdrawals in accordance with article 38;

(*d*) Of the date on which this Convention will come into force in accordance with article 39;

(*e*) Of denunciations and notifications in accordance with article 40;

(*f*) Of request for revision in accordance with article 41.

IN FAITH WHEREOF the undersigned, duly authorized, have signed this Convention on behalf of their respective Governments.

DONE at New York, this twenty-eighth day of September, one thousand nine hundred and fifty-four, in a single copy, of which the English, French and Spanish texts are equally authentic and which shall remain deposited in the archives of the United Nations, and certified true copies of which shall be delivered to all Members of the United Nations and to the non-member States referred to in article 35.

81. Convention relating to the Status of Refugees

Adopted on 28 July 1951 by the United Nations Conference of Plenipotentiaries on the Status of Refugees and Stateless Persons convened under General Assembly resolution 429 (V) of 14 December 1950

ENTRY INTO FORCE: 22 April 1954, in accordance with article 43

PREAMBLE

The High Contracting Parties,

Considering that the Charter of the United Nations and the Universal Declaration of Human Rights approved on 10 December 1948 by the General Assembly have affirmed the principle that human beings shall enjoy fundamental rights and freedoms without discrimination,

Considering that the United Nations has, on various occasions, manifested its profound concern for refugees and endeavoured to assure refugees the widest possible exercise of these fundamental rights and freedoms,

Considering that it is desirable to revise and consolidate previous international agreements relating to the status of refugees and to extend the scope of and the protection accorded by such instruments by means of a new agreement,

Considering that the grant of asylum may place unduly heavy burdens on certain countries, and that a satisfactory solution of a problem of which the United Nations has recognized the international scope and nature cannot therefore be achieved without international co-operation,

Expressing the wish that all States, recognizing the social and humanitarian nature of the problem of refugees, will do everything within their power to prevent this problem from becoming a cause of tension between States,

Noting that the United Nations High Commissioner for Refugees is charged with the task of supervising international conventions providing for the protection of refugees, and recognizing that the effective co-ordination of measures taken to deal with this problem will depend upon the co-operation of States with the High Commissioner,

Have agreed as follows:

CHAPTER I

GENERAL PROVISIONS

Article 1. — Definition of the term "refugee"

A. For the purposes of the present Convention, the term "refugee" shall apply to any person who:

(1) Has been considered a refugee under the Arrangements of 12 May 1926 and 30 June 1928 or under the Conventions of 28 October 1933 and 10 February 1938, the Protocol of 14 September 1939 or the Constitution of the International Refugee Organization;

Decisions of non-eligibility taken by the International Refugee Organization during the period of its activities shall not prevent the status of refugee being accorded to persons who fulfil the conditions of paragraph 2 of this section;

(2) As a result of events occurring before 1 January 1951 and owing to well-founded fear of being persecuted for reasons of race, religion, nationality, membership of a particular social group or political opinion, is outside the country of his nationality and is unable, or owing to such fear, is unwilling to avail himself of the protection of that country; or who, not having a nationality and being outside the country of his former habitual residence as a result of such events, is unable or, owing to such fear, is unwilling to return to it.

In the case of a person who has more than one nationality, the term "the country of his nationality" shall mean each of the countries of which he is a national, and a person shall not be deemed to be lacking the protection of the country of his nationality if, without any valid reason based on well-founded fear, he has not availed himself of the protection of one of the countries of which he is a national.

B. (1) For the purposes of this Convention, the words "events occurring before 1 January 1951" in article 1, section A, shall be understood to mean either (*a*) "events occurring in Europe before 1 January 1951"; or (*b*) "events occurring in Europe or elsewhere before 1 January 1951"; and each Contracting State shall make a declaration at the time of signature, ratification or accession, specifying which of these meanings it applies for the purpose of its obligations under this Convention.

(2) Any Contracting State which has adopted alternative (*a*) may at any time extend its obligations by adopting alternative (*b*) by means of a notification addressed to the Secretary-General of the United Nations.

C. This Convention shall cease to apply to any person falling under the terms of section A if:

(1) He has voluntarily re-availed himself of the protection of the country of his nationality; or

(2) Having lost his nationality, he has voluntarily reacquired it; or

(3) He has acquired a new nationality, and enjoys the protection of the country of his new nationality; or

(4) He has voluntarily re-established himself in the country which he left or outside which he remained owing to fear of persecution; or

(5) He can no longer, because the circumstances in connection with which he has been recognized as a refugee have ceased to exist, continue to refuse to avail himself of the protection of the country of his nationality;

Provided that this paragraph shall not apply to a refugee falling under section A (1) of this article who is able to invoke compelling reasons arising out of previous persecution for refusing to avail himself of the protection of the country of nationality;

(6) Being a person who has no nationality he is, because the circumstances in connection with which he has been recognized as a refugee have ceased to exist, able to return to the country of his former habitual residence;

Provided that this paragraph shall not apply to a refugee falling under section A (I) of this article who is able to invoke compelling reasons arising out of previous persecution for refusing to return to the country of his former habitual residence.

D. This Convention shall not apply to persons who are at present receiving from organs or agencies of the United Nations other than the United Nations High Commissioner for Refugees protection or assistance.

When such protection or assistance has ceased for any reason, without the position of such persons being definitively settled in accordance with the relevant resolutions adopted by the General Assembly of the United Nations, these persons shall *ipso facto* be entitled to the benefits of this Convention.

E. This Convention shall not apply to a person who is recognized by the competent authorities of the country in which he has taken residence as having the rights and obligations which are attached to the possession of the nationality of that country.

F. The provisions of this Convention shall not apply to any person with respect to whom there are serious reasons for considering that:

(*a*) He has committed a crime against peace, a war crime, or a crime against humanity, as defined in the international instruments drawn up to make provision in respect of such crimes;

(*b*) He has committed a serious non-political crime outside the country of refuge prior to his admission to that country as a refugee;

(*c*) He has been guilty of acts contrary to the purposes and principles of the United Nations.

Article 2. — *General obligations*

Every refugee has duties to the country in which he finds himself, which require in particular that he conform to its laws and regulations as well as to measures taken for the maintenance of public order.

Article 3. — *Non-discrimination*

The Contracting States shall apply the provisions of this Convention to refugees without discrimination as to race, religion or country of origin.

Article 4. — *Religion*

The Contracting States shall accord to refugees within their territories treatment at least as favourable as that accorded to their nationals with respect to freedom to practise their religion and freedom as regards the religious education of their children.

Article 5. — *Rights granted apart from this Convention*

Nothing in this Convention shall be deemed to impair any rights and benefits granted by a Contracting State to refugees apart from this Convention.

Article 6. — *The term "in the same circumstances"*

For the purposes of this Convention, the term "in the same circumstances" implies that any requirements (including requirements as to length and conditions of sojourn or residence) which the particular individual would have to fulfil for the enjoyment of the right in question, if he were not a refugee, must be fulfilled by him, with the exception of requirements which by their nature a refugee is incapable of fulfilling.

Article 7. — Exemption from reciprocity

1.   Except where this Convention contains more favourable provisions, a Contracting State shall accord to refugees the same treatment as is accorded to aliens generally.

2.   After a period of three years' residence, all refugees shall enjoy exemption from legislative reciprocity in the territory of the Contracting States.

3.   Each Contracting State shall continue to accord to refugees the rights and benefits to which they were already entitled, in the absence of reciprocity, at the date of entry into force of this Convention for that State.

4.   The Contracting States shall consider favourably the possibility of according to refugees, in the absence of reciprocity, rights and benefits beyond those to which they are entitled according to paragraphs 2 and 3, and to extending exemption from reciprocity to refugees who do not fulfil the conditions provided for in paragraphs 2 and 3.

5.   The provisions of paragraphs 2 and 3 apply both to the rights and benefits referred to in articles 13, 18, 19, 21 and 22 of this Convention and to rights and benefits for which this Convention does not provide.

Article 8. — Exemption from exceptional measures

With regard to exceptional measures which may be taken against the person, property or interests of nationals of a foreign State, the Contracting States shall not apply such measures to a refugee who is formally a national of the said State solely on account of such nationality. Contracting States which, under their legislation, are prevented from applying the general principle expressed in this article, shall, in appropriate cases, grant exemptions in favour of such refugees.

Article 9. — Provisional measures

Nothing in this Convention shall prevent a Contracting State, in time of war or other grave and exceptional circumstances, from taking provisionally measures which it considers to be essential to the national security in the case of a particular person, pending a determination by the Contracting State that that person is in fact a refugee and that the continuance of such measures is necessary in his case in the interests of national security.

Article 10. — Continuity of residence

1. Where a refugee has been forcibly displaced during the Second World War and removed to the territory of a Contracting State, and is resident there, the period of such enforced sojourn shall be considered to have been lawful residence within that territory.

2. Where a refugee has been forcibly displaced during the Second World War from the territory of a Contracting State and has, prior to the date of entry into force of this Convention, returned there for the purpose of taking up residence, the period of residence before and after such enforced displacement shall be regarded as one uninterrupted period for any purposes for which uninterrupted residence is required.

Article 11. — Refugee seamen

In the case of refugees regularly serving as crew members on board a ship flying the flag of a Contracting State, that State shall give sympathetic consideration to their establishment on its territory and the issue of travel documents to them or their temporary admission to its territory particularly with a view to facilitating their establishment in another country.

CHAPTER II

JURIDICAL STATUS

Article 12. — Personal status

1. The personal status of a refugee shall be governed by the law of the country of his domicile or, if he has no domicile, by the law of the country of his residence.

2. Rights previously acquired by a refugee and dependent on personal status, more particularly rights attaching to marriage, shall be respected by a Contracting State, subject to compliance, if this be necessary, with the formalities required by the law of that State, provided that the right in question is one which would have been recognized by the law of that State had he not become a refugee.

Article 13. — Movable and immovable property

The Contracting States shall accord to a refugee treatment as favourable as possible and, in any event, not less favourable than that accorded to aliens generally in the same circumstances, as regards the acquisition of movable and immovable property and other rights pertaining thereto, and to leases and other contracts relating to movable and immovable property.

Article 14. — Artistic rights and industrial property

In respect of the protection of industrial property, such as inventions, designs or models, trade marks, trade names, and of rights in literary, artistic and scientific works, a refugee shall be accorded in the country in which he has his habitual residence the same protection as is accorded to nationals of that country. In the territory of any other Contracting States, he shall be accorded the same protection as is accorded in that territory to nationals of the country in which he has his habitual residence.

Article 15. — Right of association

As regards non-political and non-profit-making associations and trade unions the Contracting States shall accord to refugees lawfully staying in their territory the most favourable treatment accorded to nationals of a foreign country, in the same circumstances.

Article 16. — Access to courts

1. A refugee shall have free access to the courts of law on the territory of all Contracting States.

2. A refugee shall enjoy in the Contracting State in which he has his habitual residence the same treatment as a national in matters pertaining to access to the courts, including legal assistance and exemption from *cautio judicatum solvi.*

3. A refugee shall be accorded in the matters referred to in paragraph 2 in countries other than that in which he has his habitual residence the treatment granted to a national of the country of his habitual residence.

CHAPTER III

GAINFUL EMPLOYMENT

Article 17. — Wage-earning employment

1. The Contracting States shall accord to refugees lawfully staying in their territory the most favourable treatment accorded to nationals of a

foreign country in the same circumstances, as regards the right to engage in wage-earning employment.

2.   In any case, restrictive measures imposed on aliens or the employment of aliens for the protection of the national labour market shall not be applied to a refugee who was already exempt from them at the date of entry into force of this Convention for the Contracting State concerned, or who fulfils one of the following conditions:

(a) He has completed three years' residence in the country;

(b) He has a spouse possessing the nationality of the country of residence. A refugee may not invoke the benefit of this provision if he has abandoned his spouse;

(c) He has one or more children possessing the nationality of the country of residence.

3.   The Contracting States shall give sympathetic consideration to assimilating the rights of all refugees with regard to wage-earning employment to those of nationals, and in particular of those refugees who have entered their territory pursuant to programmes of labour recruitment or under immigration schemes.

Article 18. — Self-employment

The Contracting States shall accord to a refugee lawfully in their territory treatment as favourable as possible and, in any event, not less favourable than that accorded to aliens generally in the same circumstances, as regards the right to engage on his own account in agriculture, industry, handicrafts and commerce and to establish commercial and industrial companies.

Article 19. — Liberal professions

1.   Each Contracting State shall accord to refugees lawfully staying in their territory who hold diplomas recognized by the competent authorities of that State, and who are desirous of practising a liberal profession, treatment as favourable as possible and, in any event, not less favourable than that accorded to aliens generally in the same circumstances.

2.   The Contracting States shall use their best endeavours consistently with their laws and constitutions to secure the settlement of such refugees in the territories, other than the metropolitan territory, for whose international relations they are responsible.

CHAPTER IV

WELFARE

Article 20. — Rationing

Where a rationing system exists, which applies to the population at large and regulates the general distribution of products in short supply, refugees shall be accorded the same treatment as nationals.

Article 21. — Housing

As regards housing, the Contracting States, in so far as the matter is regulated by laws or regulations or is subject to the control of public authorities, shall accord to refugees lawfully staying in their territory treatment as favourable as possible and, in any event, not less favourable than that accorded to aliens generally in the same circumstances.

Article 22. — Public education

1.   The Contracting States shall accord to refugees the same treatment as is accorded to nationals with respect to elementary education.

2.   The Contracting States shall accord to refugees treatment as favourable as possible, and, in any event, not less favourable than that accorded to aliens generally in the same circumstances, with respect to education other than elementary education and, in particular, as regards access to studies, the recognition of foreign school certificates, diplomas and degrees, the remission of fees and charges and the award of scholarships.

Article 23. — Public relief

The Contracting States shall accord to refugees lawfully staying in their territory the same treatment with respect to public relief and assistance as is accorded to their nationals.

Article 24. — Labour legislation and social security

1.   The Contracting States shall accord to refugees lawfully staying in their territory the same treatment as is accorded to nationals in respect of the following matters;

(a) In so far as such matters are governed by laws or regulations or are subject to the control of administrative authorities: remuneration, including family allowances where these form part of remuneration, hours of work, overtime arrangements, holidays with pay, restrictions on home work, minimum age of employment, apprenticeship and training, women's work and the work of young persons, and the enjoyment of the benefits of collective bargaining;

(*b*) Social security (legal provisions in respect of employment injury, occupational diseases, maternity, sickness, disability, old age, death, unemployment, family responsibilities and any other contingency which, according to national laws or regulations, is covered by a social security scheme), subject to the following limitations:

(i) There may be appropriate arrangements for the maintenance of acquired rights and rights in course of acquisition;

(ii) National laws or regulations of the country of residence may prescribe special arrangements concerning benefits or portions of benefits which are payable wholly out of public funds, and concerning allowances paid to persons who do not fulfil the contribution conditions prescribed for the award of a normal pension.

2. The right to compensation for the death of a refugee resulting from employment injury or from occupational disease shall not be affected by the fact that the residence of the beneficiary is outside the territory of the Contracting State.

3. The Contracting States shall extend to refugees the benefits of agreements concluded between them, or which may be concluded between them in the future, concerning the maintenance of acquired rights and rights in the process of acquisition in regard to social security, subject only to the conditions which apply to nationals of the States signatory to the agreements in question.

4. The Contracting States will give sympathetic consideration to extending to refugees so far as possible the benefits of similar agreements which may at any time be in force between such Contracting States and non-contracting States.

CHAPTER V

ADMINISTRATIVE MEASURES

Article 25. — Administrative assistance

1. When the exercise of a right by a refugee would normally require the assistance of authorities of a foreign country to whom he cannot have recourse, the Contracting States in whose territory he is residing shall arrange

that such assistance be afforded to him by their own authorities or by an international authority.

2.   The authority or authorities mentioned in paragraph 1 shall deliver or cause to be delivered under their supervision to refugees such documents or certifications as would normally be delivered to aliens by or through their national authorities.

3.   Documents or certifications so delivered shall stand in the stead of the official instruments delivered to aliens by or through their national authorities, and shall be given credence in the absence of proof to the contrary.

4.   Subject to such exceptional treatment as may be granted to indigent persons, fees may be charged for the services mentioned herein, but such fees shall be moderate and commensurate with those charged to nationals for similar services.

5.   The provisions of this article shall be without prejudice to articles 27 and 28.

Article 26. — *Freedom of movement*

Each Contracting State shall accord to refugees lawfully in its territory the right to choose their place of residence and to move freely within its territory subject to any regulations applicable to aliens generally in the same circumstances.

Article 27. — *Identity papers*

The Contracting States shall issue identity papers to any refugee in their territory who does not possess a valid travel document.

Article 28. — *Travel documents*

1.   The Contracting States shall issue to refugees lawfully staying in their territory travel documents for the purpose of travel outside their territory, unless compelling reasons of national security or public order otherwise require, and the provisions of the Schedule to this Convention shall apply with respect to such documents. The Contracting States may issue such a travel document to any other refugee in their territory; they shall in particular give sympathetic consideration to the issue of such a travel document to refugees in their territory who are unable to obtain a travel document from the country of their lawful residence.

2.   Travel documents issued to refugees under previous international agreements by Parties thereto shall be recognized and treated by the Con-

tracting States in the same way as if they had been issued pursuant to this article.

Article 29. — Fiscal charges

1.   The Contracting States shall not impose upon refugees duties, charges or taxes, of any description whatsoever, other or higher than those which are or may be levied on their nationals in similar situations.

2.   Nothing in the above paragraph shall prevent the application to refugees of the laws and regulations concerning charges in respect of the issue to aliens of administrative documents including identity papers.

Article 30. — Transfer of assets

1.   A Contracting State shall, in conformity with its laws and regula-tions, permit refugees to transfer assets which they have brought into its territory, to another country where they have been admitted for the purposes of resettlement.

2.   A Contracting State shall give sympathetic consideration to the application of refugees for permission to transfer assets wherever they may be and which are necessary for their resettlement in another country to which they have been admitted.

Article 31. — Refugees unlawfully in the country of refuge

1.   The Contracting States shall not impose penalties, on account of their illegal entry or presence, on refugees who, coming directly from a ter-ritory where their life or freedom was threatened in the sense of article 1, enter or are present in their territory without authorization, provided they present themselves without delay to the authorities and show good cause for their illegal entry or presence.

2.   The Contracting States shall not apply to the movements of such refugees restrictions other than those which are necessary and such restric-tions shall only be applied until their status in the country is regularized or they obtain admission into another country. The Contracting States shall allow such refugees a reasonable period and all the necessary facilities to obtain admission into another country.

Article 32. — Expulsion

1.   The Contracting States shall not expel a refugee lawfully in their territory save on grounds of national security or public order.

2. The expulsion of such a refugee shall be only in pursuance of a decision reached in accordance with due process of law. Except where compelling reasons of national security otherwise require, the refugee shall be allowed to submit evidence to clear himself, and to appeal to and be represented for the purpose before competent authority or a person or persons specially designated by the competent authority.

3. The Contracting States shall allow such a refugee a reasonable period within which to seek legal admission into another country. The Contracting States reserve the right to apply during that period such internal measures as they may deem necessary.

Article 33. — Prohibition of expulsion or return ("refoulement")

1. No Contracting State shall expel or return ("*refouler*") a refugee in any manner whatsoever to the frontiers of territories where his life or freedom would be threatened on account of his race, religion, nationality, membership of a particular social group or political opinion.

2. The benefit of the present provision may not, however, be claimed by a refugee whom there are reasonable grounds for regarding as a danger to the security of the country in which he is, or who, having been convicted by a final judgement of a particularly serious crime, constitutes a danger to the community of that country.

Article 34. — Naturalization

The Contracting States shall as far as possible facilitate the assimilation and naturalization of refugees. They shall in particular make every effort to expedite naturalization proceedings and to reduce as far as possible the charges and costs of such proceedings.

CHAPTER VI

EXECUTORY AND TRANSITORY PROVISIONS

Article 35. — Co-operation of the national authorities with the United Nations

1. The Contracting States undertake to co-operate with the Office of the United Nations High Commissioner for Refugees, or any other agency of the United Nations which may succeed it, in the exercise of its functions, and

shall in particular facilitate its duty of supervising the application of the provisions of this Convention.

2.   In order to enable the Office of the High Commissioner or any other agency of the United Nations which may succeed it, to make reports to the competent organs of the United Nations, the Contracting States undertake to provide them in the appropriate form with information and statistical data requested concerning:

(*a*) The condition of refugees,

(*b*) The implementation of this Convention, and

(*c*) Laws, regulations and decrees which are, or may hereafter be, in force relating to refugees.

Article 36. — *Information on national legislation*

The Contracting States shall communicate to the Secretary-General of the United Nations the laws and regulations which they may adopt to ensure the application of this Convention.

Article 37. — *Relation to previous conventions*

Without prejudice to article 28, paragraph 2, of this Convention, this Convention replaces, as between Parties to it, the Arrangements of 5 July 1922, 31 May 1924, 12 May 1926, 30 June 1928 and 30 July 1935, the Conventions of 28 October 1933 and 10 February 1938, the Protocol of 14 September 1939 and the Agreement of 15 October 1946.

CHAPTER VII

FINAL CLAUSES

Article 38. — *Settlement of disputes*

Any dispute between Parties to this Convention relating to its interpretation or application, which cannot be settled by other means, shall be referred to the International Court of Justice at the request of any one of the parties to the dispute.

Article 39. — *Signature, ratification and accession*

1.   This Convention shall be opened for signature at Geneva on 28 July 1951 and shall thereafter be deposited with the Secretary-General of the United Nations. It shall be open for signature at the European Office of the

United Nations from 28 July to 31 August 1951 and shall be re-opened for signature at the Headquarters of the United Nations from 17 September 1951 to 31 December 1952.

2.   This Convention shall be open for signature on behalf of all States Members of the United Nations, and also on behalf of any other State invited to attend the Conference of Plenipotentiaries on the Status of Refugees and Stateless Persons or to which an invitation to sign will have been addressed by the General Assembly. It shall be ratified and the instruments of ratification shall be deposited with the Secretary-General of the United Nations.

3.   This Convention shall be open from 28 July 1951 for accession by the States referred to in paragraph 2 of this article. Accession shall be effected by the deposit of an instrument of accession with the Secretary-General of the United Nations.

Article 40. — Territorial application clause

1.   Any State may, at the time of signature, ratification or accession, declare that this Convention shall extend to all or any of the territories for the international relations of which it is responsible. Such a declaration shall take effect when the Convention enters into force for the State concerned.

2.   At any time thereafter any such extension shall be made by notification addressed to the Secretary-General of the United Nations and shall take effect as from the ninetieth day after the day of receipt by the Secretary-General of the United Nations of this notification, or as from the date of entry into force of the Convention for the State concerned, whichever is the later.

3.   With respect to those territories to which this Convention is not extended at the time of signature, ratification or accession, each State concerned shall consider the possibility of taking the necessary steps in order to extend the application of this Convention to such territories, subject, where necessary for constitutional reasons, to the consent of the Governments of such territories.

Article 41. — Federal clause

In the case of a Federal or non-unitary State, the following provisions shall apply:

(a) With respect to those articles of this Convention that come within the legislative jurisdiction of the federal legislative authority, the obligations of the Federal Government shall to this extent be the same as those of parties which are not Federal States;

(*b*) With respect to those articles of this Convention that come within the legislative jurisdiction of constituent States, provinces or cantons which are not, under the constitutional system of the Federation, bound to take legislative action, the Federal Government shall bring such articles with a favourable recommendation to the notice of the appropriate authorities of States, provinces or cantons at the earliest possible moment;

(*c*) A Federal State Party to this Convention shall, at the request of any other Contracting State transmitted through the Secretary-General of the United Nations, supply a statement of the law and practice of the Federation and its constituent units in regard to any particular provision of the Convention showing the extent to which effect has been given to that provision by legislative or other action.

Article 42. — Reservations

1. At the time of signature, ratification or accession, any State may make reservations to articles of the Convention other than to articles 1, 3, 4, 16 (1), 33, 36-46 inclusive.

2. Any State making a reservation in accordance with paragraph 1 of this article may at any time withdraw the reservation by a communication to that effect addressed to the Secretary-General of the United Nations.

Article 43. — Entry into force

1. This Convention shall come into force on the ninetieth day following the day of deposit of the sixth instrument of ratification or accession.

2. For each State ratifying or acceding to the Convention after the deposit of the sixth instrument of ratification or accession, the Convention shall enter into force on the ninetieth day following the date of deposit by such State of its instrument of ratification or accession.

Article 44. — Denunciation

1. Any Contracting State may denounce this Convention at any time by a notification addressed to the Secretary-General of the United Nations.

2. Such denunciation shall take effect for the Contracting State concerned one year from the date upon which it is received by the Secretary-General of the United Nations.

3. Any State which has made a declaration or notification under article 40 may, at any time thereafter, by a notification to the Secretary-General of the United Nations, declare that the Convention shall cease to extend to such

territory one year after the date of receipt of the notification by the Secretary-General.

Article 45. — Revision

1.   Any Contracting State may request revision of this Convention at any time by a notification addressed to the Secretary-General of the United Nations.

2.   The General Assembly of the United Nations shall recommend the steps, if any, to be taken in respect of such request.

Article 46. — Notifications by the Secretary-General of the United Nations

The Secretary-General of the United Nations shall inform all Members of the United Nations and non-member States referred to in article 39:

(a) Of declarations and notifications in accordance with section B of article 1;

(b) Of signatures, ratifications and accessions in accordance with article 39;

(c) Of declarations and notifications in accordance with article 40;

(d) Of reservations and withdrawals in accordance with article 42;

(e) Of the date on which this Convention will come into force in accordance with article 43;

(f) Of denunciations and notifications in accordance with article 44;

(g) Of requests for revision in accordance with article 45.

IN FAITH WHEREOF the undersigned, duly authorized, have signed this Convention on behalf of their respective Governments.

DONE at Geneva, this twenty-eighth day of July, one thousand nine hundred and fifty-one, in a single copy, of which the English and French texts are equally authentic and which shall remain deposited in the archives of the United Nations, and certified true copies of which shall be delivered to all Members of the United Nations and to the non-member States referred to in article 39.

82. Protocol relating to the Status of Refugees

The Protocol was taken note of with approval by the Economic and Social Council in resolution 1186 (XLI) of 18 November 1966 and was taken note of by the General Assembly in resolution 2198 (XXI) of 16 December 1966. In the same resolution the General Assembly requested the Secretary-General to transmit the text of the Protocol to the States mentioned in article V thereof, with a view to enabling them to accede to the Protocol

ENTRY INTO FORCE: 4 October 1967, in accordance with article VIII

The States Parties to the present Protocol,

Considering that the Convention relating to the Status of Refugees done at Geneva on 28 July 1951 (hereinafter referred to as the Convention) covers only those persons who have become refugees as a result of events occurring before 1 January 1951,

Considering that new refugee situations have arisen since the Convention was adopted and that the refugees concerned may therefore not fall within the scope of the Convention,

Considering that it is desirable that equal status should be enjoyed by all refugees covered by the definition in the Convention irrespective of the dateline 1 January 1951,

Have agreed as follows:

Article I. — General provision

1.   The States Parties to the present Protocol undertake to apply articles 2 to 34 inclusive of the Convention to refugees as hereinafter defined.

2.   For the purpose of the present Protocol, the term "refugee" shall, except as regards the application of paragraph 3 of this article, mean any person within the definition of article 1 of the Convention as if the words "As a result of events occurring before 1 January 1951 and..." and the words "...as a result of such events", in article 1 A (2) were omitted.

3.   The present Protocol shall be applied by the States Parties hereto without any geographic limitation, save that existing declarations made by States already Parties to the Convention in accordance with article 1 B (1) (*a*) of the Convention, shall, unless extended under article 1 B (2) thereof, apply also under the present Protocol.

Article II. — Co-operation of the national authorities
with the United Nations

1.   The States Parties to the present Protocol undertake to co-operate with the Office of the United Nations High Commissioner for Refugees, or any other agency of the United Nations which may succeed it, in the exercise of its functions, and shall in particular facilitate its duty of supervising the application of the provisions of the present Protocol.

2.   In order to enable the Office of the High Commissioner or any other agency of the United Nations which may succeed it, to make reports to the competent organs of the United Nations, the States Parties to the present Protocol undertake to provide them with the information and statistical data requested, in the appropriate form, concerning:

(*a*) The condition of refugees;

(*b*) The implementation of the present Protocol;

(*c*) Laws, regulations and decrees which are, or may hereafter be, in force relating to refugees.

Article III. — Information on national legislation

The States Parties to the present Protocol shall communicate to the Secretary-General of the United Nations the laws and regulations which they may adopt to ensure the application of the present Protocol.

Article IV. — Settlement of disputes

Any dispute between States Parties to the present Protocol which relates to its interpretation or application and which cannot be settled by other means shall be referred to the International Court of Justice at the request of any one of the parties to the dispute.

Article V. — Accession

The present Protocol shall be open for accession on behalf of all States Parties to the Convention and of any other State Member of the United Nations or member of any of the specialized agencies or to which an invitation to accede may have been addressed by the General Assembly of the United Nations. Accession shall be effected by the deposit of an instrument of accession with the Secretary-General of the United Nations.

Article VI. — Federal clause

In the case of a Federal or non-unitary State, the following provisions shall apply:

(*a*) With respect to those articles of the Convention to be applied in accordance with article I, paragraph 1, of the present Protocol that come within the legislative jurisdiction of the federal legislative authority, the obligations of the Federal Government shall to this extent be the same as those of States Parties which are not Federal States;

(*b*) With respect to those articles of the Convention to be applied in accordance with article I, paragraph 1, of the present Protocol that come within the legislative jurisdiction of constituent States, provinces or cantons which are not, under the constitutional system of the Federation, bound to take legislative action, the Federal Government shall bring such articles with a favourable recommendation to the notice of the appropriate authorities of States, provinces or cantons at the earliest possible moment;

(*c*) A Federal State Party to the present Protocol shall, at the request of any other State Party hereto transmitted through the Secretary-General of the United Nations, supply a statement of the law and practice of the Federation and its constituent units in regard to any particular provision of the Convention to be applied in accordance with article I, paragraph 1, of the present Protocol, showing the extent to which effect has been given to that provision by legislative or other action.

Article VII. — Reservations and declarations

1. At the time of accession, any State may make reservations in respect of article IV of the present Protocol and in respect of the application in accordance with article I of the present Protocol of any provisions of the Convention other than those contained in articles 1, 3, 4, 16 (1) and 33 thereof, provided that in the case of a State Party to the Convention reservations made under this article shall not extend to refugees in respect of whom the Convention applies.

2. Reservations made by States Parties to the Convention in accordance with article 42 thereof shall, unless withdrawn, be applicable in relation to their obligations under the present Protocol.

3. Any State making a reservation in accordance with paragraph 1 of this article may at any time withdraw such reservation by a communication to that effect addressed to the Secretary-General of the United Nations.

4. Declarations made under article 40, paragraphs 1 and 2, of the Convention by a State Party thereto which accedes to the present Protocol shall be deemed to apply in respect of the present Protocol, unless upon accession a notification to the contrary is addressed by the State Party concerned to the Secretary-General of the United Nations. The provisions of article 40, paragraphs 2 and 3, and of article 44, paragraph 3, of the Convention shall be deemed to apply *mutatis mutandis* to the present Protocol.

Article VIII. — Entry into force

1. The present Protocol shall come into force on the day of deposit of the sixth instrument of accession.

2. For each State acceding to the Protocol after the deposit of the sixth instrument of accession, the Protocol shall come into force on the date of deposit by such State of its instrument of accession.

Article IX. — Denunciation

1. Any State Party hereto may denounce this Protocol at any time by a notification addressed to the Secretary-General of the United Nations.

2. Such denunciation shall take effect for the State Party concerned one year from the date on which it is received by the Secretary-General of the United Nations.

Article X. — Notifications by the Secretary-General of the United Nations

The Secretary-General of the United Nations shall inform the States referred to in article V above of the date of entry into force, accessions, reservations and withdrawals of reservations to and denunciations of the present Protocol, and of declarations and notifications relating hereto.

Article XI. — Deposit in the archives of the Secretariat of the United Nations

A copy of the present Protocol, of which the Chinese, English, French, Russian and Spanish texts are equally authentic, signed by the President of the General Assembly and by the Secretary-General of the United Nations, shall be deposited in the archives of the Secretariat of the United Nations. The Secretary-General will transmit certified copies thereof to all States Members of the United Nations and to the other States referred to in article V above.

83. Statute of the Office of the United Nations High Commissioner for Refugees

Adopted by General Assembly resolution 428 (V) of 14 December 1950

CHAPTER I. – GENERAL PROVISIONS

1. The United Nations High Commissioner for Refugees, acting under the authority of the General Assembly, shall assume the function of providing international protection, under the auspices of the United Nations, to refugees who fall within the scope of the present Statute and of seeking permanent solutions for the problem of refugees by assisting governments and, subject to the approval of the governments concerned, private organizations to facilitate the voluntary repatriation of such refugees, or their assimilation within new national communities.

In the exercise of his functions, more particularly when difficulties arise, and for instance with regard to any controversy concerning the international status of these persons, the High Commissioner shall request the opinion of an advisory committee on refugees if it is created.

2. The work of the High Commissioner shall be of an entirely non-political character; it shall be humanitarian and social and shall relate, as a rule, to groups and categories of refugees.

3. The High Commissioner shall follow policy directives given him by the General Assembly or the Economic and Social Council.

4. The Economic and Social Council may decide, after hearing the views of the High Commissioner on the subject, to establish an advisory committee on refugees, which shall consist of representatives of States Members and States non-members of the United Nations, to be selected by the Council on the basis of their demonstrated interest in and devotion to the solution of the refugee problem.

5. The General Assembly shall review, not later than at its eighth regular session, the arrangements for the Office of the High Commissioner with a view to determining whether the Office should be continued beyond 31 December 1963.

CHAPTER II. – FUNCTIONS OF THE HIGH COMMISSIONER

6. The competence of the High Commissioner shall extend to:

A. (i) Any person who has been considered a refugee under the Arrangements of 12 May 1926 and 30 June 1928 or under the Conventions of 28 October 1933 and 10 February 1938, the Protocol of 14 September 1939 or the Constitution of the International Refugee Organization;

(ii) Any person who, as a result of events occurring before 1 January 1951 and owing to well-founded fear of being persecuted for reasons of race, religion, nationality or political opinion, is outside the country of his nationality and is unable or, owing to such fear or for reasons other than personal convenience, is unwilling to avail himself of the protection of that country; or who, not having a nationality and being outside the country of his former habitual residence, is unable or, owing to such fear or for reasons other than personal convenience, is unwilling to return to it.

Decisions as to eligibility taken by the International Refugee Organization during the period of its activities shall not prevent the status of refugee being accorded to persons who fulfil the conditions of the present paragraph.

The competence of the High Commissioner shall cease to apply to any person defined in section A above if:

(*a*) He has voluntarily re-availed himself of the protection of the country of his nationality; or

(*b*) Having lost his nationality, he has voluntarily re-acquired it; or

(*c*) He has acquired a new nationality, and enjoys the protection of the country of his new nationality; or

(*d*) He has voluntarily re-established himself in the country which he left or outside which he remained owing to fear of persecution; or

(*e*) He can no longer, because the circumstances in connection with which he has been recognized as a refugee have ceased to exist, claim grounds other than those of personal convenience, for continuing to refuse to avail himself of the protection of the country of his nationality. Reasons of a purely economic character may not be invoked; or

(*f*) Being a person who has no nationality, he can no longer, because the circumstances in connection with which he has been recognized as a refugee have ceased to exist and he is able to return to the country of his former habitual residence, claim grounds other than those of personal convenience for continuing to refuse to return to that country.

B. Any other person who is outside the country of his nationality or, if he has no nationality, the country of his former habitual residence, because he has or had well-founded fear of persecution by reason of his race, religion, nationality or political opinion and is unable or, because of such fear, is unwilling to avail himself of the protection of the government of the country of his nationality, or, if he has no nationality, to return to the country of his former habitual residence.

7. Provided that the competence of the High Commissioner as defined in paragraph 6 above shall not extend to a person:

(*a*) Who is a national of more than one country unless he satisfies the provisions of the preceding paragraph in relation to each of the countries of which he is a national; or

(*b*) Who is recognized by the competent authorities of the country in which he has taken residence as having the rights and obligations which are attached to the possession of the nationality of that country; or

(*c*) Who continues to receive from other organs or agencies of the United Nations protection or assistance; or

(*d*) In respect of whom there are serious reasons for considering that he has committed a crime covered by the provisions of treaties of extradition or a crime mentioned in article VI of the London Charter of the International Military Tribunal or by the provisions of article 14, paragraph 2, of the Universal Declaration of Human Rights.

8. The High Commissioner shall provide for the protection of refugees falling under the competence of his Office by:

(*a*) Promoting the conclusion and ratification of international conventions for the protection of refugees, supervising their application and proposing amendments thereto;

(*b*) Promoting through special agreements with governments the execution of any measures calculated to improve the situation of refugees and to reduce the number requiring protection;

(*c*) Assisting governmental and private efforts to promote voluntary repatriation or assimilation within new national communities;

(*d*) Promoting the admission of refugees, not excluding those in the most destitute categories, to the territories of States;

(*e*) Endeavouring to obtain permission for refugees to transfer their assets and especially those necessary for their resettlement;

(*f*) Obtaining from governments information concerning the number and conditions of refugees in their territories and the laws and regulations concerning them;

(*g*) Keeping in close touch with the governments and inter-governmental organizations concerned;

(*h*) Establishing contact in such manner as he may think best with private organizations dealing with refugee questions;

(*i*) Facilitating the co-ordination of the efforts of private organizations concerned with the welfare of refugees.

9. The High Commissioner shall engage in such additional activities, including repatriation and resettlement, as the General Assembly may determine, within the limits of the resources placed at his disposal.

10. The High Commissioner shall administer any funds, public or private, which he receives for assistance to refugees, and shall distribute them among the private and, as appropriate, public agencies which he deems best qualified to administer such assistance.

The High Commissioner may reject any offers which he does not consider appropriate or which cannot be utilized.

The High Commissioner shall not appeal to governments for funds or make a general appeal, without the prior approval of the General Assembly.

The High Commissioner shall include in his annual report a statement of his activities in this field.

11. The High Commissioner shall be entitled to present his views before the General Assembly, the Economic and Social Council and their subsidiary bodies.

The High Commissioner shall report annually to the General Assembly through the Economic and Social Council; his report shall be considered as a separate item on the agenda of the General Assembly.

12. The High Commissioner may invite the co-operation of the various specialized agencies.

CHAPTER III. – ORGANIZATION AND FINANCES

13. The High Commissioner shall be elected by the General Assembly on the nomination of the Secretary-General. The terms of appointment of the

High Commissioner shall be proposed by the Secretary-General and approved by the General Assembly. The High Commissioner shall be elected for a term of three years, from 1 January 1951.

14. The High Commissioner shall appoint, for the same term, a Deputy High Commissioner of a nationality other than his own.

15. (*a*) Within the limits of the budgetary appropriations provided, the staff of the Office of the High Commissioner shall be appointed by the High Commissioner and shall be responsible to him in the exercise of their functions.

(*b*) Such staff shall be chosen from persons devoted to the purposes of the Office of the High Commissioner.

(*c*) Their conditions of employment shall be those provided under the staff regulations adopted by the General Assembly and the rules promulgated thereunder by the Secretary-General.

(*d*) Provision may also be made to permit the employment of personnel without compensation.

16. The High Commissioner shall consult the governments of the countries of residence of refugees as to the need for appointing representatives therein. In any country recognizing such need, there may be appointed a representative approved by the government of that country. Subject to the foregoing, the same representative may serve in more than one country.

17. The High Commissioner and the Secretary-General shall make appropriate arrangements for liaison and consultation on matters of mutual interest.

18. The Secretary-General shall provide the High Commissioner with all necessary facilities within budgetary limitations.

19. The Office of the High Commissioner shall be located in Geneva, Switzerland.

20. The Office of the High Commissioner shall be financed under the budget of the United Nations. Unless the General Assembly subsequently decides otherwise, no expenditure, other than administrative expenditures relating to the functioning of the Office of the High Commissioner, shall be borne on the budget of the United Nations, and all other expenditures relating to the activities of the High Commissioner shall be financed by voluntary contributions.

21. The administration of the Office of the High Commissioner shall be subject to the Financial Regulations of the United Nations and to the financial rules promulgated thereunder by the Secretary-General.

22.   Transactions relating to the High Commissioner's funds shall be subject to audit by the United Nations Board of Auditors, provided that the Board may accept audited accounts from the agencies to which funds have been allocated. Administrative arrangements for the custody of such funds and their allocation shall be agreed between the High Commissioner and the Secretary-General in accordance with the Financial Regulations of the United Nations and rules promulgated thereunder by the Secretary-General.

84. Declaration on Territorial Asylum

Adopted by General Assembly resolution 2312 (XXII) of 14 December 1967

The General Assembly,

Recalling its resolutions 1839 (XVII) of 19 December 1962, 2100 (XX) of 20 December 1965 and 2203 (XXI) of 16 December 1966 concerning a declaration on the right of asylum,

Considering the work of codification to be undertaken by the International Law Commission in accordance with General Assembly resolution 1400 (XIV) of 21 November 1959,

Adopts the following Declaration:

DECLARATION ON TERRITORIAL ASYLUM

The General Assembly,

Noting that the purposes proclaimed in the Charter of the United Nations are to maintain international peace and security, to develop friendly relations among all nations and to achieve international co-operation in solving international problems of an economic, social, cultural or humanitarian character and in promoting and encouraging respect for human rights and for fundamental freedoms for all without distinction as to race, sex, language or religion,

Mindful of the Universal Declaration of Human Rights, which declares in article 14 that:

"1. Everyone has the right to seek and to enjoy in other countries asylum from persecution.

"2. This right may not be invoked in the case of prosecutions genuinely arising from non-political crimes or from acts contrary to the purposes and principles of the United Nations",

Recalling also article 13, paragraph 2, of the Universal Declaration of Human Rights, which states:

"Everyone has the right to leave any country, including his own, and to return to his country",

Recognizing that the grant of asylum by a State to persons entitled to invoke article 14 of the Universal Declaration of Human Rights is a peaceful and humanitarian act and that, as such, it cannot be regarded as unfriendly by any other State,

Recommends that, without prejudice to existing instruments dealing with asylum and the status of refugees and stateless persons, States should base themselves in their practices relating to territorial asylum on the following principles:

Article 1

1. Asylum granted by a State, in the exercise of its sovereignty, to persons entitled to invoke article 14 of the Universal Declaration of Human Rights, including persons struggling against colonialism, shall be respected by all other States.

2. The right to seek and to enjoy asylum may not be invoked by any person with respect to whom there are serious reasons for considering that he has committed a crime against peace, a war crime or a crime against humanity, as defined in the international instruments drawn up to make provision in respect of such crimes.

3. It shall rest with the State granting asylum to evaluate the grounds for the grant of asylum.

Article 2

1. The situation of persons referred to in article 1, paragraph 1, is, without prejudice to the sovereignty of States and the purposes and principles of the United Nations, of concern to the international community.

2. Where a State finds difficulty in granting or continuing to grant asylum, States individually or jointly or through the United Nations shall consider, in a spirit of international solidarity, appropriate measures to lighten the burden on that State.

Article 3

1. No person referred to in article 1, paragraph 1, shall be subjected to measures such as rejection at the frontier or, if he has already entered the territory in which he seeks asylum, expulsion or compulsory return to any State where he may be subjected to persecution.

2. Exception may be made to the foregoing principle only for overriding reasons of national security or in order to safeguard the population, as in the case of a mass influx of persons.

3.   Should a State decide in any case that exception to the principle stated in paragraph 1 of this article would be justified, it shall consider the possibility of granting to the persons concerned, under such conditions as it may deem appropriate, an opportunity, whether by way of provisional asylum or otherwise, of going to another State.

Article 4

States granting asylum shall not permit persons who have received asylum to engage in activities contrary to the purposes and principles of the United Nations.

85. Declaration on the Human Rights of Individuals Who are not Nationals of the Country in which They Live

Adopted by General Assembly resolution 40/144 of 13 December 1985

The General Assembly,

Considering that the Charter of the United Nations encourages universal respect for and observance of the human rights and fundamental freedoms of all human beings, without distinction as to race, sex, language or religion,

Considering that the Universal Declaration of Human Rights proclaims that all human beings are born free and equal in dignity and rights and that everyone is entitled to all the rights and freedoms set forth in that Declaration, without distinction of any kind, such as race, colour, sex, language, religion, political or other opinion, national or social origin, property, birth or other status,

Considering that the Universal Declaration of Human Rights proclaims further that everyone has the right to recognition everywhere as a person before the law, that all are equal before the law and entitled without any discrimination to equal protection of the law, and that all are entitled to equal protection against any discrimination in violation of that Declaration and against any incitement to such discrimination,

Being aware that the States Parties to the International Covenants on Human Rights undertake to guarantee that the rights enunciated in these Covenants will be exercised without discrimination of any kind as to race, colour, sex, language, religion, political or other opinion, national or social origin, property, birth or other status,

Conscious that, with improving communications and the development of peaceful and friendly relations among countries, individuals increasingly live in countries of which they are not nationals,

Reaffirming the purposes and principles of the Charter of the United Nations,

Recognizing that the protection of human rights and fundamental freedoms provided for in international instruments should also be ensured for individuals who are not nationals of the country in which they live,

Proclaims this Declaration:

Article 1

For the purposes of this Declaration, the term "alien" shall apply, with due regard to qualifications made in subsequent articles, to any individual who is not a national of the State in which he or she is present.

Article 2

1. Nothing in this Declaration shall be interpreted as legitimizing the illegal entry into and presence in a State of any alien, nor shall any provision be interpreted as restricting the right of any State to promulgate laws and regulations concerning the entry of aliens and the terms and conditions of their stay or to establish differences between nationals and aliens. However, such laws and regulations shall not be incompatible with the international legal obligations of that State, including those in the field of human rights.

2. This Declaration shall not prejudice the enjoyment of the rights accorded by domestic law and of the rights which under international law a State is obliged to accord to aliens, even where this Declaration does not recognize such rights or recognizes them to a lesser extent.

Article 3

Every State shall make public its national legislation or regulations affecting aliens.

Article 4

Aliens shall observe the laws of the State in which they reside or are present and regard with respect the customs and traditions of the people of that State.

Article 5

1. Aliens shall enjoy, in accordance with domestic law and subject to the relevant international obligation of the State in which they are present, in particular the following rights:

(a) The right to life and security of person; no alien shall be subjected to arbitrary arrest or detention; no alien shall be deprived of his or her liberty except on such grounds and in accordance with such procedures as are established by law;

(b) The right to protection against arbitrary or unlawful interference with privacy, family, home or correspondence;

(c) The right to be equal before the courts, tribunals and all other organs and authorities administering justice and, when necessary, to free assistance of an interpreter in criminal proceedings and, when prescribed by law, other proceedings;

(d) The right to choose a spouse, to marry, to found a family;

(e) The right to freedom of thought, opinion, conscience and religion; the right to manifest their religion or beliefs, subject only to such limitations as are prescribed by law and are necessary to protect public safety, order, health or morals or the fundamental rights and freedoms of others;

(f) The right to retain their own language, culture and tradition;

(g) The right to transfer abroad earnings, savings or other personal monetary assets, subject to domestic currency regulations.

2. Subject to such restrictions as are prescribed by law and which are necessary in a democratic society to protect national security, public safety, public order, public health or morals or the rights and freedoms of others, and which are consistent with the other rights recognized in the relevant international instruments and those set forth in this Declaration, aliens shall enjoy the following rights:

(a) The right to leave the country;

(b) The right to freedom of expression;

(c) The right to peaceful assembly;

(d) The right to own property alone as well as in association with others, subject to domestic law.

3. Subject to the provisions referred to in paragraph 2, aliens lawfully in the territory of a State shall enjoy the right to liberty of movement and freedom to choose their residence within the borders of the State.

4. Subject to national legislation and due authorization, the spouse and minor or dependent children of an alien lawfully residing in the territory of a State shall be admitted to accompany, join and stay with the alien.

Article 6

No alien shall be subjected to torture or to cruel, inhuman or degrading treatment or punishment and, in particular, no alien shall be subjected without his or her free consent to medical or scientific experimentation.

Article 7

An alien lawfully in the territory of a State may be expelled therefrom only in pursuance of a decision reached in accordance with law and shall, except where compelling reasons of national security otherwise require, be allowed to submit the reasons why he or she should not be expelled and to have the case reviewed by, and be represented for the purpose before, the competent authority or a person or persons specially designated by the competent authority. Individual or collective expulsion of such aliens on grounds of race, colour, religion, culture, descent or national or ethnic origin is prohibited.

Article 8

1.   Aliens lawfully residing in the territory of a State shall also enjoy, in accordance with the national laws, the following rights, subject to their obligations under article 4:

(*a*) The right to safe and healthy working conditions, to fair wages and equal remuneration for work of equal value without distinction of any kind, in particular, women being guaranteed conditions of work not inferior to those enjoyed by men, with equal pay for equal work;

(*b*) The right to join trade unions and other organizations or associations of their choice and to participate in their activities. No restrictions may be placed on the exercise of this right other than those prescribed by law and which are necessary, in a democratic society, in the interests of national security or public order or for the protection of the rights and freedoms of others;

(*c*) The right to health protection, medical care, social security, social services, education, rest and leisure, provided that they fulfil the requirements under the relevant regulations for participation and that undue strain is not placed on the resources of the State.

2.   With a view to protecting the rights of aliens carrying on lawful paid activities in the country in which they are present, such rights may be specified by the Governments concerned in multilateral or bilateral conventions.

Article 9

No alien shall be arbitrarily deprived of his or her lawfully acquired assets.

Article 10

Any alien shall be free at any time to communicate with the consulate or diplomatic mission of the State of which he or she is a national or, in the absence thereof, with the consulate or diplomatic mission of any other State entrusted with the protection of the interests of the State of which he or she is a national in the State where he or she resides.

P. WAR CRIMES AND CRIMES AGAINST HUMANITY, INCLUDING GENOCIDE

86. Convention on the Prevention and Punishment of the Crime of Genocide

Approved and proposed for signature and ratification or accession by General Assembly resolution 260 A (III) of 9 December 1948

ENTRY INTO FORCE: 12 January 1951, in accordance with article XIII

The Contracting Parties,

Having considered the declaration made by the General Assembly of the United Nations in its resolution 96 (I) dated 11 December 1946 that genocide is a crime under international law, contrary to the spirit and aims of the United Nations and condemned by the civilized world,

Recognizing that at all periods of history genocide has inflicted great losses on humanity, and

Being convinced that, in order to liberate mankind from such an odious scourge, international co-operation is required,

Hereby agree as hereinafter provided:

Article I

The Contracting Parties confirm that genocide, whether committed in time of peace or in time of war, is a crime under international law which they undertake to prevent and to punish.

Article II

In the present Convention, genocide means any of the following acts committed with intent to destroy, in whole or in part, a national, ethnical, racial or religious group, as such:

(*a*) Killing members of the group;

(*b*) Causing serious bodily or mental harm to members of the group;

(*c*) Deliberately inflicting on the group conditions of life calculated to bring about its physical destruction in whole or in part;

(*d*) Imposing measures intended to prevent births within the group;

(*e*) Forcibly transferring children of the group to another group.

Article III

The following acts shall be punishable:

(*a*) Genocide;

(*b*) Conspiracy to commit gneocide;

(*c*) Direct and public incitement to commit genocide;

(*d*) Attempt to commit genocide;

(*e*) Complicity in genocide.

Article IV

Persons committing genocide or any of the other acts enumerated in article III shall be punished, whether they are constitutionally responsible rulers, public officials or private individuals.

Article V

The Contracting Parties undertake to enact, in accordance with their respective Constitutions, the necessary legislation to give effect to the provisions of the present Convention, and, in particular, to provide effective penalties for persons guilty of genocide or any of the other acts enumerated in article III.

Article VI

Persons charged with genocide or any of the other acts enumerated in article III shall be tried by a competent tribunal of the State in the territory of which the act was committed, or by such international penal tribunal as may have jurisdiction with respect to those Contracting Parties which shall have accepted its jurisdiction.

Article VII

Genocide and the other acts enumerated in article III shall not be considered as political crimes for the purpose of extradition.

The Contracting Parties pledge themselves in such cases to grant extradition in accordance with their laws and treaties in force.

Article VIII

Any Contracting Party may call upon the competent organs of the United Nations to take such action under the Charter of the United Nations as they consider appropriate for the prevention and suppression of acts of genocide or any of the other acts enumerated in article III.

Article IX

Disputes between the Contracting Parties relating to the interpretation, application or fulfilment of the present Convention, including those relating to the responsibility of a State for genocide or for any of the other acts enumerated in article III, shall be submitted to the International Court of Justice at the request of any of the parties to the dispute.

Article X

The present Convention, of which the Chinese, English, French, Russian and Spanish texts are equally authentic, shall bear the date of 9 December 1948.

Article XI

The present Convention shall be open until 31 December 1949 for signature on behalf of any Member of the United Nations and of any non-member State to which an invitation to sign has been addressed by the General Assembly.

The present Convention shall be ratified, and the instruments of ratification shall be deposited with the Secretary-General of the United Nations.

After 1 January 1950, the present Convention may be acceded to on behalf of any Member of the United Nations and of any non-member State which has received an invitation as aforesaid.

Instruments of accession shall be deposited with the Secretary-General of the United Nations.

Article XII

Any Contracting Party may at any time, by notification addressed to the Secretary-General of the United Nations, extend the application of the present Convention to all or any of the territories for the conduct of whose foreign relations that Contracting Party is responsible.

Article XIII

On the day when the first twenty instruments of ratification or accession have been deposited, the Secretary-General shall draw up a *procès-verbal* and transmit a copy thereof to each Member of the United Nations and to each of the non-member States contemplated in article XI.

The present Convention shall come into force on the ninetieth day following the date of deposit of the twentieth instrument of ratification or accession.

Any ratification or accession effected, subsequent to the latter date shall become effective on the ninetieth day following the deposit of the instrument of ratification or accession.

Article XIV

The present Convention shall remain in effect for a period of ten years as from the date of its coming into force.

It shall thereafter remain in force for successive periods of five years for such Contracting Parties as have not denounced it at least six months before the expiration of the current period.

Denunciation shall be effected by a written notification addressed to the Secretary-General of the United Nations.

Article XV

If, as a result of denunciations, the number of Parties to the present Convention should become less than sixteen, the Convention shall cease to be in force as from the date on which the last of these denunciations shall become effective.

Article XVI

A request for the revision of the present Convention may be made at any time by any Contracting Party by means of a notification in writing addressed to the Secretary-General.

The General Assembly shall decide upon the steps, if any, to be taken in respect of such request.

Article XVII

The Secretary-General of the United Nations shall notify all Members of the United Nations and the non-member States contemplated in article XI of the following:

(*a*) Signatures, ratifications and accessions received in accordance with article XI;

(*b*) Notifications received in accordance with article XII;

(*c*) The date upon which the present Convention comes into force in accordance with article XIII;

(*d*) Denunciations received in accordance with article XIV;

(*e*) The abrogation of the Convention in accordance with article XV;

(*f*) Notifications received in accordance with article XVI.

Article XVIII

The original of the present Convention shall be deposited in the archives of the United Nations.

A certified copy of the Convention shall be transmitted to each Member of the United Nations and to each of the non-member States contemplated in article XI.

Article XIX

The present Convention shall be registered by the Secretary-General of the United Nations on the date of its coming into force.

87. Convention on the Non-Applicability of Statutory Limitations to War Crimes and Crimes against Humanity

Adopted and opened for signature, ratification and accession by General Assembly resolution 2391 (XXIII) of 26 November 1968

ENTRY INTO FORCE: 11 November 1970, in accordance with article VIII

PREAMBLE

The States Parties to the present Convention,

Recalling resolutions of the General Assembly of the United Nations 3 (I) of 13 February 1946 and 170 (II) of 31 October 1947 on the extradition and punishment of war criminals, resolution 95 (I) of 11 December 1946 affirming the principles of international law recognized by the Charter of the International Military Tribunal, Nürnberg, and the judgement of the Tribunal, and resolutions 2184 (XXI) of 12 December 1966 and 2202 (XXI) of 16 December 1966 which expressly condemned as crimes against humanity the violation of the economic and political rights of the indigenous population on the one hand and the policies of *apartheid* on the other,

Recalling resolutions of the Economic and Social Council of the United Nations 1074 D (XXXIX) of 28 July 1965 and 1158 (XLI) of 5 August 1966 on the punishment of war criminals and of persons who have committed crimes against humanity,

Noting that none of the solemn declarations, instruments or conventions relating to the prosecution and punishment of war crimes and crimes against humanity made provision for a period of limitation,

Considering that war crimes and crimes against humanity are among the gravest crimes in international law,

Convinced that the effective punishment of war crimes and crimes against humanity is an important element in the prevention of such crimes, the protection of human rights and fundamental freedoms, the encouragement of confidence, the furtherance of co-operation among peoples and the promotion of international peace and security,

Noting that the application to war crimes and crimes against humanity of the rules of municipal law relating to the period of limitation for ordinary crimes is a matter of serious concern to world public opinion, since it prevents the prosecution and punishment of persons responsible for those crimes,

Recognizing that it is necessary and timely to affirm in international law, through this Convention, the principle that there is no period of limitation for war crimes and crimes against humanity, and to secure its universal application,

Have agreed as follows:

Article I

No statutory limitation shall apply to the following crimes, irrespective of the date of their commission:

(*a*) War crimes as they are defined in the Charter of the International Military Tribunal, Nürnberg, of 8 August 1945 and confirmed by resolutions 3 (I) of 13 February 1946 and 95 (I) of 11 December 1946 of the General Assembly of the United Nations, particularly the "grave breaches" enumerated in the Geneva Conventions of 12 August 1949 for the protection of war victims;

(*b*) Crimes against humanity whether committed in time of war or in time of peace as they are defined in the Charter of the International Military Tribunal, Nürnberg, of 8 August 1945 and confirmed by resolutions 3 (I) of 13 February 1946 and 95 (I) of 11 December 1946 of the General Assembly of the United Nations, eviction by armed attack or occupation and inhuman acts resulting from the policy of *apartheid,* and the crime of genocide as defined in the 1948 Convention on the Prevention and Punishment of the Crime of Genocide, even if such acts do not constitute a violation of the domestic law of the country in which they were committed.

Article II

If any of the crimes mentioned in article I is committed, the provisions of this Convention shall apply to representatives of the State authority and private individuals who, as principals or accomplices, participate in or who directly incite others to the commission of any of those crimes, or who conspire to commit them, irrespective of the degree of completion, and to representatives of the State authority who tolerate their commission.

Article III

The States Parties to the present Convention undertake to adopt all necessary domestic measures, legislative or otherwise, with a view to making possible the extradition, in accordance with international law, of the persons referred to in article II of this Convention.

Article IV

The States Parties to the present Convention undertake to adopt, in accordance with their respective constitutional processes, any legislative or other measures necessary to ensure that statutory or other limitations shall not apply to the prosecution and punishment of the crimes referred to in articles I and II of this Convention and that, where they exist, such limitations shall be abolished.

Article V

This Convention shall, until 31 December 1969, be open for signature by any State Member of the United Nations or member of any of its specialized agencies or of the International Atomic Energy Agency, by any State Party to the Statute of the International Court of Justice, and by any other State which has been invited by the General Assembly of the United Nations to become a Party to this Convention.

Article VI

This Convention is subject to ratification. Instruments of ratification shall be deposited with the Secretary-General of the United Nations.

Article VII

This Convention shall be open to accession by any State referred to in article V. Instruments of accession shall be deposited with the Secretary-General of the United Nations.

Article VIII

1.   This Convention shall enter into force on the ninetieth day after the date of the deposit with the Secretary-General of the United Nations of the tenth instrument of ratification or accession.

2.   For each State ratifying this Convention or acceding to it after the deposit of the tenth instrument of ratification or accession, the Convention shall enter into force on the ninetieth day after the date of the deposit of its own instrument of ratification or accession.

Article IX

1.   After the expiry of a period of ten years from the date on which this Convention enters into force, a request for the revision of the Convention may be made at any time by any Contracting Party by means of a notification in writing addressed to the Secretary-General of the United Nations.

2. The General Assembly of the United Nations shall decide upon the steps, if any, to be taken in respect of such a request.

Article X

1. This Convention shall be deposited with the Secretary-General of the United Nations.

2. The Secretary-General of the United Nations shall transmit certified copies of this Convention to all States referred to in article V.

3. The Secretary-General of the United Nations shall inform all States referred to in article V of the following particulars:

(*a*) Signatures of this Convention, and instruments of ratification and accession deposited under articles V, VI and VII;

(*b*) The date of entry into force of this Convention in accordance with article VIII;

(*c*) Communications received under article IX.

Article XI

This Convention, of which the Chinese, English, French, Russian and Spanish texts are equally authentic, shall bear the date of 26 November 1968.

IN WITNESS WHEREOF the undersigned, being duly authorized for that purpose, have signed this Convention.

88. Principles of international co-operation in the detection, arrest, extradition and punishment of persons guilty of war crimes and crimes against humanity

General Assembly resolution 3074 (XXVIII) of 3 December 1973

The General Assembly,

Recalling its resolutions 2583 (XXIV) of 15 December 1969, 2712 (XXV) of 15 December 1970, 2840 (XXVI) of 18 December 1971 and 3020 (XXVII) of 18 December 1972,

Taking into account the special need for international action in order to ensure the prosecution and punishment of persons guilty of war crimes and crimes against humanity,

Having considered the draft principles of international co-operation in the detection, arrest, extradition and punishment of persons guilty of war crimes and crimes against humanity,

Declares that the United Nations, in pursuance of the principles and purposes set forth in the Charter concerning the promotion of co-operation between peoples and the maintenance of international peace and security, proclaims the following principles of international co-operation in the detection, arrest, extradition and punishment of persons guilty of war crimes and crimes against humanity:

1. War crimes and crimes against humanity, wherever they are committed, shall be subject to investigation and the persons against whom there is evidence that they have committed such crimes shall be subject to tracing, arrest, trial and, if found guilty, to punishment.

2. Every State has the right to try its own nationals for war crimes against humanity.

3. States shall co-operate with each other on a bilateral and multilateral basis with a view to halting and preventing war crimes and crimes against humanity, and shall take the domestic and international measures necessary for that purpose.

4. States shall assist each other in detecting, arresting and bringing to trial persons suspected of having committed such crimes and, if they are found guilty, in punishing them.

5. Persons against whom there is evidence that they have committed war crimes and crimes against humanity shall be subject to trial and, if found guilty, to punishment, as a general rule in the countries in which they committed those crimes. In that connection, States shall co-operate on questions of extraditing such persons.

6. States shall co-operate with each other in the collection of information and evidence which would help to bring to trial the persons indicated in paragraph 5 above and shall exchange such information.

7. In accordance with article 1 of the Declaration on Territorial Asylum of 14 December 1967, States shall not grant asylum to any person with respect to whom there are serious reasons for considering that he has committed a crime against peace, a war crime or a crime against humanity.

8. States shall not take any legislative or other measures which may be prejudicial to the international obligations they have assumed in regard to the detection, arrest, extradition and punishment of persons guilty of war crimes and crimes against humanity.

9. In co-operating with a view to the detection, arrest and extradition of persons against whom there is evidence that they have committed war crimes and crimes against humanity and, if found guilty, their punishment, States shall act in conformity with the provisions of the Charter of the United Nations and of the Declaration on Principles of International Law concerning Friendly Relations and Co-operation among States in accordance with the Charter of the United Nations.

Q. HUMANITARIAN LAW

89. Geneva Convention for the Amelioration of the Condition of the Wounded and Sick in Armed Forces in the Field

Adopted on 12 August 1949 by the Diplomatic Conference for the Establishment of International Conventions for the Protection of Victims of War, held in Geneva from 21 April to 12 August, 1949

ENTRY INTO FORCE: 21 October 1950

CHAPTER I

GENERAL PROVISIONS

Article 1

The High Contracting Parties undertake to respect and to ensure respect for the present Convention in all circumstances.

Article 2

In addition to the provisions which shall be implemented in peacetime, the present Convention shall apply to all cases of declared war or of any other armed conflict which may arise between two or more of the High Contracting Parties, even if the state of war is not recognized by one of them.

The Convention shall also apply to all cases of partial or total occupation of the territory of a High Contracting Party, even if the said occupation meets with no armed resistance.

Although one of the Powers in conflict may not be a party to the present Convention, the Powers who are parties thereto shall remain bound by it in their mutual relations. They shall furthermore be bound by the Convention in relation to the said Power, if the latter accepts and applies the provisions thereof.

Article 3

In the case of armed conflict not of an international character occurring in the territory of one of the High Contracting Parties, each Party to the conflict shall be bound to apply, as a minimum, the following provisions:

1.   Persons taking no active part in the hostilities, including members of armed forces who have laid down their arms and those placed *hors de combat* by sickness, wounds, detention, or any other cause, shall in all circumstances be treated humanely, without any adverse distinction founded on race, colour, religion or faith, sex, birth or wealth, or any other similar criteria.

To this end, the following acts are and shall remain prohibited at any time and in any place whatsoever with respect to the above-mentioned persons:

(*a*)   Violence to life and person, in particular murder of all kinds, mutilation, cruel treatment and torture;

(*b*)   Taking of hostages;

(*c*)   Outrages upon personal dignity, in particular humiliating and degrading treatment;

(*d*)   The passing of sentences and the carrying out of executions without previous judgment pronounced by a regularly constituted court, affording all the judicial guarantees which are recognized as indispensable by civilized peoples.

2.   The wounded and sick shall be collected and cared for.

An impartial humanitarian body, such as the International Committee of the Red Cross, may offer its services to the Parties to the conflict.

The Parties to the conflict should further endeavour to bring into force, by means of special agreements, all or part of the other provisions of the present Convention.

The application of the preceding provisions shall not affect the legal status of the Parties to the conflict.

Article 4

Neutral Powers shall apply by analogy the provisions of the present Convention to the wounded and sick, and to members of the medical personnel and to chaplains of the armed forces of the Parties to the conflict, received or interned in their territory, as well as to dead persons found.

Article 5

For the protected persons who have fallen into the hands of the enemy, the present Convention shall apply until their final repatriation.

Article 6

In addition to the agreements expressly provided for in Articles 10, 15, 23, 28, 31, 36, 37 and 52, the High Contracting Parties may conclude other special agreements for all matters concerning which they may deem it suitable to make separate provision. No special agreement shall adversely affect the situation of the wounded and sick, of members of the medical personnel or of chaplains, as defined by the present Convention, nor restrict the rights which it confers upon them.

Wounded and sick, as well as medical personnel and chaplains, shall continue to have the benefit of such agreements as long as the Convention is applicable to them, except where express provisions to the contrary are contained in the aforesaid or in subsequent agreements, or where more favourable measures have been taken with regard to them by one or other of the Parties to the conflict.

Article 7

Wounded and sick, as well as members of the medical personnel and chaplains, may in no circumstances renounce in part or in entirety the rights secured to them by the present Convention, and by the special agreements referred to in the foregoing Article, if such there be.

Article 8

The present Convention shall be applied with the cooperation and under the scrutiny of the Protecting Powers whose duty it is to safeguard the interests of the Parties to the conflict. For this purpose, the Protecting Powers may appoint, apart from their diplomatic or consular staff, delegates from amongst their own nationals or the nationals of other neutral Powers. The said delegates shall be subject to the approval of the Power with which they are to carry out their duties.

The Parties to the conflict shall facilitate, to the greatest extent possible, the task of the representatives or delegates of the Protecting Powers.

The representatives or delegates of the Protecting Powers shall not in any case exceed their mission under the present Convention. They shall, in particular, take account of the imperative necessities of security of the State wherein they carry out their duties. Their activities shall only be restricted as an exceptional and temporary measure when this is rendered necessary by imperative military necessities.

Article 9

The provisions of the present Convention constitute no obstacle to the humanitarian activities which the International Committee of the Red Cross or any other impartial humanitarian organization may, subject to the consent of the Parties to the conflict concerned, undertake for the protection of wounded and sick, medical personnel and chaplains, and for their relief.

Article 10

The High Contracting Parties may at any time agree to entrust to an organization which offers all guarantees of impartiality and efficacy the duties incumbent on the Protecting Powers by virtue of the present Convention.

When wounded and sick, or medical personnel and chaplains do not benefit or cease to benefit, no matter for what reason, by the activities of a Protecting Power or of an organization provided for in the first paragraph above, the Detaining Power shall request a neutral State, or such an organization, to undertake the functions performed under the present Convention by a Protecting Power designated by the Parties to a conflict.

If protection cannot be arranged accordingly, the Detaining Power shall request or shall accept, subject to the provisions of this Article, the offer of the services of a humanitarian organization, such as the International Committee of the Red Cross, to assume the humanitarian functions performed by Protecting Powers under the present Convention.

Any neutral Power, or any organization invited by the Power concerned or offering itself for these purposes, shall be required to act with a sense of responsibility towards the Party to the conflict on which persons protected by the present Convention depend, and shall be required to furnish sufficient assurances that it is a position to undertake the appropriate functions and to discharge them impartially.

No derogation from the preceding provisions shall be made by special agreements between Powers one of which is restricted, even temporarily, in its freedom to negotiate with the other Power or its allies by reason of military events, more particularly where the whole, or a substantial part, of the territory of the said Power is occupied.

Whenever in the present Convention mention is made of a Protecting Power, such mention also applies to substitute organizations in the sense of the present Article.

Article 11

In cases where they deem it advisable in the interest of protected persons, particularly in cases of disagreement between the Parties to the conflict as to the application or interpretation of the provisions of the present Convention, the Protecting Powers shall lend their good offices with a view to settling the disagreement.

For this purpose, each of the Protecting Powers may, either at the invitation of one Party or on its own initiative, propose to the Parties to the conflict a meeting of their representatives, in particular of the authorities responsible for the wounded and sick, members of medical personnel and chaplains, possibly on neutral territory suitably chosen. The Parties to the conflict shall be bound to give effect to the proposals made to them for this purpose. The Protecting Powers may, if necessary, propose for approval by the Parties to the conflict a person belonging to a neutral Power or delegated by the International Committee of the Red Cross, who shall be invited to take part in such a meeting.

CHAPTER II

WOUNDED AND SICK

Article 12

Members of the armed forces and other persons mentioned in the following Article, who are wounded or sick, shall be respected and protected in all circumstances.

They shall be treated humanely and cared for by the Party to the conflict in whose power they may be, without any adverse distinction founded on sex, race, nationality, religion, political opinions, or any other similar criteria. Any attempts upon their lives, or violence to their persons, shall be strictly prohibited; in particular, they shall not be murdered or exterminated, subjected to torture or to biological experiments; they shall not wilfully be left without medical assistance and care, nor shall conditions exposing them to contagion or infection be created.

Only urgent medical reasons will authorize priority in the order of treatment to be administered.

Women shall be treated with all consideration due to their sex.

The Party to the conflict which is compelled to abandon wounded or sick to the enemy shall, as far as military considerations permit, leave with them a part of its medical personnel and material to assist in their care.

Article 13

The present Convention shall apply to the wounded and sick belonging to the following categories:

1.   Members of the armed forces of a Party to the conflict as well as members of militias or volunteer corps forming part of such armed forces.

2. Members of other militias and members of other volunteer corps, including those of organized resistance movements, belonging to a Party to the conflict and operating in or outside their own territory, even if this territory is occupied, provided that such militias or volunteer corps, including such organized resistance movements, fulfil the following conditions:

(a) That of being commanded by a person responsible for his subordinates;

(b) That of having a fixed distinctive sign recognizable at a distance;

(c) That of carrying arms openly;

(d) That of conducting their operations in accordance with the laws and customs of war.

3. Members of regular armed forces who profess allegiance to a Government or an authority not recognized by the Detaining Power.

4. Persons who accompany the armed forces without actually being members thereof, such as civil members of military aircraft crews, war correspondents, supply contractors, members of labour units or of services responsible for the welfare of the armed forces, provided that they have received authorization from the armed forces which they accompany.

5. Members of crews, including masters, pilots and apprentices of the merchant marine and the crews of civil aircraft of the Parties to the conflict, who do not benefit by more favourable treatment under any other provisions in international law.

6. Inhabitants of a non-occupied territory who on the approach of the enemy spontaneously take up arms to resist the invading forces, without having had time to form themselves into regular armed units, provided they carry arms openly and respect the laws and customs of war.

Article 14

Subject to the provisions of Article 12, the wounded and sick of a belligerent who fall into enemy hands shall be prisoners of war, and the provisions of international law concerning prisoners of war shall apply to them.

Article 15

At all times, and particularly after an engagement, Parties to the conflict shall, without delay, take all possible measures to search for and collect the wounded and sick, to protect them against pillage and ill-treatment, to ensure their adequate care, and to search for the dead and prevent their being despoiled.

Whenever circumstances permit, an armistice or a suspension of fire shall be arranged, or local arrangements made, to permit the removal, exchange and transport of the wounded left on the battlefield.

Likewise, local arrangements may be concluded between Parties to the conflict for the removal or exchange of wounded and sick from a besieged or encircled area, and for the passage of medical and religious personnel and equipment on their way to that area.

Article 16

Parties to the conflict shall record as soon as possible, in respect of each wounded, sick or dead person of the adverse Party falling into their hands, any particulars which may assist in his identification.

These records should if possible include:

(a) Designation of the Power on which he depends;

(b) Army, regimental, personal or serial number;

(c) Surname;

(d) First name or names;

(e) Date of birth;

(f) Any other particulars shown on his identity card or disc;

(g) Date and place of capture or death;

(h) Particulars concerning wounds or illness, or cause of death.

As soon as possible the above mentioned information shall be forwarded to the Information Bureau described in Article 122 of the Geneva Convention relative to the Treatment of Prisoners of War of August 12, 1949, which shall transmit this information to the Power on which these persons depend through the intermediary of the Protecting Power and of the Central Prisoners of War Agency.

Parties to the conflict shall prepare and forward to each other through the same bureau, certificates of death or duly authenticated lists of the dead. They shall likewise collect and forward through the same bureau one half of a double identity disc, last wills or other documents of importance to the next of kin, money and in general all articles of an intrinsic or sentimental value, which are found on the dead. These articles, together with unidentified articles, shall be sent in sealed packets, accompanied by statements giving all particulars necessary for the identification of the deceased owners, as well as by a complete list of the contents of the parcel.

Article 17

Parties to the conflict shall ensure that burial or cremation of the dead, carried out individually as far as circumstances permit, is preceded by a careful examination, if possible by a medical examination, of the bodies, with a view to confirming death, establishing identity and enabling a report to be made. One half of the double identity disc, or the identity disc itself if it is a single disc, should remain on the body.

Bodies shall not be cremated except for imperative reasons of hygiene or for motives based on the religion of the deceased. In case of cremation, the circumstances and reasons for cremation shall be stated in detail in the death certificate or on the authenticated list of the dead.

They shall further ensure that the dead are honourably interred, if possible according to the rites of the religion to which they belonged, that their graves are respected, grouped if possible according to the nationality of the deceased, properly maintained and marked so that they may always be found. For this purpose, they shall organize at the commencement of hostilities an Official Graves Registration Service, to allow subsequent exhumations and to ensure the identification of bodies, whatever the site of the graves, and the possible transportation to the home country. These provisions shall likewise apply to the ashes, which shall be kept by the Graves Registration Service until proper disposal thereof in accordance with the wishes of the home country.

As soon as circumstances permit, and at latest at the end of hostilities, these Services shall exchange, through the Information Bureau mentioned in the second paragraph of Article 16, lists showing the exact location and markings of the graves together with particulars of the dead interred therein.

Article 18

The military authorities may appeal to the charity of the inhabitants voluntarily to collect and care for, under their direction, the wounded and sick, granting persons who have responded to this appeal the necessary protection and facilities. Should the adverse party take or retake control of the area, he shall likewise grant these persons the same protection and the same facilities.

The military authorities shall permit the inhabitants and relief societies, even in invaded or occupied areas, spontaneously to collect and care for wounded or sick of whatever nationality. The civilian population shall respect these wounded and sick, and in particular abstain from offering them violence.

No one may ever be molested or convicted for having nursed the wounded or sick.

The provisions of the present Article do not relieve the occupying Power of its obligation to give both physical and moral care to the wounded and sick.

CHAPTER III

MEDICAL UNITS AND ESTABLISHMENTS

Article 19

Fixed establishments and mobile medical units of the Medical Service may in no circumstances be attacked, but shall at all times be respected and protected by the Parties to the conflict. Should they fall into the hands of the adverse Party, their personnel shall be free to pursue their duties, as long as the capturing Power has not itself ensured the necessary care of the wounded and sick found in such establishments and units.

The responsible authorities shall ensure that the said medical establishments and units are, as far as possible, situated in such a manner that attacks against military objectives cannot imperil their safety.

Article 20

Hospital ships entitled to the protection of the Geneva Convention for the Amelioration of the Condition of Wounded, Sick and Shipwrecked Members of Armed Forces at Sea of August 12, 1949, shall not be attacked from the land.

Article 21

The protection to which fixed establishments and mobile medical units of the Medical Service are entitled shall not cease unless they are used to commit, outside their humanitarian duties, acts harmful to the enemy. Protection may, however, cease only after a due warning has been given, naming, in all appropriate cases, a reasonable time limit and after such warning has remained unheeded.

Article 22

The following conditions shall not be considered as depriving a medical unit or establishment of the protection guaranteed by Article 19:

1. That the personnel of the unit or establishment are armed, and that they use the arms in their own defence, or in that of the wounded and sick in their charge.

2. That in the absence of armed orderlies, the unit or establishment is protected by a picket or by sentries or by an escort.

3. That small arms and ammunition taken from the wounded and sick and not yet handed to the proper service, are found in the unit or establishment.

4.   That personnel and material of the veterinary service are found in the unit or establishment, without forming an integral part thereof.

5.   That the humanitarian activities of medical units and establishments or of their personnel extend to the care of civilian wounded or sick.

Article 23

In time of peace, the High Contracting Parties and, after the outbreak of hostilities, the Parties to the conflict may establish in their own territory and, if the need arises, in occupied areas, hospital zones and localities so organized as to protect the wounded and sick from the effects of war, as well as the personnel entrusted with the organization and administration of these zones and localities and with the care of the persons therein assembled.

Upon the outbreak and during the course of hostilities, the Parties concerned may conclude agreements on mutual recognition of the hospital zones and localities they have created. They may for this purpose implement the provisions of the Draft Agreement annexed to the present Convention, with such amendments as they may consider necessary.

The Protecting Powers and the International Committee of the Red Cross are invited to lend their good offices in order to facilitate the institution and recognition of these hospital zones and localities.

Chapter IV

PERSONNEL

Article 24

Medical personnel exclusively engaged in the search for, or the collection, transport or treatment of the wounded or sick, or in the prevention of disease, staff exclusively engaged in the administration of medical units and establishments, as well as chaplains attached to the armed forces, shall be respected and protected in all circumstances.

Article 25

Members of the armed forces specially trained for employment, should the need arise, as hospital orderlies, nurses or auxiliary stretcher-bearers, in the search for or the collection, transport or treatment of the wounded and sick shall likewise be respected and protected if they are carrying out these duties at the time when they come into contact with the enemy or fall into his hands.

Article 26

The staff of National Red Cross Societies and that of other Voluntary Aid Societies, duly recognized and authorized by their Governments, who may be employed on the same duties as the personnel named in Article 24, are placed on the same footing as the personnel named in the said Article, provided that the staff of such societies are subject to military laws and regulations.

Each High Contracting Party shall notify to the other, either in time of peace or at the commencement of or during hostilities, but in any case before actually employing them, the names of the societies which it has authorized, under its responsibility, to render assistance to the regular medical service of its armed forces.

Article 27

A recognized Society of a neutral country can only lend the assistance of its medical personnel and units to a Party to the conflict with the previous consent of its own Government and the authorization of the Party to the conflict concerned. That personnel and those units shall be placed under the control of that Party to the conflict.

The neutral Government shall notify this consent to the adversary of the State which accepts such assistance. The Party to the conflict who accepts such assistance is bound to notify the adverse Party thereof before making any use of it.

In no circumstances shall this assistance be considered as interference in the conflict.

The members of the personnel named in the first paragraph shall be duly furnished with the identity cards provided for in Article 40 before leaving the neutral country to which they belong.

Article 28

Personnel designated in Articles 24 and 26 who fall into the hands of the adverse Party shall be retained only in so far as the state of health, the spiritual needs and the number of prisoners of war require.

Personnel thus retained shall not be deemed prisoners of war. Nevertheless, they shall at least benefit by all the provisions of the Geneva Convention relative to the Treatment of Prisoners of War of August 12, 1949. Within the framework of the military laws and regulations of the Detaining Power, and under the authority of its competent service, they shall continue to carry out, in accordance with their professional ethics, their medical and spiritual duties on behalf of prisoners of war, preferably those of the armed forces to which they themselves belong. They shall further enjoy the following facilities for carrying out their medical or spiritual duties:

(*a*) They shall be authorized to visit periodically the prisoners of war in labour units or hospitals outside the camp. The Detaining Power shall put at their disposal the means of transport required.

(*b*) In each camp the senior medical officer of the highest rank shall be responsible to the military authorities of the camp for the professional activity of the retained medical personnel. For this purpose, from the outbreak of hostilities, the Parties to the conflict shall agree regarding the corresponding seniority of the ranks of their medical personnel, including those of the societies designated in Article 26. In all questions arising out of their duties, this medical officer and the chaplains, shall have direct access to the military and medical authorities of the camp who shall grant them the facilities they may require for correspondence relating to these questions.

(*c*) Although retained personnel in a camp shall be subject to its internal discipline, they shall not, however, be required to perform any work outside their medical or religious duties.

During hostilities the Parties to the conflict shall make arrangements for relieving where possible retained personnel, and shall settle the procedure of such relief.

None of the preceding provisions shall relieve the Detaining Power of the obligations imposed upon it with regard to the medical and spiritual welfare of the prisoners of war.

Article 29

Members of the personnel designated in Article 25 who have fallen into the hands of the enemy shall be prisoners of war, but shall be employed on their medical duties in so far as the need arises.

Article 30

Personnel whose retention is not indispensable by virtue of the provisions of Article 28 shall be returned to the Party to the conflict to whom they belong, as soon as a road is open for their return and military requirements permit.

Pending their return, they shall not be deemed prisoners of war. Nevertheless, they shall at least benefit by all the provisions of the Geneva Convention relative to the Treatment of Prisoners of War of August 12, 1949. They shall continue to fulfil their duties under the orders of the adverse Party and shall preferably be engaged in the care of the wounded and sick of the Party to the conflict to which they themselves belong.

On their departure, they shall take with them the effects, personal belongings, valuables and instruments belonging to them.

Article 31

The selection of personnel for return under Article 30 shall be made irrespective of any consideration of race, religion or political opinion, but preferably according to the chronological order of their capture and their state of health.

As from the outbreak of hostilities, Parties to the conflict may determine by special agreement the percentage of personnel to be retained, in proportion to the number of prisoners and the distribution of the said personnel in the camps.

Article 32

Persons designated in Article 27 who have fallen into the hands of the adverse Party may not be detained.

Unless otherwise agreed, they shall have permission to return to their country, or if this is not possible, to the territory of the Party to the conflict in whose service they were, as soon as a route for their return is open and military considerations permit.

Pending their release, they shall continue their work under the direction of the adverse Party; they shall preferably be engaged in the care of the wounded and sick of the Party to the conflict in whose service they were.

On their departure, they shall take with them their effects, personal articles and valuables and the instruments, arms and if possible the means of transport belonging to them.

The Parties to the conflict shall secure to this personnel, while in their power, the same food, lodging, allowances and pay as are granted to the corresponding personnel of their armed forces. The food shall in any case be sufficient as regards quantity, quality and variety to keep the said personnel in a normal state of health.

CHAPTER V

BUILDINGS AND MATERIAL

Article 33

The material of mobile medical units of the armed forces which fall into the hands of the enemy shall be reserved for the care of wounded and sick.

The buildings, material and stores of fixed medical establishments of the armed forces shall remain subject to the laws of war, but may not be diverted from that purpose as long as they are required for the care of wounded and sick. Nevertheless, the commanders of forces in the field may make use of them, in case of urgent military necessity, provided that they make previous arrangements for the welfare of the wounded and sick who are nursed in them.

The material and stores defined in the present Article shall not be intentionally destroyed.

Article 34

The real and personal property of aid societies which are admitted to the privileges of the Convention shall be regarded as private property.

The right of requisition recognized for belligerents by the laws and customs of war shall not be exercised except in case of urgent necessity, and only after the welfare of the wounded and sick has been ensured.

CHAPTER VI

MEDICAL TRANSPORTS

Article 35

Transports of wounded and sick or of medical equipment shall be respected and protected in the same way as mobile medical units.

Should such transports or vehicles fall into the hands of the adverse Party, they shall be subject to the laws of war, on condition that the Party to the conflict who captures them shall in all cases ensure the care of the wounded and sick they contain.

The civilian personnel and all means of transport obtained by requisition shall be subject to the general rules of international law.

Article 36

Medical aircraft, that is to say, aircraft exclusively employed for the removal of wounded and sick and for the transport of medical personnel and equipment, shall not be attacked, but shall be respected by the belligerents, while flying at heights, times and on routes specifically agreed upon between the belligerents concerned.

They shall bear, clearly marked, the distinctive emblem prescribed in Article 38, together with their national colours, on their lower, upper and lateral surfaces. They shall be provided with any other markings or means of identification that may be agreed upon between the belligerents upon the outbreak or during the course of hostilities.

Unless agreed otherwise, flights over enemy or enemy-occupied territory are prohibited.

Medical aircraft shall obey every summons to land. In the event of a landing thus imposed, the aircraft with its occupants may continue its flight after examination, if any.

In the event of an involuntary landing in enemy or enemy-occupied territory, the wounded and sick, as well as the crew of the aircraft shall be prisoners of war. The medical personnel shall be treated according to Article 24, and the Articles following.

Article 37

Subject to the provisions of the second paragraph, medical aircraft of Parties to the conflict may fly over the territory of neutral Powers, land on it in case of necessity, or use it as a port of call. They shall give the neutral Powers previous notice of their passage over the said territory and obey all summons to alight, on land or water. They will be immune from attack only when flying on routes, at heights and at times specifically agreed upon between the Parties to the conflict and the neutral Power concerned.

The neutral Powers may, however, place conditions or restrictions on the passage or landing of medical aircraft on their territory. Such possible conditions or restrictions shall be applied equally to all Parties to the conflict.

Unless agreed otherwise between the neutral Power and the Parties to the conflict, the wounded and sick who are disembarked, with the consent of the local authorities, on neutral territory by medical aircraft, shall be detained by the neutral Power, where so required by international law, in such a manner that they cannot again take part in operations of war. The cost of their accommodation and internment shall be borne by the Power on which they depend.

CHAPTER VII

THE DISTINCTIVE EMBLEM

Article 38

As a compliment to Switzerland, the heraldic emblem of the red cross on a white ground, formed by reversing the Federal colours, is retained as the emblem and distinctive sign of the Medical Service of armed forces.

Nevertheless, in the case of countries which already use as emblem, in place of the red cross, the red crescent or the red lion and sun on a white ground, those emblems are also recognized by the terms of the present Convention.

Article 39

Under the direction of the competent military authority, the emblem shall be displayed on the flags, armlets and on all equipment employed in the Medical Service.

Article 40

The personnel designated in Article 24 and in Articles 26 and 27 shall wear, affixed to the left arm, a water-resistant armlet bearing the distinctive emblem, issued and stamped by the military authority.

Such personnel, in addition to wearing the identity disc mentioned in Article 16, shall also carry a special identity card bearing the distinctive emblem. This card shall be water-resistant and of such size that it can be carried in the pocket. It shall be worded in the national language, shall mention at least the surname and first names, the date of birth, the rank and the service number of the bearer, and shall state in what capacity he is entitled to the protection of the present Convention. The card shall bear the photograph of the owner and also either his signature or his finger-prints or both. It shall be embossed with the stamp of the military authority.

The identity card shall be uniform throughout the same armed forces and, as far as possible, of a similar type in the armed forces of the High Contracting Parties. The Parties to the conflict may be guided by the model which is annexed, by way of example, to the present Convention. They shall inform each other, at the outbreak of hostilities, of the model they are using. Identity cards should be made out, if possible, at least in duplicate, one copy being kept by the home country.

In no circumstances may the said personnel be deprived of their insignia or identity cards nor of the right to wear the armlet. In case of loss, they shall be entitled to receive duplicates of the cards and to have the insignia replaced.

Article 41

The personnel designated in Article 25 shall wear, but only while carrying out medical duties, a white armlet bearing in its centre the distinctive sign in miniature; the armlet shall be issued and stamped by the military authority.

Military identity documents to be carried by this type of personnel shall specify what special training they have received, the temporary character of the duties they are engaged upon, and their authority for wearing the armlet.

Article 42

The distinctive flag of the Convention shall be hoisted only over such medical units and establishments as are entitled to be respected under the Convention, and only with the consent of the military authorities.

In mobile units, as in fixed establishments, it may be accompanied by the national flag of the Party to the conflict to which the unit or establishment belongs.

Nevertheless, medical units which have fallen into the hands of the enemy shall not fly any flag other than that of the Convention.

Parties to the conflict shall take the necessary steps, in so far as military considerations permit, to make the distinctive emblems indicating medical units and establishments clearly visible to the enemy land, air or naval forces, in order to obviate the possibility of any hostile action.

Article 43

The medical units belonging to neutral countries, which may have been authorized to lend their services to a belligerent under the conditions laid down in Article 27, shall fly, along with the flag of the Convention, the national flag of that belligerent, wherever the latter makes use of the faculty conferred on him by Article 42.

Subject to orders to the contrary by the responsible military authorities, they may, on all occasions, fly their national flag, even if they fall into the hands of the adverse Party.

Article 44

With the exception of the cases mentioned in the following paragraphs of the present Article, the emblem of the Red Cross on a white ground and the words "Red Cross", or "Geneva Cross" may not be employed, either in time of peace or in time of war, except to indicate or to protect the medical units and establishments, the personnel and material protected by the present Convention and other Conventions dealing with similar matters. The same shall apply to the emblems mentioned in Article 38, second paragraph, in respect of the countries which use them. The National Red Cross Societies and other Societies designated in Article 26 shall have the right to use the distinctive emblem conferring the protection of the Convention only within the framework of the present paragraph.

Furthermore, National Red Cross (Red Crescent, Red Lion and Sun) Societies may, in time of peace, in accordance with their national legislation, make use of the name and emblem of the Red Cross for their other activities which are in conformity with the principles laid down by the International Red Cross Conferences. When those activities are carried out in time of war, the conditions for the use of the emblem shall be such that it cannot be considered as conferring the protection of the Convention; the emblem shall be comparatively small in size and may not be placed on armlets or on the roofs of buildings.

The international Red Cross organizations and their duly authorized personnel shall be permitted to make use, at all times, of the emblem of the Red Cross on a white ground.

As an exceptional measure, in conformity with national legislation and with the express permission of one of the National Red Cross (Red Crescent, Red Lion and Sun) Societies, the emblem of the Convention may be employed in time of peace to identify vehicles used as ambulances and to mark the position of aid stations exclusively assigned to the purpose of giving free treatment to the wounded or sick.

CHAPTER VIII

EXECUTION OF THE CONVENTION

Article 45

Each Party to the conflict, acting through its commanders-in-chief, shall ensure the detailed execution of the preceding Articles and provide for unforeseen cases, in conformity with the general principles of the present Convention.

Article 46

Reprisals against the wounded, sick, personnel, buildings or equipment protected by the Convention are prohibited.

Article 47

The High Contracting Parties undertake, in time of peace as in time of war, to disseminate the text of the present Convention as widely as possible in their respective countries, and, in particular, to include the study thereof in their programmes of military and, if possible, civil instruction, so that the principles thereof may become known to the entire population, in particular to the armed fighting forces, the medical personnel and the chaplains.

Article 48

The High Contracting Parties shall communicate to one another through the Swiss Federal Council and, during hostilities, through the Protecting Powers, the official translations of the present Convention, as well as the laws and regulations which they may adopt to ensure the application thereof.

CHAPTER IX

REPRESSION OF ABUSES AND INFRACTIONS

Article 49

The High Contracting Parties undertake to enact any legislation necessary to provide effective penal sanctions for persons committing, or ordering to be committed, any of the grave breaches of the present Convention defined in the following Article.

Each High Contracting Party shall be under the obligation to search for persons alleged to have committed, or to have ordered to be committed, such grave breaches, and shall bring such persons, regardless of their nationality, before its own courts. It may also, if it prefers, and in accordance with the provisions of its own legislation, hand such persons over for trial to another High Contracting Party concerned, provided such High Contracting Party has made out a *prima facie* case.

Each High Contracting Party shall take measures necessary for the suppression of all acts contrary to the provisions of the present Convention other than the grave breaches defined in the following Article.

In all circumstances, the accused persons shall benefit by safeguards of proper trial and defence, which shall not be less favourable than those provided by Article 105 and those following of the Geneva Convention relative to the Treatment of Prisoners of War of August 12, 1949.

Article 50

Grave breaches to which the preceding Article relates shall be those involving any of the following acts, if committed against persons or property protected by the Convention: wilful killing, torture or inhuman treatment, including biological experiments, wilfully causing great suffering or serious injury to body or health, and extensive destruction and appropriation of property, not justified by military necessity and carried out unlawfully and wantonly.

Article 51

No High Contracting Party shall be allowed to absolve itself or any other High Contracting Party of any liability incurred by itself or by another High Contracting Party in respect of breaches referred to in the preceding Article.

Article 52

At the request of a Party to the conflict, an enquiry shall be instituted, in a manner to be decided between the interested Parties, concerning any alleged violation of the Convention.

If agreement has not been reached concerning the procedure for the enquiry, the Parties should agree on the choice of an umpire who will decide upon the procedure to be followed.

Once the violation has been established, the Parties to the conflict shall put an end to it and shall repress it with the least possible delay.

Article 53

The use by individuals, societies, firms or companies either public or private, other than those entitled thereto under the present Convention, of the emblem or the designation ''Red Cross'' or ''Geneva Cross'', or any sign or designation constituting an imitation thereof, whatever the object of such use, and irrespective of the date of its adoption, shall be prohibited at all times.

By reason of the tribute paid to Switzerland by the adoption of the reversed Federal colours, and of the confusion which may arise between the arms of Switzerland and the distinctive emblem of the Convention, the use by private individuals, societies or firms, of the arms of the Swiss Confederation, or of marks constituting an imitation thereof, whether as trademarks or commercial marks, or as parts of such marks, or for a purpose contrary to commercial honesty, or in circumstances capable of wounding Swiss national sentiment, shall be prohibited at all times.

Nevertheless, such High Contracting Parties as were not party to the Geneva Convention of July 27, 1929, may grant to prior users of the emblems, designations, signs or marks designated in the first paragraph, a time limit not to exceed three years from the coming into force of the present Convention to discontinue such use, provided that the said use shall not be such as would appear, in time of war, to confer the protection of the Convention.

The prohibition laid down in the first paragraph of the present Article shall also apply, without effect on any rights acquired through prior use, to the emblems and marks mentioned in the second paragraph of Article 38.

Article 54

The High Contracting Parties shall, if their legislation is not already adequate, take measures necessary for the prevention and repression, at all times, of the abuses referred to under Article 53.

FINAL PROVISIONS

Article 55

The present Convention is established in English and in French. Both texts are equally authentic.

The Swiss Federal Council shall arrange for official translations of the Convention to be made in the Russian and Spanish languages.

Article 56

The present Convention, which bears the date of this day, is open to signature until February 12, 1950, in the name of the Powers represented at the Conference which opened at Geneva on April 21, 1949; furthermore, by Powers not represented at that Conference but which are parties to the Geneva Conventions of 1864, 1906 or 1929 for the Relief of the Wounded and Sick in Armies in the Field.

Article 57

The present Convention shall be ratified as soon as possible and the ratifications shall be deposited at Berne.

A record shall be drawn up of the deposit of each instrument of ratification and certified copies of this record shall be transmitted by the Swiss Federal Council to all the Powers in whose name the Convention has been signed, or whose accession has been notified.

Article 58

The present Convention shall come into force six months after not less than two instruments of ratification have been deposited.

Thereafter, it shall come into force for each High Contracting Party six months after the deposit of the instrument of ratification.

Article 59

The present Convention replaces the Convention of August 22, 1864, July 6, 1906, and July 27, 1929, in relations between the High Contracting Parties.

Article 60

From the date of its coming into force, it shall be open to any Power in whose name the present Convention has not been signed, to accede to this Convention.

Article 61

Accessions shall be notified in writing to the Swiss Federal Council, and shall take effect six months after the date on which they are received.

The Swiss Federal Council shall communicate the accessions to all the Powers in whose name the Convention has been signed, or whose accession has been notified.

Article 62

The situations provided for in Articles 2 and 3 shall give immediate effect to ratifications deposited and accessions notified by the Parties to the conflict before or after the beginning of hostilities or occupation. The Swiss Federal Council shall communicate by the quickest method any ratifications or accessions received from Parties to the conflict.

Article 63

Each of the High Contracting Parties shall be at liberty to denounce the present Convention.

The denunciation shall be notified in writing to the Swiss Federal Council, which shall transmit it to the Governments of all the High Contracting Parties.

The denunciation shall take effect one year after the notification thereof has been made to the Swiss Federal Council. However, a denunciation of which notification has been made at a time when the denouncing Power is involved in a conflict shall not take effect until peace has been concluded, and until after operations connected with the release and repatriation of the persons protected by the present Convention have been terminated.

The denunciation shall have effect only in respect of the denouncing Power. It shall in no way impair the obligations which the Parties to the conflict shall remain bound to fulfil by virtue of the principles of the law of nations, as they result from the usages established among civilized peoples, from the laws of humanity and the dictates of the public conscience.

Article 64

The Swiss Federal Council shall register the present Convention with the Secretariat of the United Nations. The Swiss Federal Council shall also inform the Secretariat of the United Nations of all ratifications, accessions and denunciations received by it with respect to the present Convention.

IN WITNESS WHEREOF the undersigned, having deposited their respective full powers, have signed the present Convention.

DONE at Geneva this twelfth day of August 1949, in the English and French languages. The original shall be deposited in the Archives of the Swiss Confederation. The Swiss Federal Council shall transmit certified copies thereof to each of the signatory and acceding States.

ANNEX I

Draft agreement relating to hospital zones and localities

Article 1

Hospital zones shall be strictly reserved for the persons named in Article 23 of the Geneva Convention for the Amelioration of the Condition of the Wounded and Sick in Armed Forces in the Field of August 12, 1949, and for the personnel entrusted with the organization and administration of these zones and localities and with the care of the persons therein assembled.

Nevertheless, persons whose permanent residence is within such zones shall have the right to stay there.

Article 2

No persons residing, in whatever capacity, in a hospital zone shall perform any work, either within or without the zone, directly connected with military operations or the production of war material.

Article 3

The Power establishing a hospital zone shall take all necessary measures to prohibit access to all persons who have no right of residence or entry therein.

Article 4

Hospital zones shall fulfil the following conditions:

(*a*) They shall comprise only a small part of the territory governed by the Power which has established them.

(*b*) They shall be thinly populated in relation to the possibilities of accommodation.

(*c*) They shall be far removed and free from all military objectives, or large industrial or administrative establishments.

(*d*) They shall not be situated in areas which, according to every probability, may become important for the conduct of the war.

Article 5

Hospital zones shall be subject to the following obligations:

(*a*) The lines of communication and means of transport which they possess shall not be used for the transport of military personnel or material, even in transit.

(*b*) They shall in no case be defended by military means.

Article 6

Hospital zones shall be marked by means of red crosses (red crescents, red lions and suns) on a white background placed on the outer precincts and on the buildings. They may be similarly marked at night by means of appropriate illumination.

Article 7

The Powers shall communicate to all the High Contracting Parties in peacetime or on the outbreak of hostilities, a list of the hospital zones in the territories governed by them. They shall also give notice of any new zones set up during hostilities.

As soon as the adverse Party has received the above-mentioned notification, the zone shall be regularly constituted.

If, however, the adverse Party considers that the conditions of the present agreement have not been fulfilled, it may refuse to recognize the zone by giving immediate notice thereof to the Party responsible for the said zone, or may make its recognition of such zone dependent upon the institution of the control provided for in Article 8.

Article 8

Any Power having recognized one or several hospital zones instituted by the adverse Party shall be entitled to demand control by one or more Special Commissions, for the purpose of ascertaining if the zones fulfil the conditions and obligations stipulated in the present agreement.

For this purpose, the members of the Special Commissions shall at all times have free access to the various zones and may even reside there permanently. They shall be given all facilities for their duties of inspection.

Article 9

Should the Special Commissions note any facts which they consider contrary to the stipulations of the present agreement, they shall at once draw the attention of the Power governing the said zone to these facts, and shall fix a time limit of five days within which the matter should be rectified. They shall duly notify the Power who has recognized the zone.

If, when the time limit has expired, the Power governing the zone has not complied with the warning, the adverse Party may declare that it is no longer bound by the present agreement in respect of the said zone.

Article 10

Any Power setting up one or more hospital zones and localities, and the adverse Parties to whom their existence has been notified, shall nominate or have nominated by neutral Powers, the persons who shall be members of the Special Commissions mentioned in Articles 8 and 9.

Article 11

In no circumstances may hospital zones be the object of attack. They shall be protected and respected at all times by the Parties to the conflict.

Article 12

In the case of occupation of a territory, the hospital zones therein shall continue to be respected and utilized as such.

Their purpose may, however, be modified by the Occupying Power, on condition that all measures are taken to ensure the safety of the persons accommodated.

Article 13

The present agreement shall also apply to localities which the Powers may utilize for the same purposes as hospital zones.

ANNEX II

Reverse Side

Photo of bearer

Embossed stamp of military authority issuing card

Signature of bearer or fingerprints or both

Height	Eyes	Hair

Other distinguishing marks

Front

(Space reserved for the name of the country and military authority issuing this card)

IDENTITY CARD

for members of medical and religious personnel attached to the armed forces

Surname ....

First names ....

Date of Birth ....

Rank ....

Army Number ....

The bearer of this card is protected by the Geneva Convention for the Amelioration of the Condition of the Wounded and Sick in Armed Forces in the Field of August 12, 1949, in his capacity as

Date of issue   Number of Card

90. Geneva Convention for the Amelioration of the Condition of Wounded, Sick and Shipwrecked Members of Armed Forces at Sea

Adopted on 12 August 1949 by the Diplomatic Conference for the Establishment of International Conventions for the Protection of Victims of War, held in Geneva from 21 April to 12 August, 1949

ENTRY INTO FORCE: 21 October 1950

CHAPTER I

GENERAL PROVISIONS

Article 1

The High Contracting Parties undertake to respect and to ensure respect for the present Convention in all circumstances.

Article 2

In addition to the provisions which shall be implemented in peacetime, the present Convention shall apply to all cases of declared war or of any other armed conflict which may arise between two or more of the High Contracting Parties, even if the state of war is not recognized by one of them.

The Convention shall also apply to all cases of partial or total occupation of the territory of a High Contracting Party, even if the said occupation meets with no armed resistance.

Although one of the Powers in conflict may not be a party to the present Convention, the Powers who are parties thereto shall remain bound by it in their mutual relations. They shall furthermore be bound by the Convention in relation to the said Power, if the latter accepts and applies the provisions thereof.

Article 3

In the case of armed conflict not of an international character occurring in the territory of one of the High Contracting Parties, each Party to the conflict shall be bound to apply, as a minimum, the following provisions:

1. Persons taking no active part in the hostilities, including members of armed forces who have laid down their arms and those placed *hors de combat* by sickness, wounds, detention, or any other cause, shall in all cir-

cumstances be treated humanely, without any adverse distinction founded on race, colour, religion or faith, sex, birth or wealth, or any other similar criteria.

To this end, the following acts are and shall remain prohibited at any time and in any place whatsoever with respect to the above-mentioned persons:

(*a*) Violence to life and person, in particular murder of all kinds, mutilation, cruel treatment and torture;

(*b*) Taking of hostages;

(*c*) Outrages upon personal dignity, in particular, humiliating and degrading treatment;

(*d*) The passing of sentences and the carrying out of executions without previous judgment pronounced by a regularly constituted court, affording all the judicial guarantees which are recognized as indispensable by civilized peoples.

2. The wounded, sick and shipwrecked shall be collected and cared for.

An impartial humanitarian body, such as the International Committee of the Red Cross, may offer its services to the Parties to the conflict.

The Parties to the conflict should further endeavour to bring into force, by means of special agreements, all or part of the other provisions of the present Convention.

The application of the preceding provisions shall not affect the legal status of the Parties to the conflict.

Article 4

In case of hostilities between land and naval forces of Parties to the conflict, the provisions of the present Convention shall apply only to forces on board ship.

Forces put ashore shall immediately become subject to the provisions of the Geneva Convention for the Amelioration of the Condition of the Wounded and Sick in Armed Forces in the Field of August 12, 1949.

Article 5

Neutral Powers shall apply by analogy the provisions of the present Convention to the wounded, sick and shipwrecked, and to members of the medical personnel and to chaplains of the armed forces of the Parties to the conflict received or interned in their territory, as well as to dead persons found.

Article 6

In addition to the agreements expressly provided for in Articles 10, 18, 31, 38, 39, 40, 43 and 53, the High Contracting Parties may conclude other special agreements for all matters concerning which they may deem it suitable to make separate provision. No special agreement shall adversely affect the situation of wounded, sick and shipwrecked persons, of members of the medical personnel or of chaplains, as defined by the present Convention, nor restrict the rights which it confers upon them.

Wounded, sick, and shipwrecked persons, as well as medical personnel and chaplains, shall continue to have the benefit of such agreements as long as the Convention is applicable to them, except where express provisions to the contrary are contained in the aforesaid or in subsequent agreements, or where more favourable measures have been taken with regard to them by one or other of the Parties to the conflict.

Article 7

Wounded, sick and shipwrecked persons, as well as members of the medical personnel and chaplains, may in no circumstances renounce in part or in entirety the rights secured to them by the present Convention, and by the special agreements referred to in the foregoing Article, if such there be.

Article 8

The present Convention shall be applied with the cooperation and under the scrutiny of the Protecting Powers whose duty it is to safeguard the interests of the Parties to the conflict. For this purpose, the Protecting Powers may appoint, apart from their diplomatic or consular staff, delegates from amongst their own nationals or the nationals of other neutral Powers. The said delegates shall be subject to the approval of the Power with which they are to carry out their duties.

The Parties to the conflict shall facilitate to the greatest extent possible the task of the representatives or delegates of the Protecting Powers.

The representatives or delegates of the Protecting Powers shall not in any case exceed their mission under the present Convention. They shall, in particular, take account of the imperative necessities of security of the State wherein they carry out their duties. Their activities shall only be restricted as an exceptional and temporary measure when this is rendered necessary by imperative military necessities.

Article 9

The provisions of the present Convention constitute no obstacle to the humanitarian activities which the International Committee of the Red Cross or any other impartial humanitarian organization may, subject to the consent of the Parties to the conflict concerned, undertake for the protection of wounded, sick and shipwrecked persons, medical personnel and chaplains, and for their relief.

Article 10

The High Contracting Parties may at any time agree to entrust to an organization which offers all guarantees of impartiality and efficacy the duties incumbent on the Protecting Powers by virtue of the present Convention.

When wounded, sick and shipwrecked, or medical personnel and chaplains do not benefit or cease to benefit, no matter for what reason, by the activities of a Protecting Power or of an organization provided for in the first paragraph above, the Detaining Power shall request a neutral State, or such an organization, to undertake the functions performed under the present Convention by a Protecting Power designated by the Parties to a conflict.

If protection cannot be arranged accordingly, the Detaining Power shall request or shall accept, subject to the provisions of this Article, the offer of the services of a humanitarian organization, such as the International Committee of the Red Cross, to assume the humanitarian functions performed by Protecting Powers under the present Convention.

Any neutral Power, or any organization invited by the Power concerned or offering itself for these purposes, shall be required to act with a sense of responsibility towards the Party to the conflict on which persons protected by the present Convention depend, and shall be required to furnish sufficient assurances that it is in a position to undertake the appropriate functions and to discharge them impartially.

No derogation from the preceding provisions shall be made by special agreements between Powers one of which is restricted, even temporarily, in its freedom to negotiate with the other Power or its allies by reason of military events, more particularly where the whole, or a substantial part, of the territory of the said Power is occupied.

Whenever, in the present Convention, mention is made of a Protecting Power, such mention also applies to substitute organizations in the sense of the present Article.

Article 11

In cases where they deem it advisable in the interest of protected persons, particularly in cases of disagreement between the Parties to the conflict as to the application or interpretation of the provisions of the present Convention, the Protecting Powers shall lend their good offices with a view to settling the disagreement.

For this purpose, each of the Protecting Powers may, either at the invitation of one Party or on its own initiative, propose to the Parties to the conflict a meeting of their representatives, in particular of the authorities responsible for the wounded, sick and shipwrecked, medical personnel and chaplains, possibly on neutral territory suitably chosen. The Parties to the conflict shall be bound to give effect to the proposals made to them for this purpose. The Protecting Powers may, if necessary, propose for approval by the Parties to the conflict, a person belonging to a neutral Power or delegated by the International Committee of the Red Cross, who shall be invited to take part in such a meeting.

CHAPTER II

WOUNDED, SICK AND SHIPWRECKED

Article 12

Members of the armed forces and other persons mentioned in the following Article, who are at sea and who are wounded, sick or shipwrecked, shall be respected and protected in all circumstances, it being understood that the term "shipwreck" means shipwreck from any cause and includes forced landings at sea by or from aircraft.

Such persons shall be treated humanely and cared for by the Parties to the conflict in whose power they may be, without any adverse distinction founded on sex, race, nationality, religion, political opinions, or any other similar criteria. Any attempts upon their lives, or violence to their persons, shall be strictly prohibited; in particular, they shall not be murdered or exterminated, subjected to torture or to biological experiments; they shall not wilfully be left without medical assistance and care, nor shall conditions exposing them to contagion or infection be created.

Only urgent medical reasons will authorize priority in the order of treatment to be administered.

Women shall be treated with all consideration due to their sex.

Article 13

The present Convention shall apply to the wounded, sick and shipwrecked at sea belonging to the following categories:

1.   Members of the armed forces of a Party to the conflict, as well as members of militias or volunteer corps forming part of such armed forces.

2. Members of other militias and members of other volunteer corps, including those of organized resistance movements, belonging to a Party to the conflict and operating in or outside their own territory, even if this territory is occupied, provided that such militias or volunteer corps, including such organized resistance movements, fulfil the following conditions:

(a) That of being commanded by a person responsible for his subordinates;

(b) That of having a fixed distinctive sign recognizable at a distance;

(c) That of carrying arms openly;

(d) That of conducting their operations in accordance with the laws and customs of war.

3. Members of regular armed forces who profess allegiance to a Government or an authority not recognized by the Detaining Power.

4. Persons who accompany the armed forces without actually being members thereof, such as civilian members of military aircraft crews, war correspondents, supply contractors, members of labour units or of services responsible for the welfare of the armed forces, provided that they have received authorization from the armed forces which they accompany.

5. Members of crews, including masters, pilots and apprentices of the merchant marine and the crews of civil aircraft of the Parties to the conflict, who do not benefit by more favourable treatment under any other provisions of international law.

6. Inhabitants of a non-occupied territory who, on the approach of the enemy, spontaneously take up arms to resist the invading forces, without having had time to form themselves into regular armed units, provided they carry arms openly and respect the laws and customs of war.

Article 14

All warships of a belligerent Party shall have the right to demand that the wounded, sick or shipwrecked on board military hospital ships, and hospital ships belonging to relief societies or to private individuals, as well as merchant vessels, yachts and other craft shall be surrendered, whatever their nationality, provided that the wounded and sick are in a fit state to be moved and that the warship can provide adequate facilities for necessary medical treatment.

Article 15

If wounded, sick or shipwrecked persons are taken on board a neutral warship or a neutral military aircraft, it shall be ensured, where so required by international law, that they can take no further part in operations of war.

Article 16

Subject to the provisions of Article 12, the wounded, sick and ship-wrecked of a belligerent who fall into enemy hands shall be prisoners of war, and the provisions of international law concerning prisoners of war shall apply to them. The captor may decide, according to circumstances, whether it is expedient to hold them, or to convey them to a port in the captor's own country, to a neutral port or even to a port in enemy territory. In the last case, prisoners of war thus returned to their home country may not serve for the duration of the war.

Article 17

Wounded, sick or shipwrecked persons who are landed in neutral ports with the consent of the local authorities, shall, failing arrangements to the contrary between the neutral and the belligerent Powers, be so guarded by the neutral Power, where so required by international law, that the said persons cannot again take part in operations of war.

The costs of hospital accommodation and internment shall be borne by the Power on whom the wounded, sick or shipwrecked persons depend.

Article 18

After each engagement, Parties to the conflict shall, without delay, take all possible measures to search for and collect the shipwrecked, wounded and sick, to protect them against pillage and ill-treatment, to ensure their adequate care, and to search for the dead and prevent their being despoiled.

Whenever circumstances permit, the Parties to the conflict shall conclude local arrangements for the removal of the wounded and sick by sea from a besieged or encircled area and for the passage of medical and religious personnel and equipment on their way to that area.

Article 19

The Parties to the conflict shall record as soon as possible, in respect of each shipwrecked, wounded, sick or dead person of the adverse Party falling into their hands, any particulars which may assist in his identification. These records should if possible include:

(*a*) Designation of the Power on which he depends;

(*b*) Army, regimental, personal or serial number;

(*c*) Surname;

(*d*) First name or names;

(*e*) Date of birth;

(*f*) Any other particulars shown on his identity card or disc;

(*g*) Date and place of capture or death;

(*h*) Particulars concerning wounds or illness, or cause of death.

As soon as possible the above-mentioned information shall be forwarded to the information bureau described in Article 122 of the Geneva Convention relative to the Treatment of Prisoners of War of August 12, 1949, which shall transmit this information to the Power on which these persons depend through the intermediary of the Protecting Power and of the Central Prisoners of War Agency.

Parties to the conflict shall prepare and forward to each other, through the same bureau, certificates of death or duly authenticated lists of the dead. They shall likewise collect and forward through the same bureau one half of the double identity disc, or the identity disc itself if it is a single disc, last wills or other documents of importance to the next of kin, money and in general all articles of an intrinsic or sentimental value, which are found on the dead. These articles, together with unidentified articles, shall be sent in sealed packets, accompanied by statements giving all particulars necessary for the identification of the deceased owners, as well as by a complete list of the contents of the parcel.

Article 20

Parties to the conflict shall ensure that burial at sea of the dead, carried out individually as far as circumstances permit, is preceded by a careful examination, if possible by a medical examination, of the bodies, with a view to confirming death, establishing identity and enabling a report to be made. Where a double identity disc is used, one half of the disc should remain on the body.

If dead persons are landed, the provisions of the Geneva Convention for the Amelioration of the Condition of the Wounded and Sick in Armed Forces in the Field of August 12, 1949, shall be applicable.

Article 21

The Parties to the conflict may appeal to the charity of commanders of neutral merchant vessels, yachts or other craft, to take on board and care for wounded, sick or shipwrecked persons, and to collect the dead.

Vessels of any kind responding to this appeal, and those having of their own accord collected wounded, sick or shipwrecked persons, shall enjoy special protection and facilities to carry out such assistance.

They may, in no case, be captured on account of any such transport; but, in the absence of any promise to the contrary, they shall remain liable to capture for any violations of neutrality they may have committed.

CHAPTER III

HOSPITAL SHIPS

Article 22

Military hospital ships, that is to say, ships built or equipped by the Powers specially and solely with a view to assisting the wounded, sick and shipwrecked, to treating them and to transporting them, may in no circumstances be attacked or captured, but shall at all times be respected and protected, on condition that their names and descriptions have been notified to the Parties to the conflict ten days before those ships are employed.

The characteristics which must appear in the notification shall include registered gross tonnage, the length from stem to stern and the number of masts and funnels.

Article 23

Establishments ashore entitled to the protection of the Geneva Convention for the Amelioration of the Condition of the Wounded and Sick in Armed Forces in the Field of August 12, 1949, shall be protected from bombardment or attack from the sea.

Article 24

Hospital ships utilized by National Red Cross Societies, by officially recognized relief societies or by private persons shall have the same protection as military hospital ships and shall be exempt from capture, if the Party to the conflict on which they depend has given them an official commission and in so far as the provisions of Article 22 concerning notification have been complied with.

These ships must be provided with certificates from the responsible authorities, stating that the vessels have been under their control while fitting out and on departure.

Article 25

Hospital ships utilized by National Red Cross Societies, officially recognized relief societies, or private persons of neutral countries shall have the same protection as military hospital ships and shall be exempt from capture, on condition that they have placed themselves under the control of one of the Parties to the conflict, with the previous consent of their own governments and with the authorization of the Party to the conflict concerned, in so far as the provisions of Article 22 concerning notification have been complied with.

Article 26

The protection mentioned in Articles 22, 24 and 25 shall apply to hospital ships of any tonnage and to their lifeboats, wherever they are operating. Nevertheless, to ensure the maximum comfort and security, the Parties to the conflict shall endeavour to utilize, for the transport of wounded, sick and shipwrecked over long distances and on the high seas, only hospital ships of over 2,000 tons gross.

Article 27

Under the same conditions as those provided for in Articles 22 and 24, small craft employed by the State or by the officially recognized lifeboat institutions for coastal rescue operations shall also be respected and protected, so far as operational requirements permit.

The same shall apply so far as possible to fixed coastal installations used exclusively by these craft for their humanitarian missions.

Article 28

Should fighting occur on board a warship, the sick-bays shall be respected and spared as far as possible. Sick-bays and their equipment shall remain subject to the laws of warfare, but may not be diverted from their purpose so long as they are required for the wounded and sick. Nevertheless, the commander into whose power they have fallen may, after ensuring the proper care of the wounded and sick who are accommodated therein, apply them to other purposes in case of urgent military necessity.

Article 29

Any hospital ship in a port which falls into the hands of the enemy shall be authorized to leave the said port.

Article 30

The vessels described in Articles 22, 24, 25 and 27 shall afford relief and assistance to the wounded, sick and shipwrecked without distinction of nationality.

The High Contracting Parties undertake not to use these vessels for any military purpose.

Such vessels shall in no wise hamper the movements of the combatants.

During and after an engagement, they will act at their own risk.

Article 31

The Parties to the conflict shall have the right to control and search the vessels mentioned in Articles 22, 24, 25 and 27. They can refuse assistance from these vessels, order them off, make them take a certain course, control the use of their wireless and other means of communication, and even detain them for a period not exceeding seven days from the time of interception, if the gravity of the circumstances so requires.

They may put a commissioner temporarily on board whose sole task shall be to see that orders given in virtue of the provisions of the preceding paragraph are carried out.

As far as possible, the Parties to the conflict shall enter in the log of the hospital ship, in a language he can understand, the orders they have given the captain of the vessel.

Parties to the conflict may, either unilaterally or by particular agreements, put on board their ships neutral observers who shall verify the strict observation of the provisions contained in the present Convention.

Article 32

Vessels described in Articles 22, 24, 25 and 27 are not classed as warships as regards their stay in a neutral port.

Article 33

Merchant vessels which have been transformed into hospital ships cannot be put to any other use throughout the duration of hostilities.

Article 34

The protection to which hospital ships and sick-bays are entitled shall not cease unless they are used to commit, outside their humanitarian duties, acts harmful to the enemy. Protection may, however, cease only after due warning has been given, naming in all appropriate cases a reasonable time limit, and after such warning has remained unheeded.

In particular, hospital ships may not possess or use a secret code for their wireless or other means of communication.

Article 35

The following conditions shall not be considered as depriving hospital ships or sick-bays of vessels of the protection due to them:

1. The fact that the crews of ships or sick-bays are armed for the maintenance of order, for their own defence or that of the sick and wounded.

2.   The presence on board of apparatus exclusively intended to facilitate navigation or communication.

3.   The discovery on board hospital ships or in sick-bays of portable arms and ammunition taken from the wounded, sick and shipwrecked and not yet handed to the proper service.

4.   The fact that the humanitarian activities of hospital ships and sick-bays of vessels or of the crews extend to the care of wounded, sick or shipwrecked civilians.

5.   The transport of equipment and of personnel intended exclusively for medical duties, over and above the normal requirements.

CHAPTER IV

PERSONNEL

Article 36

The religious, medical and hospital personnel of hospital ships and their crews shall be respected and protected; they may not be captured during the time they are in the service of the hospital ship, whether or not there are wounded and sick on board.

Article 37

The religious, medical and hospital personnel assigned to the medical or spiritual care of the persons designated in Articles 12 and 13 shall, if they fall into the hands of the enemy, be respected and protected; they may continue to carry out their duties as long as this is necessary for the care of the wounded and sick. They shall afterwards be sent back as soon as the Commander-in-Chief, under whose authority they are, considers it practicable. They may take with them, on leaving the ship, their personal property.

If, however, it proves necessary to retain some of this personnel owing to the medical or spiritual needs of prisoners of war, everything possible shall be done for their earliest possible landing.

Retained personnel shall be subject, on landing, to the provisions of the Geneva Convention for the Amelioration of the Condition of the Wounded and Sick in Armed Forces in the Field of August 12, 1949.

CHAPTER V

MEDICAL TRANSPORTS

Article 38

Ships chartered for that purpose shall be authorized to transport equipment exclusively intended for the treatment of wounded and sick members of armed forces or for the prevention of disease, provided that the particulars regarding their voyage have been notified to the adverse Power and approved by the latter. The adverse Power shall preserve the right to board the carrier ships, but not to capture them or seize the equipment carried.

By agreement amongst the Parties to the conflict, neutral observers may be placed on board such ships to verify the equipment carried. For this purpose, free access to the equipment shall be given.

Article 39

Medical aircraft, that is to say, aircraft exclusively employed for the removal of wounded, sick and shipwrecked, and for the transport of medical personnel and equipment, may not be the object of attack, but shall be respected by the Parties to the conflict, while flying at heights, at times and on routes specifically agreed upon between the Parties to the conflict concerned.

They shall be clearly marked with the distinctive emblem prescribed in Article 41, together with their national colours, on their lower, upper and lateral surfaces. They shall be provided with any other markings or means of identification which may be agreed upon between the Parties to the conflict upon the outbreak or during the course of hostilities.

Unless agreed otherwise, flights over enemy or enemy-occupied territory are prohibited.

Medical aircraft shall obey every summons to alight on land or water. In the event of having thus to alight, the aircraft with its occupants may continue its flight after examination, if any.

In the event of alighting involuntarily on land or water in enemy or enemy-occupied territory, the wounded, sick and shipwrecked, as well as the crew of the aircraft shall be prisoners of war. The medical personnel shall be treated according to Articles 36 and 37.

Article 40

Subject to the provisions of the second paragraph, medical aircraft of Parties to the conflict may fly over the territory of neutral Powers, land thereon in case of necessity, or use it as a port of call. They shall give neutral Powers prior notice of their passage over the said territory, and obey every summons to alight, on land or water. They will be immune from attack only when flying on routes, at heights and at times specifically agreed upon between the Parties to the conflict and the neutral Power concerned.

The neutral Powers may, however, place conditions or restrictions on the passage or landing of medical aircraft on their territory. Such possible conditions or restrictions shall be applied equally to all Parties to the conflict.

Unless otherwise agreed between the neutral Powers and the Parties to the conflict, the wounded, sick or shipwrecked who are disembarked with the consent of the local authorities on neutral territory by medical aircraft shall be detained by the neutral Power, where so required by international law, in such a manner that they cannot again take part in operations of war. The cost of their accommodation and internment shall be borne by the Power on which they depend.

CHAPTER VI

THE DISTINCTIVE EMBLEM

Article 41

Under the direction of the competent military authority, the emblem of the red cross on a white ground shall be displayed on the flags, armlets and on all equipment employed in the Medical Service.

Nevertheless, in the case of countries which already use as emblem, in place of the red cross, the red crescent or the red lion and sun on a white ground, these emblems are also recognized by the terms of the present Convention.

Article 42

The personnel designated in Articles 36 and 37 shall wear, affixed to the left arm, a water-resistant armlet bearing the distinctive emblem, issued and stamped by the military authority.

Such personnel, in addition to wearing the identity disc mentioned in Article 19, shall also carry a special identity card bearing the distinctive emblem. This card shall be water-resistant and of such size that it can be carried in the pocket. It shall be worded in the national language, shall mention at least the surname and first names, the date of birth, the rank and the service number of the bearer, and shall state in what capacity he is entitled to the protection of the present Convention. The card shall bear the photograph of the owner and also either his signature or his finger-prints or both. It shall be embossed with the stamp of the military authority.

The identity card shall be uniform throughout the same armed forces and, as far as possible, of a similar type in the armed forces of the High Contracting Parties. The Parties to the conflict may be guided by the model which is annexed, by way of example, to the present Convention. They shall inform each other, at the outbreak of hostilities, of the model they are using. Identity cards should be made out, if possible, at least in duplicate, one copy being kept by the home country.

In no circumstances may the said personnel be deprived of their insignia or identity cards nor of the right to wear the armlet. In cases of loss they shall be entitled to receive duplicates of the cards and to have the insignia replaced.

Article 43

The ships designated in Articles 22, 24, 25 and 27 shall be distinctively marked as follows:

(*a*) All exterior surfaces shall be white.

(*b*) One or more dark red crosses, as large as possible, shall be painted and displayed on each side of the hull and on the horizontal surfaces, so placed as to afford the greatest possible visibility from the sea and from the air.

All hospital ships shall make themselves known by hoisting their national flag and further, if they belong to a neutral state, the flag of the Party to the conflict whose direction they have accepted. A white flag with a red cross shall be flown at the mainmast as high as possible.

Lifeboats of hospital ships, coastal lifeboats and all small craft used by the Medical Service shall be painted white with dark red crosses prominently displayed and shall, in general, comply with the identification system prescribed above for hospital ships.

The above-mentioned ships and craft, which may wish to ensure by night and in times of reduced visibility the protection to which they are entitled, must, subject to the assent of the Party to the conflict under whose power they are, take the necessary measures to render their painting and distinctive emblems sufficiently apparent.

Hospital ships which, in accordance with Article 31, are provisionally detained by the enemy, must haul down the flag of the Party to the conflict in whose service they are or whose direction they have accepted.

Coastal lifeboats, if they continue to operate with the consent of the Occupying Power from a base which is occupied, may be allowed, when away from their base, to continue to fly their own national colours along with a flag carrying a red cross on a white ground, subject to prior notification to all the Parties to the conflict concerned.

All the provisions in this Article relating to the red cross shall apply equally to the other emblems mentioned in Article 41.

Parties to the conflict shall at all times endeavour to conclude mutual agreements, in order to use the most modern methods available to facilitate the identification of hospital ships.

Article 44

The distinguishing signs referred to in Article 43 can only be used, whether in time of peace or war, for indicating or protecting the ships therein mentioned, except as may be provided in any other international Convention or by agreement between all the Parties to the conflict concerned.

Article 45

The High Contracting Parties shall, if their legislation is not already adequate, take the measures necessary for the prevention and repression, at all times, of any abuse of the distinctive signs provided for under Article 43.

CHAPTER VII

EXECUTION OF THE CONVENTION

Article 46

Each Party to the conflict, acting through its Commanders-in-Chief, shall ensure the detailed execution of the preceding Articles and provide for unforeseen cases, in conformity with the general principles of the present Convention.

Article 47

Reprisals against the wounded, sick and shipwrecked persons, the personnel, the vessels or the equipment protected by the Convention are prohibited.

Article 48

The High Contracting Parties undertake, in time of peace as in time of war, to disseminate the text of the present Convention as widely as possible in their respective countries, and, in particular, to include the study thereof in their programmes of military and, if possible, civil instruction, so that the principles thereof may become known to the entire population, in particular to the armed fighting forces, the medical personnel and the chaplains.

Article 49

The High Contracting Parties shall communicate to one another through the Swiss Federal Council and, during hostilities, through the Protecting Powers, the official translations of the present Convention, as well as the laws and regulations which they may adopt to ensure the application thereof.

CHAPTER VIII

REPRESSION OF ABUSES AND INFRACTIONS

Article 50

The High Contracting Parties undertake to enact any legislation necessary to provide effective penal sanctions for persons committing, or ordering to be committed, any of the grave breaches of the present Convention defined in the following Article.

Each High Contracting Party shall be under the obligation to search for persons alleged to have committed, or to have ordered to be committed, such grave breaches, and shall bring such persons, regardless of their nationality, before its own courts. It may also, if it prefers, and in accordance with the provisions of its own legislation, hand such persons over for trial to another High Contracting Party concerned, provided such High Contracting Party has made out a *prima facie* case.

Each High Contracting Party shall take measures necessary for the suppression of all acts contrary to the provisions of the present Convention other than the grave breaches defined in the following Article.

In all circumstances, the accused persons shall benefit by safeguards of proper trial and defence, which shall not be less favourable than those provided by Article 105 and those following of the Geneva Convention relative to the Treatment of Prisoners of War of August 12, 1949.

Article 51

Grave breaches to which the preceding Article relates shall be those involving any of the following acts, if committed against persons or property protected by the Convention: wilful killing, torture or inhuman treatment, including biological experiments, wilfully causing great suffering or serious injury to body or health, and extensive destruction and appropriation of

property, not justified by military necessity and carried out unlawfully and
wantonly.

Article 52

No High Contracting Party shall be allowed to absolve itself or any
other High Contracting Party of any liability incurred by itself or by another
High Contracting Party in respect of breaches referred to in the preceding
Article.

Article 53

At the request of a Party to the conflict, an enquiry shall be instituted,
in a manner to be decided between the interested Parties, concerning any alleged violation of the Convention.

If agreement has not been reached concerning the procedure for the enquiry, the Parties should agree on the choice of an umpire, who will decide
upon the procedure to be followed.

Once the violation has been established, the Parties to the conflict shall
put an end to it and shall repress it with the least possible delay.

FINAL PROVISIONS

Article 54

The present Convention is established in English and in French. Both
texts are equally authentic.

The Swiss Federal Council shall arrange for official translations of the
Convention to be made in the Russian and Spanish languages.

Article 55

The present Convention, which bears the date of this day, is open to
signature until February 12, 1950, in the name of the Powers represented at
the Conference which opened at Geneva on April 21, 1949; furthermore, by
Powers not represented at that Conference, but which are parties to the Xth
Hague Convention of October 18, 1907, for the adaptation to Maritime Warfare of the principles of the Geneva Convention of 1906, or to the Geneva
Conventions of 1864, 1906 or 1929 for the Relief of the Wounded and Sick
in Armies in the Field.

Article 56

The present Convention shall be ratified as soon as possible and the ratifications shall be deposited at Berne.

A record shall be drawn up of the deposit of each instrument of ratification and certified copies of this record shall be transmitted by the Swiss Federal Council to all the Powers in whose name the Convention has been signed, or whose accession has been notified.

Article 57

The present Convention shall come into force six months after not less than two instruments of ratification have been deposited.

Thereafter, it shall come into force for each High Contracting Party six months after the deposit of the instruments of ratification.

Article 58

The present Convention replaces the Xth Hague Convention of October 18, 1907, for the adaptation to Maritime Warfare of the principles of the Geneva Convention of 1906, in relations between the High Contracting Parties.

Article 59

From the date of its coming into force, it shall be open to any Power in whose name the present Convention has not been signed, to accede to this Convention.

Article 60

Accessions shall be notified in writing to the Swiss Federal Council, and shall take effect six months after the date on which they are received.

The Swiss Federal Council shall communicate the accessions to all the Powers in whose name the Convention has been signed, or whose accession has been notified.

Article 61

The situations provided for in Articles 2 and 3 shall give immediate effect to ratifications deposited and accessions notified by the Parties to the conflict before or after the beginning of hostilities or occupation. The Swiss Federal Council shall communicate by the quickest method any ratifications or accessions received from Parties to the conflict.

Article 62

Each of the High Contracting Parties shall be at liberty to denounce the present Convention.

The denunciation shall be notified in writing to the Swiss Federal Council, which shall transmit it to the Governments of all the High Contracting Parties.

The denunciation shall take effect one year after the notification thereof has been made to the Swiss Federal Council. However, a denunciation of which notification has been made at a time when the denouncing Power is involved in a conflict shall not take effect until peace has been concluded, and until after operations connected with the release and repatriation of the persons protected by the present Convention have been terminated.

The denunciation shall have effect only in respect of the denouncing Power. It shall in no way impair the obligations which the Parties to the conflict shall remain bound to fulfil by virtue of the principles of the law of nations, as they result from the usages established among civilized peoples, from the laws of humanity and the dictates of the public conscience.

Article 63

The Swiss Federal Council shall register the present Convention with the Secretariat of the United Nations. The Swiss Federal Council shall also inform the Secretariat of the United Nations of all ratifications, accessions and denunciations received by it with respect to the present Convention.

IN WITNESS WHEREOF the undersigned, having deposited their respective full powers, have signed the present Convention.

DONE at Geneva this twelfth day of August 1949, in the English and French languages. The original shall be deposited in the Archives of the Swiss Confederation. The Swiss Federal Council shall transmit certified copies thereof to each of the signatory and acceding States.

ANNEX

Front

(Space reserved for the name of the country and military authority issuing this card)

IDENTITY CARD

for members of medical and religious personnel attached to the armed forces at sea

Surname ....

First names ....

Date of Birth ....

Rank ....

Army Number ....

The bearer of this card is protected by the Geneva Convention for the Amelioration of the Condition of the Wounded, Sick and Shipwrecked Members of Armed Forces at Sea of August 12, 1949, in his capacity as

Date of issue   Number of Card

....

Reverse Side

Photo of bearer

Embossed stamp of military authority issuing card

Signature of bearer or fingerprints or both

Height	Eyes	Hair

Other distinguishing marks

....

91. Geneva Convention relative to the Treatment of Prisoners of War

*Adopted on 12 August 1949 by the Diplomatic Conference for the Establishment
of International Conventions for the Protection of Victims of War,
held in Geneva from 21 April to 12 August, 1949*

ENTRY INTO FORCE: 21 October 1950

PART I

GENERAL PROVISIONS

Article 1

The High Contracting Parties undertake to respect and to ensure respect for the present Convention in all circumstances.

Article 2

In addition to the provisions which shall be implemented in peace time, the present Convention shall apply to all cases of declared war or of any other armed conflict which may arise between two or more of the High Contracting Parties, even if the state of war is not recognized by one of them.

The Convention shall also apply to all cases of partial or total occupation of the territory of a High Contracting Party, even if the said occupation meets with no armed resistance.

Although one of the Powers in conflict may not be a party to the present Convention, the Powers who are parties thereto shall remain bound by it in their mutual relations. They shall furthermore be bound by the Convention in relation to the said Power, if the latter accepts and applies the provisions thereof.

Article 3

In the case of armed conflict not of an international character occurring in the territory of one of the High Contracting Parties, each party to the conflict shall be bound to apply, as a minimum, the following provisions:

1. Persons taking no active part in the hostilities, including members of armed forces who have laid down their arms and those placed *hors de combat* by sickness, wounds, detention, or any other cause, shall in all circumstances be treated humanely, without any adverse distinction founded on race, colour, religion or faith, sex, birth or wealth, or any other similar criteria.

To this end the following acts are and shall remain prohibited at any time and in any place whatsoever with respect to the above-mentioned persons:

(*a*) Violence to life and person, in particular murder of all kinds, mutilation, cruel treatment and torture;

(*b*) Taking of hostages;

(*c*) Outrages upon personal dignity, in particular, humiliating and degrading treatment;

(*d*) The passing of sentences and the carrying out of executions without previous judgment pronounced by a regularly constituted court affording all the judicial guarantees which are recognized as indispensable by civilized peoples.

2. The wounded and sick shall be collected and cared for.

An impartial humanitarian body, such as the International Committee of the Red Cross, may offer its services to the Parties to the conflict.

The Parties to the conflict should further endeavour to bring into force, by means of special agreements, all or part of the other provisions of the present Convention.

The application of the preceding provisions shall not affect the legal status of the Parties to the conflict.

Article 4

A. Prisoners of war, in the sense of the present Convention, are persons belonging to one of the following categories, who have fallen into the power of the enemy:

1. Members of the armed forces of a Party to the conflict as well as members of militias or volunteer corps forming part of such armed forces.

2. Members of other militias and members of other volunteer corps, including those of organized resistance movements, belonging to a Party to the conflict and operating in or outside their own territory, even if this territory is occupied, provided that such militias or volunteer corps, including such organized resistance movements, fulfil the following conditions:

(*a*) That of being commanded by a person responsible for his subordinates;

(*b*) That of having a fixed distinctive sign recognizable at a distance;

(*c*) That of carrying arms openly;

(*d*) That of conducting their operations in accordance with the laws and customs of war.

3. Members of regular armed forces who profess allegiance to a government or an authority not recognized by the Detaining Power.

4. Persons who accompany the armed forces without actually being members thereof, such as civilian members of military aircraft crews, war correspondents, supply contractors, members of labour units or of services responsible for the welfare of the armed forces, provided that they have received authorization from the armed forces which they accompany, who shall provide them for that purpose with an identity card similar to the annexed model.

5. Members of crews, including masters, pilots and apprentices, of the merchant marine and the crews of civil aircraft of the Parties to the conflict, who do not benefit by more favourable treatment under any other provisions of international law.

6. Inhabitants of a non-occupied territory, who on the approach of the enemy spontaneously take up arms to resist the invading forces, without having had time to form themselves into regular armed units, provided they carry arms openly and respect the laws and customs of war.

B. The following shall likewise be treated as prisoners of war under the present Convention:

1. Persons belonging, or having belonged, to the armed forces of the occupied country, if the occupying Power considers it necessary by reason of such allegiance to intern them, even though it has originally liberated them while hostilities were going on outside the territory it occupies, in particular where such persons have made an unsuccessful attempt to rejoin the armed forces to which they belong and which are engaged in combat, or where they fail to comply with a summons made to them with a view to internment.

2. The persons belonging to one of the categories enumerated in the present Article, who have been received by neutral or non-belligerent Powers on their territory and whom these Powers are required to intern under international law, without prejudice to any more favourable treatment which these Powers may choose to give and with the exception of Articles 8, 10, 15, 30, fifth paragraph, 58-67, 92, 126 and, where diplomatic relations exist between the Parties to the conflict and the neutral or non-belligerent Power concerned, those Articles concerning the Protecting Power. Where such diplomatic relations exist, the Parties to a conflict on whom these persons depend shall be allowed to perform towards them the functions of a

Protecting Power as provided in the present Convention, without prejudice to the functions which these Parties normally exercise in conformity with diplomatic and consular usage and treaties.

C.   This Article shall in no way affect the status of medical personnel and chaplains as provided for in Article 33 of the present Convention.

Article 5

The present Convention shall apply to the persons referred to in Article 4 from the time they fall into the power of the enemy and until their final release and repatriation.

Should any doubt arise as to whether persons, having committed a belligerent act and having fallen into the hands of the enemy, belong to any of the categories enumerated in Article 4, such persons shall enjoy the protection of the present Convention until such time as their status has been determined by a competent tribunal.

Article 6

In addition to the agreements expressly provided for in Articles 10, 23, 28, 33, 60, 65, 66, 67, 72, 73, 75, 109, 110, 118, 119, 122 and 132, the High Contracting Parties may conclude other special agreements for all matters concerning which they may deem it suitable to make separate provision. No special agreement shall adversely affect the situation of prisoners of war, as defined by the present Convention, nor restrict the rights which it confers upon them.

Prisoners of war shall continue to have the benefit of such agreements as long as the Convention is applicable to them, except where express provisions to the contrary are contained in the aforesaid or in subsequent agreements, or where more favourable measures have been taken with regard to them by one or other of the Parties to the conflict.

Article 7

Prisoners of war may in no circumstances renounce in part or in entirety the rights secured to them by the present Convention, and by the special agreements referred to in the foregoing Article, if such there be.

Article 8

The present Convention shall be applied with the cooperation and under the scrutiny of the Protecting Powers whose duty it is to safeguard the interests of the Parties to the conflict. For this purpose, the Protecting Powers may appoint, apart from their diplomatic or consular staff, delegates from amongst their own nationals or the nationals of other neutral Powers. The said delegates shall be subject to the approval of the Power with which they are to carry out their duties.

The Parties to the conflict shall facilitate to the greatest extent possible the task of the representatives or delegates of the Protecting Powers.

The representatives or delegates of the Protecting Powers shall not in any case exceed their mission under the present Convention. They shall, in particular, take account of the imperative necessities of security of the State wherein they carry out their duties.

Article 9

The provisions of the present Convention constitute no obstacle to the humanitarian activities which the International Committee of the Red Cross or any other impartial humanitarian organization may, subject to the consent of the Parties to the conflict concerned, undertake for the protection of prisoners of war and for their relief.

Article 10

The High Contracting Parties may at any time agree to entrust to an organization which offers all guarantees of impartiality and efficacy the duties incumbent on the Protecting Powers by virtue of the present Convention.

When prisoners of war do not benefit or cease to benefit, no matter for what reason, by the activities of a Protecting Power or of an organization provided for in the first paragraph above, the Detaining Power shall request a neutral State, or such an organization, to undertake the functions performed under the present Convention by a Protecting Power designated by the Parties to a conflict.

If protection cannot be arranged accordingly, the Detaining Power shall request or shall accept, subject to the provisions of this Article, the offer of the services of a humanitarian organization, such as the International Committee of the Red Cross, to assume the humanitarian functions performed by Protecting Powers under the present Convention.

Any neutral Power or any organization invited by the Power concerned or offering itself for these purposes, shall be required to act with a sense of responsibility towards the Party to the conflict on which persons protected by the present Convention depend, and shall be required to furnish sufficient assurances that it is in a position to undertake the appropriate functions and to discharge them impartially.

No derogation from the preceding provisions shall be made by special agreements between Powers one of which is restricted, even temporarily, in its freedom to negotiate with the other Power or its allies by reason of military events, more particularly where the whole, or a substantial part, of the territory of the said Power is occupied.

Whenever in the present Convention mention is made of a Protecting Power, such mention applies to substitute organizations in the sense of the present Article.

Article 11

In cases where they deem it advisable in the interest of protected persons, particularly in cases of disagreement between the Parties to the conflict as to the application or interpretation of the provisions of the present Convention, the Protecting Powers shall lend their good offices with a view to settling the disagreement.

For this purpose, each of the Protecting Powers may, either at the invitation of one Party or on its own initiative, propose to the Parties to the conflict a meeting of their representatives, and in particular of the authorities responsible for prisoners of war, possibly on neutral territory suitably chosen. The Parties to the conflict shall be bound to give effect to the proposals made to them for this purpose. The Protecting Powers may, if necessary, propose for approval by the Parties to the conflict a person belonging to a neutral Power, or delegated by the International Committee of the Red Cross, who shall be invited to take part in such a meeting.

PART II

GENERAL PROTECTION OF PRISONERS OF WAR

Article 12

Prisoners of war are in the hands of the enemy Power, but not of the individuals or military units who have captured them. Irrespective of the individual responsibilities that may exist, the Detaining Power is responsible for the treatment given them.

Prisoners of war may only be transferred by the Detaining Power to a Power which is a party to the Convention and after the Detaining Power has satisfied itself of the willingness and ability of such transferee Power to apply the Convention. When prisoners of war are transferred under such circumstances, responsibility for the application of the Convention rests on the Power accepting them while they are in its custody.

Nevertheless if that Power fails to carry out the provisions of the Convention in any important respect, the Power by whom the prisoners of war were transferred shall, upon being notified by the Protecting Power, take effective measures to correct the situation or shall request the return of the prisoners of war. Such requests must be complied with.

Article 13

Prisoners of war must at all times be humanely treated. Any unlawful act or omission by the Detaining Power causing death or seriously endangering the health of a prisoner of war in its custody is prohibited, and will be regarded as a serious breach of the present Convention. In particular, no prisoner of war may be subjected to physical mutilation or to medical or scientific experiments of any kind which are not justified by the medical, dental or hospital treatment of the prisoner concerned and carried out in his interest.

Likewise, prisoners of war must at all times be protected, particularly against acts of violence or intimidation and against insults and public curiosity.

Measures of reprisal against prisoners of war are prohibited.

Article 14

Prisoners of war are entitled in all circumstances to respect for their persons and their honour.

Women shall be treated with all the regard due to their sex and shall in all cases benefit by treatment as favourable as that granted to men.

Prisoners of war shall retain the full civil capacity which they enjoyed at the time of their capture. The Detaining Power may not restrict the exercise, either within or without its own territory, of the rights such capacity confers except in so far as the captivity requires.

Article 15

The Power detaining prisoners of war shall be bound to provide free of charge for their maintenance and for the medical attention required by their state of health.

Article 16

Taking into consideration the provisions of the present Convention relating to rank and sex, and subject to any privileged treatment which may be accorded to them by reason of their state of health, age or professional qualifications, all prisoners of war shall be treated alike by the Detaining Power, without any adverse distinction based on race, nationality, religious belief or political opinions, or any other distinction founded on similar criteria.

PART III

CAPTIVITY

SECTION I

BEGINNING OF CAPTIVITY

Article 17

Every prisoner of war, when questioned on the subject, is bound to give only his surname, first names and rank, date of birth, and army, regimental, personal or serial number, or failing this, equivalent information.

If he wilfully infringes this rule, he may render himself liable to a restriction of the privileges accorded to his rank or status.

Each Party to a conflict is required to furnish the persons under its jurisdiction who are liable to become prisoners of war, with an identity card showing the owner's surname, first names, rank, army, regimental, personal or serial number or equivalent information, and date of birth. The identity card may, furthermore, bear the signature or the fingerprints, or both, of the owner, and may bear, as well, any other information the Party to the conflict may wish to add concerning persons belonging to its armed forces. As far as possible the card shall measure 6.5 x 10 cm. and shall be issued in duplicate. The identity card shall be shown by the prisoner of war upon demand, but may in no case be taken away from him.

No physical or mental torture, nor any other form of coercion, may be inflicted on prisoners of war to secure from them information of any kind whatever. Prisoners of war who refuse to answer may not be threatened, insulted, or exposed to any unpleasant or disadvantageous treatment of any kind.

Prisoners of war who, owing to their physical or mental condition, are unable to state their identity, shall be handed over to the medical service. The identity of such prisoners shall be established by all possible means, subject to the provisions of the preceding paragraph.

The questioning of prisoners of war shall be carried out in a language which they understand.

Article 18

All effects and articles of personal use, except arms, horses, military equipment and military documents, shall remain in the possession of prisoners of war, likewise their metal helmets and gas masks and like articles issued for personal protection. Effects and articles used for their clothing or feeding shall likewise remain in their possession, even if such effects and articles belong to their regulation military equipment.

At no time should prisoners of war be without identity documents. The Detaining Power shall supply such documents to prisoners of war who possess none.

Badges of rank and nationality, decorations and articles having above all a personal or sentimental value may not be taken from prisoners of war.

Sums of money carried by prisoners of war may not be taken away from them except by order of an officer, and after the amount and particulars of the owner have been recorded in a special register and an itemized receipt has been given, legibly inscribed with the name, rank and unit of the person issuing the said receipt. Sums in the currency of the Detaining Power, or which are changed into such currency at the prisoner's request, shall be placed to the credit of the prisoner's account as provided in Article 64.

The Detaining Power may withdraw articles of value from prisoners of war only for reasons of security; when such articles are withdrawn, the procedure laid down for sums of money impounded shall apply.

Such objects, likewise the sums taken away in any currency other than that of the Detaining Power and the conversion of which has not been asked for by the owners, shall be kept in the custody of the Detaining Power and shall be returned in their initial shape to prisoners of war at the end of their captivity.

Article 19

Prisoners of war shall be evacuated, as soon as possible after their capture, to camps situated in an area far enough from the combat zone for them to be out of danger.

Only those prisoners of war who, owing to wounds or sickness, would run greater risks by being evacuated than by remaining where they are, may be temporarily kept back in a danger zone.

Prisoners of war shall not be unnecessarily exposed to danger while awaiting evacuation from a fighting zone.

Article 20

The evacuation of prisoners of war shall always be effected humanely and in conditions similar to those for the forces of the Detaining Power in their changes of station.

The Detaining Power shall supply prisoners of war who are being evacuated with sufficient food and potable water, and with the necessary clothing and medical attention. The Detaining Power shall take all suitable precautions to ensure their safety during evacuation, and shall establish as soon as possible a list of the prisoners of war who are evacuated.

If prisoners of war must, during evacuation, pass through transit camps, their stay in such camps shall be as brief as possible.

SECTION II

INTERNMENT OF PRISONERS OF WAR

Chapter I

GENERAL OBSERVATIONS

Article 21

The Detaining Power may subject prisoners of war to internment. It may impose on them the obligation of not leaving, beyond certain limits, the camp where they are interned, or if the said camp is fenced in, of not going outside its perimeter. Subject to the provisions of the present Convention relative to penal and disciplinary sanctions, prisoners of war may not be held in close confinement except where necessary to safeguard their health and then only during the continuation of the circumstances which make such confinement necessary.

Prisoners of war may be partially or wholly released on parole or promise, in so far as is allowed by the laws of the Power on which they depend. Such measures shall be taken particularly in cases where this may contribute to the improvement of their state of health. No prisoner of war shall be compelled to accept liberty on parole or promise.

Upon the outbreak of hostilities, each Party to the conflict shall notify the adverse Party of the laws and regulations allowing or forbidding its own nationals to accept liberty on parole or promise. Prisoners of war who are paroled or who have given their promise in conformity with the laws and regulations so notified, are bound on their personal honour scrupulously to fulfil, both towards the Power on which they depend and towards the Power which has captured them, the engagements of their paroles or promises. In such cases, the Power on which they depend is bound neither to require nor to accept from them any service incompatible with the parole or promise given.

Article 22

Prisoners of war may be interned only in premises located on land and affording every guarantee of hygiene and healthfulness. Except in particular cases which are justified by the interest of the prisoners themselves, they shall not be interned in penitentiaries.

Prisoners of war interned in unhealthy areas, or where the climate is injurious for them, shall be removed as soon as possible to a more favourable climate.

The Detaining Power shall assemble prisoners of war in camps or camp compounds according to their nationality, language and customs, provided that such prisoners shall not be separated from prisoners of war belonging to the armed forces with which they were serving at the time of their capture, except with their consent.

Article 23

No prisoner of war may at any time be sent to or detained in areas where he may be exposed to the fire of the combat zone, nor may his presence be used to render certain points or areas immune from military operations.

Prisoners of war shall have shelters against air bombardment and other hazards of war, to the same extent as the local civilian population. With the exception of those engaged in the protection of their quarters against the aforesaid hazards, they may enter such shelters as soon as possible after the giving of the alarm. Any other protective measure taken in favour of the population shall also apply to them.

Detaining Powers shall give the Powers concerned, through the intermediary of the Protecting Powers, all useful information regarding the geographical location of prisoner of war camps.

Whenever military considerations permit, prisoner of war camps shall be indicated in the day-time by the letters PW or PG, placed so as to be clearly visible from the air. The Powers concerned may, however, agree upon any other system of marking. Only prisoner of war camps shall be marked as such.

Article 24

Transit or screening camps of a permanent kind shall be fitted out under conditions similar to those described in the present Section, and the prisoners therein shall have the same treatment as in other camps.

Chapter II

QUARTERS, FOOD AND CLOTHING OF PRISONERS OF WAR

Article 25

Prisoners of war shall be quartered under conditions as favourable as those for the forces of the Detaining Power who are billeted in the same area. The said conditions shall make allowance for the habits and customs of the prisoners and shall in no case be prejudicial to their health.

The foregoing provisions shall apply in particular to the dormitories of prisoners of war as regards both total surface and minimum cubic space, and the general installations, bedding and blankets.

The premises provided for the use of prisoners of war individually or collectively, shall be entirely protected from dampness and adequately heated and lighted, in particular between dusk and lights out. All precautions must be taken against the danger of fire.

In any camps in which women prisoners of war, as well as men, are accommodated, separate dormitories shall be provided for them.

Article 26

The basic daily food rations shall be sufficient in quantity, quality and variety to keep prisoners of war in good health and to prevent loss of weight or the development of nutritional deficiencies. Account shall also be taken of the habitual diet of the prisoners.

The Detaining Power shall supply prisoners of war who work with such additional rations as are necessary for the labour on which they are employed.

Sufficient drinking water shall be supplied to prisoners of war. The use of tobacco shall be permitted.

Prisoners of war shall, as far as possible, be associated with the preparation of their meals; they may be employed for that purpose in the kitchens. Furthermore, they shall be given the means of preparing, themselves, the additional food in their possession.

Adequate premises shall be provided for messing.

Collective disciplinary measures affecting food are prohibited.

Article 27

Clothing, underwear and footwear shall be supplied to prisoners of war in sufficient quantities by the Detaining Power, which shall make allowance for the climate of the region where the prisoners are detained. Uniforms of enemy armed forces captured by the Detaining Power should, if suitable for the climate, be made available to clothe prisoners of war.

The regular replacement and repair of the above articles shall be assured by the Detaining Power. In addition, prisoners of war who work shall receive appropriate clothing, wherever the nature of the work demands.

Article 28

Canteens shall be installed in all camps, where prisoners of war may procure foodstuffs, soap and tobacco and ordinary articles in daily use. The tariff shall never be in excess of local market prices.

The profits made by camp canteens shall be used for the benefit of the prisoners; a special fund shall be created for this purpose. The prisoners' representative shall have the right to collaborate in the management of the canteen and of this fund.

When a camp is closed down, the credit balance of the special fund shall be handed to an international welfare organization, to be employed for the benefit of prisoners of war of the same nationality as those who have contributed to the fund. In case of a general repatriation, such profits shall be kept by the Detaining Power, subject to any agreement to the contrary between the Powers concerned.

Chapter III

HYGIENE AND MEDICAL ATTENTION

Article 29

The Detaining Power shall be bound to take all sanitary measures necessary to ensure the cleanliness and healthfulness of camps and to prevent epidemics.

Prisoners of war shall have for their use, day and night, conveniences which conform to the rules of hygiene and are maintained in a constant state of cleanliness. In any camps in which women prisoners of war are accommodated, separate conveniences shall be provided for them.

Also, apart from the baths and showers with which the camps shall be furnished, prisoners of war shall be provided with sufficient water and soap for their personal toilet and for washing their personal laundry; the necessary installations, facilities and time shall be granted them for that purpose.

Article 30

Every camp shall have an adequate infirmary where prisoners of war may have the attention they require, as well as appropriate diet. Isolation wards shall, if necessary, be set aside for cases of contagious or mental disease.

Prisoners of war suffering from serious disease, or whose condition necessitates special treatment, a surgical operation or hospital care, must be admitted to any military or civilian medical unit where such treatment can be given, even if their repatriation is contemplated in the near future. Special facilities shall be afforded for the care to be given to the disabled, in particular to the blind, and for their rehabilitation, pending repatriation.

Prisoners of war shall have the attention, preferably, of medical personnel of the Power on which they depend and, if possible, of their nationality.

Prisoners of war may not be prevented from presenting themselves to the medical authorities for examination. The detaining authorities shall, upon request, issue to every prisoner who has undergone treatment, an official certificate indicating the nature of his illness or injury, and the duration and kind of treatment received. A duplicate of this certificate shall be forwarded to the Central Prisoners of War Agency.

The costs of treatment, including those of any apparatus necessary for the maintenance of prisoners of war in good health, particularly dentures and other artificial appliances, and spectacles, shall be borne by the Detaining Power.

Article 31

Medical inspections of prisoners of war shall be held at least once a month. They shall include the checking and the recording of the weight of each prisoner of war. Their purpose shall be, in particular, to supervise the general state of health, nutrition and cleanliness of prisoners and to detect contagious diseases, especially tuberculosis, malaria and venereal disease. For this purpose the most efficient methods available shall be employed, e.g. periodic mass miniature radiography for the early detection of tuberculosis.

Article 32

Prisoners of war who, though not attached to the medical service of their armed forces, are physicians, surgeons, dentists, nurses or medical orderlies, may be required by the Detaining Power to exercise their medical functions in the interests of prisoners of war dependent on the same Power. In that case they shall continue to be prisoners of war, but shall receive the same treatment as corresponding medical personnel retained by the Detaining Power. They shall be exempted from any other work under Article 49.

Chapter IV

MEDICAL PERSONNEL AND CHAPLAINS
RETAINED TO ASSIST PRISONERS OF WAR

Article 33

Members of the medical personnel and chaplains while retained by the Detaining Power with a view to assisting prisoners of war, shall not be considered as prisoners of war. They shall, however, receive as a minimum the benefits and protection of the present Convention, and shall also be granted all facilities necessary to provide for the medical care of, and religious ministration to prisoners of war.

They shall continue to exercise their medical and spiritual functions for the benefit of prisoners of war, preferably those belonging to the armed forces upon which they depend, within the scope of the military laws and regulations of the Detaining Power and under the control of its competent services, in accordance with their professional etiquette. They shall also benefit by the following facilities in the exercise of their medical or spiritual functions:

(*a*) They shall be authorized to visit periodically prisoners of war situated in working detachments or in hospitals outside the camp. For this purpose, the Detaining Power shall place at their disposal the necessary means of transport.

(*b*) The senior medical officer in each camp shall be responsible to the camp military authorities for everything connected with the activities of retained medical personnel. For this purpose, Parties to the conflict shall agree at the outbreak of hostilities on the subject of the corresponding ranks of the medical personnel, including that of societies mentioned in Article 26 of the Geneva Convention for the Amelioration of the Condition of the Wounded and Sick in Armed Forces in the Field of August 12, 1949. This senior medical officer, as well as chaplains, shall have the right to deal with the competent authorities of the camp on all questions relating to their duties. Such authorities shall afford them all necessary facilities for correspondence relating to these questions.

(*c*) Although they shall be subject to the internal discipline of the camp in which they are retained, such personnel may not be compelled to carry out any work other than that concerned with their medical or religious duties.

During hostilities, the Parties to the conflict shall agree concerning the possible relief of retained personnel and shall settle the procedure to be followed.

None of the preceding provisions shall relieve the Detaining Power of its obligations with regard to prisoners of war from the medical or spiritual point of view.

Chapter V

RELIGIOUS, INTELLECTUAL AND PHYSICAL ACTIVITIES

Article 34

Prisoners of war shall enjoy complete latitude in the exercise of their religious duties, including attendance at the service of their faith, on condition that thy comply with the disciplinary routine prescribed by the military authorities.

Adequate premises shall be provided where religious services may be held.

Article 35

Chaplains who fall into the hands of the enemy Power and who remain or are retained with a view to assisting prisoners of war, shall be allowed to minister to them and to exercise freely their ministry amongst prisoners of war of the same religion, in accordance with their religious conscience. They shall be allocated among the various camps and labour detachments containing prisoners of war belonging to the same forces, speaking the same language or practising the same religion. They shall enjoy the necessary facilities, including the means of transport provided for in Article 33, for visiting the prisoners of war outside their camp. They shall be free to correspond, subject to censorship, on matters concerning their religious duties with the ecclesiastical authorities in the country of detention and with international religious organizations. Letters and cards which they may send for this purpose shall be in addition to the quota provided for in Article 71.

Article 36

Prisoners of war who are ministers of religion, without having officiated as chaplains to their own forces, shall be at liberty, whatever their denomination, to minister freely to the members of their community. For this purpose, they shall receive the same treatment as the chaplains retained by the Detaining Power. They shall not be obliged to do any other work.

Article 37

When prisoners of war have not the assistance of a retained chaplain or of a prisoner of war minister of their faith, a minister belonging to the prisoners' or a similar denomination, or in his absence a qualified layman, if such a course is feasible from a confessional point of view, shall be appointed, at the request of the prisoners concerned, to fill this office. This appointment, subject to the approval of the Detaining Power, shall take place with the agreement of the community of prisoners concerned and, wherever necessary, with the approval of the local religious authorities of the same faith. The person thus appointed shall comply with all regulations established by the Detaining Power in the interests of discipline and military security.

Article 38

While respecting the individual preferences of every prisoner, the Detaining Power shall encourage the practice of intellectual, educational, and recreational pursuits, sports and games amongst prisoners, and shall take the measures necessary to ensure the exercise thereof by providing them with adequate premises and necessary equipment.

Prisoners shall have opportunities for taking physical exercise, including sports and games, and for being out of doors. Sufficient open spaces shall be provided for this purpose in all camps.

Chapter VI

DISCIPLINE

Article 39

Every prisoner of war camp shall be put under the immediate authority of a responsible commissioned officer belonging to the regular armed forces of the Detaining Power. Such officer shall have in his possession a copy of the present Convention; he shall ensure that its provisions are known to the camp staff and the guard and shall be responsible, under the direction of his government, for its application.

Prisoners of war, with the exception of officers, must salute and show to all officers of the Detaining Power the external marks of respect provided for by the regulations applying in their own forces.

Officer prisoners of war are bound to salute only officers of a higher rank of the Detaining Power; they must, however, salute the camp commander regardless of his rank.

Article 40

The wearing of badges of rank and nationality, as well as of decorations, shall be permitted.

Article 41

In every camp the text of the present Convention and its Annexes and the contents of any special agreement provided for in Article 6, shall be posted, in the prisoners' own language, at places where all may read them. Copies shall be supplied, on request, to the prisoners who cannot have access to the copy which has been posted.

Regulations, orders, notices and publications of every kind relating to the conduct of prisoners of war shall be issued to them in a language which they understand. Such regulations, orders and publications shall be posted in the manner described above and copies shall be handed to the prisoners' representative. Every order and command addressed to prisoners of war individually must likewise be given in a language which they understand.

Article 42

The use of weapons against prisoners of war, especially against those who are escaping or attempting to escape, shall constitute an extreme measure, which shall always be preceded by warnings appropriate to the circumstances.

Chapter VII

RANK OF PRISONERS OF WAR

Article 43

Upon the outbreak of hostilities, the Parties to the conflict shall communicate to one another the titles and ranks of all the persons mentioned in Article 4 of the present Convention, in order to ensure equality of treatment between prisoners of equivalent rank. Titles and ranks which are subsequently created shall form the subject of similar communications.

The Detaining Power shall recognize promotions in rank which have been accorded to prisoners of war and which have been duly notified by the Power on which these prisoners depend.

Article 44

Officers and prisoners of equivalent status shall be treated with the regard due to their rank and age.

In order to ensure service in officers' camps, other ranks of the same armed forces who, as far as possible, speak the same language, shall be assigned in sufficient numbers, account being taken of the rank of officers and prisoners of equivalent status. Such orderlies shall not be required to perform any other work.

Supervision of the mess by the officers themselves shall be facilitated in every way.

Article 45

Prisoners of war other than officers and prisoners of equivalent status shall be treated with the regard due to their rank and age.

Supervision of the mess by the prisoners themselves shall be facilitated in every way.

Chapter VIII

TRANSFER OF PRISONERS OF WAR AFTER THEIR ARRIVAL IN CAMP

Article 46

The Detaining Power, when deciding upon the transfer of prisoners of war, shall take into account the interests of the prisoners themselves, more especially so as not to increase the difficulty of their repatriation.

The transfer of prisoners of war shall always be effected humanely and in conditions not less favourable than those under which the forces of the Detaining Power are transferred. Account shall always be taken of the climatic conditions to which the prisoners of war are accustomed and the conditions of transfer shall in no case be prejudicial to their health.

The Detaining Power shall supply prisoners of war during transfer with sufficient food and drinking water to keep them in good health, likewise with the necessary clothing, shelter and medical attention. The Detaining Power shall take adequate precautions especially in case of transport by sea or by air, to ensure their safety during transfer, and shall draw up a complete list of all transferred prisoners before their departure.

Article 47

Sick or wounded prisoners of war shall not be transferred as long as their recovery may be endangered by the journey, unless their safety imperatively demands it.

If the combat zone draws closer to a camp, the prisoners of war in the said camp shall not be transferred unless their transfer can be carried out in adequate conditions of safety, or if they are exposed to greater risks by remaining on the spot than by being transferred.

Article 48

In the event of transfer, prisoners of war shall be officially advised of their departure and of their new postal address. Such notifications shall be given in time for them to pack their luggage and inform their next of kin.

They shall be allowed to take with them their personal effects, and the correspondence and parcels which have arrived for them. The weight of such baggage may be limited, if the conditions of transfer so require, to what each prisoner can reasonably carry, which shall in no case be more than twenty-five kilograms per head.

Mail and parcels addressed to their former camp shall be forwarded to them without delay. The camp commander shall take, in agreement with the prisoners' representative, any measures needed to ensure the transport of the prisoners' community property and of the luggage they are unable to take with them in consequence of restrictions imposed by virtue of the second paragraph of this Article.

The costs of transfers shall be borne by the Detaining Power.

SECTION III

LABOUR OF PRISONERS OF WAR

Article 49

The Detaining Power may utilize the labour of prisoners of war who are physically fit, taking into account their age, sex, rank and physical aptitude, and with a view particularly to maintaining them in a good state of physical and mental health.

Non-commissioned officers who are prisoners of war shall only be required to do supervisory work. Those not so required may ask for other suitable work which shall, so far as possible, be found for them.

If officers or persons of equivalent status ask for suitable work, it shall be found for them, so far as possible, but they may in no circumstances be compelled to work.

Article 50

Besides work connected with camp administration, installation or maintenance, prisoners of war may be compelled to do only such work as is included in the following classes:

(*a*) Agriculture;

(*b*) Industries connected with the production or the extraction of raw materials, and manufacturing industries, with the exception of metallurgical, machinery and chemical industries; public works and building operations which have no military character or purpose;

(*c*) Transport and handling of stores which are not military in character or purpose;

(*d*) Commercial business, and arts and crafts;

(*e*) Domestic service;

(*f*) Public utility services having no military character or purpose.

Should the above provisions be infringed, prisoners of war shall be allowed to exercise their right of complaint, in conformity with Article 78.

Article 51

Prisoners of war must be granted suitable working conditions, especially as regards accommodation, food, clothing and equipment; such conditions shall not be inferior to those enjoyed by nationals of the Detaining Power employed in similar work; account shall also be taken of climatic conditions.

The Detaining Power, in utilizing the labour of prisoners of war, shall ensure that in areas in which prisoners are employed, the national legislation concerning the protection of labour, and, more particularly, the regulations for the safety of workers, are duly applied.

Prisoners of war shall receive training and be provided with the means of protection suitable to the work they will have to do and similar to those accorded to the nationals of the Detaining Power. Subject to the provisions of Article 52, prisoners may be submitted to the normal risks run by these civilian workers.

Conditions of labour shall in no case be rendered more arduous by disciplinary measures.

Article 52

Unless he be a volunteer, no prisoner of war may be employed on labour which is of an unhealthy or dangerous nature.

No prisoner of war shall be assigned to labour which would be looked upon as humiliating for a member of the Detaining Power's own forces.

The removal of mines or similar devices shall be considered as dangerous labour.

Article 53

The duration of the daily labour of prisoners of war, including the time of the journey to and fro, shall not be excessive, and must in no case exceed that permitted for civilian workers in the district, who are nationals of the Detaining Power and employed on the same work.

Prisoners of war must be allowed, in the middle of the day's work, a rest of not less than one hour. This rest will be the same as that to which workers of the Detaining Power are entitled, if the latter is of longer duration. They shall be allowed in addition a rest of twenty-four consecutive hours every week, preferably on Sunday or the day of rest in their country of origin. Furthermore, every prisoner who has worked for one year shall be granted a rest of eight consecutive days, during which his working pay shall be paid him.

If methods of labour such as piece-work are employed, the length of the working period shall not be rendered excessive thereby.

Article 54

The working pay due to prisoners of war shall be fixed in accordance with the provisions of Article 62 of the present Convention.

Prisoners of war who sustain accidents in connection with work, or who contract a disease in the course, or in consequence of their work, shall receive all the care their condition may require. The Detaining Power shall furthermore deliver to such prisoners of war a medical certificate enabling them to submit their claims to the Power on which they depend, and shall send a duplicate to the Central Prisoners of War Agency provided for in Article 123.

Article 55

The fitness of prisoners of war for work shall be periodically verified by medical examinations at least once a month. The examinations shall have particular regard to the nature of the work which prisoners of war are required to do.

If any prisoner of war considers himself incapable of working, he shall be permitted to appear before the medical authorities of his camp. Physicians or surgeons may recommend that the prisoners who are, in their opinion, unfit for work, be exempted therefrom.

Article 56

The organization and administration of labour detachments shall be similar to those of prisoner of war camps.

Every labour detachment shall remain under the control of and administratively part of a prisoner of war camp. The military authorities and the commander of the said camp shall be responsible, under the direction of their government, for the observance of the provisions of the present Convention in labour detachments.

The camp commander shall keep an up-to-date record of the labour detachments dependent on his camp, and shall communicate it to the delegates of the Protecting Power, of the International Committee of the Red Cross, or of other agencies giving relief to prisoners of war, who may visit the camp.

Article 57

The treatment of prisoners of war who work for private persons, even if the latter are responsible for guarding and protecting them, shall not be inferior to that which is provided for by the present Convention. The Detaining Power, the military authorities and the commander of the camp to which such prisoners belong shall be entirely responsible for the maintenance, care, treatment, and payment of the working pay of such prisoners of war.

Such prisoners of war shall have the right to remain in communication with the prisoners' representatives in the camps on which they depend.

SECTION IV

FINANCIAL RESOURCES OF PRISONERS OF WAR

Article 58

Upon the outbreak of hostilities, and pending an arrangement on this matter with the Protecting Power, the Detaining Power may determine the maximum amount of money in cash or in any similar form, that prisoners may have in their possession. Any amount in excess, which was properly in their possession and which has been taken or withheld from them, shall be placed to their account, together with any monies deposited by them, and shall not be converted into any other currency without their consent.

If prisoners of war are permitted to purchase services or commodities outside the camp against payment in cash, such payments shall be made by the prisoner himself or by the camp administration who will charge them to the accounts of the prisoners concerned. The Detaining Power will establish the necessary rules in this respect.

Article 59

Cash which was taken from prisoners of war, in accordance with Article 18, at the time of their capture, and which is in the currency of the Detaining Power, shall be placed to their separate accounts, in accordance with the provisions of Article 64 of the present Section.

The amounts, in the currency of the Detaining Power, due to the conversion of sums in other currencies that are taken from the prisoners of war at the same time, shall also be credited to their separate accounts.

Article 60

The Detaining Power shall grant all prisoners of war a monthly advance of pay, the amount of which shall be fixed by conversion, into the currency of the said Power, of the following amounts:

Category I: Prisoners ranking below sergeant: eight Swiss francs.

Category II: Sergeants and other non-commissioned officers, or prisoners of equivalent rank: twelve Swiss francs.

Category III: Warrant officers and commissioned officers below the rank of major or prisoners of equivalent rank: fifty Swiss francs.

Category IV: Majors, lieutenant-colonels, colonels or prisoners of equivalent rank: sixty Swiss francs.

Category V: General officers or prisoners of equivalent rank: seventy-five Swiss francs.

However, the Parties to the conflict concerned may by special agreement modify the amount of advances of pay due to prisoners of the preceding categories.

Furthermore, if the amounts indicated in the first paragraph above would be unduly high compared with the pay of the Detaining Power's armed forces or would, for any reason, seriously embarrass the Detaining Power, then, pending the conclusion of a special agreement with the Power on which the prisoners depend to vary the amounts indicated above, the Detaining Power:

(*a*) Shall continue to credit the accounts of the prisoners with the amounts indicated in the first paragraph above;

(*b*) May temporarily limit the amount made available from these advances of pay to prisoners of war for their own use, to sums which are reasonable, but which, for Category I, shall never be inferior to the amount that the Detaining Power gives to the members of its own armed forces.

The reasons for any limitations will be given without delay to the Protecting Power.

Article 61

The Detaining Power shall accept for distribution as supplementary pay to prisoners of war sums which the Power on which the prisoners depend may forward to them, on condition that the sums to be paid shall be the same for each prisoner of the same category, shall be payable to all prisoners of that category depending on that Power, and shall be placed in their separate accounts, at the earliest opportunity, in accordance with the provisions of Article 64. Such supplementary pay shall not relieve the Detaining Power of any obligation under this Convention.

Article 62

Prisoners of war shall be paid a fair working rate of pay by the detaining authorities direct. The rate shall be fixed by the said authorities, but shall at no time be less than one-fourth of one Swiss franc for a full working day. The Detaining Power shall inform prisoners of war, as well as the Power on which they depend, through the intermediary of the Protecting Power, of the rate of daily working pay that it has fixed.

Working pay shall likewise be paid by the detaining authorities to prisoners of war permanently detailed to duties or to a skilled or semi-skilled occupation in connection with the administration, installation or maintenance of camps, and to the prisoners who are required to carry out spiritual or medical duties on behalf of their comrades.

The working pay of the prisoners' representative, of his advisers, if any, and of his assistants, shall be paid out of the fund maintained by canteen profits. The scale of this working pay shall be fixed by the prisoners' representative and approved by the camp commander. If there is no such fund, the detaining authorities shall pay these prisoners a fair working rate of pay.

Article 63

Prisoners of war shall be permitted to receive remittances of money addressed to them individually or collectively.

Every prisoner of war shall have at his disposal the credit balance of his account as provided for in the following Article, within the limits fixed by the Detaining Power, which shall make such payments as are requested. Subject to financial or monetary restrictions which the Detaining Power regards as essential, prisoners of war may also have payments made abroad. In this case payments addressed by prisoners of war to dependants shall be given priority.

In any event, and subject to the consent of the Power on which they depend, prisoners may have payments made in their own country, as follows: the Detaining Power shall send to the aforesaid Power through the Protecting Power a notification giving all the necessary particulars concerning the prisoners of war, the beneficiaries of the payments, and the amount of the sums to be paid, expressed in the Detaining Power's currency. The said notification shall be signed by the prisoners and countersigned by the camp commander. The Detaining Power shall debit the prisoners' account by a corresponding amount; the sums thus debited shall be placed by it to the credit of the Power on which the prisoners depend.

To apply the foregoing provisions, the Detaining Power may usefully consult the Model Regulations in Annex V of the present Convention.

Article 64

The Detaining Power shall hold an account for each prisoner of war, showing at least the following:

1.   The amounts due to the prisoner or received by him as advances of pay, as working pay or derived from any other source; the sums in the currency of the Detaining Power which were taken from him; the sums taken from him and converted at his request into the currency of the said Power.

2.   The payments made to the prisoner in cash, or in any other similar form; the payments made on his behalf and at his request; the sums transferred under Article 63, third paragraph.

Article 65

Every item entered in the account of a prisoner of war shall be countersigned or initialled by him, or by the prisoners' representative acting on his behalf.

Prisoners of war shall at all times be afforded reasonable facilities for consulting and obtaining copies of their accounts, which may likewise be inspected by the representatives of the Protecting Powers at the time of visits to the camp.

When prisoners of war are transferred from one camp to another, their personal accounts will follow them. In case of transfer from one Detaining Power to another, the monies which are their property and are not in the currency of the Detaining Power will follow them. They shall be given certificates for any other monies standing to the credit of their accounts.

The Parties to the conflict concerned may agree to notify to each other at specific intervals through the Protecting Power, the amount of the accounts of the prisoners of war.

Article 66

On the termination of captivity, through the release of a prisoner of war or his repatriation, the Detaining Power shall give him a statement, signed by an authorized officer of that Power, showing the credit balance then due to him. The Detaining Power shall also send through the Protecting Power to the government upon which the prisoner of war depends, lists giving all appropriate particulars of all prisoners of war whose captivity has been terminated by repatriation, release, escape, death or any other means, and showing the amount of their credit balances. Such lists shall be certified on each sheet by an authorized representative of the Detaining Power.

Any of the above provisions of this Article may be varied by mutual agreement between any two Parties to the conflict.

The Power on which the prisoner of war depends shall be responsible for settling with him any credit balance due to him from the Detaining Power on the termination of his captivity.

Article 67

Advances of pay, issued to prisoners of war in conformity with Article 60, shall be considered as made on behalf of the Power on which they depend. Such advances of pay, as well as all payments made by the said Power under Article 63, third paragraph, and Article 68, shall form the subject of arrangements between the Powers concerned, at the close of hostilities.

Article 68

Any claim by a prisoner of war for compensation in respect of any injury or other disability arising out of work shall be referred to the Power on which he depends, through the Protecting Power. In accordance with Article 54, the Detaining Power will, in all cases, provide the prisoner of war concerned with a statement showing the nature of the injury or disability, the circumstances in which it arose and particulars of medical or hospital treatment given for it. This statement will be signed by a responsible officer of the Detaining Power and the medical particulars certified by a medical officer.

Any claim by a prisoner of war for compensation in respect of personal effects, monies or valuables impounded by the Detaining Power under

Article 18 and not forthcoming on his repatriation, or in respect of loss alleged to be due to the fault of the Detaining Power or any of its servants, shall likewise be referred to the Power on which he depends. Nevertheless, any such personal effects required for use by the prisoners of war whilst in captivity shall be replaced at the expense of the Detaining Power. The Detaining Power will, in all cases, provide the prisoner of war with a statement, signed by a responsible officer, showing all available information regarding the reasons why such effects, monies or valuables have not been restored to him. A copy of this statement will be forwarded to the Power on which he depends through the Central Prisoners of War Agency provided for in Article 123.

SECTION V

RELATIONS OF PRISONERS OF WAR WITH THE EXTERIOR

Article 69

Immediately upon prisoners of war falling into its power, the Detaining Power shall inform them and the Powers on which they depend, through the Protecting Power, of the measures taken to carry out the provisions of the present Section. They shall likewise inform the parties concerned of any subsequent modifications of such measures.

Article 70

Immediately upon capture, or not more than one week after arrival at a camp, even if it is a transit camp, likewise in case of sickness or transfer to hospital or another camp, every prisoner of war shall be enabled to write direct to his family, on the one hand, and to the Central Prisoners of War Agency provided for in Article 123, on the other hand, a card similar, if possible, to the model annexed to the present Convention, informing his relatives of his capture, address and state of health. The said cards shall be forwarded as rapidly as possible and may not be delayed in any manner.

Article 71

Prisoners of war shall be allowed to send and receive letters and cards. If the Detaining Power deems it necessary to limit the number of letters and cards sent by each prisoner of war, the said number shall not be less than two letters and four cards monthly, exclusive of the capture cards provided for in Article 70, and conforming as closely as possible to the models annexed to the present Convention. Further limitations may be imposed only if the Protecting Power is satisfied that it would be in the interests of the prisoners of war concerned to do so owing to difficulties of translation caused by the Detaining Power's inability to find sufficient qualified linguists to carry out the necessary censorship. If limitations must be placed on the correspondence addressed to prisoners of war, they may be ordered only by the Power on which the prisoners depend, possibly at the request of the Detaining Power. Such letters and cards must be conveyed by the most rapid method at the disposal of the Detaining Power; they may not be delayed or retained for disciplinary reasons.

Prisoners of war who have been without news for a long period, or who are unable to receive news from their next of kin or to give them news by the ordinary postal route, as well as those who are at a great distance from their homes, shall be permitted to send telegrams, the fees being charged against the prisoners of war's accounts with the Detaining Power or paid in the currency at their disposal. They shall likewise benefit by this measure in cases of urgency.

As a general rule, the correspondence of prisoners of war shall be written in their native language. The Parties to the conflict may allow correspondence in other languages.

Sacks containing prisoner of war mail must be securely sealed and labelled so as clearly to indicate their contents, and must be addressed to offices of destination.

Article 72

Prisoners of war shall be allowed to receive by post or by any other means individual parcels or collective shipments containing, in particular, foodstuffs, clothing, medical supplies and articles of a religious, educational or recreational character which may meet their needs, including books, devotional articles, scientific equipment, examination papers, musical instruments, sports outfits and materials allowing prisoners of war to pursue their studies or their cultural activities.

Such shipments shall in no way free the Detaining Power from the obligations imposed upon it by virtue of the present Convention.

The only limits which may be placed on these shipments shall be those proposed by the Protecting Power in the interest of the prisoners themselves, or by the International Committee of the Red Cross or any other organization giving assistance to the prisoners, in respect of their own shipments only, on account of exceptional strain on transport or communications.

The conditions for the sending of individual parcels and collective relief shall, if necessary, be the subject of special agreements between the Powers concerned, which may in no case delay the receipt by the prisoners of relief supplies. Books may not be included in parcels of clothing and foodstuffs. Medical supplies shall, as a rule, be sent in collective parcels.

Article 73

In the absence of special agreements between the Powers concerned on the conditions for the receipt and distribution of collective relief shipments, the rules and regulations concerning collective shipments, which are annexed to the present Convention, shall be applied.

The special agreements referred to above shall in no case restrict the right of prisoners' representatives to take possession of collective relief shipments intended for prisoners of war, to proceed to their distribution or to dispose of them in the interest of the prisoners.

Nor shall such agreements restrict the right of representatives of the Protecting Power, the International Committee of the Red Cross or any other organization giving assistance to prisoners of war and responsible for the forwarding of collective shipments, to supervise their distribution to the recipients.

Article 74

All relief shipments for prisoners of war shall be exempt from import, customs and other dues.

Correspondence, relief shipments and authorized remittances of money addressed to prisoners of war or despatched by them through the post office, either direct or through the Information Bureaux provided for in Article 122 and the Central Prisoners of War Agency provided for in Article 123, shall be exempt from any postal dues, both in the countries of origin and destination, and in intermediate countries.

If relief shipments intended for prisoners of war cannot be sent through the post office by reason of weight or for any other cause, the cost of transportation shall be borne by the Detaining Power in all the territories under its control. The other Powers party to the Convention shall bear the cost of transport in their respective territories.

In the absence of special agreements between the Parties concerned, the costs connected with transport of such shipments, other than costs covered by the above exemption, shall be charged to the senders.

The High Contracting Parties shall endeavour to reduce, so far as possible, the rates charged for telegrams sent by prisoners of war, or addressed to them.

Article 75

Should military operations prevent the Powers concerned from fulfilling their obligation to assure the transport of the shipments referred to in Articles 70, 71, 72 and 77, the Protecting Powers concerned, the International Committee of the Red Cross or any other organization duly approved by the Parties to the conflict may undertake to ensure the conveyance of such shipments by suitable means (railway wagons, motor vehicles, vessels or aircraft, etc.). For this purpose, the High Contracting Parties shall endeavour to supply them with such transport and to allow its circulation, especially by granting the necessary safe-conducts.

Such transport may also be used to convey:

(*a*) Correspondence, lists and reports exchanged between the Central Information Agency referred to in Article 123 and the National Bureaux referred to in Article 122;

(*b*) Correspondence and reports relating to prisoners of war which the Protecting Powers, the International Committee of the Red Cross or any other body assisting the prisoners, exchange either with their own delegates or with the Parties to the conflict.

These provisions in no way detract from the right of any Party to the conflict to arrange other means of transport, if it should so prefer, nor preclude the granting of safe-conducts, under mutually agreed conditions, to such means of transport.

In the absence of special agreements, the costs occasioned by the use of such means of transport shall be borne proportionally by the Parties to the conflict whose nationals are benefited thereby.

Article 76

The censoring of correspondence addressed to prisoners of war or despatched by them shall be done as quickly as possible. Mail shall be censored only by the despatching State and the receiving State, and once only by each.

The examination of consignments intended for prisoners of war shall not be carried out under conditions that will expose the goods contained in them to deterioration; except in the case of written or printed matter, it shall be done in the presence of the addressee, or of a fellow-prisoner duly delegated by him. The delivery to prisoners of individual or collective consignments shall not be delayed under the pretext of difficulties of censorship.

Any prohibition of correspondence ordered by Parties to the conflict, either for military or political reasons, shall be only temporary and its duration shall be as short as possible.

Article 77

The Detaining Powers shall provide all facilities for the transmission, through the Protecting Power or the Central Prisoners of War Agency provided for in Article 123, of instruments, papers or documents intended for prisoners of war or despatched by them, especially powers of attorney and wills.

In all cases they shall facilitate the preparation and execution of such documents on behalf of prisoners of war; in particular, they shall allow them to consult a lawyer and shall take what measures are necessary for the authentication of their signatures.

SECTION VI

RELATIONS BETWEEN PRISONERS OF WAR AND THE AUTHORITIES

Chapter I

COMPLAINTS OF PRISONERS OF WAR
RESPECTING THE CONDITIONS OF CAPTIVITY

Article 78

Prisoners of war shall have the right to make known to the military authorities in whose power they are, their requests regarding the conditions of captivity to which they are subjected.

They shall also have the unrestricted right to apply to the representatives of the Protecting Powers either through their prisoners' representative or, if they consider it necessary, direct, in order to draw their attention to any points on which they may have complaints to make regarding their conditions of captivity.

These requests and complaints shall not be limited nor considered to be a part of the correspondence quota referred to in Article 71. They must be transmitted immediately. Even if they are recognized to be unfounded, they may not give rise to any punishment.

Prisoners' representatives may send periodic reports on the situation in the camps and the needs of the prisoners of war to the representatives of the Protecting Powers.

Chapter II

PRISONER OF WAR REPRESENTATIVES

Article 79

In all places where there are prisoners of war, except in those where there are officers, the prisoners shall freely elect by secret ballot, every six months, and also in case of vacancies, prisoners' representatives entrusted with representing them before the military authorities, the Protecting Powers, the International Committee of the Red Cross and any other organization which may assist them. These prisoners' representatives shall be eligible for re-election.

In camps for officers and persons of equivalent status or in mixed camps, the senior officer among the prisoners of war shall be recognized as the camp prisoners' representative. In camps for officers, he shall be assisted by one or more advisers chosen by the officers; in mixed camps, his assistants shall be chosen from among the prisoners of war who are not officers and shall be elected by them.

Officer prisoners of war of the same nationality shall be stationed in labour camps for prisoners of war, for the purpose of carrying out the camp administration duties for which the prisoners of war are responsible. These officers may be elected as prisoners' representatives under the first paragraph of this Article. In such a case the assistants to the prisoners' representatives shall be chosen from among those prisoners of war who are not officers.

Every representative elected must be approved by the Detaining Power before he has the right to commence his duties. Where the Detaining Power refuses to approve a prisoner of war elected by his fellow prisoners of war, it must inform the Protecting Power of the reason for such refusal.

In all cases the prisoners' representative must have the same nationality, language and customs as the prisoners of war whom he represents. Thus, prisoners of war distributed in different sections of a camp, according to their nationality, language or customs, shall have for each section their own prisoners' representative, in accordance with the foregoing paragraphs.

Article 80

Prisoners' representatives shall further the physical, spiritual and intellectual well-being of prisoners of war.

In particular, where the prisoners decide to organize amongst themselves a system of mutual assistance, this organization will be within the province of the prisoners' representative, in addition to the special duties entrusted to him by other provisions of the present Convention.

Prisoners' representatives shall not be held responsible, simply by reason of their duties, for any offences committed by prisoners of war.

Article 81

Prisoners' representatives shall not be required to perform any other work, if the accomplishment of their duties is thereby made more difficult.

Prisoners' representatives may appoint from amongst the prisoners such assistants as they may require. All material facilities shall be granted them, particularly a certain freedom of movement necessary for the accomplishment of their duties (inspection of labour detachments, receipt of supplies, etc.).

Prisoners' representatives shall be permitted to visit premises where prisoners of war are detained, and every prisoner of war shall have the right to consult freely his prisoners' representative.

All facilities shall likewise be accorded to the prisoners' representatives for communication by post and telegraph with the detaining authorities, the Protecting Powers, the International Committee of the Red Cross and their delegates, the Mixed Medical Commissions and with the bodies which give assistance to prisoners of war. Prisoners' representatives of labour detachments shall enjoy the same facilities for communication with the prisoners' representatives of the principal camp. Such communications shall not be restricted, nor considered as forming a part of the quota mentioned in Article 71.

Prisoners' representatives who are transferred shall be allowed a reasonable time to acquaint their successors with current affairs.

In case of dismissal, the reasons therefor shall be communicated to the Protecting Power.

Chapter III

PENAL AND DISCIPLINARY SANCTIONS

I. *General provisions*

Article 82

A prisoner of war shall be subject to the laws, regulations and orders in force in the armed forces of the Detaining Power; the Detaining Power shall be justified in taking judicial or disciplinary measures in respect of any offence committed by a prisoner of war against such laws, regulations or orders. However, no proceedings or punishments contrary to the provisions of this Chapter shall be allowed.

If any law, regulation or order of the Detaining Power shall declare acts committed by a prisoner of war to be punishable, whereas the same acts would not be punishable if committed by a member of the forces of the Detaining Power, such acts shall entail disciplinary punishments only.

Article 83

In deciding whether proceedings in respect of an offence alleged to have been committed by a prisoner of war shall be judicial or disciplinary, the Detaining Power shall ensure that the competent authorities exercise the greatest leniency and adopt, wherever possible, disciplinary rather than judicial measures.

Article 84

A prisoner of war shall be tried only by a military court, unless the existing laws of the Detaining Power expressly permit the civil courts to try a member of the armed forces of the Detaining Power in respect of the particular offence alleged to have been committed by the prisoner of war.

In no circumstances whatever shall a prisoner of war be tried by a court of any kind which does not offer the essential guarantees of independence and impartiality as generally recognized, and, in particular, the procedure of which does not afford the accused the rights and means of defence provided for in Article 105.

Article 85

Prisoners of war prosecuted under the laws of the Detaining Power for acts committed prior to capture shall retain, even if convicted, the benefits of the present Convention.

Article 86

No prisoner of war may be punished more than once for the same act, or on the same charge.

Article 87

Prisoners of war may not be sentenced by the military authorities and courts of the Detaining Power to any penalties except those provided for in respect of members of the armed forces of the said Power who have committed the same acts.

When fixing the penalty, the courts or authorities of the Detaining Power shall take into consideration, to the widest extent possible, the fact that the accused, not being a national of the Detaining Power, is not bound to it by any duty of allegiance, and that he is in its power as the result of circumstances independent of his own will. The said courts or authorities shall be at liberty to reduce the penalty provided for the violation of which the prisoner of war is accused, and shall therefore not be bound to apply the minimum penalty prescribed.

Collective punishment for individual acts, corporal punishments, imprisonment in premises without daylight and, in general, any form of torture or cruelty, are forbidden.

No prisoner of war may be deprived of his rank by the Detaining Power, or prevented from wearing his badges.

Article 88

Officers, non-commissioned officers and men who are prisoners of war undergoing a disciplinary or judicial punishment, shall not be subjected to more severe treatment than that applied in respect of the same punishment to members of the armed forces of the Detaining Power of equivalent rank.

A woman prisoner of war shall not be awarded or sentenced to a punishment more severe, or treated whilst undergoing punishment more severely, than a woman member of the armed forces of the Detaining Power dealt with for a similar offence.

In no case may a woman prisoner of war be awarded or sentenced to a punishment more severe, or treated whilst undergoing punishment more severely, than a male member of the armed forces of the Detaining Power dealt with for a similar offence.

Prisoners of war who have served disciplinary or judicial sentences may not be treated differently from other prisoners of war.

II. *Disciplinary sanctions*

Article 89

The disciplinary punishments applicable to prisoners of war are the following:

1. A fine which shall not exceed 50 per cent of the advances of pay and working pay which the prisoner of war would otherwise receive under

the provisions of Articles 60 and 62 during a period of not more than thirty days.

2. Discontinuance of privileges granted over and above the treatment provided for by the present Convention.

3. Fatigue duties not exceeding two hours daily.

4. Confinement.

The punishment referred to under (3) shall not be applied to officers.

In no case shall disciplinary punishments be inhuman, brutal or dangerous to the health of prisoners of war.

Article 90

The duration of any single punishment shall in no case exceed thirty days. Any period of confinement awaiting the hearing of a disciplinary offence or the award of disciplinary punishment shall be deducted from an award pronounced against a prisoner of war.

The maximum of thirty days provided above may not be exceeded, even if the prisoner of war is answerable for several acts at the same time when he is awarded punishment, whether such acts are related or not.

The period between the pronouncing of an award of disciplinary punishment and its execution shall not exceed one month.

When a prisoner of war is awarded a further disciplinary punishment, a period of at least three days shall elapse between the execution of any two of the punishments, if the duration of one of these is ten days or more.

Article 91

The escape of a prisoner of war shall be deemed to have succeeded when:

1. He has joined the armed forces of the Power on which he depends, or those of an allied Power;

2. He has left the territory under the control of the Detaining Power, or of an ally of the said Power;

3. He has joined a ship flying the flag of the Power on which he depends, or of an allied Power, in the territorial waters of the Detaining Power, the said ship not being under the control of the last named Power.

Prisoners of war who have made good their escape in the sense of this Article and who are recaptured, shall not be liable to any punishment in respect of their previous escape.

Article 92

A prisoner of war who attempts to escape and is recaptured before having made good his escape in the sense of Article 91 shall be liable only to a disciplinary punishment in respect of this act, even if it is a repeated offence.

A prisoner of war who is recaptured shall be handed over without delay to the competent military authority.

Article 88, fourth paragraph, notwithstanding, prisoners of war punished as a result of an unsuccessful escape may be subjected to special surveillance. Such surveillance must not affect the state of their health, must be undergone in a prisoner of war camp, and must not entail the suppression of any of the safeguards granted them by the present Convention.

Article 93

Escape or attempt to escape, even if it is a repeated offence, shall not be deemed an aggravating circumstance if the prisoner of war is subjected to trial by judicial proceedings in respect of an offence committed during his escape or attempt to escape.

In conformity with the principle stated in Article 83, offences committed by prisoners of war with the sole intention of facilitating their escape and which do not entail any violence against life or limb, such as offences against public property, theft without intention of self-enrichment, the drawing up or use of false papers, the wearing of civilian clothing, shall occasion disciplinary punishment only.

Prisoners of war who aid or abet an escape or an attempt to escape shall be liable on this count to disciplinary punishment only.

Article 94

If an escaped prisoner of war is recaptured, the Power on which he depends shall be notified thereof in the manner defined in Article 122, provided notification of his escape has been made.

Article 95

A prisoner of war accused of an offence against discipline shall not be kept in confinement pending the hearing unless a member of the armed forces of the Detaining Power would be so kept if he were accused of a similar offence, or if it is essential in the interests of camp order and discipline.

Any period spent by a prisoner of war in confinement awaiting the disposal of an offence against discipline shall be reduced to an absolute minimum and shall not exceed fourteen days.

The provisions of Articles 97 and 98 of this Chapter shall apply to prisoners of war who are in confinement awaiting the disposal of offences against discipline.

Article 96

Acts which constitute offences against discipline shall be investigated immediately.

Without prejudice to the competence of courts and superior military authorities, disciplinary punishment may be ordered only by an officer having disciplinary powers in his capacity as camp commander, or by a responsible officer who replaces him or to whom he has delegated his disciplinary powers.

In no case may such powers be delegated to a prisoner of war or be exercised by a prisoner of war.

Before any disciplinary award is pronounced, the accused shall be given precise information regarding the offences of which he is accused, and given an opportunity of explaining his conduct and of defending himself. He shall be permitted, in particular, to call witnesses and to have recourse, if necessary, to the services of a qualified interpreter. The decision shall be announced to the accused prisoner of war and to the prisoners' representative.

A record of disciplinary punishments shall be maintained by the camp commander and shall be open to inspection by representatives of the Protecting Power.

Article 97

Prisoners of war shall not in any case be transferred to penitentiary establishments (prisons, penitentiaries, convict prisons, etc.) to undergo disciplinary punishment therein.

All premises in which disciplinary punishments are undergone shall conform to the sanitary requirements set forth in Article 25. A prisoner of war undergoing punishment shall be enabled to keep himself in a state of cleanliness, in conformity with Article 29.

Officers and persons of equivalent status shall not be lodged in the same quarters as non-commissioned officers or men.

Women prisoners of war undergoing disciplinary punishment shall be confined in separate quarters from male prisoners of war and shall be under the immediate supervision of women.

Article 98

A prisoner of war undergoing confinement as a disciplinary punishment, shall continue to enjoy the benefits of the provisions of this Convention except in so far as these are necessarily rendered inapplicable by the mere fact that he is confined. In no case may he be deprived of the benefits of the provisions of Articles 78 and 126.

A prisoner of war awarded disciplinary punishment may not be deprived of the prerogatives attached to his rank.

Prisoners of war awarded disciplinary punishment shall be allowed to exercise and to stay in the open air at least two hours daily.

They shall be allowed, on their request, to be present at the daily medical inspections. They shall receive the attention which their state of health requires and, if necessary, shall be removed to the camp infirmary or to a hospital.

They shall have permission to read and write, likewise to send and receive letters. Parcels and remittances of money, however, may be withheld from them until the completion of the punishment; they shall meanwhile be entrusted to the prisoners' representative, who will hand over to the infirmary the perishable goods contained in such parcels.

III. *Judicial proceedings*

Article 99

No prisoner of war may be tried or sentenced for an act which is not forbidden by the law of the Detaining Power or by international law, in force at the time the said act was committed.

No moral or physical coercion may be exerted on a prisoner of war in order to induce him to admit himself guilty of the act of which he is accused.

No prisoner of war may be convicted without having had an opportunity to present his defence and the assistance of a qualified advocate or counsel.

Article 100

Prisoners of war and the Protecting Powers shall be informed as soon as possible of the offences which are punishable by the death sentence under the laws of the Detaining Power.

Other offences shall not thereafter be made punishable by the death penalty without the concurrence of the Power upon which the prisoners of war depend.

The death sentence cannot be pronounced on a prisoner of war unless the attention of the court has, in accordance with Article 87, second paragraph, been particularly called to the fact that since the accused is not a national of the Detaining Power, he is not bound to it by any duty of allegiance, and that he is in its power as the result of circumstances independent of his own will.

Article 101

If the death penalty is pronounced on a prisoner of war, the sentence shall not be executed before the expiration of a period of at least six months from the date when the Protecting Power receives, at an indicated address, the detailed communication provided for in Article 107.

Article 102

A prisoner of war can be validly sentenced only if the sentence has been pronounced by the same courts according to the same procedure as in the case of members of the armed forces of the Detaining Power, and if, furthermore, the provisions of the present Chapter have been observed.

Article 103

Judicial investigations relating to a prisoner of war shall be conducted as rapidly as circumstances permit and so that his trial shall take place as soon as possible. A prisoner of war shall not be confined while awaiting trial unless a member of the armed forces of the Detaining Power would be so confined if he were accused of a similar offence, or if it is essential to do so in the interests of national security. In no circumstances shall this confinement exceed three months.

Any period spent by a prisoner of war in confinement awaiting trial shall be deducted from any sentence of imprisonment passed upon him and taken into account in fixing any penalty.

The provisions of Articles 97 and 98 of this Chapter shall apply to a prisoner of war whilst in confinement awaiting trial.

Article 104

In any case in which the Detaining Power has decided to institute judicial proceedings against a prisoner of war, it shall notify the Protecting Power as soon as possible and at least three weeks before the opening of the trial. This period of three weeks shall run as from the day on which such notification reaches the Protecting Power at the address previously indicated by the latter to the Detaining Power.

The said notification shall contain the following information:

1. Surname and first names of the prisoner of war, his rank, his army, regimental, personal or serial number, his date of birth, and his profession or trade, if any;

2. Place of internment or confinement;

3. Specification of the charge or charges on which the prisoner of war is to be arraigned, giving the legal provisions applicable;

4. Designation of the court which will try the case, likewise the date and place fixed for the opening of the trial.

The same communication shall be made by the Detaining Power to the prisoners' representative.

If no evidence is submitted, at the opening of a trial, that the notification referred to above was received by the Protecting Power, by the prisoner of war and by the prisoners' representative concerned, at least three weeks before the opening of the trial, then the latter cannot take place and must be adjourned.

Article 105

The prisoner of war shall be entitled to assistance by one of his prisoner comrades, to defence by a qualified advocate or counsel of his own choice, to the calling of witnesses and, if he deems necessary, to the services of a competent interpreter. He shall be advised of these rights by the Detaining Power in due time before the trial.

Failing a choice by the prisoner of war, the Protecting Power shall find him an advocate or counsel, and shall have at least one week at its disposal for the purpose. The Detaining Power shall deliver to the said Power, on request, a list of persons qualified to present the defence. Failing a choice of an advocate or counsel by the prisoner of war or the Protecting Power, the Detaining Power shall appoint a competent advocate or counsel to conduct the defence.

The advocate or counsel conducting the defence on behalf of the prisoner of war shall have at his disposal a period of two weeks at least before the opening of the trial, as well as the necessary facilities to prepare the defence of the accused. He may, in particular, freely visit the accused and interview him in private. He may also confer with any witnesses for the defence, including prisoners of war. He shall have the benefit of these facilities until the term of appeal or petition has expired.

Particulars of the charge or charges on which the prisoner of war is to be arraigned, as well as the documents which are generally communicated to the accused by virtue of the laws in force in the armed forces of the Detaining Power, shall be communicated to the accused prisoner of war in a language which he understands, and in good time before the opening of the trial. The same communication in the same circumstances shall be made to the advocate or counsel conducting the defence on behalf of the prisoner of war.

The representatives of the Protecting Power shall be entitled to attend the trial of the case, unless, exceptionally, this is held *in camera* in the interest of State security. In such a case the Detaining Power shall advise the Protecting Power accordingly.

Article 106

Every prisoner of war shall have, in the same manner as the members of the armed forces of the Detaining Power, the right of appeal or petition from any sentence pronounced upon him, with a view to the quashing or revising of the sentence or the reopening of the trial. He shall be fully informed of his right to appeal or petition and of the time limit within which he may do so.

Article 107

Any judgment and sentence pronounced upon a prisoner of war shall be immediately reported to the Protecting Power in the form of a summary communication, which shall also indicate whether he has the right of appeal with a view to the quashing of the sentence or the reopening of the trial. This communication shall likewise be sent to the prisoners' representative concerned. It shall also be sent to the accused prisoner of war in a language he understands, if the sentence was not pronounced in his presence. The Detaining Power shall also immediately communicate to the Protecting Power the decision of the prisoner of war to use or to waive his right of appeal.

Furthermore, if a prisoner of war is finally convicted or if a sentence pronounced on a prisoner of war in the first instance is a death sentence, the Detaining Power shall as soon as possible address to the Protecting Power a detailed communication containing:

1.   The precise wording of the finding and sentence;

2.   A summarized report of any preliminary investigation and of the trial, emphasizing in particular the elements of the prosecution and the defence;

3.   Notification, where applicable, of the establishment where the sentence will be served.

The communications provided for in the foregoing subparagraphs shall be sent to the Protecting Power at the address previously made known to the Detaining Power.

Article 108

Sentences pronounced on prisoners of war after a conviction has become duly enforceable, shall be served in the same establishments and under the same conditions as in the case of members of the armed forces of the Detaining Power. These conditions shall in all cases conform to the requirements of health and humanity.

A woman prisoner of war on whom such a sentence has been pronounced shall be confined in separate quarters and shall be under the supervision of women.

In any case, prisoners of war sentenced to a penalty depriving them of their liberty shall retain the benefit of the provisions of Articles 78 and 126 of the present Convention. Furthermore, they shall be entitled to receive and despatch correspondence, to receive at least one relief parcel monthly, to take regular exercise in the open air, to have the medical care required by their state of health, and the spiritual assistance they may desire. Penalties to which they may be subjected shall be in accordance with the provisions of Article 87, third paragraph.

PART IV

TERMINATION OF CAPTIVITY

SECTION I

DIRECT REPATRIATION AND ACCOMMODATION IN NEUTRAL COUNTRIES

Article 109

Subject to the provisions of the third paragraph of this Article, Parties to the conflict are bound to send back to their own country, regardless of number or rank, seriously wounded and seriously sick prisoners of war, after having cared for them until they are fit to travel, in accordance with the first paragraph of the following Article.

Throughout the duration of hostilities, Parties to the conflict shall endeavour, with the cooperation of the neutral Powers concerned, to make arrangements for the accommodation in neutral countries of the sick and wounded prisoners of war referred to in the second paragraph of the following Article. They may, in addition, conclude agreements with a view to the direct repatriation or internment in a neutral country of able-bodied prisoners of war who have undergone a long period of captivity.

No sick or injured prisoner of war who is eligible for repatriation under the first paragraph of this Article, may be repatriated against his will during hostilities.

Article 110

The following shall be repatriated direct:

1. Incurably wounded and sick whose mental or physical fitness seems to have been gravely diminished.

2. Wounded and sick who, according to medical opinion, are not likely to recover within one year, whose condition requires treatment and whose mental or physical fitness seems to have been gravely diminished.

3. Wounded and sick who have recovered, but whose mental or physical fitness seems to have been gravely and permanently diminished.

The following may be accommodated in a neutral country:

1. Wounded and sick whose recovery may be expected within one year of the date of the wound or the beginning of the illness, if treatment in a neutral country might increase the prospects of a more certain and speedy recovery.

2. Prisoners of war whose mental or physical health, according to medical opinion, is seriously threatened by continued captivity, but whose accommodation in a neutral country might remove such a threat.

The conditions which prisoners of war accommodated in a neutral country must fulfil in order to permit their repatriation shall be fixed, as shall likewise their status, by agreement between the Powers concerned. In general, prisoners of war who have been accommodated in a neutral country, and who belong to the following categories, should be repatriated:

1. Those whose state of health has deteriorated so as to fulfil the conditions laid down for direct repatriation;

2. Those whose mental or physical powers remain, even after treatment, considerably impaired.

If no special agreements are concluded between the Parties to the conflict concerned, to determine the cases of disablement or sickness entailing direct repatriation or accommodation in a neutral country, such cases shall be settled in accordance with the principles laid down in the Model Agreement concerning direct repatriation and accommodation in neutral countries of wounded and sick prisoners of war and in the Regulations concerning Mixed Medical Commissions annexed to the present Convention.

Article 111

The Detaining Power, the Power on which the prisoners of war depend, and a neutral Power agreed upon by these two Powers, shall endeavour to conclude agreements which will enable prisoners of war to be interned in the territory of the said neutral Power until the close of hostilities.

Article 112

Upon the outbreak of hostilities, Mixed Medical Commissions shall be appointed to examine sick and wounded prisoners of war, and to make all appropriate decisions regarding them. The appointment, duties and functioning of these Commissions shall be in conformity with the provisions of the Regulations annexed to the present Convention.

However, prisoners of war who, in the opinion of the medical authorities of the Detaining Power, are manifestly seriously injured or seriously sick, may be repatriated without having to be examined by a Mixed Medical Commission.

Article 113

Besides those who are designated by the medical authorities of the Detaining Power, wounded or sick prisoners of war belonging to the categories listed below shall be entitled to present themselves for examination by the Mixed Medical Commissions provided for in the foregoing Article:

1. Wounded and sick proposed by a physician or surgeon who is of the same nationality, or a national of a Party to the conflict allied with the Power on which the said prisoners depend, and who exercises his functions in the camp.

2. Wounded and sick proposed by their prisoners' representative.

3. Wounded and sick proposed by the Power on which they depend, or by an organization duly recognized by the said Power and giving assistance to the prisoners.

Prisoners of war who do not belong to one of the three foregoing categories may nevertheless present themselves for examination by Mixed Medical Commissions, but shall be examined only after those belonging to the said categories.

The physician or surgeon of the same nationality as the prisoners who present themselves for examination by the Mixed Medical Commission, likewise the prisoners' representative of the said prisoners, shall have permission to be present at the examination.

Article 114

Prisoners of war who meet with accidents shall, unless the injury is self-inflicted, have the benefit of the provisions of this Convention as regards repatriation or accommodation in a neutral country.

Article 115

No prisoner of war on whom a disciplinary punishment has been imposed and who is eligible for repatriation or for accommodation in a neutral country, may be kept back on the plea that he has not undergone his punishment.

Prisoners of war detained in connection with a judicial prosecution or conviction and who are designated for repatriation or accommodation in a neutral country, may benefit by such measures before the end of the proceedings or the completion of the punishment, if the Detaining Power consents.

Parties to the conflict shall communicated to each other the names of those who will be detained until the end of the proceedings or the completion of the punishment.

Article 116

The costs of repatriating prisoners of war or of transporting them to a neutral country shall be borne, from the frontiers of the Detaining Power, by the Power on which the said prisoners depend.

Article 117

No repatriated person may be employed on active military service.

SECTION II

RELEASE AND REPATRIATION OF PRISONERS OF WAR
AT THE CLOSE OF HOSTILITIES

Article 118

Prisoners of war shall be released and repatriated without delay after the cessation of active hostilities.

In the absence of stipulations to the above effect in any agreement concluded between the Parties to the conflict with a view to the cessation of hostilities, or failing any such agreement, each of the Detaining Powers shall itself establish and execute without delay a plan of repatriation in conformity with the principle laid down in the foregoing paragraph.

In either case, the measures adopted shall be brought to the knowledge of the prisoners of war.

The costs of repatriation of prisoners of war shall in all cases be equitably apportioned between the Detaining Power and the Power on which the prisoners depend. This apportionment shall be carried out on the following basis:

(*a*) If the two Powers are contiguous, the Power on which the prisoners of war depend shall bear the costs of repatriation from the frontiers of the Detaining Power.

(*b*) If the two Powers are not contiguous, the Detaining Power shall bear the costs of transport of prisoners of war over its own territory as far as its frontier or its port of embarkation nearest to the territory of the Power on which the prisoners of war depend. The Parties concerned shall agree between themselves as to the equitable apportionment of the remaining costs of the repatriation. The conclusion of this agreement shall in no circumstances justify any delay in the repatriation of the prisoners of war.

Article 119

Repatriation shall be effected in conditions similar to those laid down in Articles 46 to 48 inclusive of the present Convention for the transfer of prisoners of war, having regard to the provisions of Article 118 and to those of the following paragraphs.

On repatriation, any articles of value impounded from prisoners of war under Article 18, and any foreign currency which has not been converted into the currency of the Detaining Power, shall be restored to them. Articles of value and foreign currency which, for any reason whatever, are not restored to prisoners of war on repatriation, shall be despatched to the Information Bureau set up under Article 122.

Prisoners of war shall be allowed to take with them their personal effects, and any correspondence and parcels which have arrived for them. The weight of such baggage may be limited, if the conditions of repatriation so require, to what each prisoner can reasonably carry. Each prisoner shall in all cases be authorized to carry at least twenty-five kilograms.

The other personal effects of the repatriated prisoner shall be left in the charge of the Detaining Power which shall have them forwarded to him as soon as it has concluded an agreement to this effect, regulating the conditions of transport and the payment of the costs involved, with the Power on which the prisoner depends.

Prisoners of war against whom criminal proceedings for an indictable offence are pending may be detained until the end of such proceedings, and, if necessary, until the completion of the punishment. The same shall apply to prisoners of war already convicted for an indictable offence.

Parties to the conflict shall communicate to each other the names of any prisoners of war who are detained until the end of the proceedings or until punishment has been completed.

By agreement between the Parties to the conflict, commissions shall be established for the purpose of searching for dispersed prisoners of war and of assuring their repatriation with the least possible delay.

SECTION III

DEATH OF PRISONERS OF WAR

Article 120

Wills of prisoners of war shall be drawn up so as to satisfy the conditions of validity required by the legislation of their country of origin, which will take steps to inform the Detaining Power of its requirements in this respect. At the request of the prisoner of war and, in all cases, after death, the will shall be transmitted without delay to the Protecting Power; a certified copy shall be sent to the Central Agency.

Death certificates in the form annexed to the present Convention, or lists certified by a responsible officer, of all persons who die as prisoners of war shall be forwarded as rapidly as possible to the Prisoner of War Information Bureau established in accordance with Article 122. The death certificates or certified lists shall show particulars of identity as set out in the third paragraph of Article 17, and also the date and place of death, the cause of death, the date and place of burial and all particulars necessary to identify the graves.

The burial or cremation of a prisoner of war shall be preceded by a medical examination of the body with a view to confirming death and enabling a report to be made and, where necessary, establishing identity.

The detaining authorities shall ensure that prisoners of war who have died in captivity are honourably buried, if possible according to the rites of the religion to which they belonged, and that their graves are respected, suitably maintained and marked so as to be found at any time. Wherever possible, deceased prisoners of war who depended on the same Power shall be interred in the same place.

Deceased prisoners of war shall be buried in individual graves unless unavoidable circumstances require the use of collective graves. Bodies may be cremated only for imperative reasons of hygiene, on account of the religion of the deceased or in accordance with his express wish to this effect. In case of cremation, the fact shall be stated and the reasons given in the death certificate of the deceased.

In order that graves may always be found, all particulars of burials and graves shall be recorded with a Graves Registration Service established by the Detaining Power. Lists of graves and particulars of the prisoners of war interred in cemeteries and elsewhere shall be transmitted to the Power on which such prisoners of war depended. Responsibility for the care of these graves and for records of any subsequent moves of the bodies shall rest on the Power controlling the territory, if a Party to the present Convention. These provisions shall also apply to the ashes, which shall be kept by the Graves Registration Service until proper disposal thereof in accordance with the wishes of the home country.

Article 121

Every death or serious injury of a prisoner of war caused or suspected to have been caused by a sentry, another prisoner of war, or any other person, as well as any death the cause of which is unknown, shall be immediately followed by an official enquiry by the Detaining Power.

A communication on this subject shall be sent immediately to the Protecting Power. Statements shall be taken from witnesses, especially from those who are prisoners of war, and a report including such statements shall be forwarded to the Protecting Power.

If the enquiry indicates the guilt of one or more persons, the Detaining Power shall take all measures for the prosecution of the person or persons responsible.

PART V

INFORMATION BUREAUX AND RELIEF SOCIETIES FOR PRISONERS OF WAR

Article 122

Upon the outbreak of a conflict and in all cases of occupation, each of the Parties to the conflict shall institute an official Information Bureau for prisoners of war who are in its power. Neutral or non-belligerent Powers who may have received within their territory persons belonging to one of the categories referred to in Article 4, shall take the same action with respect to such persons. The Power concerned shall ensure that the Prisoners of War Information Bureau is provided with the necessary accommodation, equipment and staff to ensure its efficient working. It shall be at liberty to employ prisoners of war in such a Bureau under the conditions laid down in the Section of the present Convention dealing with work by prisoners of war.

Within the shortest possible period, each of the Parties to the conflict shall give its Bureau the information referred to in the fourth, fifth and sixth paragraphs of this Article regarding any enemy person belonging to one of the categories referred to in Article 4, who has fallen into its power. Neutral or non-belligerent Powers shall take the same action with regard to persons belonging to such categories whom they have received within their territory.

The Bureau shall immediately forward such information by the most rapid means to the Powers concerned, through the intermediary of the Protecting Powers and likewise of the Central Agency provided for in Article 123.

This information shall make it possible quickly to advise the next of kin concerned. Subject to the provisions of Article 17, the information shall include, in so far as available to the Information Bureau, in respect of each prisoner of war, his surname, first names, rank, army, regimental, personal or serial number, place and full date of birth, indication of the Power on which he depends, first name of the father and maiden name of the mother, name and address of the person to be informed and the address to which correspondence for the prisoner may be sent.

The Information Bureau shall receive from the various departments concerned information regarding transfers, releases, repatriations, escapes, admissions to hospital, and deaths, and shall transmit such information in the manner described in the third paragraph above.

Likewise, information regarding the state of health of prisoners of war who are seriously ill or seriously wounded shall be supplied regularly, every week if possible.

The Information Bureau shall also be responsible for replying to all enquiries sent to it concerning prisoners of war, including those who have died in captivity; it will make any enquiries necessary to obtain the information which is asked for if this is not in its possession.

All written communications made by the Bureau shall be authenticated by a signature or a seal.

The Information Bureau shall furthermore be charged with collecting all personal valuables, including sums in currencies other than that of the Detaining Power and documents of importance to the next of kin, left by prisoners of war who have been repatriated or released, or who have escaped or died, and shall forward the said valuables to the Powers concerned. Such articles shall be sent by the Bureau in sealed packets which shall be accompanied by statements giving clear and full particulars of the identity of the person to whom the articles belonged, and by a complete list of the contents of the parcel. Other personal effects of such prisoners of war shall be transmitted under arrangements agreed upon between the Parties to the conflict concerned.

Article 123

A Central Prisoners of War Information Agency shall be created in a neutral country. The International Committee of the Red Cross shall, if it deems necessary, propose to the Powers concerned the organization of such an Agency.

The function of the Agency shall be to collect all the information it may obtain through official or private channels respecting prisoners of war, and to transmit it as rapidly as possible to the country of origin of the prisoners of war or to the Power on which they depend. It shall receive from the Parties to the conflict all facilities for effecting such transmissions.

The High Contracting Parties, and in particular those whose nationals benefit by the services of the Central Agency, are requested to give the said Agency the financial aid it may require.

The foregoing provisions shall in no way be interpreted as restricting the humanitarian activities of the International Committee of the Red Cross, or of the relief Societies provided for in Article 125.

Article 124

The national Information Bureaux and the Central Information Agency shall enjoy free postage for mail, likewise all the exemptions provided for in Article 74, and further, so far as possible, exemption from telegraphic charges or, at least, greatly reduced rates.

Article 125

Subject to the measures which the Detaining Powers may consider essential to ensure their security or to meet any other reasonable need, the representatives of religious organizations, relief societies, or any other organization assisting prisoners of war, shall receive from the said Powers, for themselves and their duly accredited agents, all necessary facilities for visiting the prisoners, distributing relief supplies and material, from any source, intended for religious, educational or recreative purposes, and for assisting them in organizing their leisure time within the camps. Such societies or organizations may be constituted in the territory of the Detaining Power or in any other country, or they may have an international character.

The Detaining Power may limit the number of societies and organizations whose delegates are allowed to carry out their activities in its territory

and under its supervision, on condition, however, that such limitation shall
not hinder the effective operation of adequate relief to all prisoners of war.

The special position of the International Committee of the Red Cross
in this field shall be recognized and respected at all times.

As soon as relief supplies or material intended for the above-
mentioned purposes are handed over to prisoners of war, or very shortly afterwards, receipts for each consignment, signed by the prisoners' representative, shall be forwarded to the relief society or organization making
the shipment. At the same time, receipts for these consignments shall be
supplied by the administrative authorities responsible for guarding the prisoners.

PART VI

EXECUTION OF THE CONVENTION

SECTION I

GENERAL PROVISIONS

Article 126

Representatives or delegates of the Protecting Powers shall have permission to go to all places where prisoners of war may be, particularly to
places of internment, imprisonment and labour, and shall have access to all
premises occupied by prisoners of war; they shall also be allowed to go to
the places of departure, passage and arrival of prisoners who are being transferred. They shall be able to interview the prisoners, and in particular the
prisoners' representatives, without witnesses, either personally or through an
interpreter.

Representatives and delegates of the Protecting Powers shall have full
liberty to select the places they wish to visit. The duration and frequency of
these visits shall not be restricted. Visits may not be prohibited except for
reasons of imperative military necessity, and then only as an exceptional and
temporary measure.

The Detaining Power and the Power on which the said prisoners of
war depend may agree, if necessary, that compatriots of these prisoners of
war be permitted to participate in the visits.

The delegates of the International Committee of the Red Cross shall
enjoy the same prerogatives. The appointment of such delegates shall be
submitted to the approval of the Power detaining the prisoners of war to be
visited.

Article 127

The High Contracting Parties undertake, in time of peace as in time of war, to disseminate the text of the present Convention as widely as possible in their respective countries, and, in particular, to include the study thereof in their programmes of military and, if possible, civil instruction, so that the principles thereof may become known to all their armed forces and to the entire population.

Any military or other authorities, who in time of war assume responsibilities in respect of prisoners of war, must possess the text of the Convention and be specially instructed as to its provisions.

Article 128

The High Contracting Parties shall communicate to one another through the Swiss Federal Council and, during hostilities, through the Protecting Powers, the official translations of the present Convention, as well as the laws and regulations which they may adopt to ensure the application thereof.

Article 129

The High Contracting Parties undertake to enact any legislation necessary to provide effective penal sanctions for persons committing, or ordering to be committed, any of the grave breaches of the present Convention defined in the following Article.

Each High Contracting Party shall be under the obligation to search for persons alleged to have committed, or to have ordered to be committed, such grave breaches, and shall bring such persons, regardless of their nationality, before its own courts. It may also, if it prefers, and in accordance with the provisions of its own legislation, hand such persons over for trial to another High Contracting Party concerned, provided such High Contracting Party has made out a *prima facie* case.

Each High Contracting Party shall take measures necessary for the suppression of all acts contrary to the provisions of the present Convention other than the grave breaches defined in the following Article.

In all circumstances, the accused persons shall benefit by safeguards of proper trial and defence, which shall not be less favourable than those provided by Article 105 and those following of the present Convention.

Article 130

Grave breaches to which the preceding Article relates shall be those involving any of the following acts, if committed against persons or property protected by the Convention: wilful killing, torture or inhuman treatment, including biological experiments, wilfully causing great suffering or serious injury to body or health, compelling a prisoner of war to serve in the forces of the hostile Power, or wilfully depriving a prisoner of war of the rights of fair and regular trial prescribed in this Convention.

Article 131

No High Contracting Party shall be allowed to absolve itself or any other High Contracting Party of any liability incurred by itself or by another High Contracting Party in respect of breaches referred to in the preceding Article.

Article 132

At the request of a Party to the conflict, an enquiry shall be instituted, in a manner to be decided between the interested Parties, concerning any alleged violation of the Convention.

If agreement has not been reached concerning the procedure for the enquiry, the Parties should agree on the choice of an umpire who will decide upon the procedure to be followed.

Once the violation has been established, the Parties to the conflict shall put an end to it and shall repress it with the least possible delay.

SECTION II

FINAL PROVISIONS

Article 133

The present Convention is established in English and in French. Both texts are equally authentic.

The Swiss Federal Council shall arrange for official translations of the Convention to be made in the Russian and Spanish languages.

Article 134

The present Convention replaces the Convention of 27 July 1929, in relations between the High Contracting Parties.

Article 135

In the relations between the Powers which are bound by The Hague Convention respecting the Laws and Customs of War on Land, whether that of July 29, 1899, or that of October 18, 1907, and which are parties to the present Convention, this last Convention shall be complementary to Chapter II of the Regulations annexed to the above-mentioned Conventions of The Hague.

Article 136

The present Convention, which bears the date of this day, is open to signature until February 12, 1950, in the name of the Powers represented at the Conference which opened at Geneva on April 21, 1949; furthermore, by Powers not represented at that Conference, but which are parties to the Convention of July 27, 1929.

Article 137

The present Convention shall be ratified as soon as possible and the ratifications shall be deposited at Berne.

A record shall be drawn up of the deposit of each instrument of ratification and certified copies of this record shall be transmitted by the Swiss Federal Council to all the Powers in whose name the Convention has been signed, or whose accession has been notified.

Article 138

The present Convention shall come into force six months after not less than two instruments of ratification have been deposited.

Thereafter, it shall come into force for each High Contracting Party six months after the deposit of the instrument of ratification.

Article 139

From the date of its coming into force, it shall be open to any Power in whose name the present Convention has not been signed, to accede to this Convention.

Article 140

Accessions shall be notified in writing to the Swiss Federal Council, and shall take effect six months after the date on which they are received.

The Swiss Federal Council shall communicate the accessions to all the Powers in whose name the Convention has been signed, or whose accession has been notified.

Article 141

The situations provided for in Articles 2 and 3 shall give immediate effect to ratifications deposited and accessions notified by the Parties to the conflict before or after the beginning of hostilities or occupation. The Swiss Federal Council shall communicate by the quickest method any ratifications or accessions received from Parties to the conflict.

Article 142

Each of the High Contracting Parties shall be at liberty to denounce the present Convention.

The denunciation shall be notified in writing to the Swiss Federal Council, which shall transmit it to the Governments of all the High Contracting Parties.

The denunciation shall take effect one year after the notification thereof has been made to the Swiss Federal Council. However, a denunciation of which notification has been made at a time when the denouncing Power is involved in a conflict shall not take effect until peace has been concluded, and until after operations connected with the release and repatriation of the persons protected by the present Convention have been terminated.

The denunciation shall have effect only in respect of the denouncing Power. It shall in no way impair the obligations which the Parties to the conflict shall remain bound to fulfil by virtue of the principles of the law of nations, as they result from the usages established among civilized peoples, from the laws of humanity and the dictates of the public conscience.

Article 143

The Swiss Federal Council shall register the present Convention with the Secretariat of the United Nations. The Swiss Federal Council shall also inform the Secretariat of the United Nations of all ratifications, accessions and denunciations received by it with respect to the present Convention.

IN WITNESS WHEREOF the undersigned, having deposited their respective full powers, have signed the present Convention.

DONE at Geneva this twelfth day of August 1949, in the English and French languages. The original shall be deposited in the Archives of the Swiss Confederation. The Swiss Federal Council shall transmit certified copies thereof to each of the signatory and acceding States.

ANNEX I

**Model agreement concerning direct repatriation and accommodation
in neutral countries of wounded and sick prisoners of war**

(see Article 110)

I.—PRINCIPLES FOR DIRECT REPATRIATION
AND ACCOMMODATION IN NEUTRAL COUNTRIES

A. DIRECT REPATRIATION

The following shall be repatriated direct:

1. All prisoners of war suffering from the following disabilities as the result of trauma: loss of limb, paralysis, articular or other disabilities, when this disability is at least the loss of a hand or a foot, or the equivalent of the loss of a hand or a foot.

Without prejudice to a more generous interpretation, the following shall be considered as equivalent to the loss of a hand or a foot:

(*a*) Loss of a hand or of all the fingers, or of the thumb and forefinger of one hand; loss of a foot, or of all the toes and metatarsals of one foot.

(*b*) Ankylosis, loss of osseous tissue, cicatricial contracture preventing the functioning of one of the large articulations or of all the digital joints of one hand.

(*c*) Pseudarthrosis of the long bones.

(*d*) Deformities due to fracture or other injury which seriously interfere with function and weight-bearing power.

2. All wounded prisoners of war whose condition has become chronic, to the extent that prognosis appears to exclude recovery—in spite of treatment—within one year from the date of the injury, as, for example, in case of:

(*a*) Projectile in the heart, even if the Mixed Medical Commission should fail, at the time of their examination, to detect any serious disorders.

(*b*) Metallic splinter in the brain or the lungs, even if the Mixed Medical Commission cannot, at the time of examination, detect any local or general reaction.

(*c*) Osteomyelitis, when recovery cannot be foreseen in the course of the year following the injury, and which seems likely to result in ankylosis of a joint, or other impairments equivalent to the loss of a hand or a foot.

(*d*) Perforating and suppurating injury to the large joints.

(*e*) Injury to the skull, with loss or shifting of bony tissue.

(*f*) Injury or burning of the face with loss of tissue and functional lesions.

(*g*) Injury to the spinal cord.

(*h*) Lesion of the peripheral nerves, the sequelae of which are equivalent to the loss of a hand or foot, and the cure of which requires more than a year from the date of injury, for example: injury to the brachial or lumbosacral plexus, the median or sciatic nerves, likewise combined injury to the radial and cubital nerves or to the lateral popliteal nerve (*N. peroneus communis*) and medial popliteal nerve (*N. tibialis*); etc. The separate injury of the radial (musculo-spiral), cubital, lateral or medial popliteal nerves shall not, however, warrant repatriation except in case of contractures or of serious neurotrophic disturbance.

(*i*) Injury to the urinary system, with incapacitating results.

3. All sick prisoners of war whose condition has become chronic to the extent that prognosis seems to exclude recovery—in spite of treatment—within one year from the inception of the disease, as, for example, in case of:

(*a*) Progressive tuberculosis of any organ which, according to medical prognosis, cannot be cured, or at least considerably improved, by treatment in a neutral country.

(*b*) Exudate pleurisy.

(*c*) Serious diseases of the respiratory organs of non-tubercular etiology, presumed incurable, for example: serious pulmonary emphysema, with or without bronchitis; chronic asthma;* chronic bronchitis* lasting more than one year in captivity; bronchiectasis;* etc.

(*d*) Serious chronic affections of the circulatory system, for example: valvular lesions and myocarditis,* which have shown signs of circulatory failure during captivity, even though the Mixed Medical Commission cannot detect any such signs at the time of examination; affections of the pericardium and the vessels (Buerger's disease, aneurism of the large vessels); etc.

(*e*) Serious chronic affections of the digestive organs, for example: gastric or duodenal ulcer; sequelae of gastric operations performed in captivity; chronic gastritis, enteritis or colitis, having lasted more than one year and seriously affecting the general condition; cirrhosis of the liver; chronic cholecystopathy;* etc.

(*f*) Serious chronic affections of the genito-urinary organs, for example: chronic diseases of the kidney with consequent disorders; nephrectomy because of a tubercular kidney; chronic pyelitis or chronic cystitis; hydronephrosis or pyonephrosis; chronic grave gynaecological conditions; normal pregnancy and obstetrical disorder, where it is impossible to accommodate in a neutral country; etc.

(*g*) Serious chronic diseases of the central and peripheral nervous system, for example: all obvious psychoses and psychoneuroses, such as serious hysteria, serious captivity psychoneurosis, etc., duly verified by a specialist;* any epilepsy duly verified by the camp physician;* cerebral arteriosclerosis; chronic neuritis lasting more than one year; etc.

(*h*) Serious chronic diseases of the neuro-vegetative system, with considerable diminution of mental or physical fitness, noticeable loss of weight and general asthenia.

(*i*) Blindness of both eyes, or of one eye when the vision of the other is less than 1 in spite of the use of corrective glasses; diminution of visual acuity in cases where it is impossible to restore it by correction to an acuity of 1/2 in at least one eye;* other grave ocular affections, for example: glaucoma, iritis, choroiditis; trachoma; etc.

(*k*) Auditive disorders, such as total unilateral deafness, if the other ear does not discern the ordinary spoken word at a distance of one metre;* etc.

(*l*) Serious affections of metabolism, for example: diabetes mellitus requiring insulin treatment; etc.

(*m*) Serious disorders of the endocrine glands, for example: thyrotoxicosis; hypothyrosis; Addison's disease; Simmonds' cachexia; tetany; etc.

(*n*) Grave and chronic disorders of the blood-forming organs.

(*o*) Serious cases of chronic intoxication, for example: lead poisoning, mercury poisoning, morphinism, cocainism, alcoholism; gas or radiation poisoning; etc.

(*p*) Chronic affections of locomotion, with obvious functional disorders, for example: arthritis deformans; primary and secondary progressive chronic polyarthritis; rheumatism with serious clinical symptoms; etc.

(*q*) Serious chronic skin diseases, not amenable to treatment.

---

* The decision of the Mixed Medical Commission shall be based to a great extent on the records kept by camp physicians and surgeons of the same nationality as the prisoners of war, or on an examination by medical specialists of the Detaining Power.

(*r*) Any malignant growth.

(*s*) Serious chronic infectious diseases, persisting for one year after their inception, for example: malaria with decided organic impairment, amoebic or bacillary dysentery with grave disorders; tertiary visceral syphilis resistant to treatment; leprosy; etc.

(*t*) Serious avitaminosis or serious inanition.

B. ACCOMMODATION IN NEUTRAL COUNTRIES

The following shall be eligible for accommodation in a neutral country:

1.   All wounded prisoners of war who are not likely to recover in captivity, but who might be cured or whose condition might be considerably improved by accommodation in a neutral country.

2.   Prisoners of war suffering from any form of tuberculosis, of whatever organ, and whose treatment in a neutral country would be likely to lead to recovery or at least to considerable improvement, with the exception of primary tuberculosis cured before captivity.

3.   Prisoners of war suffering from affections requiring treatment of the respiratory, circulatory, digestive, nervous, sensory, genito-urinary, cutaneous, locomotive organs, etc., if such treatment would clearly have better results in a neutral country than in captivity.

4.   Prisoners of war who have undergone a nephrectomy in captivity for a non-tubercular renal affection; cases of osteomyelitis, on the way to recovery or latent; diabetes mellitus not requiring insulin treatment; etc.

5.   Prisoners of war suffering from war or captivity neuroses.

Cases of captivity neurosis which are not cured after three months of accommodation in a neutral country, or which after that length of time are not clearly on the way to complete cure, shall be repatriated.

6.   All prisoners of war suffering from chronic intoxication (gases, metals, alkaloids, etc.), for whom the prospects of cure in a neutral country are especially favourable.

7.   All women prisoners of war who are pregnant or mothers with infants and small children.

The following cases shall not be eligible for accommodation in a neutral country:

1.   All duly verified chronic psychoses.

2.   All organic or functional nervous affections considered to be incurable.

3.   All contagious diseases during the period in which they are transmissible, with the exception of tuberculosis.

II.—GENERAL OBSERVATIONS

1.   The conditions given shall, in a general way, be interpreted and applied in as broad a spirit as possible.

Neuropathic and psychopathic conditions caused by war or captivity, as well as cases of tuberculosis in all stages, shall above all benefit by such liberal interpretation. Prisoners of war who have sustained several wounds, none of which, considered by itself, justifies repatriation, shall be examined in the same spirit, with due regard for the psychic traumatism due to the number of their wounds.

2.   All unquestionable cases giving the right to direct repatriation (amputation, total blindness or deafness, open pulmonary tuberculosis, mental disorder, malignant growth, etc.)

shall be examined and repatriated as soon as possible by the camp physicians or by military medical commissions appointed by the Detaining Power.

3.   Injuries and diseases which existed before the war and which have not become worse, as well as war injuries which have not prevented subsequent military service, shall not entitle to direct repatriation.

4.   The provisions of this Annex shall be interpreted and applied in a similar manner in all countries party to the conflict. The Powers and authorities concerned shall grant to Mixed Medical Commissions all the facilities necessary for the accomplishment of their task.

5.   The examples quoted under (I) above represent only typical cases. Cases which do not correspond exactly to these provisions shall be judged in the spirit of the provisions of Article 110 of the present Convention, and of the principles embodied in the present Agreement.

ANNEX II

Regulations concerning Mixed Medical Commissions

(see Article 112)

Article 1

The Mixed Medical Commissions provided for in Article 112 of the Convention shall be composed of three members, two of whom shall belong to a neutral country, the third being appointed by the Detaining Power. One of the neutral members shall take the chair.

Article 2

The two neutral members shall be appointed by the International Committee of the Red Cross, acting in agreement with the Protecting Power, at the request of the Detaining Power. They may be domiciled either in their country of origin, in any other neutral country, or in the territory of the Detaining Power.

Article 3

The neutral members shall be approved by the Parties to the conflict concerned, who shall notify their approval to the International Committee of the Red Cross and to the Protecting Power. Upon such notification, the neutral members shall be considered as effectively appointed.

Article 4

Deputy members shall also be appointed in sufficient number to replace the regular members in case of need. They shall be appointed at the same time as the regular members or, at least, as soon as possible.

Article 5

If for any reason the International Committee of the Red Cross cannot arrange for the appointment of the neutral members, this shall be done by the Power protecting the interests of the prisoners of war to be examined.

Article 6

So far as possible, one of the two neutral members shall be a surgeon and the other a physician.

Article 7

The neutral members shall be entirely independent of the Parties to the conflict, which shall grant them all facilities in the accomplishment of their duties.

Article 8

By agreement with the Detaining Power, the International Committee of the Red Cross, when making the appointments provided for in Articles 2 and 4 of the present Regulations, shall settle the terms of service of the nominees.

Article 9

The Mixed Medical Commissions shall begin their work as soon as possible after the neutral members have been approved, and in any case within a period of three months from the date of such approval.

Article 10

The Mixed Medical Commissions shall examine all the prisoners designated in Article 113 of the Convention. They shall propose repatriation, rejection, or reference to a later examination. Their decisions shall be made by a majority vote.

Article 11

The decisions made by the Mixed Medical Commissions in each specific case shall be communicated, during the month following their visit, to the Detaining Power, the Protecting Power and the International Committee of the Red Cross. The Mixed Medical Commissions shall also inform each prisoner of war examined of the decision made, and shall issue to those whose repatriation has been proposed, certificates similar to the model appended to the present Convention.

Article 12

The Detaining Power shall be required to carry out the decisions of the Mixed Medical Commissions within three months of the time when it receives due notification of such decisions.

Article 13

If there is no neutral physician in a country where the services of a Mixed Medical Commission seem to be required, and if it is for any reason impossible to appoint neutral doctors who are resident in another country, the Detaining Power, acting in agreement with the Protecting Power, shall set up a Medical Commission which shall undertake the same duties as a Mixed Medical Commission, subject to the provisions of Articles 1, 2, 3, 4, 5 and 8 of the present Regulations.

Article 14

Mixed Medical Commissions shall function permanently and shall visit each camp at intervals of not more than six months.

ANNEX III

Regulations concerning collective relief

(see Article 73)

Article 1

Prisoners' representatives shall be allowed to distribute collective relief shipments for which they are responsible, to all prisoners of war administered by their camp, including those who are in hospitals, or in prisons or other penal establishments.

Article 2

The distribution of collective relief shipments shall be effected in accordance with the instructions of the donors and with a plan drawn up by the prisoners' representatives. The issue of medical stores shall, however, be made for preference in agreement with the senior medical officers, and the latter may, in hospitals and infirmaries, waive the said instructions, if the needs of their patients so demand. Within the limits thus defined, the distribution shall always be carried out equitably.

Article 3

The said prisoners' representatives or their assistants shall be allowed to go to the points of arrival of relief supplies near their camps, so as to enable the prisoners' representatives or their assistants to verify the quality as well as the quantity of the goods received, and to make out detailed reports thereon for the donors.

Article 4

Prisoners' representatives shall be given the facilities necessary for verifying whether the distribution of collective relief in all sub-divisions and annexes of their camps has been carried out in accordance with their instructions.

Article 5

Prisoners' representatives shall be allowed to fill up, and cause to be filled up by the prisoners' representatives of labour detachments or by the senior medical officers of infirmaries and hospitals, forms or questionnaires intended for the donors, relating to collective relief supplies (distribution, requirements, quantities, etc.). Such forms and questionnaires, duly completed, shall be forwarded to the donors without delay.

Article 6

In order to secure the regular issue of collective relief to the prisoners of war in their camp, and to meet any needs that may arise from the arrival of new contingents of prisoners, prisoners' representatives shall be allowed to build up and maintain adequate reserve stocks of collective relief. For this purpose, they shall have suitable warehouses at their disposal; each warehouse shall be provided with two locks, the prisoners' representative holding the keys of one lock and the camp commander the keys of the other.

Article 7

When collective consignments of clothing are available each prisoner of war shall retain in his possession at least one complete set of clothes. If a prisoner has more than one set of clothes, the prisoners' representative shall be permitted to withdraw excess clothing from those with the largest number of sets, or particular articles in excess of one, if this is necessary in order to supply prisoners who are less well provided. He shall not, however, withdraw second sets of underclothing, socks or footwear, unless this is the only means of providing for prisoners of war with none.

Article 8

The High Contracting Parties, and the Detaining Powers in particular, shall authorize, as far as possible and subject to the regulations governing the supply of the population, all purchases of goods made in their territories for the distribution of collective relief to prisoners of war. They shall similarly facilitate the transfer of funds and other financial measures of a technical or administrative nature taken for the purpose of making such purchases.

Article 9

The foregoing provisions shall not constitute an obstacle to the right of prisoners of war to receive collective relief before their arrival in a camp or in the course of transfer, nor to the possibility of representatives of the Protecting Power, the International Committee of the Red Cross, or any other body giving assistance to prisoners which may be responsible for the forwarding of such supplies, ensuring the distribution thereof to the addressees by any other means that they may deem useful.

ANNEX IV

A. IDENTITY CARD

(see Article 4)

NOTICE

This identity card is issued to persons who accompany the Armed Forces of but are not part of them. The card must be carried at all times by the person to whom it is issued. If the bearer is taken prisoner, he shall at once hand the card to the Detaining Authorities, to assist in his identification.

Fingerprints (optional)

(Right forefinger)

(Left forefinger)

Any other mark of identification ....

Official seal imprint

Religion ....

Blood type ....

Hair

Eyes

Weight

Height

Photograph of the bearer

(Name of the country and military authority issuing this card)

IDENTITY CARD

FOR A PERSON WHO ACCOMPANIES
THE ARMED FORCES

Name ....

First names ....

Date and place of birth ....

Accompanies the Armed Forces as ....

Date of issue   Signature of bearer

....

Remarks. — This card should be made out for preference in two or three languages, one of which is in international use. Actual size of the card: 13 by 10 centimetres. It should be folded along the dotted line.

ANNEX IV

B. CAPTURE CARD

1. Front

(see Article 70)

PRISONER OF WAR MAIL | Postage free

CAPTURE CARD FOR PRISONER OF WAR

IMPORTANT

This card must be completed by each prisoner immediately after being taken prisoner and each time his address is changed (by reason of transfer to a hospital or to another camp).

This card is distinct from the special card which each prisoner is allowed to send to his relatives.

CENTRAL PRISONERS
OF WAR AGENCY

INTERNATIONAL COMMITTEE
OF THE RED CROSS

GENEVA

SWITZERLAND

2. Reverse side

Write legibly and in block letters

1. Power on which the prisoner depends ....

2. Name   3. First names (in full)   4. First name of father

5. Date of birth .... 6. Place of birth ....

7. Rank ....

8. Service number ....

9. Address of next of kin ....

*10. Taken prisoner on: (or)
Coming from (Camp No., hospital, etc.) ....

*11. (a) Good health—(b) Not wounded—(c) Recovered—(d) Convalescent—(e) Sick—(f) Slightly wounded—(g) Seriously wounded.

12. My present address is: Prisoner No. ....

Name of camp ....

13. Date .... 14. Signature ....

* Strike out what is not applicable—Do not add any remarks—See explanations overleaf.

Remarks.—This form should be made out in two or three languages, particularly in the prisoner's own language and in that of the Detaining Power. Actual size: 15 by 10.5 centimetres.

ANNEX IV

C. CORRESPONDENCE CARD AND LETTER

(see Article 71)

1. Front　　　　　　　　　　　　　　　　　　　　　　　　I. CARD.

PRISONER OF WAR MAIL

POST CARD

| Postage free |

To ....

Sender:
Name and first names
....

Place and date of birth
....

Prisoner of War No.
....

Name of camp
....

Country where posted
....

Place of Destination
....

Street ....

Country ....

Province or Department ....

2, Reverse side.

NAME OF CAMP .... Date ....

....

....

....

....

....

....

....

....

Write on the dotted lines only and as legibly as possible.

Remarks.—This form should be made out in two or three languages, particularly in the prisoner's own language and in that of the Detaining Power. Actual size of form: 15 by 10 centimetres.

ANNEX IV

C. CORRESPONDENCE CARD AND LETTER
(see Article 71)

2. LETTER

PRISONER OF WAR MAIL

Postage free

To ....

....

Place ....

Street ....

Country ....

Department or Province ....

Country where posted

Name of camp

Prisoner of War No.

Date and place of birth

Name and first names

Sender:

****

Remarks.—This form should be made out in two or three languages, particularly in the prisoner's own language and in that of the Detaining Power. It should be folded along the dotted line, the tab being inserted in the slit (marked by a line of asterisks); it then has the appearance of an envelope. Overleaf, it is lined like the postcard above (*Annex IV C 1*); this space can contain about 250 words which the prisoner is free to write. Actual size of the folded form: 29 by 15 centimetres.

ANNEX IV

D. NOTIFICATION OF DEATH

(see Article 120)

(Title of responsible   NOTIFICATION OF DEATH
   authority)

                                   Power on which the
                                   prisoner depended ....

Name and first names   ....

First name of father   ....

Place and date of birth   ....

Place and date of death   ....

Rank and service number (as given on
   identity disc)   ....

Address of next of kin   ....

Where and when taken prisoner   ....

Cause and circumstances of death   ....

Place of burial   ....

Is the grave marked and can it be found
   later by the relatives?   ....

Are the personal effects of the deceased   ....
   in the keeping of the Detaining Power   ....
   or are they being forwarded together   ....
   with this notification?   ....

If forwarded, through what agency? ....

Can the person who cared for the deceased   ....
   during sickness or during his last   ....
   moments (doctor, nurse, minister of   ....
   religion, fellow prisoner) give here or   ....
   on an attached sheet a short account   ....
   of the circumstances of the death and   ....
   burial?

(Date, seal and signature of responsible   Signature and address of two witnesses
   authority.)

....

Remarks.—This form should be made out in two or three languages, particularly in the prisoner's own language and in that of the Detaining Power. Actual size of the form: 21 by 30 centimetres.

ANNEX IV

E. REPATRIATION CERTIFICATE
(see Annex II, Article 11)

REPATRIATION CERTIFICATE

Date :

Camp :

Hospital :

Surname :

First names :

Date of birth :

Rank :

Army number :

P. W. number :

Injury-Disease :

Decision of the Commission :

Chairman of the
Mixed Medical Commission :

A = direct repatriation
B = accommodation in a neutral country
NC = re-examination by next Commission

ANNEX V

Model regulations concerning payments sent by prisoners to their own country

(see Article 63)

1.   The notification referred to in the third paragraph of Article 63 will show:

(*a*) Number as specified in Article 17, rank, surname and first names of the prisoner of war who is the payer;

(*b*) The name and address of the payee in the country of origin;

(*c*) The amount to be so paid in the currency of the country in which he is detained.

2.   The notification will be signed by the prisoner of war, or his witnessed mark made upon if it he cannot write, and shall be countersigned by the prisoners' representative.

3.   The camp commander will add to this notification a certificate that the prisoner of war concerned has a credit balance of not less than the amount registered as payable.

4.   The notification may be made up in lists, each sheet of such lists witnessed by the prisoners' representative and certified by the camp commander.

92. Geneva Convention relative to the Protection of Civilian Persons in Time of War

Adopted on 12 August 1949 by the Diplomatic Conference for the Establishment of International Conventions for the Protection of Victims of War, held in Geneva from 21 April to 12 August, 1949

ENTRY INTO FORCE: 21 October 1950

PART I

GENERAL PROVISIONS

Article 1

The High Contracting Parties undertake to respect and to ensure respect for the present Convention in all circumstances.

Article 2

In addition to the provisions which shall be implemented in peacetime, the present Convention shall apply to all cases of declared war or of any other armed conflict which may arise between two or more of the High Contracting Parties, even if the state of war is not recognized by one of them.

The Convention shall also apply to all cases of partial or total occupation of the territory of a High Contracting Party, even if the said occupation meets with no armed resistance.

Although one of the Powers in conflict may not be a party to the present Convention, the Powers who are parties thereto shall remain bound by it in their mutual relations. They shall furthermore be bound by the Convention in relation to the said Power, if the latter accepts and applies the provisions thereof.

Article 3

In the case of armed conflict not of an international character occurring in the territory of one of the High Contracting Parties, each Party to the conflict shall be bound to apply, as a minimum, the following provisions:

1.   Persons taking no active part in the hostilities, including members of armed forces who have laid down their arms and those placed *hors de*

combat by sickness, wounds, detention, or any other cause, shall in all circumstances be treated humanely, without any adverse distinction founded on race, colour, religion or faith, sex, birth or wealth, or any other similar criteria.

To this end, the following acts are and shall remain prohibited at any time and in any place whatsoever with respect to the above-mentioned persons:

(*a*) Violence to life and person, in particular murder of all kinds, mutilation, cruel treatment and torture;

(*b*) Taking of hostages;

(*c*) Outrages upon personal dignity, in particular humiliating and degrading treatment;

(*d*) The passing of sentences and the carrying out of executions without previous judgment pronounced by a regularly constituted court, affording all the judicial guarantees which are recognized as indispensable by civilized peoples.

2. The wounded and sick shall be collected and cared for.

An impartial humanitarian body, such as the International Committee of the Red Cross, may offer its services to the Parties to the conflict.

The Parties to the conflict should further endeavour to bring into force, by means of special agreements, all or part of the other provisions of the present Convention.

The application of the preceding provisions shall not affect the legal status of the Parties to the conflict.

Article 4

Persons protected by the Convention are those who, at a given moment and in any manner whatsoever, find themselves, in case of a conflict or occupation, in the hands of a Party to the conflict or Occupying Power of which they are not nationals.

Nationals of a State which is not bound by the Convention are not protected by it. Nationals of a neutral State who find themselves in the territory of a belligerent State, and nationals of a co-belligerent State, shall not be regarded as protected persons while the State of which they are nationals has normal diplomatic representation in the State in whose hands they are.

The provisions of Part II are, however, wider in application, as defined in Article 13.

Persons protected by the Geneva Convention for the Amelioration of the Condition of the Wounded and Sick in Armed Forces in the Field of August 12, 1949, or by the Geneva Convention for the Amelioration of the

Condition of Wounded, Sick and Shipwrecked Members of Armed Forces at Sea of August 12, 1949, or by the Geneva Convention relative to the Treatment of Prisoners of War of August 12, 1949, shall not be considered as protected persons within the meaning of the present Convention.

Article 5

Where, in the territory of a Party to the conflict, the latter is satisfied that an individual protected person is definitely suspected of or engaged in activities hostile to the security of the State, such individual person shall not be entitled to claim such rights and privileges under the present Convention as would, if exercised in the favour of such individual person, be prejudicial to the security of such State.

Where in occupied territory an individual protected person is detained as a spy or saboteur, or as a person under definite suspicion of activity hostile to the security of the Occupying Power, such person shall, in those cases where absolute military security so requires, be regarded as having forfeited rights of communication under the present Convention.

In each case, such persons shall nevertheless be treated with humanity, and in case of trial, shall not be deprived of the rights of fair and regular trial prescribed by the present Convention. They shall also be granted the full rights and privileges of a protected person under the present Convention at the earliest date consistent with the security of the State or Occupying Power, as the case may be.

Article 6

The present Convention shall apply from the outset of any conflict or occupation mentioned in Article 2.

In the territory of Parties to the conflict, the application of the present Convention shall cease on the general close of military operations.

In the case of occupied territory, the application of the present Convention shall cease one year after the general close of military operations; however, the Occupying Power shall be bound, for the duration of the occupation, to the extent that such Power exercises the functions of government in such territory, by the provisions of the following Articles of the present Convention: 1 to 12, 27, 29 to 34, 47, 49, 51, 52, 53, 59, 61 to 77, and 143.

Protected persons whose release, repatriation or re-establishment may take place after such dates shall meanwhile continue to benefit by the present Convention.

Article 7

In addition to the agreements expressly provided for in Articles 11, 14, 15, 17, 36, 108, 109, 132, 133 and 149, the High Contracting Parties may conclude other special agreements for all matters concerning which they may deem it suitable to make separate provision. No special agreement shall adversely affect the situation of protected persons, as defined by the present Convention, nor restrict the rights which it confers upon them.

Protected persons shall continue to have the benefit of such agreements as long as the Convention is applicable to them, except where express provisions to the contrary are contained in the aforesaid or in subsequent agreements, or where more favourable measures have been taken with regard to them by one or other of the Parties to the conflict.

Article 8

Protected persons may in no circumstances renounce in part or in entirety the rights secured to them by the present Convention, and by the special agreements referred to in the foregoing Article, if such there be.

Article 9

The present Convention shall be applied with the cooperation and under the scrutiny of the Protecting Powers whose duty it is to safeguard the interests of the Parties to the conflict. For this purpose, the Protecting Powers may appoint, apart from their diplomatic or consular staff, delegates from amongst their own nationals or the nationals of other neutral Powers. The said delegates shall be subject to the approval of the Power with which they are to carry out their duties.

The Parties to the conflict shall facilitate to the greatest extent possible the task of the representatives or delegates of the Protecting Powers.

The representatives or delegates of the Protecting Powers shall not in any case exceed their mission under the present Convention. They shall, in particular, take account of the imperative necessities of security of the State wherein they carry out their duties.

Article 10

The provisions of the present Convention constitute no obstacle to the humanitarian activities which the International Committee of the Red Cross or any other impartial humanitarian organization may, subject to the consent of the Parties to the conflict concerned, undertake for the protection of civilian persons and for their relief.

Article 11

The High Contracting Parties may at any time agree to entrust to an organization which offers all guarantees of impartiality and efficacy the duties incumbent on the Protecting Powers by virtue of the present Convention.

When persons protected by the present Convention do not benefit or cease to benefit, no matter for what reason, by the activities of a Protecting Power or of an organization provided for in the first paragraph above, the Detaining Power shall request a neutral State, or such an organization, to undertake the functions performed under the present Convention by a Protecting Power designated by the Parties to a conflict.

If protection cannot be arranged accordingly, the Detaining Power shall request or shall accept, subject to the provisions of this Article, the offer of the services of a humanitarian organization, such as the International Committee of the Red Cross, to assume the humanitarian functions performed by Protecting Powers under the present Convention.

Any neutral Power, or any organization invited by the Power concerned or offering itself for these purposes, shall be required to act with a sense of responsibility towards the Party to the conflict on which persons protected by the present Convention depend, and shall be required to furnish sufficient assurances that it is in a position to undertake the appropriate functions and to discharge them impartially.

No derogation from the preceding provisions shall be made by special agreements between Powers one of which is restricted, even temporarily, in its freedom to negotiate with the other Power or its allies by reason of military events, more particularly where the whole, or a substantial part, of the territory of the said Power is occupied.

Whenever in the present Convention mention is made of a Protecting Power, such mention applies to substitute organizations in the sense of the present Article.

The provisions of this Article shall extend and be adapted to cases of nationals of a neutral State who are in occupied territory or who find themselves in the territory of a belligerent State with which the State of which they are nationals has not normal diplomatic representation.

Article 12

In cases where they deem it advisable in the interest of protected persons, particularly in cases of disagreement between the Parties to the conflict as to the application or interpretation of the provisions of the present Convention, the Protecting Powers shall lend their good offices with a view to settling the disagreement.

For this purpose, each of the Protecting Powers may, either at the invitation of one Party or on its own initiative, propose to the Parties to the conflict a meeting of their representatives, and in particular of the authorities responsible for protected person, possibly on neutral territory suitably chosen. The Parties to the conflict shall be bound to give effect to the proposals made to them for this purpose. The Protecting Powers may, if necessary, propose for approval by the Parties to the conflict, a person belonging to a neutral Power or delegated by the International Committee of the Red Cross, who shall be invited to take part in such a meeting.

PART II

GENERAL PROTECTION OF POPULATIONS AGAINST CERTAIN CONSEQUENCES OF WAR

Article 13

The provisions of Part II cover the whole of the populations of the countries in conflict, without any adverse distinction based, in particular, on race, nationality, religion or political opinion, and are intended to alleviate the sufferings caused by war.

Article 14

In time of peace, the High Contracting Parties and, after the outbreak of hostilities, the Parties thereto, may establish in their own territory and, if the need arises, in occupied areas, hospital and safety zones and localities so organized as to protect from the effects of war, wounded, sick and aged persons, children under fifteen, expectant mothers and mothers of children under seven.

Upon the outbreak and during the course of hostilities, the Parties concerned may conclude agreements on mutual recognition of the zones and localities they have created. They may for this purpose implement the provisions of the Draft Agreement annexed to the present Convention, with such amendments as they may consider necessary.

The Protecting Powers and the International Committee of the Red Cross are invited to lend their good offices in order to facilitate the institution and recognition of these hospital and safety zones and localities.

Article 15

Any Party to the conflict may, either directly or through a neutral State or some humanitarian organization, propose to the adverse Party to establish, in the regions where fighting is taking place, neutralized zones intended to shelter from the effects of war the following persons, without distinction:

(*a*) Wounded and sick combatants or non-combatants;

(*b*) Civilian persons who take no part in hostilities, and who, while they reside in the zones, perform no work of a military character.

When the Parties concerned have agreed upon the geographical position, administration, food supply and supervision of the proposed neutralized zone, a written agreement shall be concluded and signed by the representatives of the Parties to the conflict. The agreement shall fix the beginning and the duration of the neutralization of the zone.

Article 16

The wounded and sick, as well as the infirm, and expectant mothers, shall be the object of particular protection and respect.

As far as military considerations allow, each Party to the conflict shall facilitate the steps taken to search for the killed and wounded, to assist the shipwrecked and other persons exposed to grave danger, and to protect them against pillage and ill-treatment.

Article 17

The Parties to the conflict shall endeavour to conclude local agreements for the removal from besieged or encircled areas, of wounded, sick, infirm, and aged persons, children and maternity cases, and for the passage of ministers of all religions, medical personnel and medical equipment on their way to such areas.

Article 18

Civilian hospitals organized to give care to the wounded and sick, the infirm and maternity cases, may in no circumstances be the object of attack, but shall at all times be respected and protected by the Parties to the conflict.

States which are Parties to a conflict shall provide all civilian hospitals with certificates showing that they are civilian hospitals and that the buildings which they occupy are not used for any purpose which would deprive these hospitals of protection in accordance with Article 19.

Civilian hospitals shall be marked by means of the emblem provided for in Article 38 of the Geneva Convention for the Amelioration of the Condition of the Wounded and Sick in Armed Forces in the Field of August 12, 1949, but only if so authorized by the State.

The Parties to the conflict shall, in so far as military considerations permit, take the necessary steps to make the distinctive emblems indicating civilian hospitals clearly visible to the enemy land, air and naval forces in order to obviate the possibility of any hostile action.

In view of the dangers to which hospitals may be exposed by being close to military objectives, it is recommended that such hospitals be situated as far as possible from such objectives.

Article 19

The protection to which civilian hospitals are entitled shall not cease unless they are used to commit, outside their humanitarian duties, acts harmful to the enemy. Protection may, however, cease only after due warning has been given, naming, in all appropriate cases, a reasonable time limit, and after such warning has remained unheeded.

The fact that sick or wounded members of the armed forces are nursed in these hospitals, or the presence of small arms and ammunition taken from such combatants which have not yet been handed to the proper service, shall not be considered to be acts harmful to the enemy.

Article 20

Persons regularly and solely engaged in the operation and administration of civilian hospitals, including the personnel engaged in the search for, removal and transporting of and caring for wounded and sick civilians, the infirm and maternity cases, shall be respected and protected.

In occupied territory and in zones of military operations, the above personnel shall be recognizable by means of an identity card certifying their status, bearing the photograph of the holder and embossed with the stamp of the responsible authority, and also by means of a stamped, water-resistant armlet which they shall wear on the left arm while carrying out their duties. This armlet shall be issued by the State and shall bear the emblem provided for in Article 38 of the Geneva Convention for the Amelioration of the Condition of the Wounded and Sick in Armed Forces in the Field of August 12, 1949.

Other personnel who are engaged in the operation and administration of civilian hospitals shall be entitled to respect and protection and to wear the armlet, as provided in and under the conditions prescribed in this Article, while they are employed on such duties. The identity card shall state the duties on which they are employed.

The management of each hospital shall at all times hold at the disposal of the competent national or occupying authorities an up-to-date list of such personnel.

Article 21

Convoys of vehicles or hospital trains on land or specially provided vessels on sea, conveying wounded and sick civilians, the infirm and maternity cases, shall be respected and protected in the same manner as the hospitals provided for in Article 18, and shall be marked, with the consent of the State, by the display of the distinctive emblem provided for in Article 38 of the Geneva Convention for the Amelioration of the Condition of the Wounded and Sick in Armed Forces in the Field of August 12, 1949.

Article 22

Aircraft exclusively employed for the removal of wounded and sick civilians, the infirm and maternity cases, or for the transport of medical personnel and equipment, shall not be attacked, but shall be respected while flying at heights, times and on routes specifically agreed upon between all the Parties to the conflict concerned.

They may be marked with the distinctive emblem provided for in Article 38 of the Geneva Convention for the Amelioration of the Condition of the Wounded and Sick in Armed Forces in the Field of August 12, 1949.

Unless agreed otherwise, flights over enemy or enemy-occupied territory are prohibited.

Such aircraft shall obey every summons to land. In the event of a landing thus imposed, the aircraft with its occupants may continue its flight after examination, if any.

Article 23

Each High Contracting Party shall allow the free passage of all consignments of medical and hospital stores and objects necessary for religious worship intended only for civilians of another High Contracting Party, even if the latter is its adversary. It shall likewise permit the free passage of all consignments of essential foodstuffs, clothing and tonics intended for children under fifteen, expectant mothers and maternity cases.

The obligation of a High Contracting Party to allow the free passage of the consignments indicated in the preceding paragraph is subject to the condition that this Party is satisfied that there are no serious reasons for fearing:

(*a*) That the consignments may be diverted from their destination;

(*b*) That the control may not be effective; or

(*c*) That a definite advantage may accrue to the military efforts or economy of the enemy through the substitution of the above-mentioned consignments for goods which would otherwise be provided or produced by the enemy or through the release of such material, services or facilities as would otherwise be required for the production of such goods.

The Power which allows the passage of the consignments indicated in the first paragraph of this Article may make such permission conditional on the distribution to the persons benefited thereby being made under the local supervision of the Protecting Powers.

Such consignments shall be forwarded as rapidly as possible, and the Power which permits their free passage shall have the right to prescribe the technical arrangements under which such passage is allowed.

Article 24

The Parties to the conflict shall take the necessary measures to ensure that children under fifteen, who are orphaned or are separated from their families as a result of the war, are not left to their own resources, and that their maintenance, the exercise of their religion and their education are facilitated in all circumstances. Their education shall, as far as possible, be entrusted to persons of a similar cultural tradition.

The Parties to the conflict shall facilitate the reception of such children in a neutral country for the duration of the conflict with the consent of the Protecting Power, if any, and under due safeguards for the observance of the principles stated in the first paragraph.

They shall, furthermore, endeavour to arrange for all children under twelve to be identified by the wearing of identity discs, or by some other means.

Article 25

All persons in the territory of a Party to the conflict, or in a territory occupied by it, shall be enabled to give news of a strictly personal nature to members of their families, wherever they may be, and to receive news from them. This correspondence shall be forwarded speedily and without undue delay.

If, as a result of circumstances, it becomes difficult or impossible to exchange family correspondence by the ordinary post, the Parties to the conflict concerned shall apply to a neutral intermediary, such as the Central Agency provided for in Article 140, and shall decide in consultation with it how to ensure the fulfilment of their obligations under the best possible conditions, in particular with the cooperation of the National Red Cross (Red Crescent, Red Lion and Sun) Societies.

If the Parties to the conflict deem it necessary to restrict family correspondence, such restrictions shall be confined to the compulsory use of standard forms containing twenty-five freely chosen words, and to the limitation of the number of these forms despatched to one each month.

Article 26

Each Party to the conflict shall facilitate enquiries made by members of families dispersed owing to the war, with the object of renewing contact with one another and of meeting, if possible. It shall encourage, in particular, the work of organizations engaged on this task provided they are acceptable to it and conform to its security regulations.

PART III

STATUS AND TREATMENT OF PROTECTED PERSONS

SECTION I

PROVISIONS COMMON TO THE TERRITORIES OF THE PARTIES TO THE CONFLICT AND TO OCCUPIED TERRITORIES

Article 27

Protected persons are entitled, in all circumstances, to respect for their persons, their honour, their family rights, their religious convictions and practices, and their manners and customs. They shall at all times be humanely treated, and shall be protected especially against all acts of violence or threats thereof and against insults and public curiosity.

Women shall be especially protected against any attack on their honour, in particular against rape, enforced prostitution, or any form of indecent assault.

Without prejudice to the provisions relating to their state of health, age and sex, all protected persons shall be treated with the same consideration by the Party to the conflict in whose power they are, without any adverse distinction based, in particular, on race, religion or political opinion.

However, the Parties to the conflict may take such measures of control and security in regard to protected persons as may be necessary as a result of the war.

Article 28

The presence of a protected person may not be used to render certain points or areas immune from military operations.

Article 29

The Party to the conflict in whose hands protected persons may be is responsible for the treatment accorded to them by its agents, irrespective of any individual responsibility which may be incurred.

Article 30

Protected persons shall have every facility for making application to the Protecting Powers, the International Committee of the Red Cross, the National Red Cross (Red Crescent, Red Lion and Sun) Society of the country where they may be, as well as to any organization that might assist them.

These several organizations shall be granted all facilities for that purpose by the authorities, within the bounds set by military or security considerations.

Apart from the visits of the delegates of the Protecting Powers and of the International Committee of the Red Cross, provided for by Article 143, the Detaining or Occupying Powers shall facilitate as much as possible visits to protected persons by the representatives of other organizations whose object is to give spiritual aid or material relief to such persons.

Article 31

No physical or moral coercion shall be exercised against protected persons, in particular to obtain information from them or from third parties.

Article 32

The High Contracting Parties specifically agree that each of them is prohibited from taking any measure of such a character as to cause the physical suffering or extermination of protected persons in their hands. This prohibition applies not only to murder, torture, corporal punishment, mutilation and medical or scientific experiments not necessitated by the medical treatment of a protected person, but also to any other measures of brutality whether applied by civilian or military agents.

Article 33

No protected person may be punished for an offence he or she has not personally committed. Collective penalties and likewise all measures of intimidation or of terrorism are prohibited.

Pillage is prohibited.

Reprisals against protected persons and their property are prohibited.

Article 34

The taking of hostages is prohibited.

SECTION II

ALIENS IN THE TERRITORY OF A PARTY TO THE CONFLICT

Article 35

All protected persons who may desire to leave the territory at the outset of, or during a conflict, shall be entitled to do so, unless their departure is contrary to the national interests of the State. The applications of such persons to leave shall be decided in accordance with regularly established procedures and the decision shall be taken as rapidly as possible. Those persons permitted to leave may provide themselves with the necessary funds for their journey and take with them a reasonable amount of their effects and articles of personal use.

If any such person is refused permission to leave the territory, he shall be entitled to have such refusal reconsidered as soon as possible by an appropriate court or administrative board designated by the Detaining Power for that purpose.

Upon request, representatives of the Protecting Power shall, unless reasons of security prevent it, or the persons concerned object, be furnished with the reasons for refusal of any request for permission to leave the territory and be given, as expeditiously as possible, the names of all persons who have been denied permission to leave.

Article 36

Departures permitted under the foregoing Article shall be carried out in satisfactory conditions as regards safety, hygiene, sanitation and food. All costs in connection therewith, from the point of exit in the territory of the Detaining Power, shall be borne by the country of destination, or, in the case of accommodation in a neutral country, by the Power whose nationals are benefited. The practical details of such movements may, if necessary, be settled by special agreements between the Powers concerned.

The foregoing shall not prejudice such special agreements as may be concluded between Parties to the conflict concerning the exchange and repatriation of their nationals in enemy hands.

Article 37

Protected persons who are confined pending proceedings or serving a sentence involving loss of liberty shall during their confinement be humanely treated.

As soon as they are released, they may ask to leave the territory in conformity with the foregoing Articles.

Article 38

With the exception of special measures authorized by the present Convention, in particular by Articles 27 and 41 thereof, the situation of protected persons shall continue to be regulated, in principle, by the provisions concerning aliens in time of peace. In any case, the following rights shall be granted to them:

1. They shall be enabled to receive the individual or collective relief that may be sent to them.

2. They shall, if their state of health so requires, receive medical attention and hospital treatment to the same extent as the nationals of the State concerned.

3. They shall be allowed to practise their religion and to receive spiritual assistance from ministers of their faith.

4. If they reside in an area particularly exposed to the dangers of war, they shall be authorized to move from that area to the same extent as the nationals of the State concerned.

5. Children under fifteen years, pregnant women and mothers of children under seven years shall benefit by any preferential treatment to the same extent as the nationals of the State concerned.

Article 39

Protected persons who, as a result of the war, have lost their gainful employment, shall be granted the opportunity to find paid employment. That opportunity shall, subject to security considerations and to the provisions of Article 40, be equal to that enjoyed by the nationals of the Power in whose territory they are.

Where a Party to the conflict applies to a protected person methods of control which result in his being unable to support himself, and especially if such a person is prevented for reasons of security from finding paid employment on reasonable conditions, the said Party shall ensure his support and that of his dependents.

Protected persons may in any case receive allowances from their home country, the Protecting Power, or the relief societies referred to in Article 30.

Article 40

Protected persons may be compelled to work only to the same extent as nationals of the Party to the conflict in whose territory they are.

If protected persons are of enemy nationality, they may only be compelled to do work which is normally necessary to ensure the feeding, sheltering, clothing, transport and health of human beings and which is not directly related to the conduct of military operations.

In the cases mentioned in the two preceding paragraphs, protected persons compelled to work shall have the benefit of the same working conditions and of the same safeguards as national workers, in particular as regards wages, hours of labour, clothing and equipment, previous training and compensation for occupational accidents and diseases.

If the above provisions are infringed, protected persons shall be allowed to exercise their right of complaint in accordance with Article 30.

Article 41

Should the Power in whose hands protected persons may be consider the measures of control mentioned in the present Convention to be inadequate, it may not have recourse to any other measure of control more severe than that of assigned residence or internment, in accordance with the provisions of Articles 42 and 43.

In applying the provisions of Article 39, second paragraph, to the cases of persons required to leave their usual places of residences by virtue of a decision placing them in assigned residence elsewhere, the Detaining Power shall be guided as closely as possible by the standards of welfare set forth in Part III, Section IV of this Convention.

Article 42

The internment or placing in assigned residence of protected persons may be ordered only if the security of the Detaining Power makes it absolutely necessary.

If any person, acting through the representatives of the Protecting Power, voluntarily demands internment, and if his situation renders this step necessary, he shall be interned by the Power in whose hands he may be.

Article 43

Any protected person who has been interned or placed in assigned residence shall be entitled to have such action reconsidered as soon as possible by an appropriate court or administrative board designated by the Detaining Power for that purpose. If the internment or placing in assigned residence is maintained, the court or administrative board shall periodically, and at least twice yearly, give consideration to his or her case, with a view to the favourable amendment of the initial decision, if circumstances permit.

Unless the protected persons concerned object, the Detaining Power shall, as rapidly as possible, give the Protecting Power the names of any protected persons who have been interned or subjected to assigned residence, or who have been released from internment or assigned residence. The decisions of the courts or boards mentioned in the first paragraph of the present Article shall also, subject to the same conditions, be notified as rapidly as possible to the Protecting Power.

Article 44

In applying the measures of control mentioned in the present Convention, the Detaining Power shall not treat as enemy aliens exclusively on the basis of their nationality *de jure* of an enemy State, refugees who do not, in fact, enjoy the protection of any government.

Article 45

Protected persons shall not be transferred to a Power which is not a party to the Convention.

This provision shall in no way constitute an obstacle to the repatriation of protected persons, or to their return to their country of residence after the cessation of hostilities.

Protected persons may be transferred by the Detaining Power only to a Power which is a party to the present Convention and after the Detaining Power has satisfied itself of the willingness and ability of such transferee Power to apply the present Convention. If protected persons are transferred under such circumstances, responsibility for the application of the present Convention rests on the Power accepting them, while they are in its custody. Nevertheless, if that Power fails to carry out the provisions of the present Convention in any important respect, the Power by which the protected persons were transferred shall, upon being so notified by the Protecting Power, take effective measures to correct the situation or shall request the return of the protected persons. Such request must be complied with.

In no circumstances shall a protected person be transferred to a country where he or she may have reason to fear persecution for his or her political opinions or religious beliefs.

The provisions of this Article do not constitute an obstacle to the extradition, in pursuance of extradition treaties concluded before the outbreak of hostilities, of protected persons accused of offences against ordinary criminal law.

Article 46

In so far as they have not been previously withdrawn, restrictive measures taken regarding protected persons shall be cancelled as soon as possible after the close of hostilities.

Restrictive measures affecting their property shall be cancelled, in accordance with the law of the Detaining Power, as soon as possible after the close of hostilities.

SECTION III

OCCUPIED TERRITORIES

Article 47

Protected persons who are in occupied territory shall not be deprived, in any case or in any manner whatsoever, of the benefits of the present Convention by any change introduced, as the result of the occupation of a territory, into the institutions or government of the said territory, nor by any agreement concluded between the authorities of the occupied territories and the Occupying Power, nor by any annexation by the latter of the whole or part of the occupied territory.

Article 48

Protected persons who are not nationals of the Power whose territory is occupied may avail themselves of the right to leave the territory subject to the provisions of Article 35, and decisions thereon shall be taken according to the procedure which the Occupying Power shall establish in accordance with the said Article.

Article 49

Individual or mass forcible transfers, as well as deportations of protected persons from occupied territory to the territory of the Occupying Power or to that of any other country, occupied or not, are prohibited, regardless of their motive.

Nevertheless, the Occupying Power may undertake total or partial evacuation of a given area if the security of the population or imperative military reasons do demand. Such evacuations may not involve the displacement of protected persons outside the bounds of the occupied territory except when for material reasons it is impossible to avoid such displacement. Persons thus evacuated shall be transferred back to their homes as soon as hostilities in the area in question have ceased.

The Occupying Power undertaking such transfers or evacuations shall ensure, to the greatest practicable extent, that proper accommodation is provided to receive the protected persons, that the removals are effected in satisfactory conditions of hygiene, health, safety and nutrition, and that members of the same family are not separated.

The Protecting Power shall be informed of any transfers and evacuations as soon as they have taken place.

The Occupying Power shall not detain protected persons in an area particularly exposed to the dangers of war unless the security of the population or imperative military reasons so demand.

The Occupying Power shall not deport or transfer parts of its own civilian population into the territory it occupies.

Article 50

The Occupying Power shall, with the cooperation of the national and local authorities, facilitate the proper working of all institutions devoted to the care and education of children.

The Occupying Power shall take all necessary steps to facilitate the identification of children and the registration of their parentage. It may not, in any case, change their personal status, nor enlist them in formations or organizations subordinate to it.

Should the local institutions be inadequate for the purpose, the Occupying Power shall make arrangements for the maintenance and education, if possible by persons of their own nationality, language and religion, of children who are orphaned or separated from their parents as a result of the war and who cannot be adequately cared for by a near relative or friend.

A special section of the Bureau set up in accordance with Article 136 shall be responsible for taking all necessary steps to identify children whose identity is in doubt. Particulars of their parents or other near relatives should always be recorded if available.

The Occupying Power shall not hinder the application of any preferential measures in regard to food, medical care and protection against the effects of war, which may have been adopted prior to the occupation in favour of children under fifteen years, expectant mothers, and mothers of children under seven years.

Article 51

The Occupying Power may not compel protected persons to serve in its armed or auxiliary forces. No pressure or propaganda which aims at securing voluntary enlistment is permitted.

The Occupying Power may not compel protected persons to work unless they are over eighteen years of age, and then only on work which is necessary either for the needs of the army of occupation, or for the public utility services, or for the feeding, sheltering, clothing, transportation or health of the population of the occupied country. Protected persons may not be compelled to undertake any work which would involve them in the obligation of taking part in military operations. The Occupying Power may not compel protected persons to employ forcible means to ensure the security of the installations where they are performing compulsory labour.

The work shall be carried out only in the occupied territory where the persons whose services have been requisitioned are. Every such person shall, so far as possible, be kept in his usual place of employment. Workers shall be paid a fair wage and the work shall be proportionate to their physical and intellectual capacities. The legislation in force in the occupied country concerning working conditions, and safeguards as regards, in particular, such matters as wages, hours of work, equipment, preliminary training and compensation for occupational accidents and diseases, shall be applicable to the protected persons assigned to the work referred to in this Article.

In no case shall requisition of labour lead to a mobilization of workers in an organization of a military or semi-military character.

Article 52

No contract, agreement or regulation shall impair the right of any worker, whether voluntary or not and wherever he may be, to apply to the representatives of the Protecting Power in order to request the said Power's intervention.

All measures aiming at creating unemployment or at restricting the opportunities offered to workers in an occupied territory, in order to induce them to work for the Occupying Power, are prohibited.

Article 53

Any destruction by the Occupying Power of real or personal property belonging individually or collectively to private persons, or to the State, or to other public authorities, or to social or cooperative organizations, is prohibited, except where such destruction is rendered absolutely necessary by military operations.

Article 54

The Occupying Power may not alter the status of public officials or judges in the occupied territories, or in any way apply sanctions to or take any measures of coercion or discrimination against them, should they abstain from fulfilling their functions for reasons of conscience.

This prohibition does not prejudice the application of the second paragraph of Article 51. It does not affect the right of the Occupying Power to remove public officials from their posts.

Article 55

To the fullest extent of the means available to it the Occupying Power has the duty of ensuring the food and medical supplies of the population; it should, in particular, bring in the necessary foodstuffs, medical stores and other articles if the resources of the occupied territory are inadequate.

The Occupying Power may not requisition foodstuffs, articles or medical supplies available in the occupied territory, except for use by the occupation forces and administration personnel, and then only if the requirements of the civilian population have been taken into account. Subject to the provisions of other international Conventions, the Occupying Power shall make arrangements to ensure that fair value is paid for any requisitioned goods.

The Protecting Power shall, at any time, be at liberty to verify the state of the food and medical supplies in occupied territories, except where temporary restrictions are made necessary by imperative military requirements.

Article 56

To the fullest extent of the means available to it, the Occupying Power has the duty of ensuring and maintaining, with the cooperation of national and local authorities, the medical and hospital establishments and services, public health and hygiene in the occupied territory, with particular reference to the adoption and application of the prophylactic and preventive measures necessary to combat the spread of contagious diseases and epidemics. Medical personnel of all categories shall be allowed to carry out their duties.

If new hospitals are set up in occupied territory and if the competent organs of the occupied State are not operating there, the occupying authorities shall, if necessary, grant them the recognition provided for in Article 18. In similar circumstances, the occupying authorities shall also grant recognition to hospital personnel and transport vehicles under the provisions of Articles 20 and 21.

In adopting measures of health and hygiene and in their implementation, the Occupying Power shall take into consideration the moral and ethical susceptibilities of the population of the occupied territory.

Article 57

The Occupying Power may requisition civilian hospitals only temporarily and only in cases of urgent necessity for the care of military wounded and sick, and then on condition that suitable arrangements are made in due time for the care and treatment of the patients and for the needs of the civilian population for hospital accommodation.

The material and stores of civilian hospitals cannot be requisitioned so long as they are necessary for the needs of the civilian population.

Article 58

The Occupying Power shall permit ministers of religion to give spiritual assistance to the members of their religious communities.

The Occupying Power shall also accept consignments of books and articles required for religious needs and shall facilitate their distribution in occupied territory.

Article 59

If the whole or part of the population of an occupied territory is inadequately supplied, the Occupying Power shall agree to relief schemes on behalf of the said population, and shall facilitate them by all the means at its disposal.

Such schemes, which may be undertaken either by States or by impartial humanitarian organizations such as the International Committee of the Red Cross, shall consist, in particular, of the provision of consignments of foodstuffs, medical supplies and clothing.

All Contracting Parties shall permit the free passage of these consignments and shall guarantee their protection.

A Power granting free passage to consignments on their way to territory occupied by an adverse Party to the conflict shall, however, have the right to search the consignments, to regulate their passage according to prescribed times and routes, and to be reasonably satisfied through the Protecting Power that these consignments are to be used for the relief of the needy population and are not to be used for the benefit of the Occupying Power.

Article 60

Relief consignments shall in no way relieve the Occupying Power of any of its responsibilities under Articles 55, 56 and 59. The Occupying Power shall in no way whatsoever divert relief consignments from the purpose for which they are intended, except in cases of urgent necessity, in the interests of the population of the occupied territory and with the consent of the Protecting Power.

Article 61

The distribution of the relief consignments referred to in the foregoing Articles shall be carried out with the cooperation and under the supervision of the Protecting Power. This duty may also be delegated, by agreement between the Occupying Power and the Protecting Power, to a neutral Power, to the International Committee of the Red Cross or to any other impartial humanitarian body.

Such consignments shall be exempt in occupied territory from all charges, taxes or customs duties unless these are necessary in the interests of the economy of the territory. The Occupying Power shall facilitate the rapid distribution of these consignments.

All Contracting Parties shall endeavour to permit the transit and transport, free of charge, of such relief consignments on their way to occupied territories.

Article 62

Subject to imperative reasons of security, protected persons in occupied territories shall be permitted to receive the individual relief consignments sent to them.

Article 63

Subject to temporary and exceptional measures imposed for urgent reasons of security by the Occupying Power:

(a) Recognized National Red Cross (Red Crescent, Red Lion and Sun) Societies shall be able to pursue their activities in accordance with Red Cross principles, as defined by the International Red Cross Conferences. Other relief societies shall be permitted to continue their humanitarian activities under similar conditions;

(b) The Occupying Power may not require any changes in the personnel or structure of these societies, which would prejudice the aforesaid activities.

The same principles shall apply to the activities and personnel of special organizations of a non-military character, which already exist or which may be established, for the purpose of ensuring the living conditions of the civilian population by the maintenance of the essential public utility services, by the distribution of relief and by the organization of rescues.

Article 64

The penal laws of the occupied territory shall remain in force, with the exception that they may be repealed or suspended by the Occupying Power in cases where they constitute a threat to its security or an obstacle to the application of the present Convention. Subject to the latter consideration and to the necessity for ensuring the effective administration of justice, the tribunals of the occupied territory shall continue to function in respect of all offences covered by the said laws.

The Occupying Power may, however, subject the population of the occupied territory to provisions which are essential to enable the Occupying Power to fulfil its obligations under the present Convention, to maintain the orderly government of the territory, and to ensure the security of the Occupying Power, of the members and property of the occupying forces or administration, and likewise of the establishments and lines of communication used by them.

Article 65

The penal provisions enacted by the Occupying Power shall not come into force before they have been published and brought to the knowledge of the inhabitants in their own language. The effect of these penal provisions shall not be retroactive.

Article 66

In case of a breach of the penal provisions promulgated by it by virtue of the second paragraph of Article 64, the Occupying Power may hand over the accused to its properly constituted, non-political military courts, on condition that the said courts sit in the occupied country. Courts of appeal shall preferably sit in the occupied country.

Article 67

The courts shall apply only those provisions of law which were applicable prior to the offence, and which are in accordance with general principles of law, in particular the principle that the penalty shall be proportioned to the offence. They shall take into consideration the fact that the accused is not a national of the Occupying Power.

Article 68

Protected persons who commit an offence which is solely intended to harm the Occupying Power, but which does not constitute an attempt on the life or limb of members of the occupying forces or administration, nor a grave collective danger, nor seriously damage the property of the occupying forces or administration or the installations used by them, shall be liable to internment or simple imprisonment, provided the duration of such internment or imprisonment is proportionate to the offence committed. Furthermore, internment or imprisonment shall, for such offences, be the only measure adopted for depriving protected persons of liberty. The courts provided for under Article 66 of the present Convention may at their discretion convert a sentence of imprisonment to one of internment for the same period.

The penal provisions promulgated by the Occupying Power in accordance with Articles 64 and 65 may impose the death penalty on a protected person only in cases where the person is guilty of espionage, of serious acts of sabotage against the military installations of the Occupying Power or of intentional offences which have caused the death of one or more persons, provided that such offences were punishable by death under the law of the occupied territory in force before the occupation began.

The death penalty may not be pronounced against a protected person unless the attention of the court has been particularly called to the fact that, since the accused is not a national of the Occupying Power, he is not bound to it by any duty of allegiance.

In any case, the death penalty may not be pronounced against a protected person who was under eighteen years of age at the time of the offence.

Article 69

In all cases, the duration of the period during which a protected person accused of an offence is under arrest awaiting trial or punishment shall be deducted from any period of imprisonment awarded.

Article 70

Protected persons shall not be arrested, prosecuted or convicted by the Occupying Power for acts committed or for opinions expressed before the occupation, or during a temporary interruption thereof, with the exception of breaches of the laws and customs of war.

Nationals of the Occupying Power who, before the outbreak of hostilities, have sought refuge in the territory of the occupied State, shall not be arrested, prosecuted, convicted or deported from the occupied territory, except for offences committed after the outbreak of hostilities, or for offences under common law committed before the outbreak of hostilities which, according to the law of the occupied State, would have justified extradition in time of peace.

Article 71

No sentence shall be pronounced by the competent courts of the Occupying Power except after a regular trial.

Accused persons who are prosecuted by the Occupying Power shall be promptly informed, in writing, in a language which they understand, of the particulars of the charges preferred against them, and shall be brought to trial as rapidly as possible. The Protecting Power shall be informed of all proceedings instituted by the Occupying Power against protected persons in respect of charges involving the death penalty or imprisonment for two years or more; it shall be enabled, at any time, to obtain information regarding the state of such proceedings. Furthermore, the Protecting Power shall be entitled, on request, to be furnished with all particulars of these and of any other proceedings instituted by the Occupying Power against protected persons.

The notification to the Protecting Power, as provided for in the second paragraph above, shall be sent immediately, and shall in any case reach the Protecting Power three weeks before the date of the first hearing. Unless, at the opening of the trial, evidence is submitted that the provisions of this Article are fully complied with, the trial shall not proceed. The notification shall include the following particulars:

(*a*) Description of the accused;

(*b*) Place of residence or detention;

(*c*) Specification of the charge or charges (with mention of the penal provisions under which it is brought);

(*d*) Designation of the court which will hear the case;

(*e*) Place and date of the first hearing.

Article 72

Accused persons shall have the right to present evidence necessary to their defence and may, in particular, call witnesses. They shall have the right to be assisted by a qualified advocate or counsel of their own choice, who shall be able to visit them freely and shall enjoy the necessary facilities for preparing the defence.

Failing a choice by the accused, the Protecting Power may provide him with an advocate or counsel. When an accused person has to meet a serious charge and the Protecting Power is not functioning, the Occupying Power, subject to the consent of the accused, shall provide an advocate or counsel.

Accused persons shall, unless they freely waive such assistance, be aided by an interpreter, both during preliminary investigation and during the hearing in court. They shall have the right at any time to object to the interpreter and to ask for his replacement.

Article 73

A convicted person shall have the right of appeal provided for by the laws applied by the court. He shall be fully informed of his right to appeal or petition and of the time limit within which he may do so.

The penal procedure provided in the present Section shall apply, as far as it is applicable, to appeals. Where the laws applied by the Court make no provision for appeals, the convicted person shall have the right to petition against the finding and sentence to the competent authority of the Occupying Power.

Article 74

Representatives of the Protecting Power shall have the right to attend the trial of any protected person, unless the hearing has, as an exceptional measure, to be held *in camera* in the interests of the security of the Occupying Power, which shall then notify the Protecting Power. A notification in respect of the date and place of trial shall be sent to the Protecting Power.

Any judgment involving a sentence of death, or imprisonment for two years or more, shall be communicated, with the relevant grounds, as rapidly as possible to the Protecting Power. The notification shall contain a reference to the notification made under Article 71, and, in the case of sentences of imprisonment, the name of the place where the sentence is to be served. A record of judgments other than those referred to above shall be kept by the court and shall be open to inspection by representatives of the Protecting Power. Any period allowed for appeal in the case of sentences involving the death penalty, or imprisonment for two years or more, shall not run until notification of judgment has been received by the Protecting Power.

Article 75

In no case shall persons condemned to death be deprived of the right of petition for pardon or reprieve.

No death sentence shall be carried out before the expiration of a period of at least six months from the date of receipt by the Protecting Power of the notification of the final judgment confirming such death sentence, or of an order denying pardon or reprieve.

The six months period of suspension of the death sentence herein prescribed may be reduced in individual cases in circumstances of grave emergency involving an organized threat to the security of the Occupying Power or its forces, provided always that the Protecting Power is notified of such reduction and is given reasonable time and opportunity to make representations to the competent occupying authorities in respect of such death sentences.

Article 76

Protected persons accused of offences shall be detained in the occupied country, and if convicted they shall serve their sentences therein. They shall, if possible, be separated from other detainees and shall enjoy conditions of food and hygiene which will be sufficient to keep them in good health, and which will be at least equal to those obtaining in prisons in the occupied country.

They shall receive the medical attention required by their state of health.

They shall also have the right to receive any spiritual assistance which they may require.

Women shall be confined in separate quarters and shall be under the direct supervision of women.

Proper regard shall be paid to the special treatment due to minors.

Protected persons who are detained shall have the right to be visited by delegates of the Protecting Power and of the International Committee of the Red Cross, in accordance with the provisions of Article 143.

Such persons shall have the right to receive at least one relief parcel monthly.

Article 77

Protected persons who have been accused of offences or convicted by the courts in occupied territory shall be handed over at the close of occupation, with the relevant records, to the authorities of the liberated territory.

Article 78

If the Occupying Power considers it necessary, for imperative reasons of security, to take safety measures concerning protected persons, it may, at the most, subject them to assigned residence or to internment.

Decisions regarding such assigned residence or internment shall be made according to a regular procedure to be prescribed by the Occupying Power in accordance with the provisions of the present Convention. This procedure shall include the right of appeal for the parties concerned. Appeals shall be decided with the least possible delay. In the event of the decision being upheld, it shall be subject to periodical review, if possible every six months, by a competent body set up by the said Power.

Protected persons made subject to assigned residence and thus required to leave their homes shall enjoy the full benefit of Article 39 of the present Convention.

REGULATIONS FOR THE TREATMENT OF INTERNEES

Chapter I

GENERAL PROVISIONS

Article 79

The Parties to the conflict shall not intern protected persons, except in accordance with the provisions of Articles 41, 42, 43, 68 and 78.

Article 80

Internees shall retain their full civil capacity and shall exercise such attendant rights as may be compatible with their status.

Article 81

Parties to the conflict who intern protected persons shall be bound to provide free of charge for their maintenance, and to grant them also the medical attention required by their state of health.

No deduction from the allowances, salaries or credits due to the internees shall be made for the repayment of these costs.

The Detaining Power shall provide for the support of those dependent on the internees, if such dependants are without adequate means of support or are unable to earn a living.

Article 82

The Detaining Power shall, as far as possible, accommodate the internees according to their nationality, language and customs. Internees who are nationals of the same country shall not be separated merely because they have different languages.

Throughout the duration of their internment, members of the same family, and in particular parents and children, shall be lodged together in the same place of internment, except when separation of a temporary nature is necessitated for reasons of employment or health or for the purposes of enforcement of the provisions of Chapter IX of the present Section. Internees may request that their children who are left at liberty without parental care shall be interned with them.

Wherever possible, interned members of the same family shall be housed in the same premises and given separate accommodation from other internees, together with facilities for leading a proper family life.

Chapter II

PLACES OF INTERNMENT

Article 83

The Detaining Power shall not set up places of internment in areas particularly exposed to the dangers of war.

The Detaining Power shall give the enemy Powers, through the intermediary of the Protecting Powers, all useful information regarding the geographical location of places of internment.

Whenever military considerations permit, internment camps shall be indicated by the letters IC, placed so as to be clearly visible in the daytime from the air. The Powers concerned may, however, agree upon any other system of marking. No place other than an internment camp shall be marked as such.

Article 84

Internees shall be accommodated and administered separately from prisoners of war and from persons deprived of liberty for any other reason.

Article 85

The Detaining Power is bound to take all necessary and possible measures to ensure that protected persons shall, from the outset of their internment, be accommodated in buildings or quarters which afford every possible safeguard as regards hygiene and health, and provide efficient protection against the rigours of the climate and the effects of the war. In no case shall permanent places of internment be situated in unhealthy areas or in districts the climate of which is injurious to the internees. In all cases where the district, in which a protected person is temporarily interned, is in an unhealthy area or has a climate which is harmful to his health, he shall be removed to a more suitable place of internment as rapidly as circumstances permit.

The premises shall be fully protected from dampness, adequately heated and lighted, in particular between dusk and lights out. The sleeping quarters shall be sufficiently spacious and well ventilated, and the internees shall have suitable bedding and sufficient blankets, account being taken of the climate, and the age, sex, and state of health of the internees.

Internees shall have for their use, day and night, sanitary conveniences which conform to the rules of hygiene and are constantly maintained in a state of cleanliness. They shall be provided with sufficient water and soap for their daily personal toilet and for washing their personal laundry; installations and facilities necessary for this purpose shall be granted to them.

Showers or baths shall also be available. The necessary time shall be set aside for washing and for cleaning.

Whenever it is necessary, as an exceptional and temporary measure, to accommodate women internees who are not members of a family unit in the same place of internment as men, the provision of separate sleeping quarters and sanitary conveniences for the use of such women internees shall be obligatory.

Article 86

The Detaining Power shall place at the disposal of interned persons, of whatever denomination, premises suitable for the holding of their religious services.

Article 87

Canteens shall be installed in every place of internment, except where other suitable facilities are available. Their purpose shall be to enable internees to make purchases, at prices not higher than local market prices, of foodstuffs and articles of everyday use, including soap and tobacco, such as would increase their personal well-being and comfort.

Profits made by canteens shall be credited to a welfare fund to be set up for each place of internment, and administered for the benefit of the internees attached to such place of internment. The Internee Committee provided for in Article 102 shall have the right to check the management of the canteen and of the said fund.

When a place of internment is closed down, the balance of the welfare fund shall be transferred to the welfare fund of a place of internment for internees of the same nationality, or, if such a place does not exist, to a central welfare fund which shall be administered for the benefit of all internees remaining in the custody of the Detaining Power. In case of a general release, the said profits shall be kept by the Detaining Power, subject to any agreement to the contrary between the Powers concerned.

Article 88

In all places of internment exposed to air raids and other hazards of war, shelters adequate in number and structure to ensure the necessary protection shall be installed. In case of alarms, the internees shall be free to enter such shelters as quickly as possible, excepting those who remain for the protection of their quarters against the aforesaid hazards. Any protective measures taken in favour of the population shall also apply to them.

All due precautions must be taken in places of internment against the danger of fire.

Chapter III

FOOD AND CLOTHING

Article 89

Daily food rations for internees shall be sufficient in quantity, quality and variety to keep internees in a good state of health and prevent the development of nutritional deficiencies. Account shall also be taken of the customary diet of the internees.

Internees shall also be given the means by which they can prepare for themselves any additional food in their possession.

Sufficient drinking water shall be supplied to internees. The use of tobacco shall be permitted.

Internees who work shall receive additional rations in proportion to the kind of labour which they perform.

Expectant and nursing mothers and children under fifteen years of age shall be given additional food, in proportion to their physiological needs.

Article 90

When taken into custody, internees shall be given all facilities to provide themselves with the necessary clothing, footwear and change of underwear, and later on, to procure further supplies if required. Should any internees not have sufficient clothing, account being taken of the climate, and be unable to procure any, it shall be provided free of charge to them by the Detaining Power.

The clothing supplied by the Detaining Power to internees and the outward markings placed on their own clothes shall not be ignominious nor expose them to ridicule.

Workers shall receive suitable working outfits, including protective clothing, whenever the nature of their work so requires.

Chapter IV

HYGIENE AND MEDICAL ATTENTION

Article 91

Every place of internment shall have an adequate infirmary, under the direction of a qualified doctor, where internees may have the attention they require, as well as an appropriate diet. Isolation wards shall be set aside for cases of contagious or mental diseases.

Maternity cases and internees suffering from serious diseases, or whose condition requires special treatment, a surgical operation or hospital care, must be admitted to any institution where adequate treatment can be given and shall receive care not inferior to that provided for the general population.

Internees shall, for preference, have the attention of medical personnel of their own nationality.

Internees may not be prevented from presenting themselves to the medical authorities for examination. The medical authorities of the Detaining Power shall, upon request, issue to every internee who has undergone treatment an official certificate showing the nature of his illness or injury, and the duration and nature of the treatment given. A duplicate of this certificate shall be forwarded to the Central Agency provided for in Article 140.

Treatment, including the provision of any apparatus necessary for the maintenance of internees in good health, particularly dentures and other artificial appliances and spectacles, shall be free of charge to the internee.

Article 92

Medical inspections of internees shall be made at least once a month. Their purpose shall be, in particular, to supervise the general state of health, nutrition and cleanliness of internees, and to detect contagious diseases, especially tuberculosis, malaria, and venereal diseases. Such inspections shall include, in particular, the checking of weight of each internee and, at least once a year, radioscopic examination.

Chapter V

RELIGIOUS, INTELLECTUAL AND PHYSICAL ACTIVITIES

Article 93

Internees shall enjoy complete latitude in the exercise of their religious duties, including attendance at the services of their faith, on condition that they comply with the disciplinary routine prescribed by the detaining authorities.

Ministers of religion who are interned shall be allowed to minister freely to the members of their community. For this purpose, the Detaining Power shall ensure their equitable allocation amongst the various places of internment in which there are internees speaking the same language and belonging to the same religion. Should such ministers be too few in number, the Detaining Power shall provide them with the necessary facilities, including means of transport, for moving from one place to another, and they shall be authorized to visit any internees who are in hospital. Ministers of religion shall be at liberty to correspond on matters concerning their ministry with the religious authorities in the country of detention and, as far as possible, with the international religious organizations of their faith. Such correspondence shall not be considered as forming a part of the quota mentioned in Article 107. It shall, however, be subject to the provisions of Article 112.

When internees do not have at their disposal the assistance of ministers of their faith, or should these latter be too few in number, the local religious authorities of the same faith may appoint, in agreement with the Detaining Power, a minister of the internees' faith or, if such a course is feasible from a denominational point of view, a minister of similar religion or a qualified layman. The latter shall enjoy the facilities granted to the ministry he has assumed. Persons so appointed shall comply with all regulations laid down by the Detaining Power in the interests of discipline and security.

Article 94

The Detaining Power shall encourage intellectual, educational and recreational pursuits, sports and games amongst internees, whilst leaving them free to take part in them or not. It shall take all practicable measures to ensure the exercise thereof, in particular by providing suitable premises.

All possible facilities shall be granted to internees to continue their studies or to take up new subjects. The education of children and young people shall be ensured; they shall be allowed to attend schools either within the place of internment or outside.

Internees shall be given opportunities for physical exercise, sports and outdoor games. For this purpose, sufficient open spaces shall be set aside in all places of internment. Special playgrounds shall be reserved for children and young people.

Article 95

The Detaining Power shall not employ internees as workers, unless they so desire. Employment which, if undertaken under compulsion by a protected person not in internment, would involve a breach of Articles 40 or 51 of the present Convention, and employment on work which is of a degrading or humiliating character are in any case prohibited.

After a working period of six weeks, internees shall be free to give up work at any moment, subject to eight days' notice.

These provisions constitute no obstacle to the right of the Detaining Power to employ interned doctors, dentists and other medical personnel in their professional capacity on behalf of their fellow internees, or to employ internees for administrative and maintenance work in places of internment and to detail such persons for work in the kitchens or for other domestic tasks, or to require such persons to undertake duties connected with the protection of internees against aerial bombardment or other war risks. No internee may, however, be required to perform tasks for which he is, in the opinion of a medical officer, physically unsuited.

The Detaining Power shall take entire responsibility for all working conditions, for medical attention, for the payment of wages, and for ensuring that all employed internees receive compensation for occupational accidents and diseases. The standards prescribed for the said working conditions and for compensation shall be in accordance with the national laws and regulations, and with the existing practice; they shall in no case be inferior to those obtaining for work of the same nature in the same district. Wages for work done shall be determined on an equitable basis by special agreements between the internees, the Detaining Power, and, if the case arises, employers other than the Detaining Power, due regard being paid to the obligation of the Detaining Power to provide for free maintenance of internees and for the medical attention which their state of health may require. Internees permanently detailed for categories of work mentioned in the third paragraph of this Article shall be paid fair wages by the Detaining Power. The working conditions and the scale of compensation for occupational accidents and diseases to internees thus detailed shall not be inferior to those applicable to work of the same nature in the same district.

Article 96

All labour detachments shall remain part of and dependent upon a place of internment. The competent authorities of the Detaining Power and the commandant of a place of internment shall be responsible for the observance in a labour detachment of the provisions of the present Convention. The commandant shall keep an up-to-date list of the labour detachments subordinate to him and shall communicate it to the delegates of the Protecting Power, of the International Committee of the Red Cross and of other humanitarian organizations who may visit the places of internment.

Chapter VI

PERSONAL PROPERTY AND FINANCIAL RESOURCES

Article 97

Internees shall be permitted to retain articles of personal use. Monies, cheques, bonds, etc., and valuables in their possession may not be taken from them except in accordance with established procedure. Detailed receipts shall be given therefor.

The amounts shall be paid into the account of every internee as provided for in Article 98. Such amounts may not be converted into any other currency unless legislation in force in the territory in which the owner is interned so requires or the internee gives his consent.

Articles which have above all a personal or sentimental value may not be taken away.

A woman internee shall not be searched except by a woman.

On release or repatriation, internees shall be given all articles, monies or other valuables taken from them during internment and shall receive in currency the balance of any credit to their accounts kept in accordance with Article 98, with the exception of any articles or amounts withheld by the Detaining Power by virtue of its legislation in force. If the property of an internee is so withheld, the owner shall receive a detailed receipt.

Family or identity documents in the possession of internees may not be taken away without a receipt being given. At no time shall internees be left without identity documents. If they have none, they shall be issued with special documents drawn up by the detaining authorities, which will serve as their identity papers until the end of their internment.

Internees may keep on their persons a certain amount of money, in cash or in the shape of purchase coupons, to enable them to make purchases.

Article 98

All internees shall receive regular allowances, sufficient to enable them to purchase goods and articles, such as tobacco, toilet requisites, etc. Such allowances may take the form of credits or purchase coupons.

Furthermore, internees may receive allowances from the Power to which they owe allegiance, the Protecting Powers, the organizations which may assist them, or their families, as well as the income on their property in accordance with the law of the Detaining Power. The amount of allowances granted by the Power to which they owe allegiance shall be the same for each category of internees (infirm, sick, pregnant women, etc.), but may not be allocated by that Power or distributed by the Detaining Power on the basis of discrimination between internees which are prohibited by Article 27 of the present Convention.

The Detaining Power shall open a regular account for every internee, to which shall be credited the allowances named in the present Article, the wages earned and the remittances received, together with such sums taken from him as may be available under the legislation in force in the territory in which he is interned. Internees shall be granted all facilities consistent with the legislation in force in such territory to make remittances to their families and to other dependants. They may draw from their accounts the amounts necessary for their personal expenses, within the limits fixed by the Detaining Power. They shall at all times be afforded reasonable facilities for consulting and obtaining copies of their accounts. A statement of accounts shall be furnished to the Protecting Power on request, and shall accompany the internee in case of transfer.

Chapter VII

ADMINISTRATION AND DISCIPLINE

Article 99

Every place of internment shall be put under the authority of a responsible officer, chosen from the regular military forces or the regular civil administration of the Detaining Power. The officer in charge of the place of internment must have in his possession a copy of the present Convention in the official language, or one of the official languages, of his country and shall be responsible for its application. The staff in control of internees shall be instructed in the provisions of the present Convention and of the administrative measures adopted to ensure its application.

The text of the present Convention and the texts of special agreements concluded under the said Convention shall be posted inside the place of internment, in a language which the internees understand, or shall be in the possession of the Internee Committee.

Regulations, orders, notices and publications of every kind shall be communicated to the internees and posted inside the places of internment, in a language which they understand.

Every order and command addressed to internees individually must likewise be given in a language which they understand.

Article 100

The disciplinary regime in places of internment shall be consistent with humanitarian principles, and shall in no circumstances include regulations imposing on internees any physical exertion dangerous to their health or involving physical or moral victimization. Identification by tattooing or imprinting signs or markings on the body is prohibited.

In particular, prolonged standing and roll-calls, punishment drill, military drill and manoeuvres, or the reduction of food rations, are prohibited.

Article 101

Internees shall have the right to present to the authorities in whose power they are any petition with regard to the conditions of internment to which they are subjected.

They shall also have the right to apply without restriction through the Internee Committee or, if they consider it necessary, direct to the representatives of the Protecting Power, in order to indicate to them any points on which they may have complaints to make with regard to the conditions of internment.

Such petitions and complaints shall be transmitted forthwith and without alteration, and even if the latter are recognized to be unfounded, they may not occasion any punishment.

Periodic reports on the situation in places of internment and as to the needs of the internees may be sent by the Internee Committees to the representatives of the Protecting Powers.

Article 102

In every place of internment, the internees shall freely elect by secret ballot every six months, the members of a Committee empowered to represent them before the Detaining and the Protecting Powers, the International Committee of the Red Cross and any other organization which may assist them. The members of the Committee shall be eligible for re-election.

Internees so elected shall enter upon their duties after their election has been approved by the detaining authorities. The reasons for any refusals or dismissals shall be communicated to the Protecting Powers concerned.

Article 103

The Internee Committees shall further the physical, spiritual and intellectual well-being of the internees.

In case the internees decide, in particular, to organize a system of mutual assistance amongst themselves, this organization would be within the competence of the Committees in addition to the special duties entrusted to them under other provisions of the present Convention.

Article 104

Members of Internee Committees shall not be required to perform any other work, if the accomplishment of their duties is rendered more difficult thereby.

Members of Internee Committees may appoint from amongst the internees such assistants as they may require. All material facilities shall be granted to them, particularly a certain freedom of movement necessary for the accomplishment of their duties (visits to labour detachments, receipt of supplies, etc.).

All facilities shall likewise be accorded to members of Internee Committees for communication by post and telegraph with the detaining authorities, the Protecting Powers, the International Committee of the Red Cross and their delegates, and with the organizations which give assistance to internees. Committee members in labour detachments shall enjoy similar facilities for communication with their Internee Committee in the principal place of internment. Such communications shall not be limited, nor considered as forming a part of the quota mentioned in Article 107.

Members of Internee Committees who are transferred shall be allowed a reasonable time to acquaint their successors with current affairs.

Chapter VIII

RELATIONS WITH THE EXTERIOR

Article 105

Immediately upon interning protected persons, the Detaining Power shall inform them, the Power to which they owe allegiance and their Protecting Power of the measures taken for executing the provisions of the present Chapter. The Detaining Power shall likewise inform the Parties concerned of any subsequent modifications of such measures.

Article 106

As soon as he is interned, or at the latest not more than one week after his arrival in a place of internment, and likewise in cases of sickness or transfer to another place of internment or to a hospital, every internee shall be enabled to send direct to his family, on the one hand, and to the Central Agency provided for by Article 140, on the other, an internment card similar, if possible, to the model annexed to the present Convention, informing his relatives of his detention, address and state of health. The said cards shall be forwarded as rapidly as possible and may not be delayed in any way.

Article 107

Internees shall be allowed to send and receive letters and cards. If the Detaining Power deems it necessary to limit the number of letters and cards sent by each internee, the said number shall not be less than two letters and four cards monthly; these shall be drawn up so as to conform as closely as possible to the models annexed to the present Convention. If limitations must be placed on the correspondence addressed to internees, they may be ordered only by the Power to which such internees owe allegiance, possibly at the request of the Detaining Power. Such letters and cards must be conveyed with reasonable despatch; they may not be delayed or retained for disciplinary reasons.

Internees who have been a long time without news, or who find it impossible to receive news from their relatives, or to give them news by the ordinary postal route, as well as those who are at a considerable distance from their homes, shall be allowed to send telegrams, the charges being paid by them in the currency at their disposal. They shall likewise benefit by this provision in cases which are recognized to be urgent.

As a rule, internees' mail shall be written in their own language. The Parties to the conflict may authorize correspondence in other languages.

Article 108

Internees shall be allowed to receive, by post or by any other means, individual parcels or collective shipments containing in particular foodstuffs, clothing, medical supplies, as well as books and objects of a devotional, educational or recreational character which may meet their needs. Such shipments shall in no way free the Detaining Power from the obligations imposed upon it by virtue of the present Convention.

Should military necessity require the quantity of such shipments to be limited, due notice thereof shall be given to the Protecting Power and to the International Committee of the Red Cross, or to any other organization giving assistance to the internees and responsible for the forwarding of such shipments.

The conditions for the sending of individual parcels and collective shipments shall, if necessary, be the subject of special agreements between the Powers concerned, which may in no case delay the receipt by the internees of relief supplies. Parcels of clothing and foodstuffs may not include books. Medical relief supplies shall, as a rule, be sent in collective parcels.

Article 109

In the absence of special agreements between Parties to the conflict regarding the conditions for the receipt and distribution of collective relief shipments, the regulations concerning collective relief which are annexed to the present Convention shall be applied.

The special agreements provided for above shall in no case restrict the right of Internee Committees to take possession of collective relief shipments intended for internees, to undertake their distribution and to dispose of them in the interests of the recipients.

Nor shall such agreements restrict the right of representatives of the Protecting Powers, the International Committee of the Red Cross, or any other organization giving assistance to internees and responsible for the forwarding of collective shipments, to supervise their distribution to the recipients.

Article 110

All relief shipments for internees shall be exempt from import, customs and other dues.

All matter sent by mail, including relief parcels sent by parcel post and remittances of money, addressed from other countries to internees or despatched by them through the post office, either direct or through the Information Bureaux provided for in Article 136 and the Central Information Agency provided for in Article 140, shall be exempt from all postal dues both in the countries of origin and destination and in intermediate countries. To this end, in particular, the exemption provided by the Universal Postal Convention of 1947 and by the agreements of the Universal Postal Union in favour of civilians of enemy nationality detained in camps or civilian prisons, shall be extended to the other interned persons protected by the present Convention. The countries not signatory to the above-mentioned agreements shall be bound to grant freedom from charges in the same circumstances.

The cost of transporting relief shipments which are intended for internees and which, by reason of their weight or any other cause, cannot be sent through the post office, shall be borne by the Detaining Power in all the territories under its control. Other Powers which are Parties to the present Convention shall bear the cost of transport in their respective territories.

Costs connected with the transport of such shipments, which are not covered by the above paragraphs, shall be charged to the senders.

The High Contracting Parties shall endeavour to reduce, so far as possible, the charges for telegrams sent by internees, or addressed to them.

Article 111

Should military operations prevent the Powers concerned from fulfilling their obligation to ensure the conveyance of the mail and relief shipments provided for in Articles 106, 107, 108 and 113, the Protecting Powers concerned, the International Committee of the Red Cross or any other organization duly approved by the Parties to the conflict may undertake the conveyance of such shipments by suitable means (rail, motor vehicles, vessels or aircraft, etc.). For this purpose, the High Contracting Parties shall endeavour to supply them with such transport, and to allow its circulation, especially by granting the necessary safe-conducts.

Such transport may also be used to convey:

(a) Correspondence, lists and reports exchanged between the Central Information Agency referred to in Article 140 and the National Bureaux referred to in Article 136;

(b) Correspondence and reports relating to internees which the Protecting Powers, the International Committee of the Red Cross or any other organization assisting the internees exchange either with their own delegates or with the Parties to the conflict.

These provisions in no way detract from the right of any Party to the conflict to arrange other means of transport if it should so prefer, nor preclude the granting of safe-conducts, under mutually agreed conditions, to such means of transport.

The costs occasioned by the use of such means of transport shall be borne, in proportion to the importance of the shipments, by the Parties to the conflict whose nationals are benefited thereby.

Article 112

The censoring of correspondence addressed to internees or despatched by them shall be done as quickly as possible.

The examination of consignments intended for internees shall not be carried out under conditions that will expose the goods contained in them to deterioration. It shall be done in the presence of the addressee, or of a fellow-internee duly delegated by him. The delivery to internees of individual or collective consignments shall not be delayed under the pretext of difficulties of censorship.

Any prohibition of correspondence ordered by the Parties to the conflict, either for military or political reasons, shall be only temporary and its duration shall be as short as possible.

Article 113

The Detaining Powers shall provide all reasonable facilities for the transmission, through the Protecting Power or the Central Agency provided for in Article 140, or as otherwise required, of wills, powers of attorney, letters of authority, or any other documents intended for internees or despatched by them.

In all cases the Detaining Power shall facilitate the execution and authentication in due legal form of such documents on behalf of internees, in particular by allowing them to consult a lawyer.

Article 114

The Detaining Power shall afford internees all facilities to enable them to manage their property, provided this is not incompatible with the conditions of internment and the law which is applicable. For this purpose, the said Power may give them permission to leave the place of internment in urgent cases and if circumstances allow.

Article 115

In all cases where an internee is a party to proceedings in any court, the Detaining Power shall, if he so requests, cause the court to be informed of his detention and shall, within legal limits, ensure that all necessary steps are taken to prevent him from being in any way prejudiced, by reason of his internment, as regards the preparation and conduct of his case or as regards the execution of any judgment of the court.

Article 116

Every internee shall be allowed to receive visitors, especially near relatives, at regular intervals and as frequently as possible.

As far as is possible, internees shall be permitted to visit their homes in urgent cases, particularly in cases of death or serious illness of relatives.

Chapter IX

PENAL AND DISCIPLINARY SANCTIONS

Article 117

Subject to the provisions of the present Chapter, the laws in force in the territory in which they are detained will continue to apply to internees who commit offences during internment.

If general laws, regulations or orders declare acts committed by internees to be punishable, whereas the same acts are not punishable when committed by persons who are not internees, such acts shall entail disciplinary punishments only.

No internee may be punished more than once for the same act, or on the same count.

Article 118

The courts or authorities shall in passing sentence take as far as possible into account the fact that the defendant is not a national of the Detaining Power. They shall be free to reduce the penalty prescribed for the offence with which the internee is charged and shall not be obliged, to this end, to apply the minimum sentence prescribed.

Imprisonment in premises without daylight, and, in general, all forms of cruelty without exception are forbidden.

Internees who have served disciplinary or judicial sentences shall not be treated differently from other internees.

The duration of preventive detention undergone by an internee shall be deducted from any disciplinary or judicial penalty involving confinement to which he may be sentenced.

Internee Committees shall be informed of all judicial proceedings instituted against internees whom they represent, and of their result.

Article 119

The disciplinary punishments applicable to internees shall be the following:

1. A fine which shall not exceed 50 per cent of the wages which the internee would otherwise receive under the provisions of Article 95 during a period of not more than thirty days.

2. Discontinuance of privileges granted over and above the treatment provided for by the present Convention.

3. Fatigue duties, not exceeding two hours daily, in connection with the maintenance of the place of internment.

4. Confinement.

In no case shall disciplinary penalties be inhuman, brutal or dangerous for the health of internees. Account shall be taken of the internee's age, sex and state of health.

The duration of any single punishment shall in no case exceed a maximum of thirty consecutive days, even if the internee is answerable for several breaches of discipline when his case is dealt with, whether such breaches are connected or not.

Article 120

Internees who are recaptured after having escaped or when attempting to escape shall be liable only to disciplinary punishment in respect of this act, even if it is a repeated offence.

Article 118, paragraph 3, notwithstanding, internees punished as a result of escape or attempt to escape, may be subjected to special surveillance, on condition that such surveillance does not affect the state of their health, that it is exercised in a place of internment and that it does not entail the abolition of any of the safeguards granted by the present Convention.

Internees who aid and abet an escape, or attempt to escape, shall be liable on this count to disciplinary punishment only.

Article 121

Escape, or attempt to escape, even if it is a repeated offence, shall not be deemed an aggravating circumstance in cases where an internee is prosecuted for offences committed during his escape.

The Parties to the conflict shall ensure that the competent authorities exercise leniency in deciding whether punishment inflicted for an offence shall be of a disciplinary or judicial nature, especially in respect of acts committed in connection with an escape, whether successful or not.

Article 122

Acts which constitute offences against discipline shall be investigated immediately. This rule shall be applied, in particular, in cases of escape or attempt to escape. Recaptured internees shall be handed over to the competent authorities as soon as possible.

In case of offences against discipline, confinement awaiting trial shall be reduced to an absolute minimum for all internees, and shall not exceed fourteen days. Its duration shall in any case be deducted from any sentence of confinement.

The provisions of Articles 124 and 125 shall apply to internees who are in confinement awaiting trial for offences against discipline.

Article 123

Without prejudice to the competence of courts and higher authorities, disciplinary punishment may be ordered only by the commandant of the place of internment, or by a responsible officer or official who replaces him, or to whom he has delegated his disciplinary powers.

Before any disciplinary punishment is awarded, the accused internee shall be given precise information regarding the offences of which he is accused, and given an opportunity of explaining his conduct and of defending himself. He shall be permitted, in particular, to call witnesses and to have recourse, if necessary, to the services of a qualified interpreter. The decision shall be announced in the presence of the accused and of a member of the Internee Committee.

The period elapsing between the time of award of a disciplinary punishment and its execution shall not exceed one month.

When an internee is awarded a further disciplinary punishment, a period of at least three days shall elapse between the execution of any two of the punishments, if the duration of one of these is ten days or more.

A record of disciplinary punishments shall be maintained by the commandant of the place of internment and shall be open to inspection by representatives of the Protecting Power.

Article 124

Internees shall not in any case be transferred to penitentiary establishments (prisons, penitentiaries, convict prisons, etc.) to undergo disciplinary punishment therein.

The premises in which disciplinary punishments are undergone shall conform to sanitary requirements; they shall in particular be provided with adequate bedding. Internees undergoing punishment shall be enabled to keep themselves in a state of cleanliness.

Women internees undergoing disciplinary punishment shall be confined in separate quarters from male internees and shall be under the immediate supervision of women.

Article 125

Internees awarded disciplinary punishment shall be allowed to exercise and to stay in the open air at least two hours daily.

They shall be allowed, if they so request, to be present at the daily medical inspections. They shall receive the attention which their state of health requires and, if necessary, shall be removed to the infirmary of the place of internment or to a hospital.

They shall have permission to read and write, likewise to send and receive letters. Parcels and remittances of money, however, may be withheld from them until the completion of their punishment; such consignments shall meanwhile be entrusted to the Internee Committee, who will hand over to the infirmary the perishable goods contained in the parcels.

No internee given a disciplinary punishment may be deprived of the benefit of the provisions of Articles 107 and 143 of the present Convention.

Article 126

The provisions of Articles 71 to 76 inclusive shall apply, by analogy, to proceedings against internees who are in the national territory of the Detaining Power.

Chapter X

TRANSFERS OF INTERNEES

Article 127

The transfer of internees shall always be effected humanely. As a general rule, it shall be carried out by rail or other means of transport, and under conditions at least equal to those obtaining for the forces of the Detaining Power in their changes of station. If, as an exceptional measure, such removals have to be effected on foot, they may not take place unless the internees are in a fit state of health, and may not in any case expose them to excessive fatigue.

The Detaining Power shall supply internees during transfer with drinking water and food sufficient in quantity, quality and variety to maintain them in good health, and also with the necessary clothing, adequate shelter and the necessary medical attention. The Detaining Power shall take all suitable precautions to ensure their safety during transfer, and shall establish before their departure a complete list of all internees transferred.

Sick, wounded or infirm internees and maternity cases shall not be transferred if the journey would be seriously detrimental to them, unless their safety imperatively so demands.

If the combat zone draws close to a place of internment, the internees in the said place shall not be transferred unless their removal can be carried out in adequate conditions of safety, or unless they are exposed to greater risks by remaining on the spot than by being transferred.

When making decisions regarding the transfer of internees, the Detaining Power shall take their interests into account and, in particular, shall not do anything to increase the difficulties of repatriating them or returning them to their own homes.

Article 128

In the event of transfer, internees shall be officially advised of their departure and of their new postal address. Such notification shall be given in time for them to pack their luggage and inform their next of kin.

They shall be allowed to take with them their personal effects, and the correspondence and parcels which have arrived for them. The weight of such baggage may be limited if the conditions of transfer so require, but in no case to less than twenty-five kilograms per internee.

Mail and parcels addressed to their former place of internment shall be forwarded to them without delay.

The commandant of the place of internment shall take, in agreement with the Internee Committee, any measures needed to ensure the transport of the internees' community property and of the luggage the internees are unable to take with them in consequence of restrictions imposed by virtue of the second paragraph.

Chapter XI

DEATHS

Article 129

The wills of internees shall be received for safe-keeping by the responsible authorities; and in the event of the death of an internee his will shall be transmitted without delay to a person whom he has previously designated.

Deaths of internees shall be certified in every case by a doctor, and a death certificate shall be made out, showing the causes of death and the conditions under which it occurred.

An official record of the death, duly registered, shall be drawn up in accordance with the procedure relating thereto in force in the territory where the place of internment is situated, and a duly certified copy of such record shall be transmitted without delay to the Protecting Power as well as to the Central Agency referred to in Article 140.

Article 130

The detaining authorities shall ensure that internees who die while interned are honourably buried, if possible according to the rites of the religion to which they belonged, and that their graves are respected, properly maintained, and marked in such a way that they can always be recognized.

Deceased internees shall be buried in individual graves unless unavoidable circumstances require the use of collective graves. Bodies may be cremated only for imperative reasons of hygiene, on account of the religion of the deceased or in accordance with his expressed wish to this effect. In case of cremation, the fact shall be stated and the reasons given in the death certificate of the deceased. The ashes shall be retained for safe-keeping by the detaining authorities and shall be transferred as soon as possible to the next of kin on their request.

As soon as circumstances permit, and not later than the close of hostilities, the Detaining Power shall forward lists of graves of deceased internees to the Powers on whom the deceased internees depended, through the Information Bureaux provided for in Article 136. Such lists shall include all particulars necessary for the identification of the deceased internees, as well as the exact location of their graves.

Article 131

Every death or serious injury of an internee, caused or suspected to have been caused by a sentry, another internee or any other person, as well as any death the cause of which is unknown, shall be immediately followed by an official enquiry by the Detaining Power.

A communication on this subject shall be sent immediately to the Protecting Power. The evidence of any witnesses shall be taken, and a report including such evidence shall be prepared and forwarded to the said Protecting Power.

If the enquiry indicates the guilt of one or more persons, the Detaining Power shall take all necessary steps to ensure the prosecution of the person or persons responsible.

Chapter XII

RELEASE, REPATRIATION AND ACCOMMODATION IN NEUTRAL COUNTRIES

Article 132

Each interned person shall be released by the Detaining Power as soon as the reasons which necessitated his internment no longer exist.

The Parties to the conflict shall, moreover, endeavour during the course of hostilities, to conclude agreements for the release, the repatriation, the return to places of residence or the accommodation in a neutral country of certain classes of internees, in particular children, pregnant women and mothers with infants and young children, wounded and sick, and internees who have been detained for a long time.

Article 133

Internment shall cease as soon as possible after the close of hostilities.

Internees, in the territory of a Party to the conflict, against whom penal proceedings are pending for offences not exclusively subject to disciplinary penalties, may be detained until the close of such proceedings and, if circumstances require, until the completion of the penalty. The same shall apply to internees who have been previously sentenced to a punishment depriving them of liberty.

By agreement between the Detaining Power and the Powers concerned, committees may be set up after the close of hostilities, or of the occupation of territories, to search for dispersed internees.

Article 134

The High Contracting Parties shall endeavour, upon the close of hostilities or occupation, to ensure the return of all internees to their last place of residence, or to facilitate their repatriation.

Article 135

The Detaining Power shall bear the expense of returning released internees to the places where they were residing when interned, or, if it took them into custody while they were in transit or on the high seas, the cost of completing their journey or of their return to their point of departure.

Where a Detaining Power refuses permission to reside in its territory to a released internee who previously had his permanent domicile therein, such Detaining Power shall pay the cost of the said internee's repatriation. If, however, the internee elects to return to his country on his own responsibility or in obedience to the Government of the Power to which he owes allegiance, the Detaining Power need not pay the expenses of his journey beyond the point of his departure from its territory. The Detaining Power need not pay the costs of repatriation of an internee who was interned at his own request.

If internees are transferred in accordance with Article 45, the transferring and receiving Powers shall agree on the portion of the above costs to be borne by each.

The foregoing shall not prejudice such special agreements as may be concluded between Parties to the conflict concerning the exchange and repatriation of their nationals in enemy hands.

SECTION V

INFORMATION BUREAUX AND CENTRAL AGENCY

Article 136

Upon the outbreak of a conflict and in all cases of occupation, each of the Parties to the conflict shall establish an official Information Bureau responsible for receiving and transmitting information in respect of the protected persons who are in its power.

Each of the Parties to the conflict shall, within the shortest possible period, give its Bureau information of any measure taken by it concerning any protected persons who are kept in custody for more than two weeks, who are subjected to assigned residence or who are interned. It shall, furthermore, require its various departments concerned with such matters to provide the aforesaid Bureau promptly with information concerning all changes pertaining to these protected persons, as, for example, transfers, release, repatriations, escapes, admittances to hospitals, births and deaths.

Article 137

Each national Bureau shall immediately forward information concerning protected persons by the most rapid means to the Powers of whom the aforesaid persons are nationals, or to Powers in whose territory they resided, through the intermediary of the Protecting Powers and likewise through the Central Agency provided for in Article 140. The Bureaux shall also reply to all enquiries which may be received regarding protected persons.

Information Bureaux shall transmit information concerning a protected person unless its transmission might be detrimental to the person concerned or to his or her relatives. Even in such a case, the information may not be withheld from the Central Agency which, upon being notified of the circumstances, will take the necessary precautions indicated in Article 140.

All communications in writing made by any Bureau shall be authenticated by a signature or a seal.

Article 138

The information received by the national Bureau and transmitted by it shall be of such a character as to make it possible to identify the protected person exactly and to advise his next of kin quickly. The information in respect of each person shall include at least his surname, first names, place and date of birth, nationality, last residence and distinguishing characteristics, the first name of the father and the maiden name of the mother, the date, place and nature of the action taken with regard to the individual, the address at which correspondence may be sent to him and the name and address of the person to be informed.

Likewise, information regarding the state of health of internees who are seriously ill or seriously wounded shall be supplied regularly and if possible every week.

Article 139

Each national Information Bureau shall, furthermore, be responsible for collecting all personal valuables left by protected persons mentioned in Article 136, in particular those who have been repatriated or released, or who have escaped or died; it shall forward the said valuables to those concerned, either direct, or, if necessary, through the Central Agency. Such articles shall be sent by the Bureau in sealed packets which shall be accompanied by statements giving clear and full identity particulars of the person to whom the articles belonged, and by a complete list of the contents of the parcel. Detailed records shall be maintained of the receipt and despatch of all such valuables.

Article 140

A Central Information Agency for protected persons, in particular for internees, shall be created in a neutral country. The International Committee of the Red Cross shall, if it deems necessary, propose to the Powers concerned the organization of such an Agency, which may be the same as that provided for in Article 123 of the Geneva Convention relative to the Treatment of Prisoners of War of August 12, 1949.

The function of the Agency shall be to collect all information of the type set forth in Article 136 which it may obtain through official or private channels and to transmit it as rapidly as possible to the countries of origin or of residence of the persons concerned, except in cases where such transmissions might be detrimental to the persons whom the said information concerns, or to their relatives. It shall receive from the Parties to the conflict all reasonable facilities for effecting such transmissions.

The High Contracting Parties, and in particular those whose nationals benefit by the services of the Central Agency, are requested to give the said Agency the financial aid it may require.

The foregoing provisions shall in no way be interpreted as restricting the humanitarian activities of the International Committee of the Red Cross and of the relief Societies described in Article 142.

Article 141

The national Information Bureaux and the Central Information Agency shall enjoy free postage for all mail, likewise the exemptions provided for in Article 110, and further, so far as possible, exemption from telegraphic charges or, at least, greatly reduced rates.

PART IV

EXECUTION OF THE CONVENTION

SECTION I

GENERAL PROVISIONS

Article 142

Subject to the measures which the Detaining Powers may consider essential to ensure their security or to meet any other reasonable need, the representatives of religious organizations, relief societies, or any other organizations assisting the protected persons, shall receive from these Powers, for themselves or their duly accredited agents, all facilities for visiting the protected persons, for distributing relief supplies and material from any source, intended for educational, recreational or religious purposes, or for assisting them in organizing their leisure time within the places of internment. Such societies or organizations may be constituted in the territory of the Detaining Power, or in any other country, or they may have an international character.

The Detaining Power may limit the number of societies and organizations whose delegates are allowed to carry out their activities in its territory and under its supervision, on condition, however, that such limitation shall not hinder the supply of effective and adequate relief to all protected persons.

The special position of the International Committee of the Red Cross in this field shall be recognized and respected at all times.

Article 143

Representatives or delegates of the Protecting Powers shall have permission to go to all places where protected persons are, particularly to places of internment, detention and work.

They shall have access to all premises occupied by protected persons and shall be able to interview the latter without witnesses, personally or through an interpreter.

Such visits may not be prohibited except for reasons of imperative military necessity, and then only as an exceptional and temporary measure. Their duration and frequency shall not be restricted.

Such representatives and delegates shall have full liberty to select the places they wish to visit. The Detaining or Occupying Power, the Protecting Power and when occasion arises the Power of origin of the persons to be visited, may agree that compatriots of the internees shall be permitted to participate in the visits.

The delegates of the International Committee of the Red Cross shall also enjoy the above prerogatives. The appointment of such delegates shall be submitted to the approval of the Power governing the territories where they will carry out their duties.

Article 144

The High Contracting Parties undertake, in time of peace as in time of war, to disseminate the text of the present Convention as widely as possible in their respective countries, and, in particular, to include the study thereof in their programmes of military and, if possible, civil instruction, so that the principles thereof may become known to the entire population.

Any civilian, military, police or other authorities, who in time of war assume responsibilities in respect of protected persons, must possess the text of the Convention and be specially instructed as to its provisions.

Article 145

The High Contracting Parties shall communicate to one another through the Swiss Federal Council and, during hostilities, through the Protecting Powers, the official translations of the present Convention, as well as the laws and regulations which they may adopt to ensure the application thereof.

Article 146

The High Contracting Parties undertake to enact any legislation necessary to provide effective penal sanctions for persons committing, or ordering to be committed, any of the grave breaches of the present Convention defined in the following Article.

Each High Contracting Party shall be under the obligation to search for persons alleged to have committed, or to have ordered to be committed, such grave breaches, and shall bring such persons, regardless of their nationality, before its own courts. It may also, if it prefers, and in accordance with the provisions of its own legislation, hand such persons over for trial to another

High Contracting Party concerned, provided such High Contracting Party has made out a *prima facie* case.

Each High Contracting Party shall take measures necessary for the suppression of all acts contrary to the provisions of the present Convention other than the grave breaches defined in the following Article.

In all circumstances, the accused persons shall benefit by safeguards of proper trial and defence, which shall not be less favourable than those provided by Article 105 and those following of the Geneva Convention relative to the Treatment of Prisoners of War of August 12, 1949.

Article 147

Grave breaches to which the preceding Article relates shall be those involving any of the following acts, if committed against persons or property protected by the present Convention: wilful killing, torture or inhuman treatment, including biological experiments, wilfully causing great suffering or serious injury to body or health, unlawful deportation or transfer or unlawful confinement of a protected person, compelling a protected person to serve in the forces of a hostile Power, or wilfully depriving a protected person of the rights of fair and regular trial prescribed in the present Convention, taking of hostages and extensive destruction and appropriation of property, not justified by military necessity and carried out unlawfully and wantonly.

Article 148

No High Contracting Party shall be allowed to absolve itself or any other High Contracting Party of any liability incurred by itself or by another High Contracting Party in respect of breaches referred to in the preceding Article.

Article 149

At the request of a Party to the conflict, an enquiry shall be instituted, in a manner to be decided between the interested Parties, concerning any alleged violation of the Convention.

If agreement has not been reached concerning the procedure for the enquiry, the Parties should agree on the choice of an umpire who will decide upon the procedure to be followed.

Once the violation has been established, the Parties to the conflict shall put an end to it and shall repress it with the least possible delay.

SECTION II

FINAL PROVISIONS

Article 150

The present Convention is established in English and in French. Both texts are equally authentic.

The Swiss Federal Council shall arrange for official translations of the Convention to be made in the Russian and Spanish languages.

Article 151

The present Convention, which bears the date of this day, is open to signature until February 12, 1950, in the name of the Powers represented at the Conference which opened at Geneva on April 21, 1949.

Article 152

The present Convention shall be ratified as soon as possible and the ratifications shall be deposited at Berne.

A record shall be drawn up of the deposit of each instrument of ratification and certified copies of this record shall be transmitted by the Swiss Federal Council to all the Powers in whose name the Convention has been signed, or whose accession has been notified.

Article 153

The present Convention shall come into force six months after not less than two instruments of ratification have been deposited.

Thereafter, it shall come into force for each High Contracting Party six months after the deposit of the instrument of ratification.

Article 154

In the relations between the Powers who are bound by The Hague Conventions respecting the Laws and Customs of War on Land, whether that of 29 July, 1899, or that of 18 October, 1907, and who are parties to the present Convention, this last Convention shall be supplementary to Sections II and III of the Regulations annexed to the above-mentioned Conventions of The Hague.

Article 155

From the date of its coming into force, it shall be open to any Power in whose name the present Convention has not been signed, to accede to this Convention.

Article 156

Accessions shall be notified in writing to the Swiss Federal Council, and shall take effect six months after the date on which they are received.

The Swiss Federal Council shall communicate the accessions to all the Powers in whose name the Convention has been signed, or whose accession has been notified.

Article 157

The situations provided for in Articles 2 and 3 shall give immediate effect to ratifications deposited and accessions notified by the Parties to the conflict before or after the beginning of hostilities or occupation. The Swiss Federal Council shall communicate by the quickest method any ratifications or accessions received from Parties to the conflict.

Article 158

Each of the High Contracting Parties shall be at liberty to denounce the present Convention.

The denunciation shall be notified in writing to the Swiss Federal Council, which shall transmit it to the Governments of all the High Contracting Parties.

The denunciation shall take effect one year after the notification thereof has been made to the Swiss Federal Council. However, a denunciation of which notification has been made at a time when the denouncing Power is involved in a conflict shall not take effect until peace has been concluded, and until after operations connected with the release, repatriation and re-establishment of the persons protected by the present Convention have been terminated.

The denunciation shall have effect only in respect of the denouncing Power. It shall in no way impair the obligations which the Parties to the conflict shall remain bound to fulfil by virtue of the principles of the law of nations, as they result from the usages established among civilized peoples, from the laws of humanity and the dictates of the public conscience.

Article 159

The Swiss Federal Council shall register the present Convention with the Secretariat of the United Nations. The Swiss Federal Council shall also inform the Secretariat of the United Nations of all ratifications, accessions and denunciations received by it with respect to the present Convention.

IN WITNESS WHEREOF the undersigned, having deposited their respective full powers, have signed the present Convention.

DONE at Geneva this twelfth day of August 1949, in the English and French languages. The original shall be deposited in the Archives of the Swiss Confederation. The Swiss Federal Council shall transmit certified copies thereof to each of the signatory and acceding States.

ANNEX I

Draft agreement relating to hospital and safety zones and localities

Article 1

Hospital and safety zones shall be strictly reserved for the persons mentioned in Article 23 of the Geneva Convention for the Amelioration of the Condition of the Wounded and Sick in Armed Forces in the Field of 12 August, 1949, and in Article 14 of the Geneva Convention relative to the Protection of Civilian Persons in Time of War of 12 August, 1949, and for the personnel entrusted with the organization and administration of these zones and localities and with the care of the persons therein assembled.

Nevertheless, persons whose permanent residence is within such zones shall have the right to stay there.

Article 2

No persons residing, in whatever capacity, in a hospital and safety zone shall perform any work, either within or without the zone, directly connected with military operations or the production of war material.

Article 3

The Power establishing a hospital and safety zone shall take all necessary measures to prohibit access to all persons who have no right of residence or entry therein.

Article 4

Hospital and safety zones shall fulfil the following conditions:

(a) They shall comprise only a small part of the territory governed by the Power which has established them.

(b) They shall be thinly populated in relation to the possibilities of accommodation.

(c) They shall be far removed and free from all military objectives, or large industrial or administrative establishments.

(d) They shall not be situated in areas which, according to every probability, may become important for the conduct of the war.

Article 5

Hospital and safety zones shall be subject to the following obligations:

(*a*) The lines of communication and means of transport which they possess shall not be used for the transport of military personnel or material, even in transit.

(*b*) They shall in no case be defended by military means.

Article 6

Hospital and safety zones shall be marked by means of oblique red bands on a white ground, placed on the buildings and outer precincts.

Zones reserved exclusively for the wounded and sick may be marked by means of the Red Cross (Red Crescent, Red Lion and Sun) emblem on a white ground.

They may be similarly marked at night by means of appropriate illumination.

Article 7

The Powers shall communicate to all the High Contracting Parties in peacetime or on the outbreak of hostilities, a list of the hospital and safety zones in the territories governed by them. They shall also give notice of any new zones set up during hostilities.

As soon as the adverse Party has received the above-mentioned notification, the zone shall be regularly established.

If, however, the adverse Party considers that the conditions of the present agreement have not been fulfilled, it may refuse to recognize the zone by giving immediate notice thereof to the Party responsible for the said zone, or may make its recognition of such zone dependent upon the institution of the control provided for in Article 8.

Article 8

Any Power having recognized one or several hospital and safety zones instituted by the adverse Party shall be entitled to demand control by one or more Special Commissions, for the purpose of ascertaining if the zones fulfil the conditions and obligations stipulated in the present agreement.

For this purpose, members of the Special Commissions shall at all times have free access to the various zones and may even reside there permanently. They shall be given all facilities for their duties of inspection.

Article 9

Should the Special Commissions note any facts which they consider contrary to the stipulations of the present agreement, they shall at once draw the attention of the Power governing the said zone to these facts, and shall fix a time limit of five days within which the matter should be rectified. They shall duly notify the Power who has recognized the zone.

If, when the time limit has expired, the Power governing the zone has not complied with the warning, the adverse Party may declare that it is no longer bound by the present agreement in respect of the said zone.

Article 10

Any Power setting up one or more hospital and safety zones, and the adverse Parties to whom their existence has been notified, shall nominate or have nominated by the Protecting Powers or by other neutral Powers, persons eligible to be members of the Special Commissions mentioned in Articles 8 and 9.

Article 11

In no circumstances may hospital and safety zones be the object of attack. They shall be protected and respected at all times by the Parties to the conflict.

Article 12

In the case of occupation of a territory, the hospital and safety zones therein shall continue to be respected and utilized as such.

Their purpose may, however, be modified by the Occupying Power, on condition that all measures are taken to ensure the safety of the persons accommodated.

Article 13

The present agreement shall also apply to localities which the Powers may utilize for the same purposes as hospital and safety zones.

ANNEX II

Draft regulations concerning collective relief

Article 1

The Internee Committees shall be allowed to distribute collective relief shipments for which they are responsible, to all internees who are dependent for administration on the said Committee's place of internment, including those internees who are in hospitals, or in prisons or other penitentiary establishments.

Article 2

The distribution of collective relief shipments shall be effected in accordance with the instructions of the donors and with a plan drawn up by the Internee Committees. The issue of medical stores shall, however, be made for preference in agreement with the senior medical officers, and the latter may, in hospitals and infirmaries, waive the said instructions, if the needs of their patients so demand. Within the limits thus defined, the distribution shall always be carried out equitably.

Article 3

Members of Internee Committees shall be allowed to go to the railway stations or other points of arrival of relief supplies near their places of internment so as to enable them to verify the quantity as well as the quality of the goods received and to make out detailed reports thereon for the donors.

Article 4

Internee Committees shall be given the facilities necessary for verifying whether the distribution of collective relief in all subdivisions and annexes of their places of internment has been carried out in accordance with their instructions.

Article 5

Internee Committees shall be allowed to complete, and to cause to be completed by members of the Internee Committees in labour detachments or by the senior medical officers of infirmaries and hospitals, forms or questionnaires intended for the donors, relating to collective relief supplies (distribution, requirements, quantities, etc.). Such forms and questionnaires, duly completed, shall be forwarded to the donors without delay.

Article 6

In order to secure the regular distribution of collective relief supplies to the internees in their place of internment, and to meet any needs that may arise through the arrival of fresh parties of internees, the Internee Committees shall be allowed to create and maintain sufficient reserve stocks of collective relief. For this purpose, they shall have suitable warehouses at their disposal; each warehouse shall be provided with two locks, the Internee Committee holding the keys of one lock, and the commandant of the place of internment the keys of the other.

Article 7

The High Contracting Parties, and the Detaining Powers in particular, shall, so far as is in any way possible and subject to the regulations governing the food supply of the population, authorize purchases of goods to be made in their territories for the distribution of collective relief to the internees. They shall likewise facilitate the transfer of funds and other financial measures of a technical or administrative nature taken for the purpose of making such purchases.

Article 8

The foregoing provisions shall not constitute an obstacle to the right of internees to receive collective relief before their arrival in a place of internment or in the course of their transfer, nor to the possibility of representatives of the Protecting Power, or of the International Committee of the Red Cross or any other humanitarian organization giving assistance to internees and responsible for forwarding such supplies, ensuring the distribution thereof to the recipients by any other means they may deem suitable.

I. INTERNMENT CARD   ANNEX III

1. Front

CIVILIAN INTERNEE MAIL

Postage free

POST CARD

IMPORTANT

This card must be completed by each internee immediately on being interned and each time his address is altered by reason of transfer to another place of internment or to a hospital.

This card is not the same as the special card which each internee is allowed to send to his relatives.

CENTRAL INFORMATION AGENCY
FOR PROTECTED PERSONS

INTERNATIONAL COMMITTEE
OF THE RED CROSS

2. Reverse side

Write legibly and in block letters—1. Nationality

2. Surname   3. First names (in full)   4. First name of father

5. Date of birth   6. Place of birth

7. Occupation

8. Address before detention

9. Address of next of kin

*10. Interned on :
        (or)
     Coming from (hospital, etc.) on :

*11. State of health

12. Present address

13. Date   14. Signature

*Strike out what is not applicable — Do not add any remarks — See explanations on other side of card

(Size of internment card—10 × 15 cm.)

II. ANNEX III

LETTER

Civilian Internee Service

Postage free

> To
>
> Street and number
>
> Place of destination *(in block capitals)*
>
> Province or Department
>
> Country *(in block capitals)*

Internment address

Date and place of birth

Surname and first names

Sender:

(Size of letter — 29 × 15 cm.)

III. CORRESPONDENCE CARD

1. Front

CIVILIAN INTERNEE MAIL

Postage free

POST CARD

To

Street and number

Place of destination *(in block capitals)*

Province or Department

Country *(in block capitals)*

Sender :

Surname and first names

Place and date of birth

Internment address

2. Reverse side

Date :

....

....

....

....

....

Write on the dotted lines only and as legibly as possible.

(Size of correspondence card—10 × 15 cm.)

93. Protocol Additional to the Geneva Conventions of 12 August 1949, and relating to the Protection of Victims of International Armed Conflicts (Protocol I)

Adopted on 8 June 1977 by the Diplomatic Conference on the Reaffirmation and Development of International Humanitarian Law applicable in Armed Conflicts

ENTRY INTO FORCE: 7 December 1978, in accordance with Article 95

PREAMBLE

The High Contracting Parties,

Proclaiming their earnest wish to see peace prevail among peoples,

Recalling that every State has the duty, in conformity with the Charter of the United Nations, to refrain in its international relations from the threat or use of force against the sovereignty, territorial integrity or political independence of any State, or in any other manner inconsistent with the purposes of the United Nations,

Believing it necessary nevertheless to reaffirm and develop the provisions protecting the victims of armed conflicts and to supplement measures intended to reinforce their application,

Expressing their conviction that nothing in this Protocol or in the Geneva Conventions of 12 August 1949 can be construed as legitimizing or authorizing any act of aggression or any other use of force inconsistent with the Charter of the United Nations,

Reaffirming further that the provisions of the Geneva Conventions of 12 August 1949 and of this Protocol must be fully applied in all circumstances to all persons who are protected by those instruments, without any adverse distinction based on the nature or origin of the armed conflict or on the causes espoused by or attributed to the Parties to the conflicts,

Have agreed on the following:

PART I

GENERAL PROVISIONS

Article 1.— General principles and scope of application

1. The High Contracting Parties undertake to respect and to ensure respect for this Protocol in all circumstances.

2. In cases not covered by this Protocol or by other international agreements, civilians and combatants remain under the protection and authority of the principles of international law derived from established custom, from the principles of humanity and from the dictates of public conscience.

3. This Protocol, which supplements the Geneva Conventions of 12 August 1949 for the protection of war victims, shall apply in the situations referred to in Article 2 common to those Conventions.

4. The situations referred to in the preceding paragraph include armed conflicts in which peoples are fighting against colonial domination and alien occupation and against racist régimes in the exercise of their right of self-determination, as enshrined in the Charter of the United Nations and the Declaration on Principles of International Law concerning Friendly Relations and Co-operation among States in accordance with the Charter of the United Nations.

Article 2.— Definitions

For the purposes of this Protocol:

(*a*) "First Convention", "Second Convention", "Third Convention" and "Fourth Convention" mean, respectively, the Geneva Convention for the Amelioration of the Condition of the Wounded and Sick in Armed Forces in the Field of 12 August 1949; the Geneva Convention for the Amelioration of the Condition of Wounded, Sick and Shipwrecked Members of Armed Forces at Sea of 12 August 1949; the Geneva Convention relative to the Treatment of Prisoners of War of 12 August 1949; the Geneva Convention relative to the Protection of Civilian Persons in Time of War of 12 August 1949; "the Conventions" means the four Geneva Conventions of 12 August 1949; for the protection of war victims;

(*b*) "Rules of international law applicable in armed conflict" means the rules applicable in armed conflict set forth in international agreements to which the Parties to the conflict are Parties and the generally recognized principles and rules of international law which are applicable to armed conflict;

(*c*) ''Protecting Power'' means a neutral or other State not a Party to the conflict which has been designated by a Party to the conflict and accepted by the adverse Party and has agreed to carry out the functions assigned to a Protecting Power under the Conventions and this Protocol;

(*d*) ''Substitute'' means an organization acting in place of a Protecting Power in accordance with Article 5.

Article 3.— Beginning and end of application

Without prejudice to the provisions which are applicable at all times:

(*a*) The Conventions and this Protocol shall apply from the beginning of any situation referred to in Article 1 of this Protocol;

(*b*) The application of the Conventions and of this Protocol shall cease, in the territory of Parties to the conflict, on the general close of military operations and, in the case of occupied territories, on the termination of the occupation, except, in either circumstance, for those persons whose final release, repatriation or re-establishment takes place thereafter. These persons shall continue to benefit from the relevant provisions of the Conventions and of this Protocol until their final release, repatriation or re-establishment.

Article 4.— Legal status of the Parties to the conflict

The application of the Conventions and of this Protocol, as well as the conclusion of the agreements provided for therein, shall not affect the legal status of the Parties to the conflict. Neither the occupation of a territory nor the application of the Conventions and this Protocol shall affect the legal status of the territory in question.

Article 5.— Appointment of Protecting Powers and of their substitute

1. It is the duty of the Parties to a conflict from the beginning of that conflict to secure the supervision and implementation of the Conventions and of this Protocol by the application of the system of Protecting Powers, including *inter alia* the designation and acceptance of those Powers, in accordance with the following paragraphs. Protecting Powers shall have the duty of safeguarding the interests of the Parties to the conflict.

2. From the beginning of a situation referred to in Article 1, each Party to the conflict shall without delay designate a Protecting Power for the purpose of applying the Conventions and this Protocol and shall, likewise without delay and for the same purpose, permit the activities of a Protecting Power which has been accepted by it as such after designation by the adverse Party.

3. If a Protecting Power has not been designated or accepted from the beginning of a situation referred to in Article 1, the International Committee

of the Red Cross, without prejudice to the right of any other impartial humanitarian organization to do likewise, shall offer its good offices to the Parties to the conflict with a view to the designation without delay of a Protecting Power to which the Parties to the conflict consent. For that purpose it may, *inter alia,* ask each Party to provide it with a list of at least five States which that Party considers acceptable to act as Protecting Power on its behalf in relation to an adverse Party, and ask each adverse Party to provide a list of at least five States which it would accept as the Protecting Power of the first Party; these lists shall be communicated to the Committee within two weeks after the receipt of the request; it shall compare them and seek the agreement of any proposed State named on both lists.

4. If, despite the foregoing, there is no Protecting Power, the Parties to the conflict shall accept without delay an offer which may be made by the International Committee of the Red Cross or by any other organization which offers all guarantees of impartiality and efficacy, after due consultations with the said Parties and taking into account the result of these consultations, to act as a substitute. The functioning of such a substitute is subject to the consent of the Parties to the conflict; every effort shall be made by the Parties to the conflict to facilitate the operations of the substitute in the performance of its tasks under the Conventions and this Protocol.

5. In accordance with Article 4, the designation and acceptance of Protecting Powers for the purpose of applying the Conventions and this Protocol shall not affect the legal status of the Parties to the conflict or of any territory, including occupied territory.

6. The maintenance of diplomatic relations between Parties to the conflict or the entrusting of the protection of a Party's interests and those of its nationals to a third State in accordance with the rules of international law relating to diplomatic relations is no obstacle to the designation of Protecting Powers for the purpose of applying the Conventions and this Protocol.

7. Any subsequent mention in this Protocol of a Protecting Power includes also a substitute.

Article 6.— *Qualified persons*

1. The High Contracting Parties shall, also in peacetime, endeavour, with the assistance of the national Red Cross (Red Crescent, Red Lion and Sun) Societies, to train qualified personnel to facilitate the application of the Conventions and of this Protocol, and in particular the activities of the Protecting Powers.

2. The recruitment and training of such personnel are within domestic jurisdiction.

3. The International Committee of the Red Cross shall hold at the disposal of the High Contracting Parties the lists of persons so trained which

the High Contracting Parties may have established and may have transmitted to it for that purpose.

4.   The conditions governing the employment of such personnel outside the national territory shall, in each case, be the subject of special agreements between the Parties concerned.

Article 7.— Meetings

The depositary of this Protocol shall convene a meeting of the High Contracting Parties, at the request of one or more of the said Parties and upon the approval of the majority of the said Parties, to consider general problems concerning the application of the Conventions and of the Protocol.

PART II

WOUNDED, SICK AND SHIPWRECKED

SECTION I. — GENERAL PROTECTION

Article 8.— Terminology

For the purposes of this Protocol:

(a) "Wounded" and "sick" mean persons, whether military or civilian, who, because of trauma, disease or other physical or mental disorder or disability, are in need of medical assistance or care and who refrain from any act of hostility. These terms also cover maternity cases, new-born babies and other persons who may be in need of immediate medical assistance or care, such as the infirm or expectant mothers, and who refrain from any act of hostility;

(b) "Shipwrecked" means persons, whether military or civilian, who are in peril at sea or in other waters as a result of misfortune affecting them or the vessel or aircraft carrying them and who refrain from any act of hostility. These persons, provided that they continue to refrain from any act of hostility, shall continue to be considered shipwrecked during their rescue until they acquire another status under the Conventions or this Protocol;

(c) "Medical personnel" means those persons assigned, by a Party to the conflict, exclusively to the medical purposes enumerated under subparagraph (e) or to the administration of medical units or to the operation or administration of medical transports. Such assignments may be either permanent or temporary. The term includes:

(i) Medical personnel of a Party to the conflict, whether military or civilian, including those described in the First and Second Conventions, and those assigned to civil defence organizations;

(ii) Medical personnel of national Red Cross (Red Crescent, Red Lion and Sun) Societies and other national voluntary aid societies duly recognized and authorized by a Party to the conflict;

(iii) Medical personnel of medical units or medical transports described in Article 9, paragraph 2;

(*d*) ''Religious personnel'' means military or civilian persons, such as chaplains, who are exclusively engaged in the work of their ministry and attached:

(i) To the armed forces of a Party to the conflict;

(ii) To medical units or medical transports of a Party to the conflict;

(iii) To medical units or medical transports described in Article 9, paragraph 2; or

(iv) To civil defence organizations of a Party to the conflict.

The attachment of religious personnel may be either permanent or temporary, and the relevant provisions mentioned under sub-paragraph (*k*) apply to them;

(*e*) ''Medical units'' means establishments and other units, whether military or civilian, organized for medical purposes, namely the search for, collection, transportation, diagnosis or treatment—including first-aid treatment—of the wounded, sick and shipwrecked, or for the prevention of disease. The term includes, for example, hospitals and other similar units, blood transfusion centres, preventive medicine centres and institutes, medical depots and the medical and pharmaceutical stores of such units. Medical units may be fixed or mobile, permanent or temporary;

(*f*) ''Medical transportation'' means the conveyance by land, water or air of the wounded, sick, shipwrecked, medical personnel, religious personnel, medical equipment or medical supplies protected by the Conventions and by this Protocol;

(*g*) ''Medical transports'' means any means of transportation, whether military or civilian, permanent or temporary, assigned exclusively to medical transportation and under the control of a competent authority of a Party to the conflict;

(*h*) ''Medical vehicles'' means any medical transports by land;

(*i*) ''Medical ships and craft'' means any medical transports by water;

(*j*) ''Medical aircraft'' means any medical transports by air;

(*k*) ''Permanent medical personnel'', ''permanent medical units'' and ''permanent medical transports'' mean those assigned exclusively to medical purposes for an indeterminate period. ''Temporary medical personnel'', "temporary medical units" and "temporary medical transports" mean those devoted exclusively to medical purposes for limited periods during the whole of such periods. Unless otherwise specified, the terms "medical personnel", " medical units" and "medical transports" cover both permanent and temporary categories;

(*l*) "Distinctive emblem" means the distinctive emblem of the red cross, red crescent or red lion and sun on a white ground when used for the protection of medical units and transports, or medical and religious personnel, equipment or supplies;

(*m*) "Distinctive signal" means any signal or message specified for the identification exclusively of medical units or transports in Chapter III of Annex I to this Protocol.

Article 9.— Field of application

1.   This Part, the provisions of which are intended to ameliorate the condition of the wounded, sick and shipwrecked, shall apply to all those affected by a situation referred to in Article 1, without any adverse distinction founded on race, colour, sex, language, religion or belief, political or other opinion, national or social origin, wealth, birth or other status, or on any other similar criteria.

2.   The relevant provisions of Articles 27 and 32 of the First Convention shall apply to permanent medical units and transports (other than hospital ships, to which Article 25 of the Second Convention applies) and their personnel made available to a Party to the conflict for humanitarian purposes:

(*a*) By a neutral or other State which is not a Party to that conflict;

(*b*) By a recognized and authorized aid society of such a State;

(*c*) By an impartial international humanitarian organization.

Article 10.— Protection and care

1.   All the wounded, sick and shipwrecked, to whichever Party they belong, shall be respected and protected.

2.   In all circumstances they shall be treated humanely and shall receive, to the fullest extent practicable and with the least possible delay, the medical care and attention required by their condition. There shall be no distinction among them founded on any grounds other than medical ones.

Article 11.— Protection of persons

1.   The physical or mental health and integrity of persons who are in the power of the adverse Party or who are interned, detained or otherwise deprived of liberty as a result of a situation referred to in Article 1 shall not

be endangered by any unjustified act or omission. Accordingly, it is prohibited to subject the persons described in this Article to any medical procedure which is not indicated by the state of health of the person concerned and which is not consistent with generally accepted medical standards which would be applied under similar medical circumstances to persons who are nationals of the Party conducting the procedure and who are in no way deprived of liberty.

2.   It is, in particular, prohibited to carry out on such persons, even with their consent:

(a) Physical mutilations;

(b) Medical or scientific experiments;

(c) Removal of tissue or organs for transplantation,

except where these acts are justified in conformity with the conditions provided for in paragraph 1.

3.   Exceptions to the prohibition in paragraph 2 (c) may be made only in the case of donations of blood for transfusion or of skin for grafting, provided that they are given voluntarily and without any coercion or inducement, and then only for therapeutic purposes, under conditions consistent with generally accepted medical standards and controls designed for the benefit of both the donor and the recipient.

4.   Any wilful act or omission which seriously endangers the physical or mental health or integrity of any person who is in the power of a Party other than the one on which he depends and which either violates any of the prohibitions in paragraphs 1 and 2 or fails to comply with the requirements of paragraph 3 shall be a grave breach of this Protocol.

5.   The persons described in paragraph 1 have the right to refuse any surgical operation. In case of refusal, medical personnel shall endeavour to obtain a written statement to that effect, signed or acknowledged by the patient.

6.   Each Party to the conflict shall keep a medical record for every donation of blood for transfusion or skin for grafting by persons referred to in paragraph 1, if that donation is made under the responsibility of that Party. In addition, each Party to the conflict shall endeavour to keep a record of all medical procedures undertaken with respect to any person who is interned, detained or otherwise deprived of liberty as a result of a situation referred to in Article 1. These records shall be available at all times for inspection by the Protecting Power.

Article 12.— Protection of medical units

1.   Medical units shall be respected and protected at all times and shall not be the object of attack.

2. Paragraph 1 shall apply to civilian medical units, provided that they:

(*a*) Belong to one of the Parties to the conflict;

(*b*) Are recognized and authorized by the competent authority of one of the Parties to the conflict; or

(*c*) Are authorized in conformity with Article 9, paragraph 2, of this Protocol or Article 27 of the First Convention.

3. The Parties to the conflict are invited to notify each other of the location of their fixed medical units. The absence of such notification shall not exempt any of the Parties from the obligation to comply with the provisions of paragraph 1.

4. Under no circumstances shall medical units be used in an attempt to shield military objectives from attack. Whenever possible, the Parties to the conflict shall ensure that medical units are so sited that attacks against military objectives do not imperil their safety.

Article 13.—Discontinuance of protection of civilian medical units

1. The protection to which civilian medical units are entitled shall not cease unless they are used to commit, outside their humanitarian function, acts harmful to the enemy. Protection may, however, cease only after a warning has been given setting, whenever appropriate, a reasonable time-limit, and after such warning has remained unheeded.

2. The following shall not be considered as acts harmful to the enemy;

(*a*) That the personnel of the unit are equipped with light individual weapons for their own defence or for that of the wounded and sick in their charge;

(*b*) That the unit is guarded by a picket or by sentries or by an escort;

(*c*) That small arms and ammunition taken from the wounded and sick, and not yet handed to the proper service, are found in the units;

(*d*) That members of the armed forces or other combatants are in the unit for medical reasons.

Article 14.—Limitations on requisition of civilian medical units

1. The Occupying Power has the duty to ensure that the medical needs of the civilian population in occupied territory continue to be satisfied.

2. The Occupying Power shall not, therefore, requisition civilian medical units, their equipment, their *matériel* or the services of their personnel, so long as these resources are necessary for the provision of adequate

medical services for the civilian population and for the continuing medical care of any wounded and sick already under treatment.

3. Provided that the general rule in paragraph 2 continues to be observed, the Occupying Power may requisition the said resources, subject to the following particular conditions:

(a) That the resources are necessary for the adequate and immediate medical treatment of the wounded and sick members of the armed forces of the Occupying Power or of prisoners of war;

(b) That the requisition continues only while such necessity exists; and

(c) That immediate arrangements are made to ensure that the medical needs of the civilian population, as well as those of any wounded and sick under treatment who are affected by the requisition, continue to be satisfied.

Article 15.— Protection of civilian medical and religious personnel

1. Civilian medical personnel shall be respected and protected.

2. If needed, all available help shall be afforded to civilian medical personnel in an area where civilian medical services are disrupted by reason of combat activity.

3. The Occupying Power shall afford civilian medical personnel in occupied territories every assistance to enable them to perform, to the best of their ability, their humanitarian functions. The Occupying Power may not require that, in the performance of those functions, such personnel shall give priority to the treatment of any person except on medical grounds. They shall not be compelled to carry out tasks which are not compatible with their humanitarian mission.

4. Civilian medical personnel shall have access to any place where their services are essential, subject to such supervisory and safety measures as the relevant Party to the conflict may deem necessary.

5. Civilian religious personnel shall be respected and protected. The provisions of the Conventions and of this Protocol concerning the protection and identification of medical personnel shall apply equally to such persons.

Article 16.— General protection of medical duties

1. Under no circumstances shall any person be punished for carrying out medical activities compatible with medical ethics, regardless of the person benefiting therefrom.

2. Persons engaged in medical activities shall not be compelled to perform acts or to carry out work contrary to the rules of medical ethics or to other medical rules designed for the benefit of the wounded and sick or to

the provisions of the Conventions or of this Protocol, or to refrain from performing acts or from carrying out work required by those rules and provisions.

3. No person engaged in medical activities shall be compelled to give to anyone belonging either to an adverse Party, or to his own Party except as required by the law of the latter Party, any information concerning the wounded and sick who are, or who have been, under his care, if such information would, in his opinion, prove harmful to the patients concerned or to their families. Regulations for the compulsory notification of communicable diseases shall, however, be respected.

Article 17.— Role of the civilian population and of aid societies

1. The civilian population shall respect the wounded, sick and shipwrecked, even if they belong to the adverse Party, and shall commit no act of violence against them. The civilian population and aid societies, such as national Red Cross (Red Crescent, Red Lion and Sun) Societies, shall be permitted, even on their own initiative, to collect and care for the wounded, sick and shipwrecked, even in invaded or occupied areas. No one shall be harmed, prosecuted, convicted or punished for such humanitarian acts.

2. The Parties to the conflict may appeal to the civilian population and the aid societies referred to in paragraph 1 to collect and care for the wounded, sick and shipwrecked, and to search for the dead and report their location; they shall grant both protection and the necessary facilities to those who respond to this appeal. If the adverse Party gains or regains control of the area, that Party also shall afford the same protection and facilities for so long as they are needed.

Article 18.— Identification

1. Each Party to the conflict shall endeavour to ensure that medical and religious personnel and medical units and transports are identifiable.

2. Each Party to the conflict shall also endeavour to adopt and to implement methods and procedures which will make it possible to recognize medical units and transports which use the distinctive emblem and distinctive signals.

3. In occupied territory and in areas where fighting is taking place or is likely to take place, civilian medical personnel and civilian religious personnel should be recognizable by the distinctive emblem and an identity card certifying their status.

4. With the consent of the competent authority, medical units and transports shall be marked by the distinctive emblem. The ships and craft re-

ferred to in Article 22 of this Protocol shall be marked in accordance with the provisions of the Second Convention.

5.   In addition to the distinctive emblem, a Party to the conflict may, as provided in Chapter III of Annex I to this Protocol, authorize the use of distinctive signals to identify medical units and transports. Exceptionally, in the special cases covered in that Chapter, medical transports may use distinctive signals without displaying the distinctive emblem.

6.   The application of the provisions of paragraphs 1 to 5 of this Article is governed by Chapters I to III of Annex I to this Protocol. Signals designated in Chapter III of the Annex for the exclusive use of medical units and transports shall not, except as provided therein, be used for any purpose other than to identify the medical units and transports specified in that Chapter.

7.   This Article does not authorize any wider use of the distinctive emblem in peacetime than is prescribed in Article 44 of the First Convention.

8.   The provisions of the Conventions and of this Protocol relating to supervision of the use of the distinctive emblem and to the prevention and repression of any misuse thereof shall be applicable to distinctive signals.

Article 19.— Neutral and other States not Parties to the conflict

Neutral and other States not Parties to the conflict shall apply the relevant provisions of this Protocol to persons protected by this Part who may be received or interned within their territory, and to any dead of the Parties to that conflict whom they may find.

Article 20.— Prohibition of reprisals

Reprisals against the persons and objects protected by this Part are prohibited.

SECTION II. — MEDICAL TRANSPORTATION

Article 21.— Medical vehicles

Medical vehicles shall be respected and protected in the same way as mobile medical units under the Conventions and this Protocol.

Article 22.— Hospitals ships and coastal rescue craft

1.   The provisions of the Conventions relating to:

(*a*) Vessels described in Articles 22, 24, 25 and 27 of the Second Convention,

(*b*) Their lifeboats and small craft,

(*c*) Their personnel and crews; and

(*d*) The wounded, sick and shipwrecked on board,

shall also apply where these vessels carry civilian wounded, sick and shipwrecked who do not belong to any of the categories mentioned in Article 13 of the Second Convention. Such civilians shall not, however, be subject to surrender to any Party which is not their own, or to capture at sea. If they find themselves in the power of a Party to the conflict other than their own they shall be covered by the Fourth Convention and by this Protocol.

2. The protection provided by the Conventions to vessels described in Article 25 of the Second Convention shall extend to hospital ships made available for humanitarian purposes to a Party to the conflict:

(*a*) By a neutral or other State which is not a Party to that conflict; or

(*b*) By an impartial international humanitarian organization,

provided that, in either case, the requirements set out in that Article are complied with.

3. Small craft described in Article 27 of the Second Convention shall be protected even if the notification envisaged by that Article has not been made. The Parties to the conflict are, nevertheless, invited to inform each other of any details of such craft which will facilitate their identification and recognition.

Article 23.— Other medical ships and craft

1. Medical ships and craft other than those referred to in Article 22 of this Protocol and Article 38 of the Second Convention shall, whether at sea or in other waters, be respected and protected in the same way as mobile medical units under the Conventions and this Protocol. Since this protection can only be effective if they can be identified and recognized as medical ships or craft, such vessels should be marked with the distinctive emblem and as far as possible comply with the second paragraph of Article 43 of the Second Convention.

2. The ships and craft referred to in paragraph 1 shall remain subject to the laws of war. Any warship on the surface able immediately to enforce its command may order them to stop, order them off, or make them take a certain course, and they shall obey every such command. Such ships and craft may not in any other way be diverted from their medical mission so long as they are needed for the wounded, sick and shipwrecked on board.

3. The protection provided in paragraph 1 shall cease only under the conditions set out in Articles 34 and 35 of the Second Convention. A clear

refusal to obey a command given in accordance with paragraph 2 shall be an act harmful to the enemy under Article 34 of the Second Convention.

4.   A Party to the conflict may notify any adverse Party as far in advance of sailing as possible of the name, description, expected time of sailing, course and estimated speed of the medical ship or craft, particularly in the case of ships of over 2,000 gross tons, and may provide any other information which would facilitate identification and recognition. The adverse Party shall acknowledge receipt of such information.

5.   The provisions of Article 37 of the Second Convention shall apply to medical and religious personnel in such ships and craft.

6.   The provisions of the Second Convention shall apply to the wounded, sick and shipwrecked belonging to the categories referred to in Article 13 of the Second Convention and in Article 44 of this Protocol who may be on board such medical ships and craft. Wounded, sick and shipwrecked civilians who do not belong to any of the categories mentioned in Article 13 of the Second Convention shall not be subject, at sea, either to surrender to any Party which is not their own, or to removal from such ships or craft; if they find themselves in the power of a Party to the conflict other than their own, they shall be covered by the Fourth Convention and by this Protocol.

Article 24.— Protection of medical aircraft

Medical aircraft shall be respected and protected, subject to the provisions of this Part.

Article 25.— Medical aircraft in areas not controlled by an adverse Party

In and over land areas physically controlled by friendly forces, or in and over sea areas not physically controlled by an adverse Party, the respect and protection of medical aircraft of a Party to the conflict is not dependent on any agreement with an adverse Party. For greater safety, however, a Party to the conflict operating its medical aircraft in these areas may notify the adverse Party, as provided in Article 29, in particular when such aircraft are making flights bringing them within range of surface-to-air weapons systems of the adverse Party.

Article 26.— Medical aircraft in contact or similar zones

1.   In and over those parts of the contact zone which are physically controlled by friendly forces and in and over those areas the physical control of which is not clearly established, protection for medical aircraft can be fully effective only by prior agreement between the competent military authorities of the Parties to the conflict, as provided for in Article 29. Al-

though, in the absence of such an agreement, medical aircraft operate at their own risk, they shall nevertheless be respected after they have been recognized as such.

2.   "Contact zone" means any area on land where the forward elements of opposing forces are in contact with each other, especially where they are exposed to direct fire from the ground.

Article 27.— Medical aircraft in areas controlled by an adverse Party

1.   The medical aircraft of a Party to the conflict shall continue to be protected while flying over land or sea areas physically controlled by an adverse Party, provided that prior agreement to such flights has been obtained from the competent authority of the adverse Party.

2.   A medical aircraft which flies over an area physically controlled by an adverse Party without, or in deviation from the terms of, an agreement provided for in paragraph 1, either through navigational error or because of an emergency affecting the safety of the flight, shall make every effort to identify itself and to inform the adverse Party of the circumstances. As soon as such medical aircraft has been recognized by the adverse Party, that Party shall make all reasonable efforts to given the order to land or to alight on water, referred to in Article 30, paragraph 1, or to take other measures to safeguard its own interests, and, in either case, to allow the aircraft time for compliance, before resorting to an attack against the aircraft.

Article 28.— Restrictions on operations of medical aircraft

1.   The Parties to the conflict are prohibited from using their medical aircraft to attempt to acquire any military advantage over an adverse Party. The presence of medical aircraft shall not be used in an attempt to render military objectives immune from attack.

2.   Medical aircraft shall not be used to collect or transmit intelligence data and shall not carry any equipment intended for such purposes. They are prohibited from carrying any persons or cargo not included within the definition in Article 8, subparagraph (f). The carrying on board of the personal effects of the occupants or of equipment intended solely to facilitate navigation, communication or identification shall not be considered as prohibited.

3.   Medical aircraft shall not carry any armament except small arms and ammunition taken from the wounded, sick and shipwrecked on board and not yet handed to the proper service, and such light individual weapons as may be necessary to enable the medical personnel on board to defend themselves and the wounded, sick and shipwrecked in their charge.

4. While carrying out the flights referred to in Articles 26 and 27, medical aircraft shall not, except by prior agreement with the adverse Party, be used to search for the wounded, sick and shipwrecked

Article 29.—Notifications and agreements concerning medical aircraft

1. Notifications under Article 25, or requests for prior agreement under Articles 26, 27, 28 (paragraph 4), or 31 shall state the proposed number of medical aircraft, their flight plans and means of identification, and shall be understood to mean that every flight will be carried out in compliance with Article 28.

2. A Party which receives a notification given under Article 25 shall at once acknowledge receipt of such notification.

3. A Party which receives a request for prior agreement under Articles 26, 27, 28 (paragraph 4), or 31 shall, as rapidly as possible, notify the requesting Party:

(*a*) That the request is agreed to;

(*b*) That the request is denied; or

(*c*) Of reasonable alternative proposals to the request. It may also propose a prohibition or restriction of other flights in the area during the time involved. If the Party which submitted the request accepts the alternative proposals, it shall notify the other Party of such acceptance.

4. The Parties shall take the necessary measures to ensure that notifications and agreements can be made rapidly.

5. The Parties shall also take the necessary measures to disseminate rapidly the substance of any such notifications and agreements to the military units concerned and shall instruct those units regarding the means of identification that will be used by the medical aircraft in question.

Article 30.—Landing and inspection of medical aircraft

1. Medical aircraft flying over areas which are physically controlled by an adverse Party, or over areas the physical control of which is not clearly established, may be ordered to land or to alight on water, as appropriate, to permit inspection in accordance with the following paragraphs. Medical aircraft shall obey any such order.

2. If such an aircraft lands or alights on water, whether ordered to do so or for other reasons, it may be subjected to inspection solely to determine the matters referred to in paragraphs 3 and 4. Any such inspection shall be commenced without delay and shall be conducted expeditiously. The inspecting Party shall not require the wounded and sick to be removed from the aircraft unless their removal is essential for the inspection. That Party

shall in any event ensure that the condition of the wounded and sick is not adversely affected by the inspection or by the removal.

3. If the inspection discloses that the aircraft:

(*a*) Is a medical aircraft within the meaning of Article 8, sub-paragraph (*j*);

(*b*) Is not in violation of the conditions prescribed in Article 28; and

(*c*) Has not flown without or in breach of a prior agreement where such agreement is required;

the aircraft and those of its occupants who belong to the adverse Party or to a neutral or other State not a Party to the conflict shall be authorized to continue the flight without delay.

4. If the inspection discloses that the aircraft:

(*a*) Is not a medical aircraft within the meaning of Article 8, sub-paragraph (*j*);

(*b*) Is in violation of the conditions prescribed in Article 28; or,

(*c*) Has flown without or in breach of a prior agreement where such agreement is required;

the aircraft may be seized. Its occupants shall be treated in conformity with the relevant provisions of the Conventions and of this Protocol. Any aircraft seized which had been assigned as a permanent medical aircraft may be used thereafter only as a medical aircraft.

Article 31.— Neutral or other States not Parties to the conflict

1. Except by prior agreement, medical aircraft shall not fly over or land in the territory of a neutral or other State not a Party to the conflict. However, with such an agreement, they shall be respected throughout their flight and also for the duration of any calls in the territory. Nevertheless they shall obey any summons to land or to alight on water, as appropriate.

2. Should a medical aircraft, in the absence of an agreement or in deviation from the terms of an agreement, fly over the territory of a neutral or other State not a Party to the conflict, either through navigational error or because of an emergency affecting the safety o the flight, it shall make every effort to give notice of the flight and to identify itself. As soon as such medical aircraft is recognized, that State shall make all reasonable efforts to give the order to land or to alight on water referred to in Article 30, paragraph 1, or to take other measures to safeguard its own interests, and in either case, to allow the aircraft time for compliance, before resorting to an attack against the aircraft.

3. If a medical aircraft, either by agreement or in the circumstances mentioned in paragraph 2, lands or alights on water in the territory of a neutral or other State not Party to the conflict, whether ordered to do so or for

other reasons, the aircraft shall be subject to inspection for the purposes of determining whether it is in fact a medical aircraft. The inspection shall be commenced without delay and shall be conducted expeditiously. The inspecting Party shall not require the wounded and sick of the Party operating the aircraft to be removed from it unless their removal is essential for the inspection. The inspecting Party shall in any event ensure that the condition of the wounded and sick is not adversely affected by the inspection or the removal. If the inspection discloses that the aircraft is in fact a medical aircraft, the aircraft with its occupants, other than those who must be detained in accordance with the rules of international law applicable in armed conflict, shall be allowed to resume its flight, and reasonable facilities shall be given for the continuation of the flight. If the inspection discloses that the aircraft is not a medical aircraft, it shall be seized and the occupants treated in accordance with paragraph 4.

4. The wounded, sick and shipwrecked disembarked, otherwise than temporarily, from a medical aircraft with the consent of the local authorities in the territory of a neutral or other State not a Party to the conflict shall, unless agreed otherwise between that State and the Parties to the conflict, be detained by that Sate where so required by the rules of international law applicable in armed conflict, in such a manner that they cannot again take part in the hostilities. The cost of hospital treatment and internment shall be borne by the State to which those persons belong.

5. Neutral or other States not Parties to the conflict shall apply any conditions and restrictions on the passage of medical aircraft over, or on the landing of medical aircraft in, their territory equally to all Parties to the conflict.

SECTION III.—MISSING AND DEAD PERSONS

Article 32.— General principle

In the implementation of this Section, the activities of the High Contracting Parties, of the Parties to the conflict and of the international humanitarian organizations mentioned in the Conventions and in this Protocol shall be prompted mainly by the right of families to know the fate of their relatives.

Article 33.— Missing persons

1. As soon as circumstances permit, and at the latest from the end of active hostilities, each Party to the conflict shall search for the persons who have been reported missing by an adverse Party. Such adverse Party shall

transmit all relevant information concerning such persons in order to facilitate such searches.

2.   In order to facilitate the gathering of information pursuant to the preceding paragraph, each Party to the conflict shall, with respect to persons who would not receive more favourable consideration under the Conventions and this Protocol:

(*a*) Record the information specified in Article 138 of the Fourth Convention in respect of such persons who have been detained, imprisoned or otherwise held in captivity for more than two weeks as a result of hostilities or occupation, or who have died during any period of detention;

(*b*) To the fullest extent possible, facilitate and, if need be, carry out the search for and the recording of information concerning such persons if they have died in other circumstances as a result of hostilities or occupation.

3.   Information concerning persons reported missing pursuant to paragraph 1 and requests for such information shall be transmitted either directly or through the Protecting Power or the Central Tracing Agency of the International Committee of the Red Cross or national Red Cross (Red Crescent, Red Lion and Sun) Societies. Where the information is not transmitted through the International Committee of the Red Cross and its Central Tracing Agency, each Party to the conflict shall ensure that such information is also supplied to the Central Tracing Agency.

4.   The Parties to the conflict shall endeavour to agree on arrangements for teams to search for, identify and recover the dead from battlefied areas, including arrangements, if appropriate, for such teams to be accompanied by personnel of the adverse Party while carrying out the missions in areas controlled by the adverse Party. Personnel of such teams shall be respected and protected while exclusively carrying out these duties.

Article 34.— *Remains of deceased*

1.   The remains of persons who have died for reasons related to occupation or in detention resulting from occupation or hostilities and those of persons not nationals of the country in which they have died as a result of hostilities shall be respected, and the gravesites of all such persons shall be respected, maintained and marked as provided for in Article 130 of the Fourth Convention, where their remains or gravesites would not receive more favourable consideration under the Conventions and this Protocol.

2.   As soon as circumstances and the relations between the adverse Parties permit, the High Contracting Parties in whose territories graves and, as the case may be, other locations of the remains of persons who have died as a result of hostilities or during occupation or in detention are situated, shall conclude agreements in order:

(*a*) To facilitate access to the gravesites by relatives of the deceased and by representatives of official graves registration services and to regulate the practical arrangements for such access;

(*b*) To protect and maintain such gravesites permanently;

(*c*) To facilitate the return of the remains of the deceased and of personal effects to the home country upon its request or, unless that country objects, upon the request of the next of kin.

3. In the absence of the agreements provided for in paragraph 2 (*b*) or (*c*) and if the home country of such deceased is not willing to arrange at its expense for the maintenance of such gravesites, the High Contracting Party in whose territory the gravesites are situated may offer to facilitate the return of the remains of the deceased to the home country. Where such an offer has not been accepted the High Contracting Party may, after the expiry of five years from the date of the offer and upon due notice to the home country, adopt the arrangements laid down in its own laws relating to cemeteries and graves.

4. A High Contracting Party in whose territory the gravesites referred to in this Article are situated shall be permitted to exhume the remains only:

(*a*) In accordance with paragraphs 2 (*c*) and 3; or

(*b*) Where exhumation is a matter of overriding public necessity, including cases of medical and investigative necessity, in which case the High Contracting Party shall at all times respect the remains, and shall give notice to the home country of its intention to exhume the remains together with details of the intended place of reinterment.

PART III

METHODS AND MEANS OF WARFARE
COMBATANT AND PRISONER-OF-WAR STATUS

SECTION I.—METHODS AND MEANS OF WARFARE

Article 35.—Basic rules

1. In any armed conflict, the right of the Parties to the conflict to choose methods or means of warfare is not unlimited.

2. It is prohibited to employ weapons, projectiles and material and methods of warfare of a nature to cause superfluous injury or unnecessary suffering.

3. It is prohibited to employ methods or means of warfare which are intended, or may be expected, to cause widespread, long-term and severe damage to the natural environment.

Article 36.— New weapons

In the study, development, acquisition or adoption of a new weapon, means or method of warfare, a High Contracting Party is under an obligation to determine whether its employment would, in some or all circumstances, be prohibited by this Protocol or by any other rule of international law applicable to the High Contracting Party.

Article 37.— Prohibition of perfidy

1. It is prohibited to kill, injure or capture an adversary by resort to perfidy. Acts inviting the confidence of an adversary to lead him to believe that he is entitled to, or is obliged to accord, protection under the rules of international law applicable in armed conflict, with intent to betray that confidence, shall constitute perfidy. The following acts are examples of perfidy:

(a) The feigning of an intent to negotiate under a flag of truce or of a surrender;

(b) The feigning of an incapacitation by wounds or sickness;

(c) The feigning of civilian, non-combatant status; and

(d) The feigning of protected status by the use of signs, emblems or uniforms of the United Nations or of neutral or other States not Parties to the conflict.

2. Ruses of war are not prohibited. Such ruses are acts which are intended to mislead an adversary or to induce him to act recklessly but which infringe no rule of international law applicable in armed conflict and which are not perfidious because they do not invite the confidence of an adversary with respect to protection under that law. The following are examples of such ruses: the use of camouflage, decoys, mock operations and misinformation

Article 38.— Recognized emblems

1. It is prohibited to make improper use of the distinctive emblem of the red cross, red crescent or red lion and sun or of other emblems, signs or signals provided for by the Conventions or by this Protocol. It is also prohibited to misuse deliberately in an armed conflict other internationally recognized protective emblems, signs or signals, including the flag of truce, and the protective emblem of cultural property.

2. It is prohibited to make use of the distinctive emblem of the United Nations, except as authorized by that Organization.

Article 39.— Emblems of nationality

1. It is prohibited to make use in an armed conflict of the flags or military emblems, insignia or uniforms of neutral or other States not Parties to the conflict.

2. It is prohibited to make use of the flags or military emblems, insignia or uniforms of adverse Parties while engaging in attacks or in order to shield, favour, protect or impede military operations.

3. Nothing in this Article or in Article 37, paragraph 1 (d), shall affect the existing generally recognized rules of international law applicable to espionage or to the use of flags in the conduct of armed conflict at sea.

Article 40.— Quarter

It is prohibited to order that there shall be no survivors, to threaten an adversary therewith or to conduct hostilities on this basis.

Article 41.— Safeguard of an enemy hors de combat

1. A person who is recognized or who, in the circumstances, should be recognized to be *hors de combat* shall not be made the object of attack.

2. A person is *hors de combat* if:

(a) He is in the power of an adverse Party;

(b) He clearly expresses an intention to surrender; or

(c) He has been rendered unconscious or is otherwise incapacitated by wounds or sickness, and therefore is incapable of defending himself;

provided that in any of these cases he abstains from any hostile act and does not attempt to escape.

3. When persons entitled to protection as prisons of war have fallen into the power of an adverse Party under unusual conditions of combat which prevent their evacuation as provided for in Part III, Section I, of the Third Convention, they shall be released and all feasible precautions shall be taken to ensure their safety.

Article 42.— Occupants of aircraft

1. No person parachuting from an aircraft in distress shall be made the object of attack during his descent.

2. Upon reaching the ground in territory controlled by an adverse Party, a person who has parachuted from an aircraft in distress shall be given an opportunity to surrender before being made the object of attack, unless it is apparent that he is engaging in a hostile act.

3. Airborne troops are not protected by this Article.

SECTION II.—COMBATANT AND PRISONER-OF-WAR STATUS

Article 43. — Armed forces

1.　The armed forces of a Party to a conflict consist of all organized armed forces, groups and units which are under a command responsible to that Party for the conduct of its subordinates, even if that Party is represented by a government or an authority not recognized by an adverse Party. Such armed forces shall be subject to an internal disciplinary system which, *inter alia,* shall enforce compliance with the rules of international law applicable in armed conflict.

2.　Members of the armed forces of a Party to a conflict (other than medical personnel and chaplains covered by Article 33 of the Third Convention) are combatants, that is to say, they have the right to participate directly in hostilities.

3.　Whenever a Party to a conflict incorporates a paramilitary or armed law enforcement agency into its armed forces it shall so notify the other Parties to the conflict.

Article 44. — Combatants and prisoners of war

1.　Any combatant, as defined in Article 43, who falls into the power of an adverse Party shall be a prisoner of war.

2.　While all combatants are obliged to comply with the rules of international law applicable in armed conflict, violations of these rules shall not deprive a combatant of his right to be a combatant or, if he falls into the power of an adverse Party, of his right to be a prisoner of war, except as provided in paragraphs 3 and 4.

3.　In order to promote the protection of the civilian population from the effects of hostilities, combatants are obliged to distinguish themselves from the civilian population while they are engaged in an attack or in a military operation preparatory to an attack. Recognizing, however, that there are situations in armed conflicts where, owing to the nature of the hostilities an armed combatant cannot so distinguish himself, he shall retain his status as a combatant, provided that, in such situations, he carries his arms openly:

(*a*) During each military engagement, and

(*b*) During such time as he is visible to the adversary while he is engaged in a military deployment preceding the launching of an attack in which he is to participate.

Acts which comply with the requirements of this paragraph shall not be considered as perfidious within the meaning of Article 37, paragraph 1 (*c*).

4.   A combatant who falls into the power of an adverse Party while failing to meet the requirements set forth in the second sentence of paragraph 3 shall forfeit his right to be a prisoner of war, but he shall, nevertheless, be given protections equivalent in all respects to those accorded to prisoners of war by the Third Convention and by this Protocol. This protection includes protections equivalent to those accorded to prisoners of war by the Third Convention in the case where such a person is tried and punished for any offences he has committed.

5.   Any combatant who falls into the power of an adverse Party while not engaged in an attack or in a military operation preparatory to an attack shall not forfeit his rights to be a combatant and a prisoner of war by virtue of his prior activities.

6.   This Article is without prejudice to the right of any person to be a prisoner of war pursuant to Article 4 of the Third Convention.

7.   This Article is not intended to change the generally accepted practice of States with respect to the wearing of the uniform by combatants assigned to the regular, uniformed armed units of a Party to the conflict.

8.   In addition to the categories of persons mentioned in Article 13 of the First and Second Conventions, all members of the armed forces of a Party to the conflict, as defined in Article 43 of this Protocol, shall be entitled to protection under those Conventions if they are wounded or sick or, in the case of the Second Convention, shipwrecked at sea or in other waters.

Article 45.— Protection of persons who have taken part in hostilities

1.   A person who takes part in hostilities and falls into the power of an adverse Party shall be presumed to be a prisoner of war, and therefore shall be protected by the Third Convention, if he claims the status of prisoner of war, or if he appears to be entitled to such status, or if the Party on which he depends claims such status on his behalf by notification to the detaining Power or to the Protecting Power. Should any doubt arise as to whether any such person is entitled to the status of prisoner of war, he shall continue to have such status and, therefore, to be protected by the Third Convention and this Protocol until such time as his status has been determined by a competent tribunal.

2.   If a person who has fallen into the power of an adverse Party is not held as a prisoner of war and is to be tried by that Party for an offence arising out of the hostilities, he shall have the right to assert his entitlement to prisoner-of-war status before a judicial tribunal and to have that question adjudicated. Whenever possible under the applicable procedure, this adjudication shall occur before the trial for the offence. The representatives of the Protecting Power shall be entitled to attend the proceedings in which that question is adjudicated, unless, exceptionally, the proceedings are held *in*

camera in the interest of State security. In such a case the detaining Power shall advise the Protecting Power accordingly.

3. Any person who has taken part in hostilities, who is not entitled to prisoner-of-war status and who does not benefit from more favourable treatment in accordance with the Fourth Convention shall have the right at all times to the protection of Article 75 of this Protocol. In occupied territory, an such person, unless he is held as a spy, shall also be entitled, notwithstanding Article 5 of the Fourth Convention, to his rights of communication under that Convention.

Article 46.— Spies

1. Notwithstanding any other provision of the Conventions or of this Protocol, any member of the armed forces of a Party to the conflict who falls into the power of an adverse Party while engaging in espionage shall not have the right to the status of prisoner of war and may be treated as a spy.

2. A member of the armed forces of a Party to the conflict who, on behalf of that Party and in territory controlled by an adverse Party, gathers or attempts to gather information shall not be considered as engaging in espionage if, while so acting, he is in the uniform of his armed forces.

3. A member of the armed forces of a Party to the conflict who is a resident of territory occupied by an adverse Party and who, on behalf of the Party on which he depends, gathers or attempts to gather information of military value within that territory shall not be considered as engaging in espionage unless he does so through an act of false pretences or deliberately in a clandestine manner. Moreover, such a resident shall not lose his right to the status of prisoner of war and may not be treated as a spy unless he is captured while engaging in espionage.

4. A member of the armed forces of a Party to the conflict who is not a resident of territory occupied by an adverse Party and who has engaged in espionage in that territory shall not lose his right to the status of prisoner of war and may not be treated as a spy unless he is captured before he has rejoined the armed forces to which he belongs.

Article 47.— Mercenaries

1. A mercenary shall not have the right to be a combatant or a prisoner of war.

2. A mercenary is any person who:

(*a*) Is specially recruited locally or abroad in order to fight in an armed conflict;

(*b*) Does, in fact, take a direct part in the hostilities;

(*c*) Is motivated to take part in the hostilities essentially by the desire for private gain and, in fact, is promised, by or on behalf of a Party to the conflict, material compensation substantially in excess of that promised or paid to combatants of similar ranks and functions in the armed forces of that Party;

(*d*) Is neither a national of a Party to the conflict nor a resident of territory controlled by a Party to the conflict;

(*e*) Is not a member of the armed forces of a Party to the conflict; and

(*f*) Has not been sent by a State which is not a Party to the conflict on official duty as a member of its armed forces.

PART IV

CIVILIAN POPULATION

SECTION I.—GENERAL PROTECTION AGAINST EFFECTS OF HOSTILITIES

CHAPTER I.— BASIC RULE AND FIELD OF APPLICATION

Article 48.— Basic rule

In order to ensure respect for and protection of the civilian population and civilian objects, the Parties to the conflict shall at all times distinguish between the civilian population and combatants and between civilian objects and military objectives and accordingly shall direct their operations only against military objectives.

Article 49.— Definition of attacks and scope of application

1. "Attacks" means acts of violence against the adversary, whether in offence or in defence.

2. The provisions of this Protocol with respect to attacks apply to all attacks in whatever territory conducted, including the national territory belonging to a Party to the conflict but under the control of an adverse Party.

3. The provisions of this Section apply to any land, air or sea warfare which may affect the civilian population, individual civilians or civilian objects on land. They further apply to all attacks from the sea or from the air

against objectives on land but do not otherwise affect the rules of international law applicable in armed conflict at sea or in the air.

4.   The provisions of this Section are additional to the rules concerning humanitarian protection contained in the Fourth Convention, particularly in Part II thereof, and in other international agreements binding upon the High Contracting Parties, as well as to other rules of international law relating to the protection of civilians and civilian objects on land, at sea or in the air against the effects of hostilities.

CHAPTER II.— CIVILIANS AND CIVILIAN POPULATION

Article 50.— Definition of civilians and civilian population

1.   A civilian is any person who does not belong to one of the categories of persons referred to in Article 4 A (1), (2), (3) and (6) of the Third Convention and in Article 43 of this Protocol. In case of doubt whether a person is a civilian, that person shall be considered to be a civilian.

2.   The civilian population comprises all persons who are civilians.

3.   The presence within the civilian population of individuals who do not come within the definition of civilians does not deprive the population of its civilian character.

Article 51.— Protection of the civilian population

1.   The civilian population and individual civilians shall enjoy general protection against dangers arising from military operations. To give effect to this protection, the following rules, which are additional to other applicable rules of international law, shall be observed in circumstances.

2.   The civilian population as such, as well as individual civilians, shall not be the object of attack. Acts or threats of violence the primary purpose of which is to spread terror among the civilian population are prohibited.

3.   Civilians shall enjoy the protection afforded by this Section, unless and for such time as they take a direct part in hostilities.

4.   Indiscriminate attacks are prohibited. Indiscriminate attacks are:

(*a*) Those which are not directed at a specific military objective;

(*b*) Those which employ a method or means of combat which cannot be directed at a specific military objective; or

(c) Those which employ a method or means of combat the effects of which cannot be limited as required by this Protocol;

and consequently, in each such case, are of a nature to strike military objectives and civilians or civilian objects without distinction.

5. Among others, the following types of attacks are to be considered as indiscriminate:

(a) An attack by bombardment by any methods or means which treats as a single military objective a number of clearly separated and distinct military objectives located in a city, town, village or other area containing a similar concentration of civilians or civilian objects; and

(b) An attack which may be expected to cause incidental loss of civilian life, injury to civilians, damage to civilian objects, or a combination thereof, which would be excessive in relation to the concrete and direct military advantage anticipated.

6. Attacks against the civilian population or civilians by way of reprisals are prohibited.

7. The presence or movements of the civilian population or individual civilians shall not be used to render certain points or areas immune from military operations, in particular in attempts to shield military objectives from attacks or to shield, favour or impede military operations. The Parties to the conflict shall not direct the movement of the civilian population or individual civilians in order to attempt to shield military objectives from attacks or to shield military operations.

8. Any violation of these prohibitions shall not release the Parties to the conflict from their legal obligations with respect to the civilian population and civilians, including the obligation to take the precautionary measures provided for in Article 57.

CHAPTER III.— CIVILIAN OBJECTS

Article 52.— General protection of civilian objects

1. Civilian objects shall not be the object of attack or of reprisals. Civilian objects are all objects which are not military objectives as defined in paragraph 2.

2. Attacks shall be limited strictly to military objectives. In so far as objects are concerned, military objectives are limited to those objects which by their nature, location, purpose or use make an effective contribution to military action and whose total or partial destruction, capture or neutraliza-

tion, in the circumstances ruling at the time, offers a definite military of advantage.

3. In case of doubt whether an object which is normally dedicated to civilian purposes, such as a place of worship, a house or other dwelling or a school, is being used to make an effective contribution to military action, it shall be presumed not to be so used.

Article 53.— Protection of cultural objects and of places of worship

Without prejudice to the provisions of the Hague Convention for the Protection of Cultural Property in the Event of Armed Conflict of 14 May 1954, and of other relevant international instruments, it is prohibited:

(*a*) To commit any acts of hostility directed against the historic monuments, works of art or places of worship which constitute the cultural or spiritual heritage of peoples;

(*b*) To use such objects in support of the military effort;

(*c*) To make such objects the object of reprisals.

Article 54.— Protection of objects indispensable to the survival
of the civilian population

1. Starvation of civilians as a method of warfare is prohibited.

2. It is prohibited to attack, destroy, remove or render useless objects indispensable to the survival of the civilian population, such as foodstuffs, agricultural areas for the production of foodstuffs, crops, livestock, drinking water installations and supplies and irrigation works, for the specific purpose of denying them for their sustenance value to the civilian population or to the adverse Party, whatever the motive, whether in order to starve out civilians, to cause them to move away, or for any other motive.

3. The prohibitions in paragraph 2 shall not apply to such of the objects covered by it as are used by an adverse Party:

(*a*) As sustenance solely for the members of its armed forces; or

(*b*) If not as sustenance, then in direct support of military action, provided, however, that in no event shall actions against these objects be taken which may be expected to leave the civilian population with such inadequate food or water as to cause its starvation or force its movement.

4. These objects shall not be made the object of reprisals.

5. In recognition of the vital requirements of any Party to the conflict in the defence of its national territory against invasion, derogation from the prohibitions contained in paragraph 2 may be made by a Party to the conflict within such territory under its own control where required by imperative military necessity.

Article 55.—Protection of the natural environment

1. Care shall be taken in warfare to protect the natural environment against widespread, long-term and severe damage. This protection includes a prohibition of the use of methods or means of warfare which are intended or may be expected to cause such damage to the natural environment and thereby to prejudice the health or survival of the population.

2. Attacks against the natural environment by way of reprisals are prohibited.

Article 56.—Protection of works and installations
containing dangerous forces

1. Works or installations containing dangerous forces, namely dams, dykes and nuclear electrical generating stations, shall not be made the object of attack, even where these objects are military objectives, if such attack may cause the release of dangerous forces and consequent severe losses among the civilian population. Other military objectives located at or in the vicinity of these works or installations shall not be made the object of attack if such attack may cause the release of dangerous forces from the works or installations and consequent severe losses among the civilian population.

2. The special protection against attack provided by paragraph 1 shall cease:

(*a*) For a dam or a dyke only if it is used for other than its normal function and in regular, significant and direct support of military operations and if such attack is the only feasible way to terminate such support;

(*b*) For a nuclear electrical generating station only if it provides electric power in regular, significant and direct support of military operations and if such attack is the only feasible way to terminate such support;

(*c*) For other military objectives located at or in the vicinity of these works or installations only if they are used in regular, significant and direct support of military operations and if such attack is the only feasible way to terminate such support.

3. In all cases, the civilian population and individual civilians shall remain entitled to all the protection accorded them by international law, including the protection of the precautionary measures provided for in Article 57. If the protection ceases and any of the works, installations or military objectives mentioned in paragraph 1 is attacked, all practical precautions shall be taken to avoid the release of the dangerous forces.

4. It is prohibited to make any of the works, installations or military objectives mentioned in paragraph 1 the object of reprisals.

5. The Parties to the conflict shall endeavour to avoid locating any military objectives in the vicinity of the works or installations mentioned in

paragraph 1. Nevertheless, installations erected for the sole purpose of defending the protected works or installations from attack are permissible and shall not themselves be made the object of attack, provided that they are not used in hostilities except for defensive actions necessary to respond to attacks against the protected works or installations and that their armament is limited to weapons capable only of repelling hostile action against the protected works or installations.

6. The High Contracting Parties and the Parties to the conflict are urged to conclude further agreements among themselves to provide additional protection for objects containing dangerous forces.

7. In order to facilitate the identification of the objects protected by this article, the Parties to the conflict may mark them with a special sign consisting of a group of three bright orange circles placed on the same axis, as specified in Article 16 of Annex I to this Protocol. The absence of such marking in no way relieves any Party to the conflict of its obligations under this Article.

CHAPTER IV.— PRECAUTIONARY MEASURES

Article 57.— Precautions in attack

1. In the conduct of military operations, constant care shall be taken to spare the civilian population, civilians and civilian objects.

2. With respect to attacks, the following precautions shall be taken:

(*a*) Those who plan or decide upon an attack shall:

(i) Do everything feasible to verify that the objectives to be attacked are neither civilians nor civilian objects and are not subject to special protection but are military objectives within the meaning of paragraph 2 of Article 52 and that it is not prohibited by the provisions of this Protocol to attack them;

(ii) Take all feasible precautions in the choice of means and methods of attack with a view to avoiding, and in any event to minimizing, incidental loss of civilian life, injury to civilians and damage to civilian objects;

(iii) Refrain from deciding to launch any attack which may be expected to cause incidental loss of civilian life, injury to civilians, damage to civilian objects, or a combination thereof, which would be excessive in relation to the concrete and direct military advantage anticipated;

(*b*) An attack shall be cancelled or suspended if it becomes apparent that the objective is not a military one or is subject to special protection or that the attack may be expected to cause incidental loss of civilian life, injury to civilians, damage to civilian objects, or a combination thereof, which would be excessive in relation to the concrete and direct military advantage anticipated;

(*c*) Effective advance warning shall be given of attacks which may affect the civilian population, unless circumstances do not permit.

3. When a choice is possible between several military objectives for obtaining a similar military advantage, the objective to be selected shall be that the attack on which may be expected to cause the least danger to civilian lives and to civilian objects.

4. In the conduct of military operations at sea or in the air, each Party to the conflict shall, in conformity with its rights and duties under the rules of international law applicable in armed conflict, take all reasonable precautions to avoid losses of civilian lives and damage to civilian objects.

5. No provision of this Article may be construed as authorizing any attacks against the civilian population, civilians or civilian objects.

Article 58.— Precautions against the effects of attacks

The Parties to the conflict shall, to the maximum extent feasible:

(*a*) Without prejudice to Article 49 of the Fourth Convention, endeavour to remove the civilian population, individual civilians and civilian objects under their control from the vicinity of military objectives;

(*b*) Avoid locating military objectives within or near densely populated areas;

(*c*) Take the other necessary precautions to protect the civilian population, individual civilians and civilian objects under their control against the dangers resulting from military operations.

CHAPTER V.— LOCALITIES AND ZONES UNDER SPECIAL PROTECTION

Article 59.— Non-defended localities

1. It is prohibited for the Parties to the conflict to attack, by any means whatsoever, non-defended localities.

2. The appropriate authorities of a Party to the conflict may declare as a non-defended locality any inhabited place near or in a zone where armed forces are in contact which is open for occupation by an adverse Party. Such a locality shall fulfil the following conditions:

(*a*) All combatants, as well as mobile weapons and mobile military equipment must have been evacuated;

(*b*) No hostile use shall be made of fixed military installations or establishments;

(*c*) No acts of hostility shall be committed by the authorities or by the population; and

(*d*) No activities in support of military operations shall be undertaken.

3. The presence, in this locality, of persons specially protected under the Conventions and this Protocol, and of police forces retained for the sole purpose of maintaining law and order, is not contrary to the conditions laid down in paragraph 2.

4. The declaration made under paragraph 2 shall be addressed to the adverse Party and shall define and describe, as precisely as possible, the limits of the non-defended locality. The Party to the conflict to which the declaration is addressed shall acknowledge its receipt and shall treat the locality as a non-defended locality unless the conditions laid down in paragraph 2 are not in fact fulfilled, in which event it shall immediately so inform the Party making the declaration. Even if the conditions laid down in paragraph 2 are not fulfilled, the locality shall continue to enjoy the protection provided by the other provisions of this Protocol and the other rules of international law applicable in armed conflict.

5. The Parties to the conflict may agree on the establishment of non-defended localities even if such localities do not fulfil the conditions laid down in paragraph 2. The agreement should define and describe, as precisely as possible, the limits of the non-defended locality; if necessary, it may lay down the methods of supervision.

6. The Party which is in control of a locality governed by such an agreement shall mark it, so far as possible, by such signs as may be agreed upon with the other Party, which shall be displayed where they are clearly visible, especially on its perimeter and limits and on highways.

7. A locality loses its status as a non-defended locality when it ceases to fulfil the conditions laid down in paragraph 2 or in the agreement referred to in paragraph 5. In such an eventuality, the locality shall continue to enjoy the protection provided by the other provisions of this Protocol and the other rules of international law applicable in armed conflict.

Article 60.— Demilitarized zones

1. It is prohibited for the Parties to the conflict to extend their military operations to zones on which they have conferred by agreement the status of demilitarized zone, if such extension is contrary to the terms of this agreement.

2. The agreement shall be an express agreement, may be concluded verbally or in writing, either directly or through a Protecting Power or any impartial humanitarian organization, and may consist of reciprocal and concordant declarations. The agreement may be concluded in peacetime, as well as after the outbreak of hostilities, and should define and describe, as precisely as possible, the limits of the demilitarized zone and, if necessary, lay down the methods of supervision.

3. The subject of such an agreement shall normally be any zone which fulfils the following conditions:

(*a*) All combatants, as well as mobile weapons and mobile military equipment, must have been evacuated;

(*b*) No hostile use shall be made of fixed military installations or establishments;

(*c*) No acts of hostility shall be committed by the authorities or by the population; and

(*d*) Any activity linked to the military effort must have ceased.

The Parties to the conflict shall agree upon the interpretation to be given to the condition laid down in sub-paragraph (*d*) and upon persons to be admitted to the demilitarized zone other than those mentioned in paragraph 4.

4. The presence, in this zone, of persons specially protected under the Conventions and this Protocol, and of police forces retained for the sole purpose of maintaining law and order, is not contrary to the conditions laid down in paragraph 3.

5. The Party which is in control of such a zone shall mark it, so far as possible, by such signs as may be agreed upon with the other Party, which shall be displayed where they are clearly visible, especially on its perimeter and limits and on highways.

6. If the fighting draws near to a demilitarized zone, and if the Parties to the conflict have so agreed, none of them may use the zone for purposes related to the conduct of military operations or unilaterally revoke its status.

7. If one of the Parties to the conflict commits a material breach of the provisions of paragraphs 3 or 6, the other Party shall be released from its obligations under the agreement conferring upon the zone the status of demilitarized zone. In such an eventuality, the zone loses its status but shall continue to enjoy the protection provided by the other provisions of this Protocol and the other rules of international law applicable in armed conflict.

CHAPTER VI.—CIVIL DEFENCE

Article 61.—Definitions and scope

For the purposes of this Protocol:

(*a*) ''Civil defence'' means the performance of some or all of the undermentioned humanitarian tasks intended to protect the civilian population against the dangers, and to help it to recover from the immediate effects, of hostilities or disasters and also to provide the conditions necessary for its survival. These tasks are:

(i) Warning;

(ii) Evacuation;

  (iii) Management of shelters;

  (iv) Management of blackout measures;

  (v) Rescue;

  (vi) Medical services, including first aid, and religious assistance;

  (vii) Fire-fighting;

(viii) Detection and marking of danger areas;

  (ix) Decontamination and similar protective measures;

  (x) Provision of emergency accommodation and supplies;

  (xi) Emergency assistance in the restoration and maintenance of order in distressed areas;

  (xii) Emergency repair of indispensable public utilities;

(xiii) Emergency disposal of the dead;

(xiv) Assistance in the preservation of objects essential for survival;

  (xv) Complementary activities necessary to carry out any of the tasks mentioned above, including, but not limited to, planning and organization;

(*b*) ''Civil defence organizations'' means those establishments and other units which are organized or authorized by the competent authorities of a Party to the conflict to perform any of the tasks mentioned under sub-paragraph (*a*), and which are assigned and devoted exclusively to such tasks;

(*c*) ''Personnel'' of civil defence organizations means those persons assigned by a Party to the conflict exclusively to the performance of the tasks mentioned under sub-paragraph (*a*), including personnel assigned by the competent authority of that Party exclusively to the administration of these organizations;

(*d*) ''*Matériel*'' of civil defence organizations means equipment, supplies and transports used by these organizations for the performance of the tasks mentioned under sub-paragraph (*a*).

Article 62.— *General protection*

   1. Civilian civil defence organizations and their personnel shall be respected and protected, subject to the provisions of this Protocol, particularly the provisions of this Section. They shall be entitled to perform their civil defence tasks except in case of imperative military necessity.

   2. The provisions of paragraph 1 shall also apply to civilians who, although not members of civilian civil defence organizations, respond to an appeal from the competent authorities and perform civil defence tasks under their control.

   3. Buildings and *matériel* used for civil defence purposes and shelters provided for the civilian population are covered by Article 52. Objects

used for civil defence purposes may not be destroyed or diverted from their proper use except by the Party to which they belong.

Article 63.— Civil defence in occupied territories

1. In occupied territories, civilian civil defence organizations shall receive from the authorities the facilities necessary for the performance of their tasks. In no circumstances shall their personnel be compelled to perform activities which would interfere with the proper performance of these tasks. The Occupying Power shall not change the structure or personnel of such organizations in any way which might jeopardize the efficient performance of their mission. These organizations shall not be required to give priority to the nationals or interests of that Power.

2. The Occupying Power shall not compel, coerce or induce civilian civil defence organizations to perform their tasks in an manner prejudicial to the interests of the civilian population.

3. The Occupying Power may disarm civil defence personnel for reasons of security.

4. The Occupying Power shall neither divert from their proper use nor requisition buildings or *matériel* belonging to or used by civil defence organizations if such diversion or requisition would be harmful to the civilian population.

5. Provided that the general rule in paragraph 4 continues to be observed, the Occuping Power may requisition or divert these resources, subject to the following particular conditions:

(*a*) That the buildings or *matériel* are necessary for other needs of the civilian population; and

(*b*) That the requisition or diversion continues only while such necessity exists.

6. The Occupying Power shall neither divert nor requisition shelters provided for the use of the civilian population or needed by such population.

Article 64.— Civilian civil defence organizations of neutral or other States not Parties to the conflict and international co-ordinating organizations

1. Articles 62, 63, 65 and 66 shall also apply to the personnel and *matériel* of civilian civil defence organizations of neutral or other States not Parties to the conflict which perform civil defence tasks mentioned in Article 61 in the territory of a Party to the conflict, with the consent and under the control of that Party. Notification of such assistance shall be given as soon as possible to any adverse Party concerned. In no circumstances shall this activity be deemed to be an interference in the conflict. This activity

should, however, be performed with due regard to the security interests of the Parties to the conflict concerned.

2. The Parties to the conflict receiving the assistance referred to in paragraph 1 and the High Contracting Parties granting it should facilitate international co-ordination of such civil defence actions when appropriate. In such cases the relevant international organizations are covered by the provisions of this Chapter.

3. In occupied territories, the Occupying Power may only exclude or restrict the activities of civilian civil defence organizations of neutral or other States not Parties to the conflict and of international co-ordinating organizations if it can ensure the adequate performance of civil defence tasks from its own resources or those of the occupied territory.

Article 65. — Cessation of protection

1. The protection to which civilian civil defence organizations, their personnel, buildings, shelters and *matériel* are entitled shall not cease unless they commit or are used to commit, outside their proper tasks, acts harmful to the enemy. Protection may, however, cease only after a warning has been given setting, whenever appropriate, a reasonable time-limit, and after such warning has remained unheeded.

2. The following shall not be considered as acts harmful to the enemy:

(*a*) That civil defence tasks are carried out under the direction or control of military authorities;

(*b*) That civilian civil defence personnel co-operate with military personnel in the performance of civil defence tasks, or that some military personnel are attached to civilian civil defence organizations;

(*c*) That the performance of civil defence tasks may incidentally benefit military victims, particularly those who are *hors de combat.*

3. It shall also not be considered as an act harmful to the enemy that civilian defence personnel bear light individual weapons for the purpose of maintaining order or for self-defence. However, in areas where land fighting it taking place or is likely to take place, the Parties to the conflict shall undertake the appropriate measures to limit these weapons to handguns, such as pistols or revolvers, in order to assist in distinguishing between civil defence personnel and combatants. Although civil defence personnel bear other light individual weapons in such areas, they shall nevertheless be respected and protected as soon as they have been recognized as such.

4. The formation of civilian civil defence organizations along military lines, and compulsory service in them, shall also not deprive them of the protection conferred by this Chapter.

Article 66.— Identification

1.   Each Party to the conflict shall endeavour to ensure that its civil defence organizations, their personnel, buildings and *matériel,* are identifiable while they are exclusively devoted to the performance of civil defence tasks. Shelters provided for the civilian population should be similarly identifiable.

2.   Each Party to the conflict shall also endeavour to adopt and implement methods and procedures which will make it possible to recognize civilian shelters as well as civil defence personnel, buildings and *matériel* on which the international distinctive sign of civil defence is displayed.

3.   In occupied territories and in areas where fighting is taking place or is likely to take place, civilian civil defence personnel should be recognizable by the international distinctive sign of civil defence and by an identity and certifying their status.

4.   The international distinctive sign of civil defence is an equilateral blue triangle on an orange ground when used for the protection of civil defence organizations, their personnel, buildings and *matériel* and for civilian shelters.

5.   In addition to the distinctive sign, Parties to the conflict may agree upon the use of distinctive signals for civil defence identification purposes.

6.   The application of the provisions of paragraphs 1 to 4 is governed by Chapter V of Annex I to this Protocol.

7.   In time of peace, the sign described in paragraph 4 may, with the consent of the competent national authorities, be used for civil defence identification purposes.

8.   The High Contracting Parties and the Parties to the conflict shall take the measures necessary to supervise the display of the international distinctive sign of civil defence and to prevent and repress any misuse thereof.

9.   The identification of civil defence medical and religious personnel, medical units and medical transports is also governed by Article 18.

Article 67.— Members of the armed forces and military units assigned to civil defence organizations

1.   Members of the armed forces and military units assigned to civil defence organizations shall be respected and protected, provided that:

(*a*) Such personnel and such units are permanently assigned and exclusively devoted to the performance of any of the tasks mentioned in Article 61;

(*b*) If so assigned, such personnel do not perform any other military duties during the conflict;

(c) Such personnel are clearly distinguishable from the other members of the armed forces by prominently displaying the international distinctive sign of civil defence, which shall be as large as appropriate, and such personnel are provided with the identity card referred to in Chapter V of Annexe I to this Protocol certifying their status;

(d) Such personnel and such units are equipped only with light individual weapons for the purpose of maintaining order or for self-defence. The provisions of Article 65, paragraph 3 shall also apply in this case;

(e) Such personnel do not participate directly in hostilities, and do not commit, or are not used to commit, outside their civil defence tasks, acts harmful to the adverse Party;

(f) Such personnel and such units perform their civil defence tasks only within the national territory of their Party.

The non-observance of the conditions stated in (e) above by any member of the armed forces who is bound by the conditions prescribed in (a) and (b) above is prohibited.

2. Military personnel serving within civil defence organizations shall, if they fall into the power of an adverse Party, be prisoners of war. In occupied territory they may, but only in the interest of the civilian population of that territory, be employed on civil defence tasks in so far as the need arises, provided however that, if such work is dangerous, they volunteer for such tasks.

3. The buildings and major items of equipment and transports of military units assigned to civil defence organizations shall be clearly marked with the international distinctive sign of civil defence. This distinctive sign shall be as large as appropriate.

4. The *matériel* and buildings of military units permanently assigned to civil defence organizations and exclusively devoted to the performance of civil defence tasks shall, if they fall into the hands of an adverse Party, remain subject to the laws of war. They may not be diverted from their civil defence purpose so long as they are required for the performance of civil defence tasks, except in case of imperative military necessity, unless previous arrangements have been made for adequate provision for the needs of the civilian population.

SECTION II.— RELIEF IN FAVOUR OF THE CIVILIAN POPULATION

Article 68.— Field of application

The provisions of this Section apply to the civilian population as defined in this Protocol and are supplementary to Articles 23, 55, 59, 60, 61 and 62 and other relevant provisions of the Fourth Convention.

Article 69.— Basic needs in occupied territories

1. In addition to the duties specified in Article 55 of the Fourth Convention concerning food and medical supplies, the Occupying Power shall, to the fullest extent of the means available to it and without any adverse distinction, also ensure the provision of clothing, bedding, means of shelter, other supplies essential to the survival of the civilian population of the occupied territory and objects necessary for religious worship.

2. Relief actions for the benefit of the civilian population of occupied territories are governed by Articles 59, 60, 61, 62, 108, 109, 110 and 111 of the Fourth Convention, and by Article 71 of this Protocol, and shall be implemented without delay.

Article 70.— Relief actions

1. If the civilian population of any territory under the control of a Party to the conflict, other than occupied territory, is not adequately provided with the supplies mentioned in Article 69, relief actions which are humanitarian and impartial in character and conducted without any adverse distinction shall be undertaken, subject to the agreement of the Parties concerned in such relief actions. Offers of such relief shall not be regarded as interference in the armed conflict or as unfriendly acts. In the distribution of relief consignments, priority shall be given to those persons, such as children, expectant mothers, maternity cases and nursing mothers, who, under the Fourth Convention or under this Protocol, are to be accorded privileged treatment or special protection.

2. The Parties to the conflict and each High Contracting Party shall allow and facilitate rapid and unimpeded passage of all relief consignments, equipment and personnel provided in accordance with this Section, even if such assistance is destined for the civilian population of the adverse Party.

3. The Parties to the conflict and each High Contracting Party which allow the passage of relief consignments, equipment and personnel in accordance with paragraph 2:

(*a*) Shall have the right to prescribe the technical arrangements, including search, under which such passage is permitted;

(*b*) May make such permission conditional on the distribution of this assistance being made under the local supervision of a Protecting Power;

(*c*) Shall, in no way whatsoever, divert relief consignments from the purpose for which they are intended nor delay their forwarding, except in cases of urgent necessity in the interest of the civilian population concerned.

4. The Parties to the conflict shall protect relief consignments and facilitate their rapid distribution.

5. The Parties to the conflict and each High Contracting Party concerned shall encourage and facilitate effective international co-ordination of the relief actions referred to in paragraph 1.

Article 71.— Personnel participating in relief actions

1. Where necessary, relief personnel may form part of the assistance provided in any relief action, in particular for the transportation and distribution of relief consignments; the participation of such personnel shall be subject to the approval of the Party in whose territory they will carry out their duties.

2. Such personnel shall be respected and protected.

3. Each Party in receipt of relief consignments shall, to the fullest extent practicable, assist the relief personnel referred to in paragraph 1 in carrying out their relief mission. Only in case of imperative military necessity may the activities of the relief personnel be limited or their movements temporarily restricted.

4. Under no circumstances may relief personnel exceed the terms of their mission under this Protocol. In particular they shall take account of the security requirements of the Party in whose territory they are carrying out their duties. The mission of any of the personnel who do not respect these conditions may be terminated.

SECTION III.—TREATMENT OF PERSONS IN THE POWER
OF A PARTY TO THE CONFLICT

CHAPTER I.— FIELD OF APPLICATION AND PROTECTION
OF PERSONS AND OBJECTS

Article 72.— Field of application

The provisions of this Section are additional to the rules concerning humanitarian protection of civilians and civilian objects in the power of a Party to the conflict contained in the Fourth Convention, particularly Parts I and III thereof, as well as to other applicable rules of international law relating to the protection of fundamental human rights during international armed conflict.

Article 73.— Refugees and stateless persons

Persons who, before the beginning of hostilities, were considered as stateless persons or refugees under the relevant international instruments accepted by the Parties concerned or under the national legislation of the State of refuge or State of residence shall be protected persons within the meaning of Parts I and III of the Fourth Convention, in all circumstances and without any adverse distinction.

Article 74.— Reunion of dispersed families

The High Contracting Parties and the Parties to the conflict shall facilitate in every possible way the reunion of families dispersed as a result of armed conflicts and shall encourage in particular the work of the humanitarian organizations engaged in this task in accordance with the provisions of the Conventions and of this Protocol and in conformity with their respective security regulations.

Article 75.— Fundamental guarantees

1. In so far as they are affected by a situation referred to in Article 1 of this Protocol, persons who are in the power of a Party to the conflict and who do not benefit from more favourable treatment under the Conventions or under this Protocol shall be treated humanely in all circumstances and shall enjoy, as a minimum, the protection provided by this Article without any adverse distinction based upon race, colour, sex, language, religion or belief, political or other opinion, national or social origin, wealth, birth or other status, or on any other similar criteria. Each Party shall respect the person, honour, convictions and religious practices of all such persons.

2. The following acts are and shall remain prohibited at any time and in any place whatsoever, whether committed by civilian or by military agents:

(a) Violence to the life, health, or physical or mental well-being of persons, in particular:

(i) Murder;

(ii) Torture of all kinds, whether physical or mental;

(iii) Corporal punishment; and

(iv) Mutilation;

(b) Outrages upon personal dignity, in particular humiliating and degrading treatment, enforced prostitution and any form of indecent assault;

(c) The taking of hostages;

(d) Collective punishments; and

(e) Threats to commit any of the foregoing acts.

3. Any person arrested, detained or interned for actions related to the armed conflict shall be informed promptly, in a language he understands, of the reasons why these measures have been taken. Except in cases of arrest or detention for penal offences, such persons shall be released with the min-

imum delay possible and in any event as soon as the circumstances justify-
ing the arrest, detention or internment have ceased to exist.

4. No sentence may be passed and no penalty may be executed on a
person found guilty of a penal offence related to the armed conflict except
pursuant to a conviction pronounced by an impartial and regularly constituted court respecting the generally recognized principles of regular judicial
procedure, which include the following:

(*a*) The procedure shall provide for an accused to be informed without
delay of the particulars of the offence alleged against him and shall afford
the accused before and during his trial all necessary rights and means of defence;

(*b*) No one shall be convicted of an offence except on the basis of individual penal responsibility;

(*c*) No one shall be accused or convicted of a criminal offence on account of any act or omission which did not constitute a criminal offence under the national or international law to which he was subject at the time
when it was committed; nor shall a heavier penalty be imposed than that
which was applicable at the time when the criminal offence was committed;
if, after the commission of the offence, provision is made by law for the imposition of a lighter penalty, the offender shall benefit thereby;

(*d*) Anyone charged with an offence is presumed innocent until
proved guilt according to law;

(*e*) Anyone charged with an offence shall have the right to be tried in
his presence;

(*f*) No one shall be compelled to testify against himself or to confess
guilt;

(*g*) Anyone charged with an offence shall have the right to examine,
or have examined, the witnesses against him and to obtain the attendance
and examination of witnesses on his behalf under the same conditions as
witnesses against him;

(*h*) No one shall be prosecuted or punished by the same Party for an
offence in respect of which a final judgement acquitting or convicting that
person has been previously pronounced under the same law and judicial procedure;

(*i*) Anyone prosecuted for an offence shall have the right to have the
judgement pronounced publicly; and

(*j*) A convicted person shall be advised on conviction of his judicial
and other remedies and of the time-limits within which they may be exercised.

5. Women whose liberty has been restricted for reasons related to the
armed conflict shall be held in quarters separated from men's quarters. They
shall be under the immediate supervision of women. Nevertheless, in cases

where families are detained or interned, they shall, whenever possible, be held in the same place and accommodated as family units.

6. Persons who are arrested, detained or interned for reasons related to the armed conflict shall enjoy the protection provided by this Article until their final release, repatriation or re-establishment, even after the end of the armed conflict.

7. In order to avoid any doubt concerning the prosecution and trial of persons accused of war crimes or crimes against humanity, the following principles shall apply:

(a) Persons who are accused of such crimes should be submitted for the purpose of prosecution and trial in accordance with the applicable rules of international law; and

(b) Any such persons who do not benefit from more favourable treatment under the Conventions or this Protocol shall be accorded the treatment provided by this Article, whether or not the crimes of which they are accused constitute grave breaches of the Conventions or of this Protocol.

8. No provision of this Article may be construed as limiting or infringing any other more favourable provision granting greater protection, under any applicable rules of international law, to persons covered by paragraph 1.

CHAPTER II.— MEASURES IN FAVOUR OF WOMEN AND CHILDREN

Article 76.— Protection of women

1. Women shall be the object of special respect and shall be protected in particular against rape, forced prostitution and any other form of indecent assault.

2. Pregnant women and mothers having dependent infants who are arrested, detained or interned for reasons related to the armed conflict, shall have their cases considered with the utmost priority.

3. To the maximum extent feasible, the Parties to the conflict shall endeavour to avoid the pronouncement of the death penalty on pregnant women or mothers having dependent infants, for an offence related to the armed conflict. The death penalty for such offences shall not be executed on such women.

Article 77.— Protection of children

1. Children shall be the object of special respect and shall be protected against any form of indecent assault. The Parties to the conflict shall

provide them with the care and aid they require, whether because of their age or for any other reason.

2. The Parties to the conflict shall take all feasible measures in order that children who have not attained the age of fifteen years do not take a direct part in hostilities and, in particular, they shall refrain from recruiting them into their armed forces. In recruiting among those persons who have attained the age of fifteen years but who have not attained the age of eighteen years, the Parties to the conflict shall endeavour to give priority to those who are oldest.

3. If, in exceptional cases, despite the provisions of paragraph 2, children who have not attained the age of fifteen years take a direct part in hostilities and fall into the power of an adverse Party, they shall continue to benefit from the special protection accorded by this Article, whether or not they are prisoners of war.

4. If arrested, detained or interned for reasons related to the armed conflict, children shall be held in quarters separate from the quarters of adults, except where families are accommodated as family units as provided in Article 75, paragraph 5.

5. The death penalty for an offence related to armed conflict shall not be executed on persons who had not attained the age of eighteen years at the time the offence was committed.

Article 78.— Evacuation of children

1. No Party to the conflict shall arrange for the evacuation of children, other than its own nationals, to a foreign country except for a temporary evacuation where compelling reasons of the health or medical treatment of the children or, except in occupied territory, their safety, so require. Where the parents or legal guardians can be found, their written consent to such evacuation is required. If these persons cannot be found, the written consent to such evacuation of the persons who by law or custom are primarily responsible for the care of the children is required. Any such evacuation shall be supervised by the Protecting Power in agreement with the Parties concerned, namely, the Party arranging for the evacuation, the Party receiving the children and any Parties whose nationals are being evacuated. In each case, all Parties to the conflict shall take all feasible precautions to avoid endangering the evacuation.

2. Whenever an evacuation occurs pursuant to paragraph 1, each child's education, including his religious and moral education as his parents desire, shall be provided while he is away with the greatest possible continuity.

3. With a view to facilitating the return to their families and country of children evacuated pursuant to this Article, the authorities of the Party ar-

ranging for the evacuation and, as appropriate, the authorities of the receiving country shall establish for each child a card with photographs, which they shall send to the Central Tracing Agency of the International Committee of the Red Cross. Each card shall bear, whenever possible, and whenever it involves no risk of harm to the child, the following information:

(*a*) Surname(s) of the child;

(*b*) The child's first name(s);

(*c*) The child's sex;

(*d*) The place and date of birth (or, if that date is not known, the approximate age);

(*e*) The father's full name;

(*f*) The mother's full name and her maiden name;

(*g*) The child's next-of-kin;

(*h*) The child's nationality;

(*i*) The child's native language, and any other languages he speaks;

(*j*) The address of the child's family;

(*k*) Any identification number for the child;

(*l*) The child's state of health;

(*m*) The child's blood group;

(*n*) Any distinguishing features;

(*o*) The date on which and the place where the child was found;

(*p*) The date on which and the place from which the child left the country;

(*q*) The child's religion, if any;

(*r*) The child's present address in the receiving country;

(*s*) Should the child die before his return, the date, place and circumstances of death and place of interment.

CHAPTER III.— *JOURNALISTS*

Article 79.— Measures of protection for journalists

1. Journalists engaged in dangerous professional missions in areas of armed conflict shall be considered as civilians within the meaning of Article 50, paragraph 1.

2. They shall be protected as such under the Conventions and this Protocol, provided that they take no action adversely affecting their status as civilians, and without prejudice to the right of war correspondents accredited to the armed forces to the status provided for in Article 4 A (4) of the Third Convention.

3.   They may obtain an identity card similar to the model in Annex II of this Protocol. This card, which shall be issued by the government of the State of which the journalist is a national or in whose territory he resides or in which the news medium employing him is located, shall attest to his status as a journalist.

PART V

EXECUTION OF THE CONVENTIONS AND OF THIS PROTOCOL

SECTION I.—GENERAL PROVISIONS

Article 80.— Measures for execution

1.   The High Contracting Parties and the Parties to the conflict shall without delay take all necessary measures for the execution of their obligations under the Conventions and this Protocol.

2.   The High Contracting Parties and the Parties to the conflict shall give orders and instructions to ensure observance of the Conventions and this Protocol, and shall supervise their execution.

Article 81.— Activities of the Red Cross and other humanitarian organizations

1.   The Parties to the conflict shall grant to the International Committee of the Red Cross all facilities within their power so as to enable it to carry out the humanitarian functions assigned to it by the Conventions and this Protocol in order to ensure protection and assistance to the victims of conflicts; the International Committee of the Red Cross may also carry out any other humanitarian activities in favour of these victims, subject to the consent of the Parties to the conflict concerned.

2.   The Parties to the conflict shall grant to their respective Red Cross (Red Crescent, Red Lion and Sun) organizations the facilities necessary for carrying out their humanitarian activities in favour of the victims of the conflict, in accordance with the provisions of the Conventions and this Protocol and the fundamental principles of the Red Cross as formulated by the International Conferences of the Red Cross.

3.   The High Contracting Parties and the Parties to the conflict shall facilitate in every possible way the assistance which Red Cross (Red Crescent, Red Lion and Sun) organizations and the League of Red Cross Societies extend to the victims of conflicts in accordance with the provisions of

the Conventions and this Protocol and with the fundamental principles of the Red Cross as formulated by the International Conferences of the Red Cross.

4. The High Contracting Parties and the Parties to the conflict shall, as far as possible, make facilities similar to those mentioned in paragraphs 2 and 3 available to the other humanitarian organizations referred to in the Conventions and this Protocol which are duly authorized by the respective Parties to the conflict and which perform their humanitarian activities in accordance with the provisions of the Conventions and this Protocol.

Article 82.— Legal advisers in armed forces

The High Contracting Parties at all times, and the Parties to the conflict in time of armed conflict, shall ensure that legal advisers are available, when necessary, to advise military commanders at the appropriate level on the application of the Conventions and this Protocol and on the appropriate instruction to be given to the armed forces on this subject.

Article 83.— Dissemination

1. The High Contracting Parties undertake, in time of peace as in time of armed conflict, to disseminate the Conventions and this Protocol as widely as possible in their respective countries and, in particular, to include the study thereof in their programmes of military instruction and to encourage the study thereof by the civilian population, so that those instruments may become known to the armed forces and to the civilian population.

2. Any military or civilian authorities who, in time of armed conflict, assume responsibilities in respect of the application of the Conventions and this Protocol shall be fully acquainted with the text thereof.

Article 84.— Rules of application

The High Contracting Parties shall communicate to one another, as soon as possible, through the depositary and, as appropriate, through the Protecting Powers, their official translations of this Protocol, as well as the laws and regulations which they may adopt to ensure its application.

SECTION II.—REPRESSION OF BREACHES OF THE CONVENTIONS
AND OF THIS PROTOCOL

Article 85.— Repression of breaches of this Protocol

1. The provisions of the Conventions relating to the repression of breaches and grave breaches, supplemented by this Section, shall apply to the repression of breaches and grave breaches of this Protocol.

2. Acts described as grave breaches in the Conventions are grave breaches of this Protocol if committed against persons in the power of an adverse Party protected by Articles 44, 45 and 73 of this Protocol, or against the wounded, sick and shipwrecked of the adverse Party who are protected by this Protocol, or against those medical or religious personnel, medical units or medical transports which are under the control of the adverse Party and are protected by this Protocol.

3. In addition to the grave breaches defined in Article 11, the following acts shall be regarded as grave breaches of this Protocol, when committed wilfully, in violation of the relevant provisions of this Protocol, and causing death or serious injury to body or health:

(*a*) Making the civilian population or individual civilians the object of attack;

(*b*) Launching an indiscriminate attack affecting the civilian population or civilian objects in the knowledge that such attack will cause excessive loss of life, injury to civilians or damage to civilian objects, as defined in Article 57, paragraph 2 (*a*) (iii);

(*c*) Launching an attack against works or installations containing dangerous forces in the knowledge that such attack will cause excessive loss of life, injury to civilians or damage to civilian objects, as defined in Article 57, paragraph 2 (*a*) (iii);

(*d*) Making non-defended localities and demilitarized zones the object of attack;

(*e*) Making a person the object of attack in the knowledge that he is *hors de combat*;

(*f*) The perfidious use, in violation of Article 37, of the distinctive emblem of the red cross, red crescent or red lion and sun or of other protective signs recognized by the Conventions or this Protocol.

4. In addition to the grave breaches defined in the preceding paragraphs and in the Conventions, the following shall be regarded as grave breaches of this Protocol, when committed wilfully and in violation of the Conventions of the Protocol;

(*a*) The transfer by the Occupying Power of parts of its own civilian population into the territory it occupies, or the deportation or transfer of all or parts of the population of the occupied territory within or outside this territory, in violation of Article 49 of the Fourth Convention;

(*b*) Unjustifiable delay in the repatriation of prisoners of war or civilians;

(*c*) Practices of *apartheid* and other inhuman and degrading practices involving outrages upon personal dignity, based on racial discrimination;

(*d*) Making the clearly-recognized historic monuments, works of art or places of worship which constitute the cultural or spiritual heritage of peoples and to which special protection has been given by special arrangement, for example, within the framework of a competent international organization, the object of attack, causing as a result extensive destruction thereof, where there is no evidence of the violation by the adverse Party of Article 53, sub-paragraph (b), and when such historic monuments, works of art and places of worship are not located in the immediate proximity of military objectives:

(*e*) Depriving a person protected by the Conventions or referred to in paragraph 2 of this Article of the rights of fair and regular trial.

5. Without prejudice to the application of the Conventions and of this Protocol, grave breaches of these instruments shall be regarded as war crimes.

Article 86.— Failure to act

1. The High Contracting Parties and the Parties to the conflict shall repress grave breaches, and take measures necessary to suppress all other breaches, of the Conventions or of this Protocol which result from a failure to act when under a duty to do so.

2. The fact that a breach of the Conventions or of this Protocol was committed by a subordinate does not absolve his superiors from penal or disciplinary responsibility, as the case may be, if they knew, or had information which should have enabled them to conclude in the circumstances at the time, that he was committing or was going to commit such a breach and if they did not take all feasible measures within their power to prevent or repress the breach.

Article 87.— Duty of commanders

1. The High Contracting Parties and the Parties to the conflict shall require military commanders, with respect to members of the armed forces under their command and other persons under their control, to prevent and, where necessary, to suppress and to report to competent authorities breaches of the Conventions and of this Protocol.

2. In order to prevent and suppress breaches, High Contracting Parties and Parties to the conflict shall require that, commensurate with their level of responsibility, commanders ensure that members of the armed forces under their command are aware of their obligations under the Conventions and this Protocol.

3. The High Contracting Parties and Parties to the conflict shall require any commander who is aware that subordinates or other persons under his control are going to commit or have committed a breach of the Conven-

tions or of this Protocol, to initiate such steps as are necessary to prevent such violations of the Conventions or this Protocol, and, where appropriate, to initiate disciplinary or penal action against violators thereof.

Article 88.— Mutual assistance in criminal matters

1.   The High Contracting Parties shall afford one another the greatest measure of assistance in connexion with criminal proceedings brought in respect of grave breaches of the Conventions or of this Protocol.

2.   Subject to the rights and obligations established in the Conventions and in Article 85, paragraph 1, of this Protocol, and when circumstances permit, the High Contracting Parties shall co-operate in the matter of extradition. They shall give due consideration to the request of the State in whose territory the alleged offence has occurred.

3.   The law of the High Contracting Party requested shall apply in all cases. The provisions of the preceding paragraphs shall not, however, affect the obligations arising from the provisions of any other treaty of a bilateral or multilateral nature which governs or will govern the whole or part of the subject of mutual assistance in criminal matters.

Article 89.— Co-operation

In situations of serious violations of the Conventions or of this Protocol, the High Contracting Parties undertake to act, jointly or individually, in co-operation with the United Nations and in conformity with the United Nations Charter.

Article 90.— International Fact-Finding Commission

1.   (a) An International Fact-Finding Commission (hereinafter referred to as ''the Commission'') consisting of fifteen members of high moral standing and acknowledged impartiality shall be established.

(b) When not less than twenty High Contracting Parties have agreed to accept the competence of the Commission pursuant to paragraph 2, the depositary shall then, and at intervals of five years thereafter, convene a meeting of representatives of those High Contracting Parties for the purpose of electing the members of the Commission. At the meeting, the representatives shall elect the members of the Commission by secret ballot from a list of persons to which each of those High Contracting Parties may nominate one person.

(c) The members of the Commission shall serve in their personal capacity and shall hold office until the election of new members at the ensuing meeting.

(*d*) At the election, the High Contracting Parties shall ensure that the persons to be elected to the Commission individually possess the qualifications required and that, in the Commission as a whole, equitable geographical representation is assured.

(*e*) In the case of a casual vacancy, the Commission itself shall fill the vacancy, having due regard to the provisions of the preceding sub-paragraphs.

(*f*) the depositary shall make available to the Commission the necessary administrative facilities for the performance of its functions.

2. (*a*) The High Contracting Parties may at the time of signing, ratifying or acceding to the Protocol, or at any other subsequent time, declare that they recognize *ipso facto* and without special agreement, in relation to any other High Contracting Party accepting the same obligation, the competence of the Commission to enquire into allegations by such other Party, as authorized by this Article.

(*b*) The declarations referred to above shall be deposited with the depositary, which shall transmit copies thereof to the High Contracting Parties.

(*c*) The Commission shall be competent to:

(i) Enquire into any facts alleged to be a grave breach as defined in the Conventions and this Protocol or other serious violation of the Conventions or of this Protocol;

(ii) Facilitate, through its good offices, the restoration of an attitude of respect for the Conventions and this Protocol.

(*d*) In other situations, the Commission shall institute an enquiry at the request of a Party to the conflict only with the consent of the other Party or Parties concerned.

(*e*) Subject to the foregoing provisions of this paragraph, the provisions of Article 52 of the First Convention, Article 53 of the Second Convention, Article 132 of the Third Convention and Article 149 of the Fourth Convention shall continue to apply to any alleged violation of the Conventions and shall extend to any alleged violation of this Protocol.

3. (*a*) Unless otherwise agreed by the Parties concerned, all enquiries shall be undertaken by a Chamber consisting of seven members appointed as follows:

(i) Five members of the Commission, not nationals of any Party to the conflict, appointed by the President of the Commission on the basis of equitable representation of the geographical areas, after consultation with the Parties to the conflict;

(ii) Two *ad hoc* members, not nationals of any Party to the conflict, one to be appointed by each side.

(*b*) Upon receipt of the request for an enquiry, the President of the Commission shall specify an appropriate time limit for setting up a Chamber. If any *ad hoc* member has not been appointed within the time limit, the President shall immediately appoint such additional member or members of the Commission as may be necessary to complete the membership of the Chamber.

4.   (*a*) The Chamber set up under paragraph 3 to undertake an enquiry shall invite the Parties to the conflict to assist it and to present evidence. The Chamber may also seek such other evidence as it deems appropriate and may carry out an investigation of the situation *in loco*.

(*b*) All evidence shall be fully disclosed to the Parties, which shall have the right to comment on it to the Commission.

(*c*) Each Party shall have the right to challenge such evidence.

5.   (*a*) The Commission shall submit to the Parties a report on the findings of fact of the Chamber, with such recommendations as it may deem appropriate.

(*b*) If the Chamber is unable to secure sufficient evidence for factual and impartial findings, the Commission shall state the reasons for that inability.

(*c*) The Commission shall not report its findings publicly, unless all the Parties to the conflict have requested the Commission to do so.

6.   The Commission shall establish its own rules, including rules for the presidency of the Commission and the presidency of the Chamber. Those rules shall ensure that the functions of the President of the Commission are exercised at all times and that, in the case of an enquiry, they are exercised by a person who is not a national of a Party to the conflict.

7.   The administrative expenses of the Commission shall be met by contributions from the High Contracting Parties which made declarations under paragraph 2, and by voluntary contributions. The Party or Parties to the conflict requesting an enquiry shall advance the necessary funds for expenses incurred by a Chamber and shall be reimbursed by the Party or Parties against which the allegations are made to the extent of fifty per cent of the costs of the Chamber. Where there are counter-allegations before the Chamber each side shall advance fifty per cent of the necessary funds.

Article 91.— Responsibility

A Party to the conflict which violates the provisions of the Conventions or of this Protocol shall, if the case demands, be liable to pay compensation. It shall be responsible for all acts committed by persons forming part of its armed forces.

PART VI

FINAL PROVISIONS

Article 92.— Signature

This Protocol shall be open for signature by the Parties to the Conventions six months after the signing of the Final Act and will remain open for a period of twelve months.

Article 93.— Ratification

This Protocol shall be ratified as soon as possible. The instruments of ratification shall be deposited with the Swiss Federal Council, depositary of the Conventions.

Article 94.— Accession

This Protocol shall be open for accession by any Party to the Conventions which has not signed it. The instruments of accession shall be deposited with the depositary.

Article 95.— Entry into force

1.   This Protocol shall enter into force six months after two instruments of ratification or accession have been deposited.

2.   For each Party to the Conventions thereafter ratifying or acceding to this Protocol, it shall enter into force six months after the deposit by such Party of its instrument of ratification or accession.

Article 96.— Treaty relations upon entry into force of this Protocol

1.   When the Parties to the Conventions are also Parties to this Protocol, the Conventions shall apply as supplemented by this Protocol.

2.   When one of the Parties to the conflict is not bound by this Protocol, the Parties to the Protocol shall remain bound by it in their mutual relations. They shall furthermore be bound by this Protocol in relation to each of the Parties which are not bound by it, if the latter accepts and applies the provisions thereof.

3.   The authority representing a people engaged against a High Contracting Party in an armed conflict of the type referred to in Article 1, paragraph 4, may undertake to apply the Conventions and this Protocol in relation to that conflict by means of a unilateral declaration addressed to the depositary. Such declaration shall, upon its receipt by the depositary, have in relation to that conflict the following effects:

(*a*) The Conventions and this Protocol are brought into force for the said authority as a Party to the conflict with immediate effect;

(*b*) The said authority assumes the same rights and obligations as those which have been assumed by a High Contracting Party to the Conventions and this Protocol; and

(*c*) The Conventions and this Protocol are equally binding upon all Parties to the conflict.

Article 97.— Amendment

1.   Any High Contracting Party may propose amendments to this Protocol. The text of any proposed amendment shall be communicated to the depositary, which shall decide, after consultation with all the High Contracting Parties and the International Committee of the Red Cross, whether a conference should be convened to consider the proposed amendment.

2.   The depositary shall invite to that conference all the High Contracting Parties as well as the Parties to the Conventions, whether or not they are signatories of this Protocol.

Article 98.— Revision of Annex I

1.   Not later than four years after the entry into force of this Protocol and thereafter at intervals of not less than four years, the International Committee of the Red Cross shall consult the High Contracting Parties concerning Annex I to this Protocol and, if it considers it necessary, may propose a meeting of technical experts to review Annex I and to propose such amendments to it as may appear to be desirable. Unless, within six months of the communication of a proposal for such a meeting to the High Contracting Parties, one third of them object, the International Committee of the Red Cross shall convene the meeting, inviting also observers of appropriate international organizations. Such a meeting shall also be convened by the International Committee of the Red Cross at any time at the request of one third of the High Contracting Parties.

2.   The depositary shall convene a conference of the High Contracting Parties and the Parties to the Conventions to consider amendments proposed by the meeting of technical experts if, after that meeting, the International Committee of the Red Cross or one third of the High Contracting Parties so request.

3.   Amendments to Annex I may be adopted at such a conference by a two-thirds majority of the High Contracting Parties present and voting.

4.   The depositary shall communicate any amendment so adopted to the High Contracting Parties and to the Parties to the Conventions. The amendment shall be considered to have been accepted at the end of a period

of one year after it has been so communicated, unless within that period a declaration of non-acceptance of the amendment has been communicated to the depositary by not less than one third of the High Contracting Parties.

5.   An amendment considered to have been accepted in accordance with paragraph 4 shall enter into force three months after its acceptance for all High Contracting Parties other than those which have made a declaration of non-acceptance in accordance with that paragraph. Any Party making such a declaration may at any time withdraw it and the amendment shall then enter into force for that Party three months thereafter.

6.   The depositary shall notify the High Contracting Parties and the Parties to the Conventions of the entry into force of any amendment, of the Parties bound thereby, of the date of its entry into force in relation to each Party, of declarations of non-acceptance made in accordance with paragraph 4, and of withdrawals of such declarations.

Article 99.— Denunciation

1.   In case a High Contracting Party should denounce this Protocol, the denunciation shall only take effect one year after receipt of the instrument of denunciation. If, however, on the expiry of that year the denouncing Party is engaged in one of the situations referred to in Article 1, the denunciation shall not take effect before the end of the armed conflict or occupation and not, in any case, before operations connected with the final release, repatriation or re-establishment of the persons protected by the Conventions or this Protocol have been terminated.

2.   The denunciation shall be notified in writing to the depositary, which shall transmit it to all the High Contracting Parties.

3.   The denunciation shall have effect only in respect of the denouncing Party.

4.   Any denunciation under paragraph 1 shall not affect the obligations already incurred, by reason of the armed conflict, under this Protocol by such denouncing Party in respect of any act committed before this denunciation becomes effective.

Article 100.— Notifications

The depositary shall inform the High Contracting Parties as well as the Parties to the Conventions, whether or not they are signatories of this Protocol, of:

(a) Signatures affixed to this Protocol and the deposit of instruments of ratification and accession under Articles 93 and 94;

(b) The date of entry into force of this Protocol under Article 95;

(*c*) Communications and declarations received under Articles 84, 90 and 97.

(*d*) Declarations received under Article 96, paragraph 3, which shall be communicated by the quickest methods; and

(*e*) Denunciations under Article 99.

Article 101.— Registration

1. After its entry into force, this Protocol shall be transmitted by the depositary to the Secretariat of the United Nations for registration and publication, in accordance with Article 102 of the Charter of the United Nations.

2. The depositary shall also inform the Secretariat of the United Nations of all ratifications, accessions and denunciations received by it with respect to this Protocol.

Article 102.— Authentic texts

The original of this Protocol, of which the Arabic, Chinese, English, French, Russian and Spanish texts are equally authentic, shall be deposited with the depositary, which shall transmit certified true copies thereof to all the Parties to the Conventions.

ANNEX I

Regulations concerning identification

CHAPTER I.—IDENTITY CARDS

Article 1.— Identity card for permanent civilian medical and religious personnel

1. The identity card for permanent civilian medical and religious personnel referred to in Article 18, paragraph 3, of the Protocol should:

(*a*) Bear the distinctive emblem and be of such size that it can be carried in the pocket;

(*b*) Be as durable as practicable;

(*c*) Be worded in the national or official language (and may in addition be worded in other languages);

(*d*) Mention the name, the date of birth (or, if that date is not available, the age at the time of issue) and the identity number, if any, of the holder;

(*e*) State in what capacity the holder is entitled to the protection of the Conventions and of the Protocol;

(*f*) Bear the photograph of the holder as well as his signature or this thumbprint, or both;

(*g*) Bear the stamp and signature of the competent authority;

(*h*) State the date of issue and date of expiry of the card.

2.   The identity card shall be uniform throughout the territory of each High Contracting Party and, as far as possible, of the same type for all Parties to the conflict. The Parties to the conflict may be guided by the single-language model shown in Figure 1. At the outbreak of hostilities, they shall transmit to each other a specimen of the model they are using, if such model differs from that shown in Figure 1. The identity card shall be made out, if possible, in duplicate, one copy being kept by the issuing authority, which should maintain control of the cards which it has issued.

3.   In no circumstances may permanent civilian medical and religious personnel be deprived of their identity cards. In the event of the loss of a card, they shall be entitled to obtain a duplicate copy.

Article 2.— *Identity card for temporary civilian medical and religious personnel*

1.   The identity card for temporary civilian medical and religious personnel should, whenever possible, be similar to that provided for in Article 1 of these Regulations. The Parties to the conflict may be guided by the model shown in Figure 1.

2.   When circumstances preclude the provision to temporary civilian medical and religious personnel of identity cards similar to those described in Article 1 of these Regulations, the said personnel may be provided with a certificate signed by the competent authority certifying that the person to whom it is issued is assigned to duty as temporary personnel and stating, if possible, the duration of such assignment and his right to wear the distinctive emblem. The certificate should mention the holder's name and date of birth (or if that date is not available, his age at the time when the certificate was issued), his function and identity number, if any. It shall bear his signature or his thumbprint, or both.

REVERSE SIDE

Height	Eyes	Hair . . . .

Other distinguishing marks or information:

. . . .
. . . .
. . . .

PHOTO OF HOLDER

Stamp

Signature of holder or thumbprint or both

FRONT

(space reserved for the name of the country and authority issuing this card)

IDENTITY CARD

for PERMANENT civilian medical personnel
    TEMPORARY religious

Name . . . .
. . . .

Date of birth (or age) . . . .

Identity No. (if any) . . . .

The holder of this card is protected by the Geneva Conventions of 12 August 1949 and by the Protocol Additional to the Geneva Conventions of 12 August 1949, and relating to the Protection of Victims of International Armed Conflicts (Protocol I) in his capacity as . . . .

. . . .

Date of issue . . . . No. of card . . . .

Signature of issuing authority

Date of expiry . . . .

Fig. 1 : Model of identity card (format: 74 mm × 105 mm)

CHAPTER II.—THE DISTINCTIVE EMBLEM

Article 3.—— Shape and nature

1. The distinctive emblem (red on a white ground) shall be as large as appropriate under the circumstances. For the shapes of the cross, the crescent or the lion and sun, the High Contracting Parties may be guided by the models shown in Figure 2.

2. At night or when visibility is reduced, the distinctive emblem may be lighted or illuminated; it may also be made of materials rendering it recognizable by technical means of detection.

Fig. 2: Distinctive emblems in red on a white ground

Article 4.—— Use

1. The distinctive emblem shall, whenever possible, be displayed on a flat surface or on flags visible from as many directions and from as far away as possible.

2. Subject to the instructions of the competent authority, medical and religious personnel carrying out their duties in the battle area shall, as far as possible, wear headgear and clothing bearing the distinctive emblem.

CHAPTER III.—DISTINCTIVE SIGNALS

Article 5.— Optional Use

1.   Subject to the provisions of Article 6 of these Regulations, the signals specified in this Chapter for exclusive use by medical units and transports shall not be used for any other purpose. The use of all signals referred to in this Chapter is optional.

2.   Temporary medical aircraft which cannot, either for lack of time or because of their characteristics, be marked with the distinctive emblem, may use the distinctive signals authorized in this Chapter. The best method of effective identification and recognition of medical aircraft is, however, the use of a visual signal, either the distinctive emblem or the light signal specified in Article 6, or both, supplemented by the other signals referred to in Articles 7 and 8 of these Regulations.

Article 6.— Light signal

1.   The light signal, consisting of a flashing blue light, is established for the use of medical aircraft to signal their identity. No other aircraft shall use this signal. The recommended blue colour is obtained by using, as trichromatic co-ordinates:

$$\text{green boundary} \quad y \;=\; 0.065 + 0.805x$$
$$\text{white boundary} \quad y \;=\; 0.400 - x$$
$$\text{purple boundary} \quad x \;=\; 0.133 + 0.600y$$

The recommended flashing rate of the blue light is between sixty and one hundred flashes per minute.

2.   Medical aircraft should be equipped with such lights as may be necessary to make the light signal visible in as many directions as possible.

3.   In the absence of a special agreement between the Parties to the conflict reserving the use of flashing blue lights for the identification of medical vehicles and ships and craft, the use of such signals for other vehicles or ships is not prohibited.

Article 7.— Radio signal

1.   The radio signal shall consist of a radiotelephonic or radiotelegraphic message preceded by a distinctive priority signal to be designated and approved by a World Administrative Radio Conference of the International Telecommunication Union. It shall be transmitted three times before the call sign of the medical transport involved. This message shall be transmitted in English at appropriate intervals on a frequency or frequencies specified pursuant to paragraph 3. The use of the priority signal shall be restricted exclusively to medical units and transports.

2.   The radio message preceded by the distinctive priority signal mentioned in paragraph 1 shall convey the following data:

(*a*) Call sign of the medical transport;

(*b*) Position of the medical transport;

(*c*) Number and type of medical transports;

(*d*) Intended route;

(*e*) Estimated time en route and of departure and arrival, as appropriate;

(*f*) Any other information such as flight altitude, radio frequencies guarded, languages and secondary surveillance radar modes and codes.

3.   In order to facilitate the communications referred to in paragraphs 1 and 2, as well as the communications referred to in Articles 22, 23, 25, 26, 27, 28, 29, 30 and 31 of the Protocol, the High Contracting Parties, the Parties to a conflict, or one of the Parties to a conflict, acting in agreement or alone, may designate, in accordance with the Table of Frequency Allocations in the Radio Regulations annexed to the International Telecommunication Convention, and publish selected national frequencies to be used by them for such communications. These frequencies shall be notified to the International Telecommunication Union in accordance with procedures to be approved by a World Administrative Radio Conference.

Article 8. — Electronic identification

1.   The Secondary Surveillance Radar (SSR) system, as specified in Annex 10 to the Chicago Convention on International Civil Aviation of 7 December 1944, as amended from time to time, may be used to identify and to follow the course of medical aircraft. The SSR mode and code to be reserved for the exclusive use of medical aircraft shall be established by the High Contracting Parties, the Parties to a conflict, or one of the Parties to a conflict, acting in agreement or alone, in accordance with procedures to be recommended by the International Civil Aviation Organization.

2.   Parties to a conflict may, by special agreement between them, establish for their use a similar electronic system for the identification of medical vehicles, and medical ships and craft.

CHAPTER IV.—COMMUNICATIONS

Article 9. — Radiocommunications

The priority signal provided for in Article 7 of these Regulations may precede appropriate radiocommunications by medical units and transports in the application of the procedures carried out under Articles 22, 23, 25, 26, 27, 28, 29, 30 and 31 of the Protocol.

Article 10. — Use of international codes

Medical units and transports may also use the codes and signals laid down by the International Telecommunication Union, the International Civil Aviation Organization and the Inter-Governmental Maritime Consultative Organization. These codes and signals shall be used in accordance with the standards, practices and procedures established by these Organizations.

Article 11. — Other means of communication

When two-way radiocommunication is not possible, the signals provided for in the International Code of Signals adopted by the Inter-Governmental Maritime Consultative Organization or in the appropriate Annex to the Chicago Convention on International Civil Aviation of 7 December 1944, as amended from time to time, may be used.

Article 12. — Flight plans

The agreements and notifications relating to flight plans provided for in Article 29 of the Protocol shall as far as possible be formulated in accordance with procedures laid down by the International Civil Aviation Organization.

Article 13. — *Signals and procedures for the interception of medical aircraft*

If an intercepting aircraft is used to verify the identity of a medical aircraft in flight or to require it to land in accordance with Articles 30 and 31 of the Protocol, the standard visual and radio interception procedures prescribed by Annex 2 to the Chicago Convention on International Civil Aviation of 7 December 1944, as amended from time to time, should be used by the intercepting and the medical aircraft.

CHAPTER V.—CIVIL DEFENCE

Article 14. — *Identity card*

1.   The identity card of the civil defence personnel provided for in Article 66, paragraph 3, of the Protocol is governed by the relevant provisions of Article 1 of these Regulations.

2.   The identity card for civil defence personnel may follow the model shown in Figure 3.

3.   If civil defence personnel are permitted to carry light individual weapons, an entry to that effect should be made on the card mentioned.

REVERSE SIDE

FRONT

(space reserved for the name of the country and authority issuing this card)

IDENTITY CARD
for civil defence personnel

Name . . . .
. . . .

Date of birth (or age) . . . .

Identity No. (if any) . . . .

The holder of this card is protected by the Geneva Conventions of 12 August 1949 and by the Protocol Additional to the Geneva Conventions of 12 August 1949, and relating to the Protection of Victims of International Armed Conflicts (Protocol I) in his capacity as . . . . .

. . . .

Date of issue . . . . No. of card . . . .

Signature of issuing authority

Date of expiry . . . .

Height . . . . . | Eyes . . . . . | Hair . . . . . .

Other distinguishing marks or information:

. . . .
. . . .
Weapons . . . .

PHOTO OF HOLDER

Stamp

Signature of holder or thumbprint or both

Fig. 3: Model of identity card for civil defence personnel
(format: 74 mm × 105 mm)

Article 15.— International distinctive sign

1.   The international distinctive sign of civil defence provided for in Article 66, paragraph 4, of the Protocol is an equilateral blue triangle on an orange ground. A model is shown in Figure 4:

Fig. 4: Blue triangle on an orange ground.

2.   It is recommended that:

(*a*) If the blue triangle is on a flag or armlet or tabard, the ground to the triangle be the orange flag, armlet or tabard;

(*b*) One of the angles of the triangle be pointed vertically upwards;

(*c*) No angle of the triangle touch the edge of the orange ground.

3.   The international distinctive sign shall be as large as appropriate under the circumstances. The distinctive sign shall, whenever possible, be displayed on flat surfaces or on flags visible from as many directions and from as far away as possible. Subject to the instructions of the competent authority, civil defence personnel shall, as far as possible, wear headgear and clothing bearing the international distinctive sign. At night or when visibility is reduced, the sign may be lighted or illuminated; it may also be made of materials rendering it recognizable by technical means of detection.

CHAPTER VI.—WORKS AND INSTALLATIONS CONTAINING DANGEROUS FORCES

Article 16. — International special sign

1.   The international special sign for works and installations containing dangerous forces, as provided for in Article 56, paragraph 7, of the Protocol, shall be a group of three bright orange circles of equal size, placed on the same axis, the distance between each circle being one radius, in accordance with Figure 5 illustrated below.

2.   The sign shall be as large as appropriate under the circumstances. When displayed over an extended surface it may be repeated as often as appropriate under the circumstances. It shall, whenever possible, be displayed on flat surfaces or on flags so as to be visible from as many directions and from as far away as possible.

3.   On a flag, the distance between the outer limits of the sign and the adjacent sides of the flag shall be one radius of a circle. The flag shall be rectangular and shall have a white ground.

4.   At night or when visibility is reduced, the sign may be lighted or illuminated. It may also be made of materials rendering it recognizable by technical means of detection.

Fig. 5: International special sign for works and installations containing dangerous forces.

ANNEX II

Identity card for journalists on dangerous professional missions

FRONT

(Name of country issuing this card)

(Nombre del país que expide esta tarjeta)

(Nom du pays qui a délivré cette carte)

(Название страны, выдавшей настоящее удостоверение)

IDENTITY CARD FOR JOURNALISTS
ON DANGEROUS PROFESSIONAL MISSIONS

بطاقة الهوية الخاصة بالصحفيين
الكائنين بمهمات مهنية خطرة

TARJETA DE IDENTIDAD DE PERIODISTA
EN MISION PELIGROSA

CARTE D'IDENTITÉ DE JOURNALISTE
EN MISSION PÉRILLEUSE

УДОСТОВЕРЕНИЕ ЖУРНАЛИСТА,
НАХОДЯЩЕГОСЯ В ОПАСНОЙ
КОМАНДИРОВКЕ

NOTICE

This identity card is issued to journalists on dangerous professional missions in areas of armed conflict. The holder is entitled to be treated as a civilian under the Geneva Conventions of 12 August 1949, and their Additional Protocol I. The card must be carried at all times by the bearer. If he is detained, he shall at once hand it to the Detaining Authorities, to assist in his identification.

ملحوظة

تصرف هذه البطاقة للصحفيين الكائنين بمهمات مهنية خطرة في مناطق النزاعات المسلحة ويحق لحاملها أن يعامل معاملة الشخص المدني وفقا لاتفاقيات جنيف المؤرخة في ١٢ آب/أغسطس ١٩٤٩ وبروتوكولها الإضافي الأول. ويجب أن يحمل صاحب البطاقة هذه البطاقة على الدوام. وإذا ما قبض عليه وجب أن يسلم فورا إلى سلطة الاحتجاز لتساعد على تحديد هويته.

NOTA

La presente tarjeta de identidad se expide a los periodistas en misión profesional peligrosa en zonas de conflictos armados. Su titular tiene derecho a ser tratado como persona civil conforme a los Convenios de Ginebra del 12 de agosto de 1949 y su Protocolo adicional I. El titular debe llevar la tarjeta consigo, en todo momento. En caso de ser detenido, la entregará inmediatamente a las autoridades que lo detengan a fin de facilitar su identificación.

AVIS

La présente carte d'identité est délivrée aux journalistes en mission professionnelle périlleuse dans des zones de conflit armé. Le porteur a le droit d'être traité comme une personne civile au terme des Conventions de Genève du 12 août 1949 et de leur Protocole additionnel I. La carte doit être portée en tout temps par son titulaire. Si celui-ci est arrêté, il la remettra immédiatement aux autorités qui le détiennent afin qu'elles puissent l'identifier.

ПРИМЕЧАНИЕ

Настоящее удостоверение выдается журналистам, находящимся в опасных профессиональных командировках в районах вооруженного конфликта. Его обладатель имеет право на обращение с ним как с гражданским лицом в соответствии с Женевскими Конвенциями от 12 августа 1949 г. и Дополнительным Протоколом 1 к ним. Владелец настоящего удостоверения должен постоянно иметь его при себе. В случае задержания он немедленно вручает его задерживающим властям для содействия установлению его личности.

REVERSE SIDE

Issued by (competent authority) / Espedida por (autoridad competente) / Délivrée par (autorité compétente) / Выдано (компетентными властями)

Photograph of bearer / Fotografía del titular / Photographie du porteur / Фотография предъявителя

(Official seal imprint) / (Sello oficial) / (Timbre de l'autorité délivrant la carte) / (Официальная печать)

Name / Apellidos / Nom / Фамилия

First names / Nombre / Prénoms / Имя, Отчество

Place & date of birth / Lugar y fecha de nacimiento / Lieu & date de naissance / Дата и место рождения

Correspondent of / Corresponsal de / Correspondant de / Корреспондент

Specific occupation / Categoría profesional / Catégorie professionnelle / Род занятий

Valid for / Válido por / Durée de validité / Действительно

Place / Lugar / Lieu / Место

Date / Fecha / Date / Дата

(Signature of bearer) / (Firma del titular) / (Signature du porteur) / (Подпись владельца)

Height / Estatura / Taille / Рост

Eyes / Ojos / Yeux / Глаза

Weight / Peso / Poids / Вес

Hair / Cabello / Cheveux / Волосы

Blood type / Grupo sanguíneo / Groupe sanguin / Группа крови

Rh factor / Factor Rh / Facteur Rh / Rh-фактор

Religion (optional) / Religión (optativa) / Religion (facultatif) / Религия (факультативно)

Fingerprint (optional) / Huellas dactilares (optativo) / Empreintes digitales (facultatif) / Отпечатки пальцев (факультативно)

(Left forefinger) / (Dedo índice izquierdo) / (Index gauche) / (Левый указательный палец)

(Right forefinger) / (Dedo índice derecho) / (Index droit) / (Правый указательный палец)

Special marks of identification / Señas particulares / Signes particuliers / Особые приметы

94. Protocol Additional to the Geneva Conventions of 12 August 1949, and relating to the Protection of Victims of Non-International Armed Conflicts (Protocol II)

Adopted on 8 June 1977 by the Diplomatic Conference on the Reaffirmation and Development of International Humanitarian Law applicable in Armed Conflicts

ENTRY INTO FORCE: 7 December 1978, in accordance with Article 23

PREAMBLE

The High Contracting Parties,

Recalling that the humanitarian principles enshrined in Article 3 common to the Geneva Conventions of 12 August 1949 constitute the foundation of respect for the human person in cases of armed conflict not of an international character,

Recalling furthermore that international instruments relating to human rights offer a basic protection to the human person,

Emphasizing the need to ensure a better protection for the victims of those armed conflicts,

Recalling that, in cases not covered by the law in force, the human person remains under the protection of the principles of humanity and the dictates of the public conscience,

Have agreed on the following:

PART I

SCOPE OF THIS PROTOCOL

Article 1.— Material field of application

1. This Protocol, which develops and supplements Article 3 common to the Geneva Conventions of 12 August 1949 without modifying its existing conditions of application, shall apply to all armed conflicts which are not covered by Article 1 of the Protocol Additional to the Geneva Conventions of 12 August 1949, and relating to the Protection of Victims of International

Armed Conflicts (Protocol I) and which take place in the territory of a High Contracting Party between its armed forces and dissident armed forces or other organized armed groups which, under responsible command, exercise such control over a part of its territory as to enable them to carry out sustained and concerted military operations and to implement this Protocol.

2. This Protocol shall not apply to situations of internal disturbances and tensions, such as riots, isolated and sporadic acts of violence and other acts of a similar nature, as not being armed conflicts.

Article 2.— Personal field of application

1. This Protocol shall be applied without any adverse distinction founded on race, colour, sex, language, religion or belief, political or other opinion, national or social origin, wealth, birth or other status, or on any other similar criteria (hereinafter referred to as "adverse distinction") to all persons affected by an armed conflict as defined in Article 1.

2. At the end of the armed conflict, all the persons who have been deprived of their liberty or whose liberty has been restricted for reasons related to such conflict, as well as those deprived of their liberty or whose liberty is restricted after the conflict for the same reasons, shall enjoy the protection of Articles 5 and 6 until the end of such deprivation or restriction of liberty.

Article 3.— Non-intervention

1. Nothing in this Protocol shall be invoked for the purpose of affecting the sovereignty of a State or the responsibility of the government, by all legitimate means, to maintain or re-establish law and order in the State or to defend the national unity and territorial integrity of the State.

2. Nothing in this Protocol shall be invoked as a justification for intervening, directly or indirectly, for any reason whatever, in the armed conflict or in the internal or external affairs of the High Contracting Party in the territory of which that conflict occurs.

PART II

HUMANE TREATMENT

Article 4.— Fundamental guarantees

1. All persons who do not take a direct part or who have ceased to take part in hostilities, whether or not their liberty has been restricted, are

entitled to respect for their person, honour and convictions and religious practices. They shall in all circumstances be treated humanely, without any adverse distinction. It is prohibited to order that there shall be no survivors.

2. Without prejudice to the generality of the foregoing, the following acts against the persons referred to in paragraph 1 are and shall remain prohibited at any time and in any place whatsoever:

(*a*) Violence to the life, health and physical or mental well-being of persons, in particular murder as well as cruel treatment such as torture, mutilation or any form of corporal punishment;

(*b*) Collective punishments;

(*c*) Taking of hostages;

(*d*) Acts of terrorism;

(*e*) Outrages upon personal dignity, in particular humiliating and degrading treatment, rape, enforced prostitution and any form of indecent assault;

(*f*) Slavery and the slave trade in all their forms;

(*g*) Pillage;

(*h*) Threats to commit any of the foregoing acts.

3. Children shall be provided with the care and aid they require, and in particular:

(*a*) They shall receive an education, including religious and moral education, in keeping with the wishes of their parents, or in the absence of parents, of those responsible for their care;

(*b*) All appropriate steps shall be taken to facilitate the reunion of families temporarily separated;

(*c*) Children who have not attained the age of fifteen years shall neither be recruited in the armed forces or groups nor allowed to take part in hostilities;

(*d*) The special protection provided by this Article to children who have not attained the age of fifteen years shall remain applicable to them if they take a direct part in hostilities despite the provisions of sub-paragraph (*c*) and are captured;

(*e*) Measures shall be taken, if necessary, and whenever possible with the consent of their parents or persons who by law or custom are primarily responsible for their care, to remove children temporarily from the area in which hostilities are taking place to a safer area within the country and ensure that they are accompanied by persons responsible for their safety and well-being.

Article 5.— Persons whose liberty has been restricted

1.   In addition to the provisions of Article 4, the following provisions shall be respected as a minimum with regard to persons deprived of their liberty for reasons related to the armed conflict, whether they are interned or detained:

(*a*) The wounded and the sick shall be treated in accordance with Article 7;

(*b*) The persons referred to in this paragraph shall, to the same extent as the local civilian population, be provided with food and drinking water and be afforded safeguards as regards health and hygiene and protection against the rigours of the climate and the dangers of the armed conflict;

(*c*) They shall be allowed to receive individual or collective relief;

(*d*) They shall be allowed to practise their religion and, if requested and appropriate, to receive spiritual assistance from persons, such as chaplains, performing religious functions;

(*e*) They shall, if made to work, have the benefit of working conditions and safeguards similar to those enjoyed by the local civilian population.

2.   Those who are responsible for the internment or detention of the persons referred to in paragraph 1 shall also, within the limits of their capabilities, respect the following provisions relating to such persons:

(*a*) Except when men and women of a family are accommodated together, women shall be held in quarters separated from those of men and shall be under the immediate supervision of women;

(*b*) They shall be allowed to send and receive letters and cards, the number of which may be limited by the competent authority if it deems necessary;

(*c*) Places of internment and detention shall not be located close to the combat zone. The persons referred to in paragraph 1 shall be evacuated when the places where they are interned or detained become particularly exposed to danger arising out of the armed conflict, if their evacuation can be carried out under adequate conditions of safety;

(*d*) They shall have the benefit of medical examinations;

(*e*) Their physical or mental health and integrity shall not be endangered by an unjustified act or omission. Accordingly, it is prohibited to subject the persons described in this Article to any medical procedure which is not indicated by the state of health of the person concerned, and which is not consistent with the generally accepted medical standards applied to free persons under similar medical circumstances.

3.   Persons who are not covered by paragraph 1 but whose liberty has been restricted in any way whatsoever for reasons related to the armed con-

flict shall be treated humanely in accordance with Article 4 and with paragraphs 1 (*a*), (*c*) and (*d*), and 2 (*b*) of this Article.

4.   If it is decided to release persons deprived of their liberty, necessary measures to ensure their safety shall be taken by those so deciding.

Article 6.—*Penal prosecutions*

1.   This Article applies to the prosecution and punishment of criminal offences related to the armed conflict.

2.   No sentence shall be passed and no penalty shall be executed on a person found guilty of an offence except pursuant to a conviction pronounced by a court offering the essential guarantees of independence and impartiality. In particular:

(*a*) The procedure shall provide for an accused to be informed without delay of the particulars of the offence alleged against him and shall afford the accused before and during his trial all necessary rights and means of defence;

(*b*) No one shall be convicted of an offence except on the basis of individual penal responsibility;

(*c*) No one shall be held guilty of any criminal offence on account of any act or omission which did not constitute a criminal offence, under the law, at the time when it was committed; nor shall a heavier penalty be imposed than that which was applicable at the time when the criminal offence was committed; if, after the commission of the offence, provision is made by law for the imposition of a lighter penalty, the offender shall benefit thereby;

(*d*) Anyone charged with an offence is presumed innocent until proved guilty according to law;

(*e*) Anyone charged with an offence shall have the right to be tried in his presence;

(*f*) No one shall be compelled to testify against himself or to confess guilt.

3.   A convicted person shall be advised on conviction of his judicial and other remedies and of the time-limits within which they may be exercised.

4.   The death penalty shall not be pronounced on persons who were under the age of eighteen years at the time of the offence and shall not be carried out on pregnant women or mothers of young children.

5.   At the end of hostilities, the authorities in power shall endeavour to grant the broadest possible amnesty to persons who have participated in the armed conflict, or those deprived of their liberty for reasons related to the armed conflict, whether they are interned or detained.

PART III

WOUNDED, SICK AND SHIPWRECKED

Article 7.— Protection and care

1.   All the wounded, sick and shipwrecked, whether or not they have taken part in the armed conflict, shall be respected and protected.

2.   In all circumstances they shall be treated humanely and shall receive, to the fullest extent practicable and with the least possible delay, the medical care and attention required by their condition. There shall be no distinction among them founded on any grounds other than medical ones.

Article 8.— Search

Whenever circumstances permit, and particularly after an engagement, all possible measures shall be taken, without delay, to search for and collect the wounded, sick and shipwrecked, to protect them against pillage and ill-treatment, to ensure their adequate care, and to search for the dead, prevent their being despoiled, and decently dispose of them.

Article 9.— Protection of medical and religious personnel

1.   Medical and religious personnel shall be respected and protected and shall be granted all available help for the performance of their duties. They shall not be compelled to carry out tasks which are not compatible with their humanitarian mission.

2.   In the performance of their duties medical personnel may not be required to give priority to any person except on medical grounds.

Article 10.— General protection of medical duties

1.   Under no circumstances shall any person be punished for having carried out medical activities compatible with medical ethics, regardless of the person benefiting therefrom.

2.   Persons engaged in medical activities shall neither be compelled to perform acts or to carry out work contrary to, nor be compelled to refrain from acts required by, the rules of medical ethics or other rules designed for the benefit of the wounded and sick, or this Protocol.

3.   The professional obligations of persons engaged in medical activities regarding information which they may acquire concerning the wounded and sick under their care shall, subject to national law, be respected.

4.   Subject to national law, no person engaged in medical activities may be penalized in any way for refusing or failing to give information concerning the wounded and sick who are, or who have been, under his care.

Article 11.— Protection of medical units and transports

1.   Medical units and transports shall be respected and protected at all times and shall not be the object of attack.

2.   The protection to which medical units and transports are entitled shall not cease unless they are used to commit hostile acts, outside their humanitarian function. Protection may, however, cease only after a warning has been given setting, whenever appropriate, a reasonable time-limit, and after such warning has remained unheeded.

Article 12.— The distinctive emblem

Under the direction of the competent authority concerned, the distinctive emblem of the red cross, red crescent or red lion and sun on a white ground shall be displayed by medical and religious personnel and medical units, and on medical transports. It shall be respected in all circumstances. It shall not be used improperly.

PART IV

CIVILIAN POPULATION

Article 13.— Protection of the civilian population

1.   The civilian population and individual civilians shall enjoy general protection against the dangers arising from military operations. To give effect to this protection, the following rules shall be observed in all circumstances.

2.   The civilian population as such, as well as individual civilians, shall not be the object of attack. Acts or threats of violence the primary purpose of which is to spread terror among the civilian population are prohibited.

3.   Civilians shall enjoy the protection afforded by this Part, unless and for such time as they take a direct part in hostilities.

Article 14.— Protection of objects indispensable to the survival of the civilian population

Starvation of civilians as a method of combat is prohibited. It is therefore prohibited to attack, destroy, remove or render useless, for that purpose, objects indispensable to the survival of the civilian population, such as food-stuffs, agricultural areas for the production of foodstuffs, crops, livestock, drinking water installations and supplies and irrigation works.

Article 15.— Protection of works and installations containing dangerous forces

Works or installations containing dangerous forces, namely dams, dykes and nuclear electrical generating stations, shall not be made the object of attack, even where these objects are military objectives, if such attack may cause the release of dangerous forces and consequent severe losses among the civilian population.

Article 16.— Protection of cultural objects and of places of worship

Without prejudice to the provisions of The Hague Convention for the Protection of Cultural Property in the Event of Armed Conflict of 14 May 1954, it is prohibited to commit any acts of hostility directed against historic monuments, works of art or places of worship which constitute the cultural or spiritual heritage of peoples, and to use them in support of the military effort.

Article 17.— Prohibition of forced movement of civilians

1. The displacement of the civilian population shall not be ordered for reasons related to the conflict unless the security of the civilians involved or imperative military reasons so demand. Should such displacements have to be carried out, all possible measures shall be taken in order that the civilian population may be received under satisfactory conditions of shelter, hygiene, health, safety and nutrition.

2. Civilians shall not be compelled to leave their own territory for reasons connected with the conflict.

Article 18.— Relief societies and relief actions

1. Relief societies located in the territory of the High Contracting Party, such as Red Cross (Red Crescent, Red Lion and Sun) organizations, may offer their services for the performance of their traditional functions in relation to the victims of the armed conflict. The civilian population may, even on its own initiative, offer to collect and care for the wounded, sick and shipwrecked.

2. If the civilian population is suffering undue hardship owing to a lack of the supplies essential for its survival, such as foodstuffs and medical supplies, relief actions for the civilian population which are of an exclusively humanitarian and impartial nature and which are conducted without

any adverse distinction shall be undertaken subject to the consent of the High Contracting Party concerned.

PART V

FINAL PROVISIONS

Article 19.— Dissemination

This Protocol shall be disseminated as widely as possible.

Article 20.— Signature

This Protocol shall be open for signature by the Parties to the Conventions six months after the signing of the Final Act and will remain open for a period of twelve months.

Article 21.— Ratification

This Protocol shall be ratified as soon as possible. The instruments of ratification shall be deposited with the Swiss Federal Council, depositary of the Conventions.

Article 22.— Accession

This Protocol shall be open for accession by any Party to the Conventions which has not signed it. The instruments of accession shall be deposited with the depositary.

Article 23.— Entry into force

1.   This Protocol shall enter into force six months after two instruments of ratification or accession have been deposited.

2.   For each Party to the Conventions thereafter ratifying or acceding to this Protocol, it shall enter into force six months after the deposit by such Party of its instrument of ratification or accession.

Article 24.— Amendment

1.   Any High Contracting Party may propose amendments to this Protocol. The text of any proposed amendment shall be communicated to the depositary which shall decide, after consultation with all the High Contracting Parties and the International Committee of the Red Cross, whether a conference should be convened to consider the proposed amendment.

2. The depositary shall invite to that conference all the High Contracting Parties as well as the Parties to the Conventions, whether or not they are signatories of this Protocol.

Article 25.—Denunciation

1. In case a High Contracting Party should denounce this Protocol, the denunciation shall only take effect six months after receipt of the instrument of denunciation. If, however, on the expiry of six months, the denouncing Party is engaged in the situation referred to in Article 1, the denunciation shall not take effect before the end of the armed conflict. Persons who have been deprived of liberty, or whose liberty has been restricted, for reasons related to the conflict shall nevertheless continue to benefit from the provisions of this Protocol until their final release.

2. The denunciation shall be notified in writing to the depositary, which shall transmit it to all the High Contracting Parties.

Article 26.—Notifications

The depositary shall inform the High Contracting Parties as well as the Parties to the Conventions, whether or not they are signatories of this Protocol, of:

(*a*) Signatures affixed to this Protocol and the deposit of instruments of ratification and accession under Articles 21 and 22;

(*b*) The date of entry into force of this Protocol under Article 23; and

(*c*) Communications and declarations received under Article 24.

Article 27.—Registration

1. After its entry into force, this Protocol shall be transmitted by the depositary to the Secretariat of the United Nations for registration and publication, in accordance with Article 102 of the Charter of the United Nations.

2. The depositary shall also inform the Secretariat of the United Nations of all ratifications and accessions received by it with respect to this Protocol.

Article 28.—Authentic texts

The original of this Protocol, of which the Arabic, Chinese, English, French, Russian and Spanish texts are equally authentic shall be deposited with the depositary, which shall transmit certified true copies thereof to all the Parties to the Conventions.

LIST OF INSTRUMENTS IN CHRONOLOGICAL
ORDER OF ADOPTION

CORRIGENDUM

Ref.: Sales No. E.93.XIV.1
ST/HR/1/Rev.4
(Vol. I, Part 1)

Geneva, 1993

Centre for Human Rights, Geneva

HUMAN RIGHTS
A COMPILATION OF INTERNATIONAL INSTRUMENTS
Volume I (First Part)
UNIVERSAL INSTRUMENTS

Corrigendum

Page viii, *in* **Contents**, *after*

insert the following text:

*
* *

Page 401, *after the subtitle*

Adopted by General Assembly resolution 47/133 of 18 December 1992

add the following text:

The General Assembly,

Considering that, in accordance with the principles proclaimed in the Charter of the United Nations and other international instruments, recognition of the inherent dignity and of the equal and inalienable rights of all members of the human family is the foundation of freedom, justice and peace in the world,

Bearing in mind the obligation of States under the Charter, in particular Article 55, to promote universal respect for, and observance of, human rights and fundamental freedoms,

Deeply concerned that in many countries, often in a persistent manner, enforced disappearances occur, in the sense that persons are arrested, detained or abducted against their will or otherwise deprived of their liberty by officials of different branches or levels of Government, or by organized groups or private individuals acting on behalf of, or with the support, direct or indirect, consent or acquiescence of the Government, followed by a refusal to disclose the fate or whereabouts of the persons concerned or a refusal to acknowledge the deprivation of their liberty, which places such persons outside the protection of the law,

Considering that enforced disappearance undermines the deepest values of any society committed to respect for the rule of law, human rights and fundamental freedoms, and that the systematic practice of such acts is of the nature of a crime against humanity,

Recalling its resolution 33/173 of 20 December 1978, in which it expressed concern about the reports from various parts of the world relating to enforced or involuntary disappearances, as well as about the anguish and sorrow caused by those disappearances, and called upon Governments to hold law enforcement and security forces legally responsible for excesses which might lead to enforced or involuntary disappearances of persons,

Recalling also the protection afforded to victims of armed conflicts by the Geneva Conventions of 12 August 1949 and the Additional Protocols thereto, of 1977,

Having regard in particular to the relevant articles of the Universal Declaration of Human Rights and the International Covenant on Civil and Political Rights, which protect the right to life, the right to liberty and security of the person, the right not to be subjected to torture and the right to recognition as a person before the law,

Having regard also to the Convention against Torture and Other Cruel, Inhuman or Degrading Treatment or Punishment, which provides that States parties shall take effective measures to prevent and punish acts of torture,

Bearing in mind the Code of Conduct for Law Enforcement Officials, the Basic Principles on the Use of Force and Firearms by Law

Enforcement Officials, the Declaration of Basic Principles of Justice for Victims of Crime and Abuse of Power and the Standard Minimum Rules for the Treatment of Prisoners,

Affirming that, in order to prevent enforced disappearances, it is necessary to ensure strict compliance with the Body of Principles for the Protection of All Persons under Any Form of Detention or Imprisonment contained in the annex to its resolution 43/173 of 9 December 1988, and with the Principles on the Effective Prevention and Investigation of Extra-legal, Arbitrary and Summary Executions, set forth in the annex to Economic and Social Council resolution 1989/65 of 24 May 1989 and endorsed by the General Assembly in its resolution 44/162 of 15 December 1989,

Bearing in mind that, while the acts which comprise enforced disappearance constitute a violation of the prohibitions found in the aforementioned international instruments, it is none the less important to devise an instrument which characterizes all acts of enforced disappearance of persons as very serious offences and sets forth standards designed to punish and prevent their commission,

1. *Proclaims* the present Declaration on the Protection of all Persons from Enforced Disappearance, as a body of principles for all States;

2. *Urges* that all efforts be made so that the Declaration becomes generally known and respected;

*
* *

Page 408, *insert the following text*:

54. Principles on the Effective Prevention and Investigation of Extra-legal, Arbitrary and Summary Executions

Recommended by Economic and Social Council
resolution 1989/65 of 24 May 1989*

Prevention

1.   Governments shall prohibit by law all extra-legal, arbitrary and summary executions and shall ensure that any such executions are

---

* In resolution 1989/65, paragraph 1, the Economic and Social Council recommended that the Principles on the Effective Prevention and Investigation of Extra-legal, Arbitrary and Summary Executions should be taken into account and respected by Governments within the framework of their national legislation and practices.

recognized as offences under their criminal laws, and are punishable by appropriate penalties which take into account the seriousness of such offences. Exceptional circumstances including a state of war or threat of war, internal political instability or any other public emergency may not be invoked as a justification of such executions. Such executions shall not be carried out under any circumstances including, but not limited to, situations of internal armed conflict, excessive or illegal use of force by a public official or other person acting in an official capacity or by a person acting at the instigation, or with the consent or acquiescence of such person, and situations in which deaths occur in custody. This prohibition shall prevail over decrees issued by governmental authority.

2. In order to prevent extra-legal, arbitrary and summary executions, Governments shall ensure strict control, including a clear chain of command over all officials responsible for apprehension, arrest, detention, custody and imprisonment, as well as those officials authorized by law to use force and firearms.

3. Governments shall prohibit orders from superior officers or public authorities authorizing or inciting other persons to carry out any such extra-legal, arbitrary or summary executions. All persons shall have the right and the duty to defy such orders. Training of law enforcement officials shall emphasize the above provisions.

4. Effective protection through judicial or other means shall be guaranteed to individuals and groups who are in danger of extra-legal, arbitrary or summary executions, including those who receive death threats.

5. No one shall be involuntarily returned or extradited to a country where there are substantial grounds for believing that he or she may become a victim of extra-legal, arbitrary or summary execution in that country.

6. Governments shall ensure that persons deprived of their liberty are held in officially recognized places of custody, and that accurate information on their custody and whereabouts, including transfers, is made promptly available to their relatives and lawyer or other persons of confidence.

7. Qualified inspectors, including medical personnel, or an equivalent independent authority, shall conduct inspections in places of custody on a regular basis, and be empowered to undertake unan-

nounced inspections on their own initiative, with full guarantees of independence in the exercise of this function. The inspectors shall have unrestricted access to all persons in such places of custody, as well as to all their records.

8.   Governments shall make every effort to prevent extra-legal, arbitrary and summary executions through measures such as diplomatic intercession, improved access of complainants to intergovernmental and judicial bodies, and public denunciation. Intergovernmental mechanisms shall be used to investigate reports of any such executions and to take effective action against such practices. Governments, including those of countries where extra-legal, arbitrary and summary executions are reasonably suspected to occur, shall cooperate fully in international investigations on the subject.

Investigation

9.   There shall be thorough, prompt and impartial investigation of all suspected cases of extra-legal, arbitrary and summary executions, including cases where complaints by relatives or other reliable reports suggest unnatural death in the above circumstances. Governments shall maintain investigative offices and procedures to undertake such inquiries. The purpose of the investigation shall be to determine the cause, manner and time of death, the person responsible, and any pattern or practice which may have brought about that death. It shall include an adequate autopsy, collection and analysis of all physical and documentary evidence and statements from witnesses. The investigation shall distinguish between natural death, accidental death, suicide and homicide.

10.   The investigative authority shall have the power to obtain all the information necessary to the inquiry. Those persons conducting the investigation shall have at their disposal all the necessary budgetary and technical resources for effective investigation. They shall also have the authority to oblige officials allegedly involved in any such executions to appear and testify. The same shall apply to any witness. To this end, they shall be entitled to issue summonses to witnesses, including the officials allegedly involved and to demand the production of evidence.

11.   In cases in which the established investigative procedures are inadequate because of lack of expertise or impartiality, because of

the importance of the matter or because of the apparent existence of a pattern of abuse, and in cases where there are complaints from the family of the victim about these inadequacies or other substantial reasons, Governments shall pursue investigations through an independent commission of inquiry or similar procedure. Members of such a commission shall be chosen for their recognized impartiality, competence and independence as individuals. In particular, they shall be independent of any institution, agency or person that may be the subject of the inquiry. The commission shall have the authority to obtain all information necessary to the inquiry and shall conduct the inquiry as provided for under these Principles.

12.   The body of the deceased person shall not be disposed of until an adequate autopsy is conducted by a physician, who shall, if possible, be an expert in forensic pathology. Those conducting the autopsy shall have the right of access to all investigative data, to the place where the body was discovered, and to the place where the death is thought to have occurred. If the body has been buried and it later appears that an investigation is required, the body shall be promptly and competently exhumed for an autopsy. If skeletal remains are discovered, they should be carefully exhumed and studied according to systematic anthropological techniques.

13.   The body of the deceased shall be available to those conducting the autopsy for a sufficient amount of time to enable a thorough investigation to be carried out. The autopsy shall, at a minimum, attempt to establish the identity of the deceased and the cause and manner of death. The time and place of death shall also be determined to the extent possible. Detailed colour photographs of the deceased shall be included in the autopsy report in order to document and support the findings of the investigation. The autopsy report must describe any and all injuries to the deceased including any evidence of torture.

14.   In order to ensure objective results, those conducting the autopsy must be able to function impartially and independently of any potentially implicated persons or organizations or entities.

15.   Complainants, witnesses, those conducting the investigation and their families shall be protected from violence, threats of violence or any other form of intimidation. Those potentially implicated in extra-legal, arbitrary or summary executions shall be removed from any position of control or power, whether direct or indirect, over com-

plainants, witnesses and their families, as well as over those conducting investigations.

16.   Families of the deceased and their legal representatives shall be informed of, and have access to, any hearing as well as to all information relevant to the investigation, and shall be entitled to present other evidence. The family of the deceased shall have the right to insist that a medical or other qualified representative be present at the autopsy. When the identity of a deceased person has been determined, a notification of death shall be posted, and the family or relatives of the deceased shall be informed immediately. The body of the deceased shall be returned to them upon completion of the investigation.

17.   A written report shall be made within a reasonable period of time on the methods and findings of such investigations. The report shall be made public immediately and shall include the scope of the inquiry, procedures and methods used to evaluate evidence as well as conclusions and recommendations based on findings of fact and on applicable law. The report shall also describe in detail specific events that were found to have occurred and the evidence upon which such findings were based, and list the names of witnesses who testified, with the exception of those whose identities have been withheld for their own protection. The Government shall, within a reasonable period of time, either reply to the report of the investigation, or indicate the steps to be taken in response to it.

Legal proceedings

18.   Governments shall ensure that persons identified by the investigation as having participated in extra-legal, arbitrary or summary executions in any territory under their jurisdiction are brought to justice. Governments shall either bring such persons to justice or cooperate to extradite any such persons to other countries wishing to exercise jurisdiction. This principle shall apply irrespective of who and where the perpetrators or the victims are, their nationalities or where the offence was committed.

19.   Without prejudice to principle 3 above, an order from a superior officer or a public authority may not be invoked as a justification for extra-legal, arbitrary or summary executions. Superiors, officers or other public officials may be held responsible for acts committed by officials under their authority if they had a reasonable

opportunity to prevent such acts. In no circumstances, including a state of war, siege or other public emergency, shall blanket immunity from prosecution be granted to any person allegedly involved in extra-legal, arbitrary or summary executions.

20.   The families and dependents of victims of extra-legal, arbitrary or summary executions shall be entitled to fair and adequate compensation within a reasonable period of time.

*

*   *

Page 414, *insert under* **1989** *the following text*:

Printed at United Nations, Geneva   ST/HR/1/Rev.4/Corr.1
GE.93-18852   Corrigendum to United Nations publication
November 1993—4,750   Sales No. E.93.XIV.1

ST/HR/1/Rev.4 (Vol. I, Part 1)   English only

HUMAN RIGHTS

Status of International Instruments

as at 31 December 1990

Update: Chart of ratification, see foreword to *Human Rights − Status of International Instruments* (ST/HR/5), United Nations publication (Sales No. E.87.XIV.2); replaces text of 1 March 1990.

States	International Covenant on Economic, Social and Cultural Rights (1)	International Covenant on Civil and Political Rights (2)	Optional Protocol to the International Covenant on Civil and Political Rights (3)	Second Optional Protocol to the International Covenant on Civil and Political Rights aiming at the abolition of the death penalty (4)	International Convention on the Elimination of All Forms of Racial Discrimination (5)	International Convention on the Suppression and Punishment of the Crime of Apartheid (6)	International Convention against Apartheid in Sports (7)	Convention on the Prevention and Punishment of the Crime of Genocide (8)	Convention on the Non-Applicability of Statutory Limitations to War Crimes and Crimes against Humanity (9)	Convention on the Rights of the Child (10)	Convention on the Elimination of All Forms of Discrimination against Women (11)	Convention on the Political Rights of Women (12)
Afghanistan	X	X			X	X		X	X	s	s	X
Albania								X	X	s		X
Algeria	X	Xa	X		Xb	X	X	X		s		
Angola							X			X	X	X
Antigua and Barbuda					X	X	X	X			X	X
Argentina	X	Xa	X		X	X		X		X	X	X
Australia	X	X			X			X		X	X	X
Austria	X	Xa	X		X			X		s	X	X
Bahamas					X	X	X	X		s	X	X
Bahrain					X	X		X				
Bangladesh					X	X				X	X	
Barbados	X	X	X		X	X	X	X		X	X	X
Belgium	X	Xa		s	X			X		s	X	X
Belize										X	X	
Benin					s	X	s			X	s	
Bhutan					s					X	X	
Bolivia	X	X	X		X	X	X	s	X	X	s	X
Botswana					X							
Brazil					X			X		X	X	X
Brunei Darussalam												
Bulgaria	X	X			X	X	X	X	X	s	X	X
Burkina Faso					X	X	X	X		X	X	
Burma, *See* Myanmar												
Burundi	X	X			X	X	s			X	s	
Byelorussian SSR	X	X			X	X	X	X	X	X	X	X
Cambodia	s	s			X	X		X			X	
Cameroon	X	X	X		X	X	s		X	s	s	
Canada	X	Xa	X		X			X		s	X	X
Cape verde					X	X	s				X	
Central African Republic	X	X	X		X	X	s			s		X
Chad					X	X				X		
Chile	X	Xa			X			X		X	X	X
China					X	X	s	X		s	X	X
Colombia	X	X	X		X	X	s	X		s	X	X

2

(14)	(15)	(16)	(17)	(18)	(19)	(20)	(21)	(22)	(23)	States
						X				Afghanistan
						X				Albania
						X		X		Algeria
								X		Angola
)		;						X		Antigua and Barbuda
>						X		X		Argentina
X		>		>	<	X		X		Australia
X		X		>	X				;	Austria
X		X		X	X					Bahamas
				X	X					Bahrain
		X		X	X	X				Bangladesh
X		X		X	X			X		Barbados
s		X		X	X	X		X	X	Belgium
									X	Belize
		X							X	Benin
										Bhutan
		X		X	X	X	X	X	X	Bolivia
								X	X	Botswana
X				X	X	X		s	X	Brazil
										Brunei Darussalam
X		X				X				Bulgaria
	;					X			X	Burkina Faso
										Burma, *See* Myanmar
									X	Burundi
X	<			X	X	X				Byelorussian SSR
						X				Cambodia
		X	X	X	X	X	X		X	Cameroon
X	Xc	X	X	X	X		X		X	Canada
									X	Cape Verde
		X		X		X		X	X	Central African Republic
								X	X	Chad
s	s	X						X	X	Chile
	X							X	X	China
s		X						s	X	Colombia

3

States	International Covenant on Economic, Social and Cultural Rights (1)	International Covenant on Civil and Political Rights (2)	Optional Protocol to the International Covenant on Civil and Political Rights (3)	Second Optional Protocol to the International Covenant on Civil and Political Rights aiming at the abolition of the death penalty (4)	International Convention on the Elimination of All Forms of Racial Discrimination (5)	International Convention on the Suppression and Punishment of the Crime of Apartheid (6)	International Convention against Apartheid in Sports (7)	Convention on the Prevention and Punishment of the Crime of Genocide (8)	Convention on the Non-Applicability of Statutory Limitations to War Crimes and Crimes against Humanity (9)	Convention on the Rights of the Child (10)	Convention on the Elimination of All Forms of Discrimination against Women (11)	Convention on the Political Rights of Women (12)
Comoros										s		
Congo	X	Xa	X		X	X					X	X
Costa Rica	X	X	X	s	Xb	X		X		X	X	X
Côte d'Ivoire					X					s	s	
Cuba					X	X	X	X	X	s	X	X
Cyprus	X	X	s		X		s	X		s	X	X
Czech and slovakia Fed. Rep.	X	X			X	X	X	X	X	s	X	X
Dem. People's Rep. of Korea	X	X					X	X		X		
Denmark	X	Xa	X	s	Xb			X		s	X	X
Djibouti										X		
Dominica										s	X	
Dominican Rep.	X	X	X		X			s		s	X	X
Ecuador	X	Xa	X		Xb	X	s	X		X	X	X
Egypt	X	X			X	X	s	X		X	X	X
El Salvador	X	X	s		X	X		X		X	X	s
Equatorial Guinea	X	X	X			X					X	
Ethiopia					X	X	X	X			X	X
Fiji					X			X				X
Finland	X	Xa	X	s	X			X		s	X	X
France	X	X	X		Xb			X		X	X	X
Gabon	X	X			X	X	s	X	X	s	X	X
Gambia	X	Xa	X		X	X		X	X	X	s	
Germany	X	Xa		X*	X	X*	X*	X	X*	X*	X	X
Ghana					X	X		X		X	X	X
Greece	X				X			X		s	X	X
Grenada					s					X	X	
Guatemala	X				X			X	X	X	X	X
Guinea	X	X	s		X	X	X		X	X	X	X
Guinea-Bissau							s			X	X	
Guyana	X	X			X	X	X			s	X	
Haïti					X	X	s	X		s	X	X
Holy See					X					X		

4

Convention on the Nationality of Married Women	Convention on Consent to Marriage, Minimum Age for Marriage and Registration of Marriages	Convention against Torture and other Cruel, Inhuman or Degrading Treatment or Punishment	Slavery Convention of 1926	1953 Protocol amending the 1926 Convention	Slavery Convention of 1926 as amended	Supplementary Convention on the Abolition of Slavery, the Slave Trade, and Institutions and Practices Similar to Slavery	Convention for the Suppression of the Traffic in Persons and of the Exploitation of the Prostitution of others	Convention on the Reduction of Statelessness	Convention relating to the Status of Stateless Persons	Convention relating to the Status of Refugees	Protocol relating to the Status of Refugees	States
(13)	(14)	(15)	(16)	(17)	(18)	(19)	(20)	(21)	(22)	(23)	(24)	States
			X			X	X			X	X	Comoros
		s						X	X	X	X	Congo
			X			X				X	X	Costa Rica
X	X	s	X	X	X	X	X					Côte d'Ivoire
X	X	s	X	X	X	X	X			X	X	Cuba
X	X	s				X	X			X	X	Cyprus
X	X	X	X			X	X					Czech and Slovakia Fed. Rep.
												Dem. People's Rep. of Korea
X	X	Xc	X	X	X	X	s	X	X	X	X	Denmark
						X	X			X	X	Djibouti
										X	X	Dominica
X	X	s	s			X	s			X	X	Dominican Rep.
X		Xc	X	X	X	X	X		X	X	X	Ecuador
	X		X	X	X	X	X			X	X	Egypt
							s		s	X	X	El Salvador
										X	X	Equatorial Guinea
			X			X	X			X	X	Ethiopia
X	X		X	X	X	X			X	X	X	Fiji
X	X	Xc	X	X	X	X	X		X	X	X	Finland
	s	Xc	X	X	X	X	X	s	X	X	X	France
		s								X	X	Gabon
		s								X	X	Gambia
X	X	X	X	X	X	X	X*	X	X	X	X	Germany
X			X			X				X	X	Ghana
	s	Xc	X	X	X	X			X	X	X	Greece
												Grenada
X	X	X	X	X	X	X			s	X	X	Guatemala
s	X	X	X	X	X	X	X		X	X	X	Guinea
										X	X	Guinea-Bissau
		X										Guyana
			X			X	X			X	X	Haïti
									s	X	X	Holy See

5

States	International Covenant on Economic, Social and Cultural Rights (1)	International Covenant on Civil and Political Rights (2)	Optional Protocol to the International Covenant on Civil and Political Rights (3)	Second Optional Protocol to the International Covenant on Civil and Political Rights aiming at the abolition of the death penalty (4)	International Convention on the Elimination of All Forms of Racial Discrimination (5)	International Convention on the Suppression and Punishment of the Crime of Apartheid (6)	International Convention against Apartheid in Sports (7)	Convention on the Prevention and Punishment of the Crime of Genocide (8)	Convention on the Non-Applicability of Statutory Limitations to War Crimes and Crimes against Humanity (9)	Convention on the Rights of the Child (10)	Convention on the Elimination of All Forms of Discrimination against Women (11)	Convention on the Political Rights of Women (12)
Honduras	X	s	s	s				X		X	X	
Hungary	X	Xa	X		Xb	X	s	X	X	s	X	X
Iceland	X	Xa	X		Xb			X		s	X	X
India	X	X			X	X	X	X	X		s	X
Indonesia							s			X	X	X
Iran (Islamic R.)	X	X			X	X	X	X				
Iraq	X	X			X	X	X	X			X	
Ireland	X	Xa	X		s			X		s	X	X
Israel	s	s			X			X		s	s	X
Italy	X	Xa	X	s	Xb			X		s	X	X
Jamaica	X	X	X		X	X	X	X		s	X	X
Japon	X	X								s	X	X
Jordan	X	X			X	s	X	X		s	s	
Kenya	X	X				s	s		X	X	X	
Kiribati												
Kuwait					X	X				s		
Lao People's Dem. Rep.					X	X		X	X		X	X
Lebanon	X	X			X		s	X		s		X
Lesotho					X	X		X		s	s	X
Liberia	s	s			X	X	s	X		s	X	s
Libyan Arab Jamahiriya	X	X	X		X	X	X	X	X	s	X	X
Liechtenstein										s		
Luxembourg	X	Xa	X	s	X			X		s	X	X
Madagascar	X	X	X		X	X	s			s	X	X
Malawi											X	X
Malaysia							s					
Maldives					X	X	s	X		s		
Mali	X	X			X	X	X	X		X	X	X
Malta	X	Xa	X		X					X		X
Mauritania					X	X	X			s		X
Mauritius	X	X	X		X			X		X	X	X
Mexico	X	X			X	X	X	X	s	X	X	X
Monaco								X				

6

(13) Convention on the Nationality of Married Women	(14) Convention on Consent to Marriage, Minimum Age for Marriage and Registration of Marriages	(15) Convention against Torture and other Cruel, Inhuman or Degrading Treatment or Punishment	(16) Slavery Convention of 1926	(17) 1953 Protocol amending the 1926 Convention	(18) Slavery Convention of 1926 as amended	(19) Supplementary Convention on the Abolition of Slavery, the Slave Trade, and Institutions and Practices Similar to Slavery	(20) Convention for the Suppression of the Traffic in Persons and of the Exploitation of the Prostitution of others	(21) Convention on the Reduction of Statelessness	(22) Convention relating to the Status of Stateless Persons	(23) Convention relating to the Status of Refugees	(24) Protocol relating to the Status of Refugees	States
							s		s			Honduras
X	X	Xc	X	X	X	X	X			X	X	Hungary
X	X	s				X	X			X	X	Iceland
s			X	X	X	X	X					India
		s										Indonesia
			s			X	s			X	X	Iran (Islamic R.)
			X	X	X	X	X					Iraq
			X	X	X	X	X	X	X	X	X	Ireland
X	s	s	X	X	X	X	X	s	X	X	X	Israel
	s	Xc	X	X	X	X	X		X	X	X	Italy
X					X	X				X	X	Jamaica
							X			X	X	Japon
					X	X	X					Jordan
										X	X	Kenya
								X	X			Kiribati
					X	X	X					Kuwait
						X	X					Lao People's Dem. Rep.
			X									Lebanon
X					X	X			X	X	X	Lesotho
		X		X	X	s	s		X	X	X	Liberia
X	X				X	X	X	X	X			Libyan Arab Jamahiriya
	Xc								s	X	X	Liechtenstein
X	Xc					X	X		X	X	X	Luxembourg
					X	X				X		Madagascar
X				X	X	X	X			X	X	Malawi
X						X						Malaysia
												Maldives
X	X		X	X	X	X	X			X	X	Mali
X		Xc	X	X	X					X	X	Malta
		X	X	X	X	X	X			X	X	Mauritania
X				X	X							Mauritius
X	X	X	X	X	X	X	X					Mexico
			X	X	X					X		Monaco

7

States	International Covenant on Economic, Social and Cultural Rights (1)	International Covenant on Civil and Political Rights (2)	Optional Protocol to the International Covenant on Civil and Political Rights (3)	Second Optional Protocol to the International Covenant on Civil and Political Rights aiming at the abolition of the death penalty (4)	International Convention on the Elimination of All Forms of Racial Discrimination (5)	International Convention on the Suppression and Punishment of the Crime of Apartheid (6)	International Convention against Apartheid in Sports (7)	Convention on the Prevention and Punishment of the Crime of Genocide (8)	Convention on the Non-Applicability of Statutory Limitations to War Crimes and Crimes against Humanity (9)	Convention on the Rights of the Child (10)	Convention on the Elimination of All Forms of Discrimination against Women (11)	Convention on the Political Rights of Women (12)
Mongolia	X	X			X	X	X	X	X	X	X	X
Morocco	X	X			X		s	X		s		X
Mozambique					X	X		X		s		
Myanmar								X				s
Namibia					X	X				X		
Nauru												
Nepal					X	X	X	X		X		X
Netherlands	X	Xa	X	s	Xb			X		s	s	X
New Zealand	X	Xa	X	X	X			X		s	X	X
Nicaragua	X	X	X	s	X	X	s	X	X	X	X	X
Niger	X	X	X		X	X	X			X		X
Nigeria					X	X	X		X	s	X	X
Norway	X	Xa	X	s	Xb			X		s	X	X
Oman						s						
Pakistan					X	X		X		X		X
Panama	X	X	X		X	X	s	X		X	X	
Papua New Guinea					X			X		s		X
Paraguay							s			X	X	X
Peru	X	Xa	X		Xb	X	X	X		X	X	X
Philippines	X	Xa	X		X	X	X	X	X	X	X	X
Poland	X	Xa			X	X	X	X	X	s	X	X
Portugal	X	X	X	X	X					X	X	
Qatar					X	X	X					
Republic of Korea	X	Xa	X		X			X		s	X	X
Romania	X	X		s	X	X		X	X	X	X	X
Rwanda	X	X			X	X	s	X	X	s	X	
Saint Kitts & Nevis							X			X	X	
Saint Lucia					X		s			s	X	
Saint Vincent et Grenadines	X	X	X		X	X		X	X		X	
Samoa										s		
San Marino	X	X	X									
Sao Tome & Principe						X						
Saudi Arabia								X				

8

(13)	(14)	(15)	(16)	(17)	(18)	(19)	(20)	(21)	(22)	(23)	(24)	States
					X	X						Mongolia
		s	X	X	X	X	X			X	X	Morocco
										X	X	Mozambique
			X	X	X		s					Myanmar
												Namibia
												Nauru
					X	X						Nepal
X	X	Xc	X	X	X	X		X	X	X	X	Netherlands
X	X	Xc	X	X	X	X				X	X	New Zealand
X		s	X	X	X	X				X	X	Nicaragua
	X	s	X	X	X	X	X	X		X	X	Niger
		s			X	X				X	X	Nigeria
X	X	Xc	X	X	X	X	X	X	X	X	X	Norway
												Oman
s					X	X	X					Pakistan
	X	s								X	X	Panama
					X					X	X	Papua New Guinea
		X								X	X	Paraguay
		X				s				X	X	Peru
	X	X			X	X	X		s	X	X	Philippines
X	X	X	X			X	X					Poland
s		Xc	X			X				X	X	Portugal
												Qatar
						X	X		X			Republic of Korea
X	s	X	X	X	X	X	X					Romania
										X	X	Rwanda
												Saint Kitts & Nevis
		X	X	X	X							Saint Lucia
		X	X	X	X							Saint Vincent et Grenadines
	X									X		Samoa
						X						San Marino
										X	X	Sao Tome & Principe
					X	X						Saudi Arabia

9

States	International Covenant on Economic, Social and Cultural Rights (1)	International Covenant on Civil and Political Rights (2)	Optional Protocol to the International Covenant on Civil and Political Rights (3)	Second Optional Protocol to the International Covenant on Civil and Political Rights aiming at the abolition of the death penalty (4)	International Convention on the Elimination of All Forms of Racial Discrimination (5)	International Convention on the Suppression and Punishment of the Crime of Apartheid (6)	International Convention against Apartheid in Sports (7)	Convention on the Prevention and Punishment of the Crime of Genocide (8)	Convention on the Non-Applicability of Statutory Limitations to War Crimes and Crimes against Humanity (9)	Convention on the Rights of the Child (10)	Convention on the Elimination of All Forms of Discrimination against Women (11)	Convention on the Political Rights of Women (12)
Senegal	X	Xa	X		Xb	X	X	X		X	X	X
Seychelles					X	X				X		
Sierra Leone					X		s			X	X	X
Singapore												
Solomon Islands	X				X							X
Somalia	X	X	X		X	X	s					
South Africa												
Spain	X	Xa	X	s	X			X		X	X	X
Sri Lanka	X	Xa			X	X		X		s	X	
Sudan	X	X			X	X	X			X		
Suriname	X	X	X		X	X				s		
Swaziland					X					s		X
Sweden	X	xa	X	X	Xb			X		X	X	X
Switzerland											s	
Syrian Arab Rep.	X	X			X	X	X	X		s		
Thailand											X	X
Togo	X	X	X		X	X	X	X		X	X	
Tonga					X			X				
Trinidad & Tobago	X	X	X		X	X	X			s	X	X
Tunisia	X	X			X	X	X	X	X	s	X	X
Turkey					s			X		s	X	X
Tuvalu												
Uganda	X				X	X	X			X	X	
Ukrainian SSR	X	X			X	X	X	X	X	s	X	X
Union of Soviet Socialist Rep.	X	X			X	X	X	X	X	X	X	X
United Arab Emirates					X	X						
United Kingdom of Great Britain and North Ireland	X	Xa			X			X		s	X	X
United Republic of Tanziana	X	X			X	X	X	X		s	X	X
United States of America	s	s			s			X			s	X
Uruguay	X	X	X	s	Xb			X		X	X	s
Vanuatu										s		
Venezuela	X	X	X	s	X	X	X	X		X	X	X

10

	(13) Convention on the Nationality of Married Women	(14) Convention on Consent to Marriage, Minimum Age for Marriage and Registration of Marriages	(15) Convention against Torture and other Cruel, Inhuman or Degrading Treatment or Punishment	(16) Slavery Convention of 1926	(17) 1953 Protocol amending the 1926 Convention	(18) Slavery Convention of 1926 as amended	(19) Supplementary Convention on the Abolition of Slavery, the Slave Trade, and Institutions and Practices Similar to Slavery	(20) Convention for the Suppression of the Traffic in Persons and of the Exploitation of the Prostitution of others	(21) Convention on the Reduction of Statelessness	(22) Convention relating to the Status of Stateless Persons	(23) Convention relating to the Status of Refugees	(24) Protocol relating to the Status of Refugees	States
			X	X			X	X			X	X	Senegal
											X	X	Seychelles
	X		s			X	X				X	X	Sierra Leone
	X						X	X					Singapore
				X	X	X	X						Solomon Islands
				X							X	X	Somalia
				X	X	X		X					South Africa
		X	Xc	X	X	X	X	X			X	X	Spain
	X	s				X	X	X					Sri Lanka
			s	X		X	X				X	X	Sudan
				X		X		X			X	X	Suriname
	X											X	Swaziland
	X	X	Xc	X	X	X	X		X	X	X	X	Sweden
			Xc	X	X	X	X			X	X	X	Switzerland
				X	X	X	X	X					Syrian Arab Rep.
													Thailand
			Xc	X			X	X			X	X	Togo
													Tonga
	X	X				X	X			X			Trinidad & Tobago
	X	X	Xc			X	X			X	X	X	Tunisia
			Xc	X	X	X	X				X	X	Turkey
											X	X	Tuvalu
	X		X			X	X			X	X	X	Uganda
	X		X			X	X	X					Ukrainian SSR
	X		X			X	X	X					Union of Soviet Socialist Rep.
													United Arab Emirates
		X	Xc	X	X	X	X		X	X	X	X	United Kingdom of Great Britain and North Ireland
	X					X	X				X	X	United Republic of Tanzania
		s	s	X	X	X	X					X	United States of America
	s		Xc	s							X	X	Uruguay
													Vanuatu
	X	X	s					X				X	Venezuela

11

States	International Covenant on Economic, Social and Cultural Rights (1)	International Covenant on Civil and Political Rights (2)	Optional Protocol to the International Covenant on Civil and Political Rights (3)	Second Optional Protocol to the International Covenant on Civil and Political Rights aiming at the abolition of the death penalty (4)	International Convention on the Elimination of All Forms of Racial Discrimination (5)	International Convention on the Suppression and Punishment of the Crime of Apartheid (6)	International Convention against Apartheid in Sports (7)	Convention on the Prevention and Punishment of the Crime of Genocide (8)	Convention on the Non-Applicability of Statutory Limitations to War Crimes and Crimes against Humanity (9)	Convention on the Rights of the Child (10)	Convention on the Elimination of All Forms of Discrimination against Women (11)	Convention on the Political Rights of Women (12)
Viet Nam	X	X			X	X		X	X	X	X	
Yemen	X	X			X	X*	s	X	X	s	X	X
Yugoslavia	X	X	s		X	X	X	X	X	s	X	X
Zaïre	X	X	X		X	X	s	X		X	X	X
Zambia	X	X	X		X	X	X			s	X	X
Zimbabwe							X			X		
TOTAL NUMBER OF STATES PARTIES	96	92	51	5	130	89	51	101	31	64	105	96
Signatures not followed by ratification	4	5	5	14	6	3	30	3	1	69	13	4

Convention on the Nationality of Married Women (13)	Convention on Consent to Marriage, Minimum Age for Marriage and Registration of Marriages (14)	Convention against Torture and other Cruel, Inhuman or Degrading Treatment or Punishment (15)	Slavery Convention of 1926 (16)	1953 Protocol amending the 1926 Convention (17)	Slavery Convention of 1926 as amended (18)	Supplementary Convention on the Abolition of Slavery, the Slave Trade, and Institutions and Practices Similar to Slavery (19)	Convention for the Suppression of the Traffic in Persons and of the Exploitation of the Prostitution of others (20)	Convention on the Reduction of Statelessness (21)	Convention relating to the Status of Stateless Persons (22)	Convention relating to the Status of Refugees (23)	Protocol relating to the Status of Refugees (24)	States
	X				X		X**			X**	X**	Viet Nam
X	X	s	X	X	X	X	X		X	X	X	Yemen
						X				X	X	Yugoslavia
						X				X	X	Zaïre
X					X	X			X	X	X	Zambia
										X	X	Zimbabwe
56	35	55	68	53	87	105	61	15	36	104	105	**TOTAL NUMBER OF STATES PARTIES**
8	8	20	6	0	0	3	5	3	8	0	0	**Signatures not followed by ratification**

× Ratification, accession, approval, notification or succession, acceptance or definitive signature.

s Signature not yet followed by ratification.

a Declaration recognizing the competence of the Human Rights Committee under article 41 of the International Covenant on Civil and Political Rights.

b Declaration recognizing the competence of the Committee on the Elimination of Racial Discrimination under article 14 of the International Convention on the Elimination of All Forms of Racial Discrimination.

c Declarations recognizing the competence of the Committee against Torture under articles 21 and 22 of the Convention against Torture and Other Cruel, Inhuman or Degrading Treatment or Punishment.

c Declaration under article 21 only.

* Ratification, accession, approval, notification or succession, acceptance or definitive signature which have been given only by the former German Democratic Republic before the reunification.

** Ratification, accession, approval, notification or succession, acceptance or definitive signature which have been given only by the former Republic of Yemen.

ST/HR/5

Printed at United Nations, Geneva
GE.91-15216—February 1991—4,770